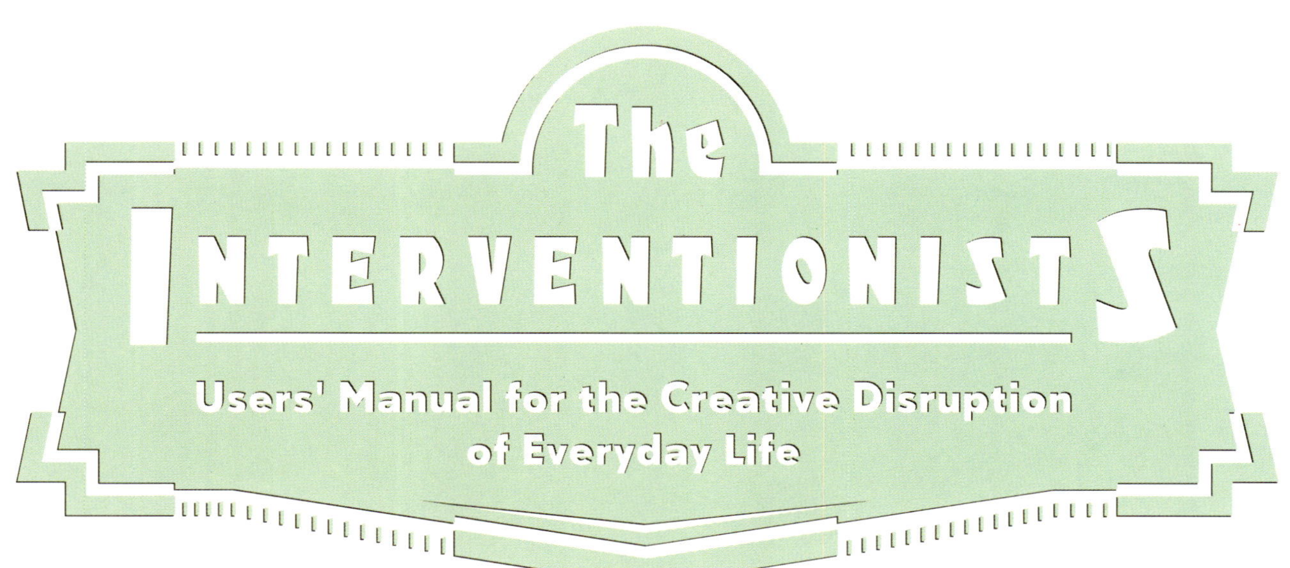

edited by Nato Thompson and Gregory Sholette
with
Joseph Thompson,
Nicholas Mirzoeff and C. Ondine Chavoya

graphic design by Arjen Noordeman

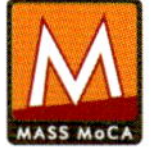

MASS MoCA Publications
North Adams, Massachusetts

The MIT Press
Cambridge, Massachusetts
London, England

This publication accompanies the exhibition *The Interventionists: Art in the Social Sphere,* organized by MASS MoCA. It was presented at MASS MoCA from May 2004 until March 2005.

The Interventionists: Art in the Social Sphere has been funded in part by grants from: the MetLife Foundation Museum Connections Program; Horace W. Goldsmith Foundation; LEF New England; The Porches Inn; Nimoy Foundation; Mondriaan Foundation, Amsterdam; Peter Norton Family Foundation; Elizabeth Firestone Graham Foundation; the Artists' Resource Trust (a Fund of the Berkshire Taconic Community Foundation); Massachusetts Foundation for the Humanities; Evelyn Stefansson Nef; and Holly Angell Hardman.

Special thanks to The Nathan Cummings Foundation.

MetLife Foundation

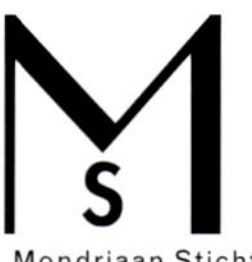
Mondriaan Stichting
(Mondriaan Foundation)

MASS MoCA would like to thank the artists, copyright holders and rights holders of all of the images in *The Interventionists, Users' Manual for the Creative Disruption of Everyday Life.* Every effort has been made to contact copyright holders prior to publication.

Book design by Arjen Noordeman
Printed and bound in Hong Kong by Palace Press International

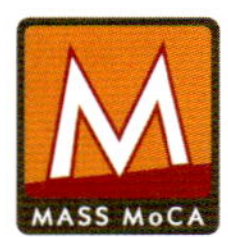

MASS MoCA
1040 MASS MoCA Way
North Adams, Massachusetts 01247
PH 413-664-4481
FAX 413-663-8548

www.massmoca.org

Library of Congress Control Number: 2004100295
ISBN 978-0-262-20150-6

10 9 8 7 6 5 4 3

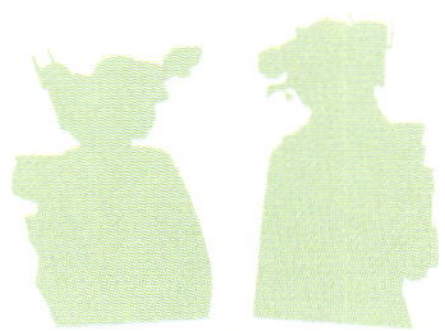

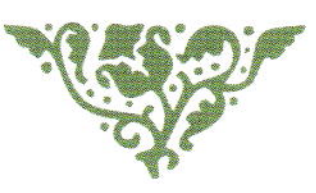

Foreword
to the Second Printing

By Nato Thompson and Gregory Sholette
Editors

The appearance of this catalogue coincides with a deepening interest in cultural practices that directly engage social and political issues. New programs dedicated to teaching interventionist forms of art have appeared on college curricula, while an increasing number of young people are exploring such things as tactical media, collective art-making, radical fashions and public reclamation projects. Granted, little of this is truly new. The 1920s, late 1960s and early 1980s witnessed scores of politically committed artists and groups who invented, and frequently re-invented, the forms and organizational methods of art activism. Perhaps this new wave of engaged art will find a way to sustain this momentum as well as pass along the lessons that previous artists could not? This book is our contribution to that aspiration.

Our early discussions about this book were preoccupied with producing a catalogue raisonné that was anything but predictable or conventional. Instead, our objective was to offer the reader a modest intervention that was similar in spirit to the work it was charged to represent. We were fortunate to have Arjen Noordeman, the newly hired MASS MoCA designer, enthusiastically embrace this mission, and the results are what follows. Nevertheless, all of this serious play was unexpectedly interrupted by the tragic events that unfolded shortly after the book's first print run went to press. As if to underscore the urgency of interventionist art, these events have once again placed issues of free speech and political dissent at the center of the contemporary art world.

On the morning of May 11, 2004, Professor Steven Kurtz, a member of the Critical Art Ensemble (CAE), awoke to find his wife lying beside him unresponsive. Kurtz called 911. But as paramedics arrived they also took notice of assorted laboratory equipment, some of it intended for use in Free Range Grain, an art project that was to be installed in MASS MoCA's upcoming exhibition *The Interventionists: Art in the Social Sphere*. Within hours, the FBI and the Joint Terrorism Task Force arrived at Kurtz's home wearing white Haz-Mat (hazardous materials) suits. Locking down the Kurtz home, they confiscated lab supplies, passports, computers and the body of Kurtz's wife, Hope, who was later found to have died of a heart attack in her sleep. They even impounded Kurtz's cat. Meanwhile, Kurtz was whisked off to a nearby hotel for 22 hours of questioning.

Within a day, government laboratory tests proved that the confiscated samples were of three common bacteria bacillus globigii, serratia marcenscens and e.coli – all routinely used in college biology classrooms. At this point the Eerie County Health Department announced that Kurtz's house posed no public danger. Officials gave Kurtz back his wife's body for burial. The FBI, however, continued to hold onto his passport, art supplies and other personal possessions. Nevertheless, Kurtz and many in the art community believed that the situation amounted to an overreaction by the government and that once Kurtz's identity as a university professor was known the matter would be dropped. Instead, the bizarre saga was only just beginning.

On May 30, 2004 as the Critical Art Ensemble gathered in North Adams for the MASS MoCA exhibition opening, two of the members were handed subpoenas by federal agents ordering them to appear before a grand jury on June 15th. It was now a little over two weeks since the loss of Kurtz's wife of 20 years, and, as if mirroring one of the CAE's own surreal parodies, Kurtz found himself under a full-blown investigation by the U.S. Attorney General's office. Eight more people were soon served subpoenas and, while neither the FBI nor the Attorney General would make public the details of the grand jury probe, it was evident from the wording of the documents that Kurtz was being investigated under US Code Title 18, Part I, Chapter #10, Sec. 175: Prohibitions with respect to Biological Weapons. The scope of this particular statute was expanded under the USA Patriot Act of 2001 to such a degree that the words "biological agent" might be interpreted to include the harmless bacteria Kurtz purchased for his art projects. After the hearings on June 15th the grand jury rejected all charges of bioterrorism. However, just as the entire incident seemed to finally end, Kurtz and a colleague, Professor Robert Ferrell, were charged with alleged mail and wire fraud for mishandling the purchase of bacterial samples obtained from a commercial supply house. If convicted, each could face up to twenty years in prison.

The Steve Kurtz case has garnered widespread media attention. While initially baffled at the language of biotechnology, the mainstream press sympathized with the artist as they rapidly connected the trail of dots between his wife's unfortunate death, his art, his trial and basic civic freedoms. Indeed, Steven Kurtz is but one of hundreds of individuals, many of Muslim background, but also artists, academics and scientists who have come under increased surveillance and investigation by the government since the passing of the USA Patriot Act of 2001. By calling attention to the shrinking of civil liberties in America today, the CAE investigation has served to politically awaken a portion of the art community while underscoring the risks that come with the creative disruption of everyday life.

Acknowledgements

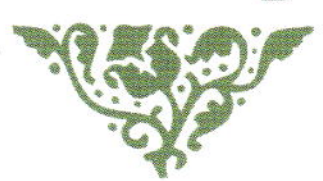

We would like to thank the following for their tremendous assistance on the catalogue and exhibition: Jessica Barthel, Gilly Barnes, Jeff Barnum, Al Bashevkin and his colleagues at Northern Berkshire Community Coalition, Gene Carlson and the North Adams Historical Society, Karyn Behnke and the Contemporary Artists Center, Creative Capital, Will Gelinas, Julie Hammond, Karl Hinojosa, Shawn Fogarty, Guenivere Johnson, Shea Kiley, Smith College Professors Lisa Armstrong and Donna Riley and their classes, Rebecca Uchill, Kathy and Tom Wallace and Elizabeth Zepp.

Foreword

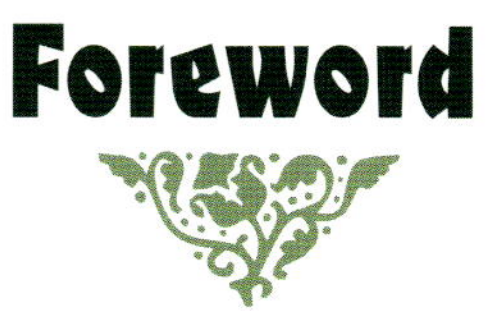

By Joseph Thompson
Director, MASS MoCA

The organized disruption of the World Trade Organization's 1999 meeting in Seattle always mystified me. Resorting to civil disobedience over the ambivalent concept of "globalism", breaking storefront glass in response to the workings of the international capital market, and wreaking havoc over the ubiquity of multinational corporate brands made as much sense to me as protesting the existence of jet stream, or the laws of thermodynamics.

Yet the depth of conviction of the protest movement was unmistakable. I could watch it on TV, as it played from Switzerland to Mexico.

At the same time, politically inspired art (and worse, political action running under art's banner) almost always leaves one cold. Nothing can suck the air around it like political art: so many words, so much ideology worn so transparently on the sleeve, so much certainty, and so little of interest to look at. For every artist like Jenny Holzer, whose works slice through the social sphere in ways that are as resistant as they are elegant, there are a hundred artist-activists whose work dead-ends at truisms asserting truth.

So why this show, which is about social engagement, and which, by and large, features practitioners who work more comfortably on the street and within a community of activists than in the gallery? Several answers: William Pope.L offered to help me get the black out, and I didn't know what he meant, the elliptical quality of his venture yielding something like mystery. I was intrigued when artist collective subRosa asked North Adams women — who, in other circumstances, might still have been producing the electronic components now being made by women in Juarez, Mexico — whether their jobs had really been lost, and what circumstances they might share with the Mexican ghosts of their labors, the inquiry re-casting macroeconomic issues of free trade in personal terms. J. Morgan Puett responded to our impossibly low budget by proposing to embed a sly business enterprise within our gallery space, an entrepreneurial fashion venture that literally turns the socioeconomic history of MASS MoCA's site inside out. And the riotous, pie-throwing, rascal-revelry of the Seattle protest — and some of the intellectual underpinnings of its political critique — surfaced in ways I could begin to fathom in the work of The Yes Men, YOMANGO, and the Institute of Applied Technology (many of whom have wry humor at the core of their work). In

short, Curator Nato Thompson kept showing up with fresh art that did indeed allow air in. The practice was ubiquitous and varied enough to demand survey.

And the timing seemed right. In a period when the doubly offensive phrase "culture war" is used to describe the controversy arising from Janet Jackson's strange televised breast misadventure, and, in the same breath, gay marriage rights; at a time when both those topics take bandwidth from debate about the nation's failing health care system, the survival of Social Security, and the outsourcing of technically sophisticated jobs from the United States to India, it's not inappropriate to see how some of the more thoughtful and politically acute artists respond.

And there is another skirmish going on, this one actually about culture: for the past few years, the most powerful critical winds have favored a self-referential art of beauty, craft, abstract luster, and evocative detail. The markets are responding: commercial galleries and museum exhibitions are overflowing with rich painting, lovely draftsmanship, and video installations of exquisite production values, MASS MoCA's own galleries included. With this ascendancy of form, our contrarian nature got the better of us.

Interventionist art does not always sit well in museums, produced, as much as it was, to create situations in the world at large. In some cases, we resort to documentary evidence of previous actions. In others, artists offer clever reconstructions. In yet others, this ephemeral work has no presence at all at MASS MoCA, having manifested itself on the streets of North Adams and surrounding towns. In all cases, however, we trust that some of the spirit of these interventionists (who no doubt shudder at the grouping, if not the term) shines through. You will no doubt smile a few times as you enjoy this show, and you might even get the black out. And by all means, feel free to leave our museum campus before getting too down with YOMANGO.

Table of Contents

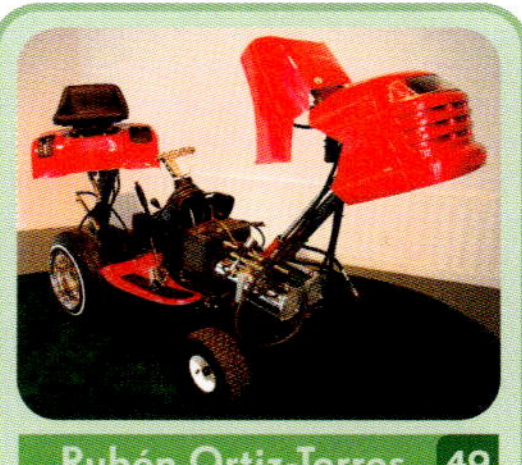
Rubén Ortiz-Torres 49

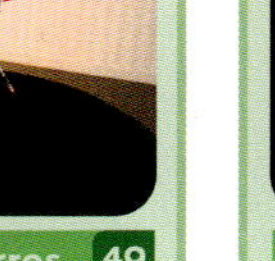
Michael Rakowitz 33

Artist Entries
Nato Thompson
and Rebecca Uchill

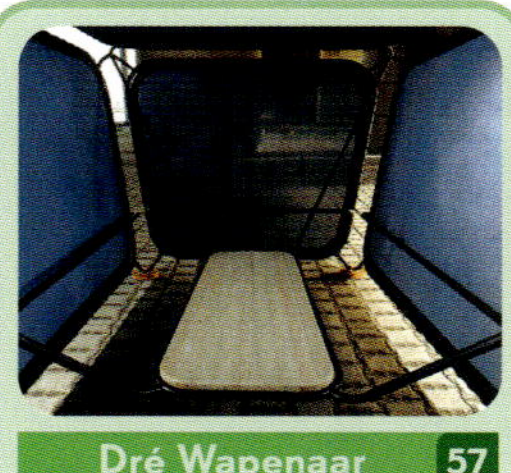
Dré Wapenaar 57

Nomads: Artists who produce work that encourages individual mobility and freedom: Krzysztof Wodiczko, Lucy Orta, Michael Rakowitz, William Pope.L, e-Xplo, Haha, Rubén Ortiz-Torres, Dré Wapenaar, N55

Reclaim the Streets:
Artists who produce actions that occur within the public sphere (sidewalks, parks, streets, malls, etc.): Craig Baldwin's Billboard Outlaws, Alex Villar, The Biotic Baking Brigade, God Bless Graffiti Coalition, Institute for Applied Autonomy, Oliver Ressler and Dario Azzellini, StreetRec, The Surveillance Camera Players, The Reverend Billy, Valerie Tevere, William Pope.L

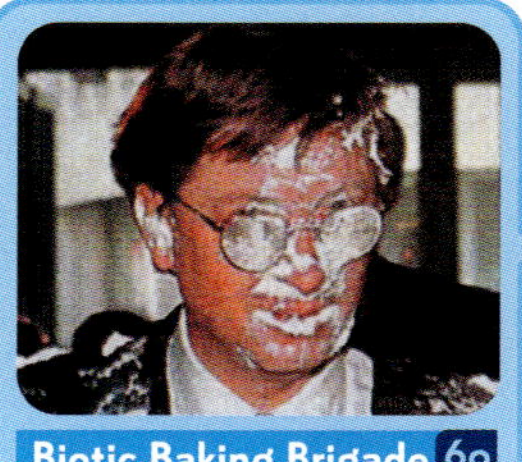
Biotic Baking Brigade 69

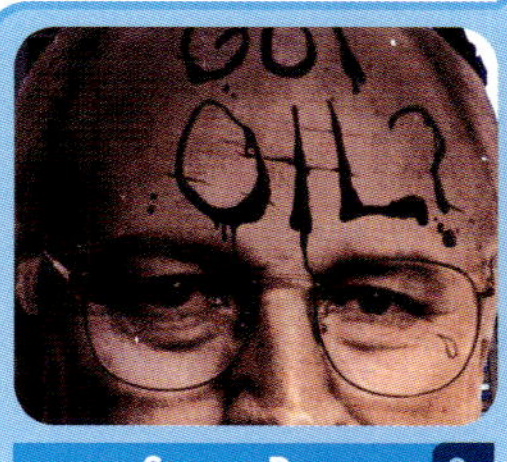

Street Rec 81

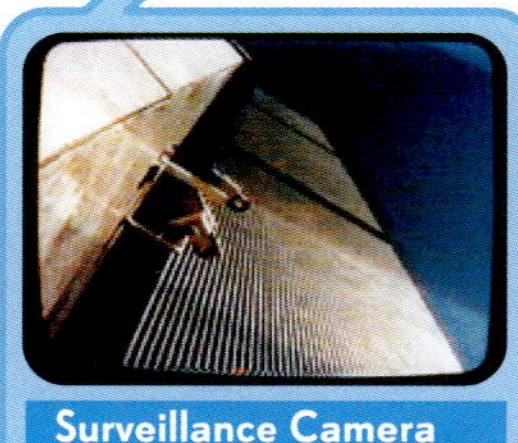
Surveillance Camera Players 83

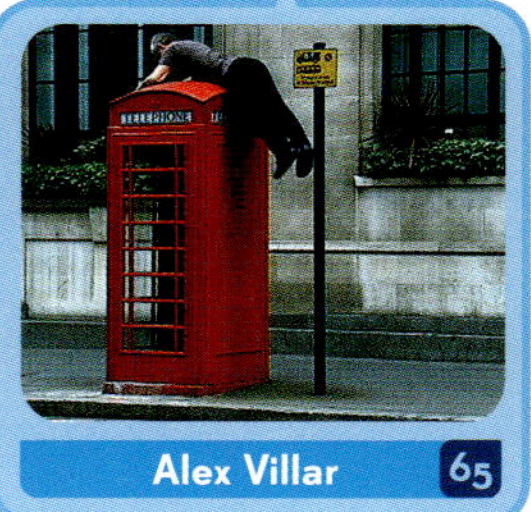
Alex Villar 65

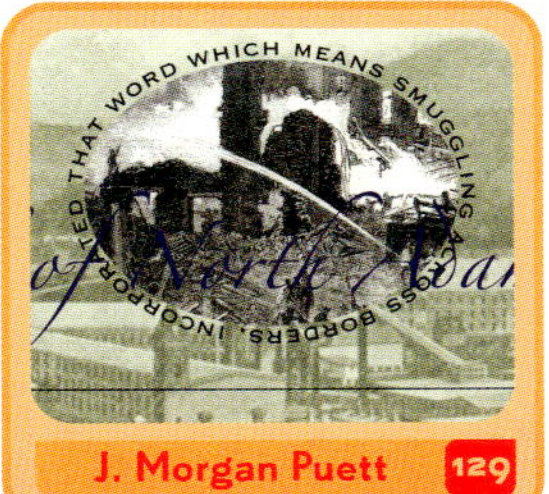

J. Morgan Puett 129

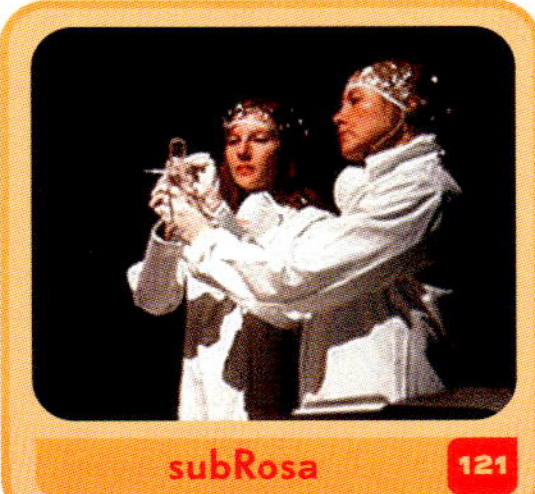

subRosa 121

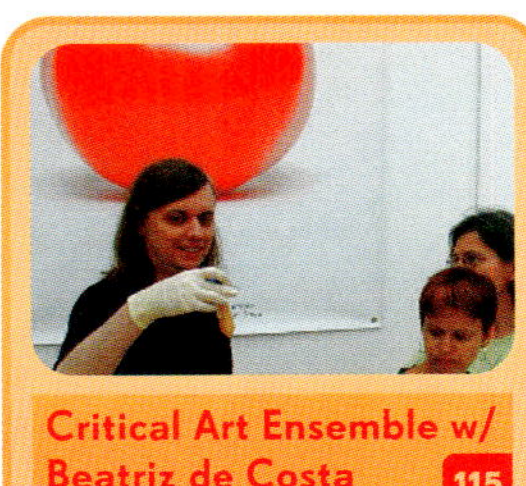

Critical Art Ensemble w/ Beatriz de Costa 115

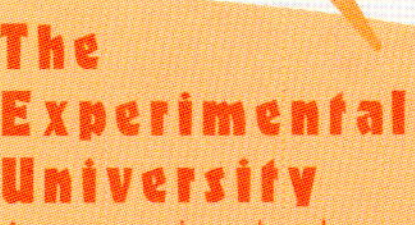

The Experimental University

Artists who deploy aesthetic strategies in other discourses including anthropology, biotechnology and urban geography: 16 Beaver St., The Atlas Group, Critical Art Ensemble with Beatriz de Costa, Spurse, subRosa, Tana Hargest, J. Morgan Puett

Ready to Wear:
Artists who produce tools and clothing to augment the wearer's sense of personal autonomy: Center for Tactical Magic, Lucy Orta, Rubén Ortiz-Torres, Krzysztof Wodiczko, The Yes Men, YOMANGO

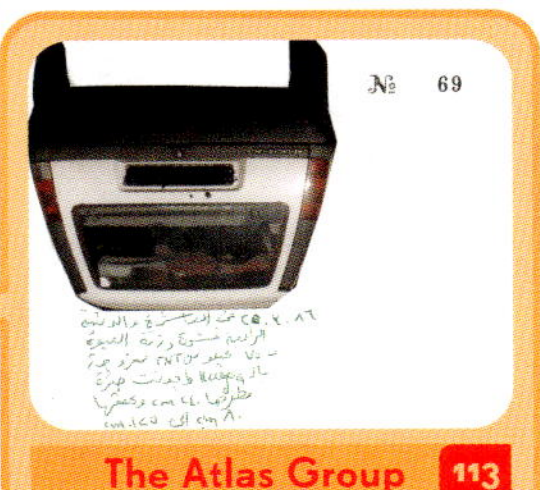

The Atlas Group 113

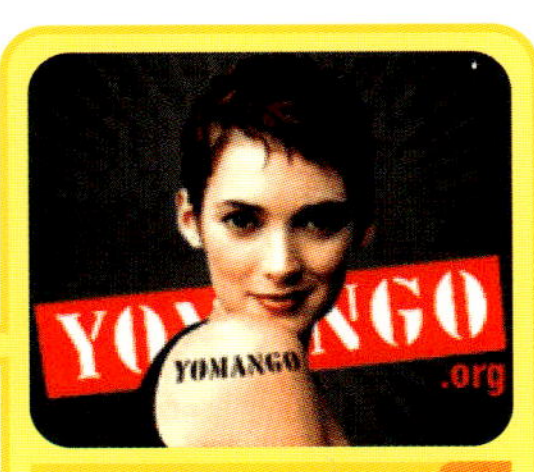

YOMANGO 107

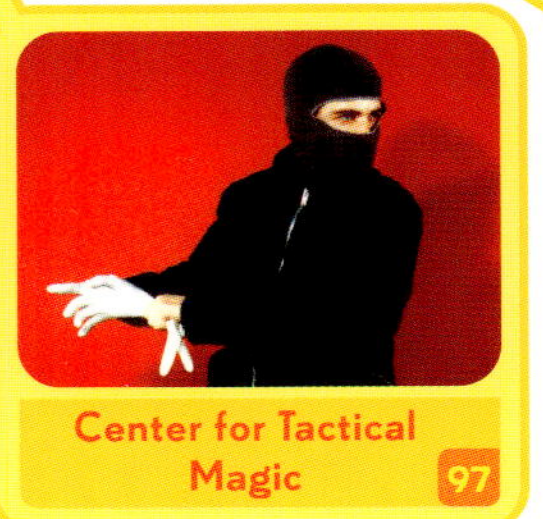

Center for Tactical Magic 97

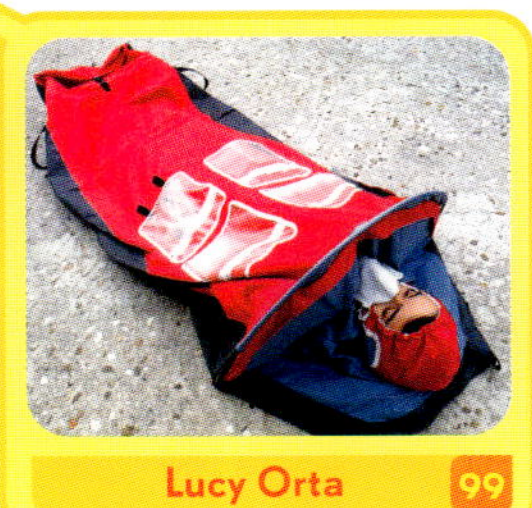

Lucy Orta 99

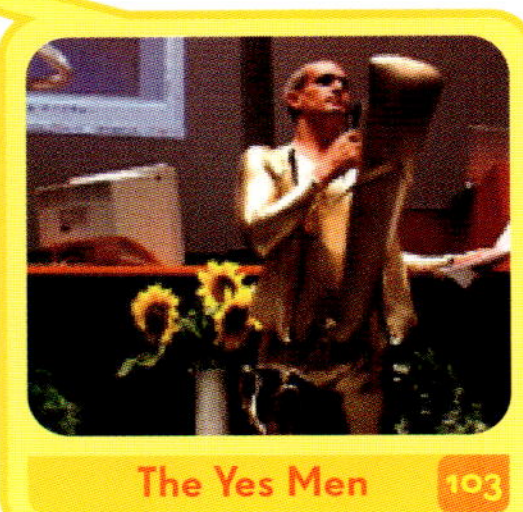

The Yes Men 103

Appendix:

Trespassing Relevance

By Nato Thompson

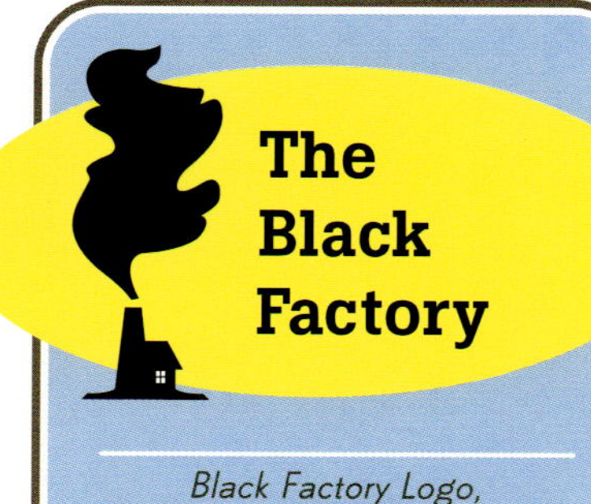

The Black Factory

Black Factory Logo,
William Pope.L

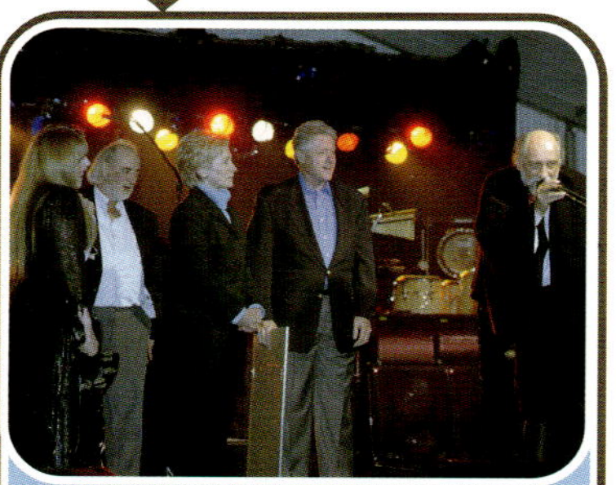

Bill Clinton and Fleetwood Mac
Photographer: Barbara Kinney
Courtesy of Barbara Kinney

You heard about its arrival but never expected it to work like this. The flyer asked you to "get the black out. Bring three to ten items that you associate with blackness to the Black Factory." Now you stand there watching a white box truck pull up to the local YMCA, wondering what on earth this truck wants with your coffee grounds, dominoes and Missy Elliot CDs. You watch the crew get out of the truck and unload a large table adorned with blenders, scissors and pulverizers. Then, suddenly, a white balloon begins to inflate from the back of the truck. To your total surprise, the balloon takes the shape of a massive igloo. You can faintly see the workers setting up display booths inside it. Instead of the Black Panther Willie Wonka you expected, the artist William Pope.L is friendly. He talks and laughs with the people beginning to bring their items of "blackness" for pulverization. You nervously approach and hear Pope.L say, "Well, the Black Factory is here to provide opportunity."

The *Black Factory* epitomizes the work of the interventionists, touring the New England countryside, "bringing the politics of difference where it is needed most," as William Pope.L advertises. At each stop, it offers the local community a set of tools for disrupting expectations. People contribute their items of blackness only to have them transformed into unlikely objects: rubber duckies, prayer rugs, drinking water. The *Black Factory* experience is ambiguous, ambivalent, even confusing, but it delivers the one thing that it promotes: opportunity.

The Interventionists: Art in the Social Sphere is a survey, in limited form, of tactical practices in contemporary visual culture beginning in the late 1980s. The timing of this exhibition is not without a sense of urgency; the entire world feels "unsettled" (to use globalism theorist Saskia Sassen's term)[1] due in no small part to the recent wars in Iraq and Afghanistan. If it's true that artists operate as both a social litmus of politics today and a harbinger of politics tomorrow, then this is a good time to survey the field.

A cursory scan over the last ten years of American art may lead one to believe that "political art" has fallen out of fashion since artists like Barbara Kruger, Hans Haacke, Leon Golub and Jenny Holzer took center stage in the early 1980s. Fashionable or not, however, political art has continued, albeit off the art world radar screen, throughout the 1990s.[2] The most telling point of departure for this "off the radar" art practice is its increasing emphasis on the tactics of intervention. Instead of representing politics (whether through language or through visual imagery), many political artists of the 1990s enter physically; that is, they place their work into the heart of the political situation itself. "Tactics" is the key term for discussing interventionist practices, and it will be examined at greater depth later in this essay. For now, let us think of the term "tactic" as a maneuver within a game which, for the interventionists, is almost always the real world. Their projects are made to operate within and upon systems of power and trade using the techniques of art. Driving around the United States with a factory for grinding up expectations about race is just one example.

In an era shaped by the phenomenon known as globalism, the aesthetic of tactical intervention has been more warmly received outside the U.S. than in it. However, the dialogue about tactics amplified by the internet and global exhibitions and conventions — has flowed across oceans and nations. Thus, this exhibition spotlights what is a worldwide tendency to insert the practice of art into the social realm.

Tactics can be thought of as a set of tools. Like a hammer, a glue gun, or a screwdriver, they are means for building and deconstructing a given situation. Interventionists are informed both by art and (more importantly) by a broad range of visual, spatial and cultural experiences.[3] They are a motley assemblage of methods for bringing political issues to an audience outside the insular art world's doors. They appeal to a viewer who is confronted by an increasingly privatized and controlled visual world. Humor, sleight of hand and high design are used to interrupt this confrontation and bring socially imperative issues to the very feet of their audiences.

If one had to make a generalization about the political art of the 1990s, it would be a near unanimous refusal to restrict their actions to mere representation. The images of violence and exploitation that so often, rightfully, move people to political action are conspicuously absent. Instead, laboratory experiments, perplexing archives, mobile homes, and bags designed to facilitate shoplifting fill MASS MoCA's gallery spaces. That these things "present," as opposed to "represent," is not an accident. When the words "political art" are spoken, most people imagine a unilateral institutional critique - depressing refugee photographs, or possibly graphic statements attacking the viewer for ignorant complicity. The symbolically charged image or overtly political text no longer feels adequate as a communicative device. Preaching is suspect. But why? In short, visual exhaustion, such pivotal factors as the rise of the culture industry, the demise of the Soviet Union, and the increasing privatization of public visual and social space have dramatically transformed the cultural landscape of the 1990s.

The '90s: A Taco Revolution

The sixties are more than merely the homeland of hip, they are a commercial template for our times, a historical prototype for the construction of cultural machines that transform alienation and despair into consent.
                    - Thomas Frank, *Conquest of Cool*.[4]

The various analyses of "new social movements" have done a great service in insisting on the political importance of cultural movements against narrowly economic perspectives that minimize their significance. These analysis, however, are extremely limited themselves because, just like the perspectives they oppose, they perpetuate narrow understandings of the economic and the cultural. Most importantly, they fail to recognize the profound economic power of the cultural movements, or really the increasing indistinguishability of economic and cultural phenomena.
                    - Antonio Negri and Michael Hardt, *Empire*.[5]

"A taco revolution, I am there."
                    - -Taco Bell Chihuahua dog.

In 1992, Bill Clinton assumed the U.S. presidency to the rock and roll sounds of Fleetwood Mac. Baby boomers were in the ascendancy, and the horn of victory Clinton raised was his own saxophone. The moment was prescient. Just three years earlier, the Berlin Wall fell and the "end of history," as Francis Fukuyama had so famously described it, was upon the world. The 1990s were a complex decade known for the rise of the dot-coms, the generational switch in power to the baby boomers, the end of the Cold War, and the end of revolutions. Yet, revolutions were still occurring. They were marketing revolutions, as the most popular marketing campaign of the 1990s — the Che Guevarian-clad Taco Bell Chihuahua — so glamorously made known. The United States officially shifted toward an "information economy", with the often contested but frequently used term "globalism" as its dancing partner.

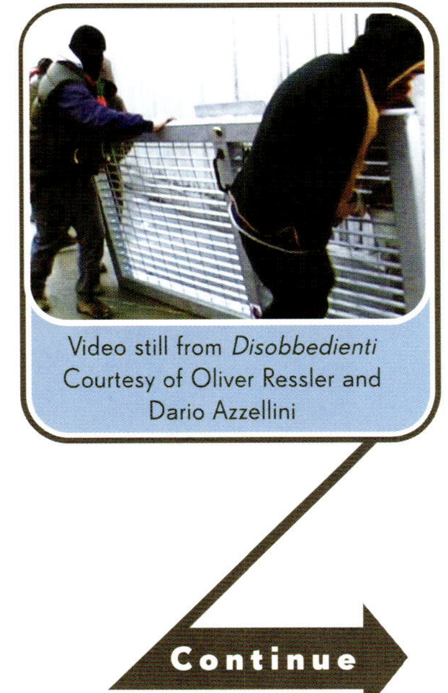

Video still from *Disobbedienti*
Courtesy of Oliver Ressler and
Dario Azzellini

Continue

Theodore Adorno, the genuinely cynical member of the German Frankfurt School, dubbed the commercialization of culture "the culture industry," a derogatory catchall term for everything from film to television to music to advertising to fashion to, of course, art. In short, the culture industry — so defined — comprises most of the service industry markets we encounter every day. The fact that "culture" became a primary industry of global capitalism was not lost on many of the artists across the globe. Globalism and the culture industry combined to form a fertile ground for the growth of interventionist practices. Through the 1990s, the branding of culture took an especially strong step forward. As Naomi Klein writes in her insightful book, *No Logo*, "The effect, if not always the original intent, of advanced branding is to nudge the hosting culture into the background and make the brand the star. It is not to sponsor culture but to be the culture."[6]

The fact that the visual and cultural apparatuses of the globe were honing in on the once rarified niche of artistic practice could only have dramatic effects on the terms in which artists saw themselves.

A signature element of this growth of the culture industry was the emphatic co-opting of all forms of America's counterculture. The major powers in the U.S. economy were now standing side by side with beatniks, ravers, punks, gangsters, and revolutionaries. The culture industry found resonance in promoting the likes of Jack Kerouac and Mahatma Ghandi in advertisements for The Gap and Apple Computer, respectively. When Stevie Nicks sang "Don't Stop" to a captivated audience, with Hillary and Bill clapping in the background, we got a clue as to the tenor of the next decade. We were entering a period of rebels, repackaged. The heroic alternative culture of the 1960s (the easy rider, the beatnik, the lonestar, the hippie, the drag queen, the revolutionary) became the poster children of the 1990s.

A particularly telling point occurred in December 1991 when underground band Nirvana reached number one on the pop charts. Alternative music had officially become mainstream. Black culture, feminist culture, and queer culture gradually followed. For the first time in music history, in October 2003 none of the artists on the top ten singles charts were white.[7] The music industry embraced all points of view, and yet still just one reaped the cornucopia of American difference.

This switch in the role of cultural production radically affected the way in which cultural producers, including visual artists, saw their "content." In 1915, a person might go entire weeks without observing an advertisement. The average adult today sees some three thousand a day.[8] The dramatic increase in popular visual inundation, coupled with the growing use of symbols of political action (like Che Guevara, Mao or Bob Dylan) for commercial purposes, meant that artists needed to reconfigure their tactics to make themselves heard. How could any artist compete with image juggernauts like Nike, Gap, Starbucks, McDonald's, or MTV? Terms like "content provider" became common, as anything resistant and edgy was used to sell an underlying not-so-hip consumerism agenda. If Che Guevara could

be turned into a marketing-Chihuahua for Taco Bell, left-leaning political artists had no more air to breathe. The counterculture was out of room.

At the same time, globalism became a household word. While interconnectedness between nations had been increasing over the past century, the 1990s saw a rapid acceleration of these processes. The Treaty on European Union signed in Maastricht (1992), the creation of the North American Free Trade Agreement (1994), and the introduction of the Euro (1999) are just a few notable examples. Accompanying these processes was the now-familiar movement of factories to nations with cheaper labor pools, the increased hybridization and displacement of cultures and the boom of global cities like New York City, Buenos Aires, Tokyo, Berlin, and London, to name a few.[9] The sudden conclusion of the Cold War elicited from leaders in the West a "full steam ahead" approach to neo-liberal economic models across the globe. And, in the art world specifically, the rise of biennials created the sense that art was being de-centered, and this de-centered quality was big business.

Activists across the world reconceived their practices in reaction to the changing political climate. The effects of globalism were not without oppositional political responses, as the Seattle protests against the World Trade Organization in November 1999 made clear. The Seattle protests marked a critical moment in progressive political history because the rallying cry was not against a specific government, but against the intangible and relatively abstract international finance organizations that so perfectly represented the shift toward an unchecked, diffuse, international power. Since that pivotal event in 1999, the global justice movement has tracked the movement of international finance: the International Monetary Fund meeting in Washington DC (2000); World Bank/IMF meeting, Prague (2000); G20 meeting in Quebec (2000); World Economic Forum, Davos, Switzerland (2001); FTAA Summit of the Americas, Quebec City (2001); EU Summit, Gothenburg, Sweden (2001); G8 Summit, Genoa, Italy (2001); World Economic Forum, New York City (2002); EU Summit, Barcelona (2002); and WTO, Cancun, Mexico (2003), to name a few. Power and resistance have obviously gone global.

While creation of cultural content was absorbed by the cultural industry, physical urban space underwent a parallel co-opting. In the major American cities of New York, Los Angeles, and Chicago, as well as internationally, artists began to register the effects of globalism in their neighborhoods. Gentrification became a buzz-word to describe the efforts by many cities to remake their downtowns into inviting hot spots for global capital. Artists found their own housing habits complicit with renewal strategies for evicting lower-income families in larger metropolitan areas. Rosalyn Deutsche writes in *Evictions: Art and Spatial Politics*, "When galleries and artists, assuming the role of the proverbial 'shock troops' of gentrification, moved into inexpensive storefronts and apartments, they aided the mechanism by driving up rents and displacing residents."[10] While housing increasingly felt the brunt of expanded privatization, so too did the arts (see Gregory Sholette's essay in this book). The space for non-commercially driven art, generally the haven for supporting and legitimating political art practice, rapidly decreased. As Brian Wallis, Chief Curator at the International Center for Photography in New York, writes, "In recent years, the gradual withdrawal and relocation of NEA funds has created a sort of Darwinian ethos in the world of alternative spaces. Many of the smaller and more fragile spaces have ceased to operate or have become 'virtual spaces.' Those that have survived have become larger and more like those institutions they once challenged."[11] While political representation was being depoliticized, space, it seemed, was becoming radically politicized. This twist is the critical turn.[12]

The '60s Malcontent Speak Out

This is not to say that these conditions - the increasing banality of revolutionary images coupled with the increasing politicization of urban space - arose out of the 1990s, but rather that they became all the more acute during this period. It is instructive to look at the writings of the Situationists (1957-1972), an avant-garde collective inspired by Dada, CoBRA (acronym meaning: Copenhagen, Brussels, and Amsterdam) and the International Movement for an Imaginist Bauhaus. The Situationists included the Danish painter Asger Jorn (1914-1973), the Dutch urban designer Constant Nieuwenhuys (born in 1920), and theorist Raoul Vaneigem (born in 1934).

In his seminal work, *Society of the Spectacle,* Guy Debord (1932-1994), the most outspoken member of the Situationists, warned of the spectacle nature of late capitalist society. By spectacle (a key term for the Situationists), Debord meant the overtly visual and alienating aspect of late capital. While more orthodox Marxists of the period were haggling over the alienation caused by the rise of consumerism, the Situationists asserted that culture itself was fast becoming the ultimate commodity. Clothing, music, film, television, and even walking were all forms of commodification. Their hysteria finds validity in the increasing privatization of culture, in the form of intellectual copyright, and in the shrinkage, policing, and control of public space. If culture was turning into a commodity, then the Situationists were determined to develop methods to confront and reverse this trend.

The Tools

The Situationists' aspirations resulted in the development of two key tactics subsequently embraced by most of the artists in this exhibition. The first is the *detourné*, which is the rearranging of popular sign-systems in order to produce new meanings. For the Situationists, this took the form of reinserting their own language into the thought bubbles of popular comic strips. In the comic strip on the following page, the gentleman is saying "The very development from class society to the spectacular organization of non-life leads the revolutionary project to become visibly what it already was essentially." This form found new relevance in the 1990s when "culture jammers" and, later, magazines like *AdBusters* began rampantly re-articulating popular advertising to produce an underlying message, such as the McDeath logo.

The second tactic was the *dérive:* a short meandering walk determined by one's desires. The *dérive* was designed to resist the work and control-oriented design of Paris that had been put in place by Baron Haussmann in the 19th century. The *dérive* would reveal hints of what the Situationists called psycho-geography, "the study of the precise effects of geographical setting, consciously managed or not, acting directly on the mood and behavior of the individual."[13] While at first such meanderings may seem fairly leisurely and not the least bit political, they propose the radical idea that ways of being in physical space (particularly in the cities) are political acts. The confluence of the détourne and the dérive manages to territorialize the visual. The spectacle is a territory. The city is a spectacle. Both tactics, *dérive* and *detourné*, take trespassing as their essential character. They must cross into the territory of others, whether these are the advertisements of Nike or the orderly storefronts of Paris, to produce new meanings. This sensibility becomes visually apparent in the video performances of Alex Villar. In his 2001 project *Temporary Occupations*, Villar performs movements that resist the structuring of public space. He clambers up, hops over, crawls into, and slides past fences and walls designed to prevent one from entering particular spaces in the city. These actions bring to light the nature of the built environment and how strongly it is developed around the boundaries of public and private.

As we know, the political upheavals of the adolescent baby boomer generation (born between 1946 and 1964) were not simply occurring in the streets of Paris, but around the world. In the United States, foremost "culture jammers" were the extraordinary yippies Abbie Hoffman and Jerry Rubin, whose pranksterish antics foreshadow much of the interventionist work of the 1990s. One of their most enduring actions took place on August 24, 1967, when Hoffman led a group to the New York Stock Exchange and dropped dollar bills to the traders below. The sudden appearance of money flittering down from the sky caused eager traders to pile on top of each other as they instinctually chased the cash. As planned, news of the Wall Street action was quickly broadcast around the globe. As Jerry Rubin states, "You can't be a revolutionary today without a television set - it's as important as a gun! Every guerilla must know how to use the terrain of culture that he is trying to destroy!"[14] The Yippies understood the connection between the spectacle, media, and political action, and their influence can be seen in much of the work in this exhibition.

Hoffman and Rubin understood the importance of mixing wit with drama in their actions (the Situationists, on the contrary, did not possess much of a sense of humor). The yippies' politics, while just as heartfelt and real as those of the Students for a Democratic Society, were tempered by an understanding of how they would be interpreted on a national media front. Humor was a tactic. Antics were a tool. Their actions were a manipulation of visual codes in a specific time and in a specific place that produced a critical result. The codes were redesigned, for application in the streets, on a billboard, on one's body, or in a classroom.

Continue

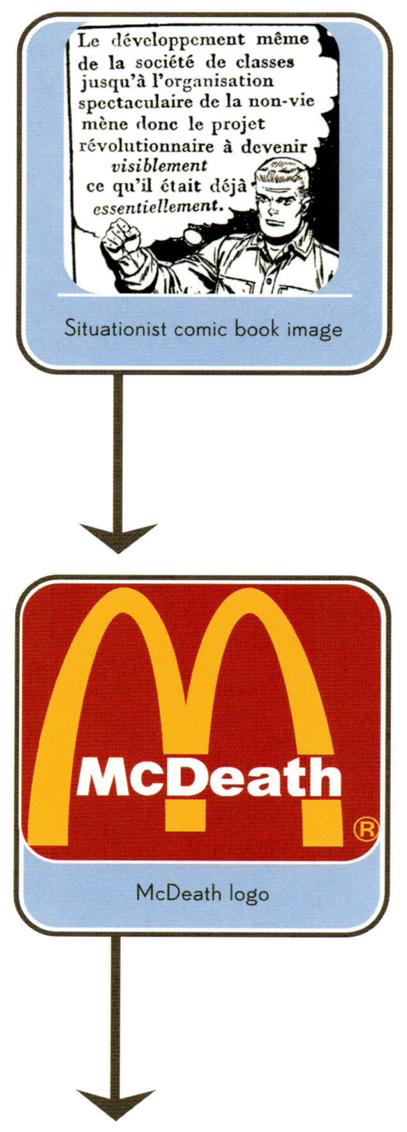

Situationist comic book image

McDeath logo

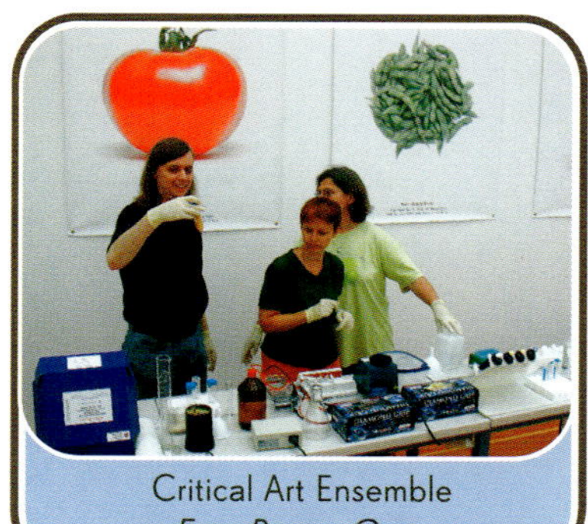

Critical Art Ensemble
Free Range Grain

Indeed, Rubin and Hoffman thought of life as a game, and they played well. To assure success, their clever projects were designed for the media and for public consumption. They calculated that if they could get the audience to laugh, the political message would follow.

Art in the Social Sphere

In *Free Range Grain*, the collective Critical Art Ensemble with Beatriz de Costa has transported a genetically modified organism (GMO) testing lab to the gallery space, where they will test for GMOs "organic" foods bought from stores. They anticipate that many of the foods labeled "organic" will test positive for GMOs. This revelation is not meant as an exposé on inaccurate packaging of organic foods so much as an amateur experiment that makes visible the extent to which the complex science of agro-business has inserted itself into the food chain, even where we least expect it.

For the last decade, Critical Art Ensemble has made the field of biotechnology its focus. Biotechnology is a system of knowledge that has particular rules and advantages for those who have control over it. The members of Critical Art Ensemble are amateur researchers purposefully operating in a system controlled by someone else. They are "intervening" in biotechnology and reworking the premises of how science should progress. This is the inflection point at which the reworking of a system, or language, can become a social or political happening. When Critical Art Ensemble inserts its own home-brewed science techniques into the field of genetically modified foods, it does so in order to challenge the role of the individuals, corporations, and scientific systems that determine the rules of the game of biotechnology.

The Interventionists illustrates a broad field of approaches, categorized into four sections: Reclaim the Streets, Nomads, Ready to Wear, and the Experimental University. Almost every project in the exhibition could fit into more than one category. Generally, the combination of a series of tactics is used to produce a result.

The reader will note that the catalogue is designed like a users' manual. Recalling Russian Constructivist Vladimir Mayakovsky's (1893-1930) book of poems designed by Lazar "El" Lissitzky (1890-1941), the book has thumb tabs which allow the "user/reader" to flip to specific sections.

Reclaim the Streets (RTS)

"Today, street action groups such as the Tutte Bianche use spectacular forms of conflict and theatrical actions designed for filming, such as climbing up a huge crane and risking one's own life to hang a banner." -Encrico Ludovici, from the film Disobbedienti *by Oliver Ressler and Dario Azzellini, 2002.*

The streets have long embodied the public sphere: a space where the entire citizenry can participate democratically and freely. Most political artists desire to reach the general public, and so the streets are their most natural field of action (far more hospitable than the museum, which remains anathema to many.) The section "Reclaim the Streets" (RTS) is named after the radical form of protest begun in London in 1991. RTS began as a logging protest that rearranged the rules of dissent by introducing DJs, dancing, wild costumes and pleasure to radical politics in the streets. Influenced in large part by the boom of rave culture in England, the combination of pageantry and civil disobedience has since become a signature characteristic of political participation in the 1990s. Art and radical politics appeared to merge under the famous anarchist Emma Goldman's dictum, "If I can't dance, I don't want to be in your revolution."[15]

This pageantry takes on a remarkable performative quality in the sermons of the Reverend Billy. A disillusioned performance-artist-turned-street-activist, Bill Talen donned the disguise of a white-haired fanatical priest to preach his over-the-top brand of anti-consumerism gospel in the heart of capitalism: Disney Stores and Starbucks. Much like the Brazilian Augusto Boal's Invisible Theater, the Reverend Billy's actions use daily life, whether it is a corporate franchise or public sidewalk, as the stage. He delivers diabolical sermons against globalization, consumerism, and the privatization of daily life:

"I am preaching here in the Disney Store today because I am a tourist myself. Like all New Yorkers I am allowing this apocalypse to take place. I know that Manhattan in fourteen months will be entirely within the hellishly expanded Disney Store. This is Manhattan as suburban mall. This is a fatal disease known as Involuntary Entertainment."[16]

Since 2000, the Reverend Billy's unexpected appearances at various multinational corporations have won a cult following. His sermons at Starbucks have been so successful that the company developed a document for its employees letting them know the proper protocol for dealing with Reverend Billy appearances.

The urban environment has also been home to a variety of ad-hoc decorations, such as graffiti, wheatpaste posters, stickers, and stencils. This do-it-yourself (DIY) aesthetic is often relegated to an "outsider" part of the art world since it is predicated on unsanctioned space. Or to speak plainly, these projects often shine brightest when they are illegal. The street aesthetic thrives on the antagonisms of public space, and retains allegiance to more traditional forms of social resistance such as broadsheets, manifesto's, political posters, and leaflets. For this exhibition the God Bless Graffiti Coalition has assembled over 200 of these projects that range from the more directly political work of Claude Moller to the simply beautiful work of Swoon.

The street can be a forum for discussion or — in the case of the collective e-Xplo — a subject in itself. E-Xplo uses the bus tour, a more down-to-earth version of the Situationist *dérive*, to transform preconceived notions of the collective environment. As e-Xplo member Rene Gabri says of their project, "We try to take familiar sites and open them up to new readings and possibilities. These sites range from the physical sites we explore to the discursive sites we inhabit; even the 'tour' itself becomes something to interrogate and question. Rather than an end point, the tour is really a tool for introducing questions, a familiar departing point for a set of overlapping journeys."[17]

In their project for the exhibition, *Roundabout - Love at Leisure: Help Me Stranger* (2004), e-Xplo's tour bus meanders between MASS MoCA and the Sterling and Francine Clark Art Institute in nearby Williamstown. The passengers listen to a Global Positioning System (GPS)-triggered soundtrack designed to enliven the side streets between the two cultural institutions. As one travels between these areas, the auditory environment encourages a contemplative form of viewing: an abandoned factory: a drive-through cemetery, a family's front yard all are seen in a new light. Geography becomes contested and re-interpretable. For a brief period, the means/ends of commuter travel is reworked as the living landscape. Its meaning is tossed up for grabs during a delightful ride.

And at other times, cultivating public participation becomes an interventionist project in and of itself, as in the work of collective Haha and their project *Taxi, North Adams* (2004). Haha collected submissions of short phrases from North Adams residents and community groups relating to specific sites in their neighborhoods. The taxi provided free rides for community members while displaying — through computer-assisted flash animation on LCD screens atop the taxi — these site-sensitive statements. With the assistance of geographically sensitive technology, Haha transformed what is usually a space for advertisements into a space for public expression. In essence, they encouraged North Adams to talk to itself about itself.

Nomads
The Situationists may have walked the streets, but today many artists prefer wheels. These interventionists are nomads cruising through the homeland to discover and support dissonant forms of existence. As described earlier, William Pope.L's extraordinary *Black Factory* (2004) serves as one of the most elaborate forms of the Situationists' *dérive* existing today.

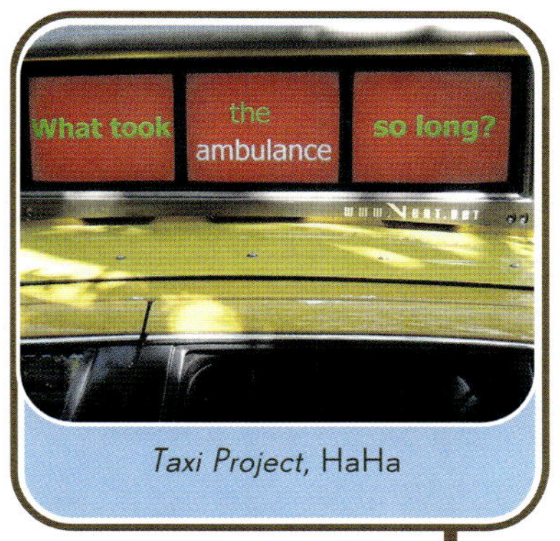

Taxi Project, HaHa

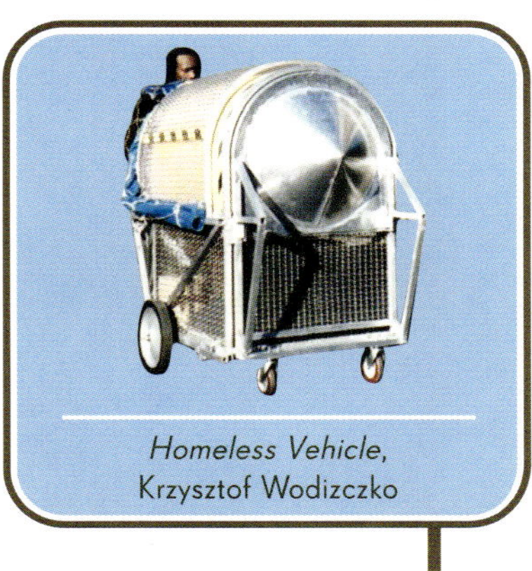

Homeless Vehicle,
Krzysztof Wodiczko

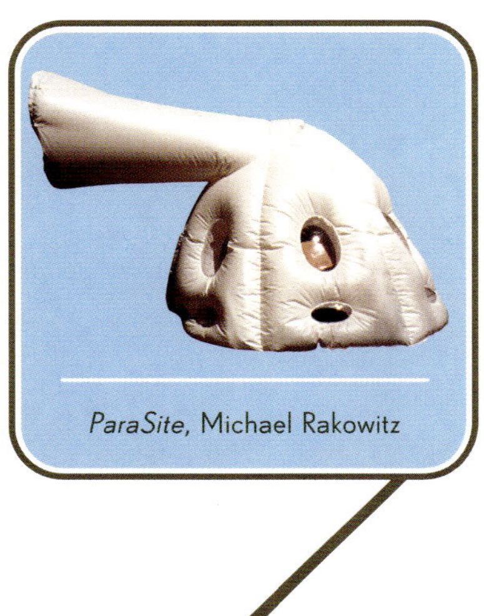

ParaSite, Michael Rakowitz

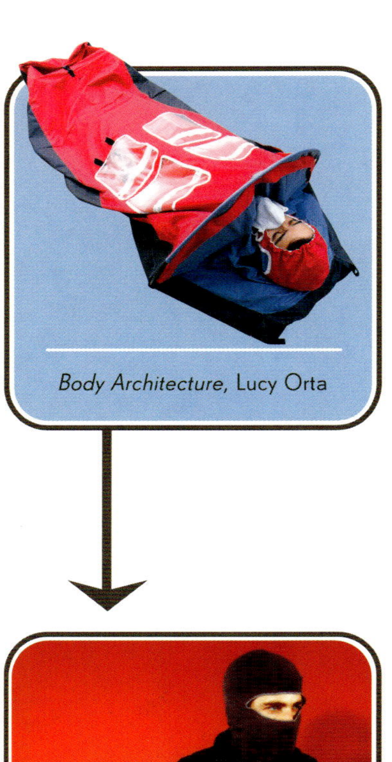

Body Architecture, Lucy Orta

Center for Tactical Magic,
The Ultimate Jacket

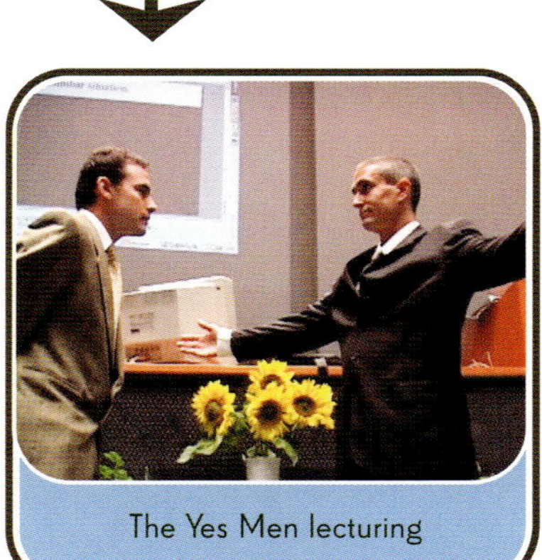

The Yes Men lecturing

For many artists, the use of vehicles (often coupled with advanced technologies) owes much to Krzysztof Wodiczko, who developed many of the milestone ideas of transport-based art.

For over thirty years, Polish-born Wodiczko has expanded the Russian Constructivists' notion of utility and technology for the public good. As Wodiczko acknowledges, his work is a mix of Situationism and Constructivism with design. "Designers must work in the world rather than 'about' or upon it."[18] His preferred term is "interrogative design," which he has incorporated into his teaching at the Center for Advanced Visual Studies (CAVS) at MIT. With a shift away from representation and an emphasis on "use" in the social sphere, Wodiczko has not only given interventionist artists some of the most powerful visual forms, but also an ideological foundation. By emphasizing use over representation, Wodiczko's projects reveal his inherent suspicions of capital and control. His projects tend to augment individual autonomy and make visible certain forms of social oppression. As an émigré from Poland, Wodiczko tempers his political affinities with a suspicion of all large systems, communist and capitalist.

Wodiczko's *Homeless Vehicle Project* (1988-89) was a critical point of departure for much interventionist political art of the 1990s. The design of the vehicle was inspired by the 1987 mandate by New York Mayor Ed Koch that all homeless people in New York must undergo psychiatric evaluations, and, if they failed, would face hospitalization. Wodiczko decided to focus on the issue of homelessness and used the shopping cart as his form. After conversations with homeless people, Wodiczko designed the *Homeless Vehicle* for multiple purposes. The *Homeless Vehicle* not only provided a user-friendly place for sleeping and can-collection, but also gave symbolic form to the social issue of homelessness. Wodiczko is under no illusion that he is capable of acting as a social service agency. He believes this is the job of a properly functioning government. The artist's job is different: "The oldest and most common reference to this kind of design is the bandage. A bandage covers and treats a wound while at the same time exposing its presence, signifying both the experience of pain and the hope of recovery."[19]

"Mobile" projects have followed the example of Wodiczko's *Homeless Vehicle*. Michael Rakowitz, a student of Wodiczko's at CAVS, is the author of one such project called *paraSITE* (1998) which, as the name implies, literally feeds off the urban environment. Using the heating, ventilation and air conditioning exhausts of buildings, the homeless shelter inflates with this "found air." Rakowitz produced many *paraSITE* projects in consultation with homeless people who helped design the inflatable home so that it could be folded into a small bundle and carried in one's pocket.

Many of these "mobile" projects have affinities in displaced populations. The mobile nature of the works point, in function, to a nomadic populace who become *de facto* parasites of the urban environment. Tools for mobility are prescient in a world increasingly forced to stay on the move. There is, for example, an abundance of tents in *The Interventionists*. The tent is mobile architecture. The tent provides a home for those trespassing or camping out in public space. It facilitates autonomy and, like Wodiczko's bandage, points to the need for self-sufficiency in displaced populations. Perhaps no one, except Buckminster Fuller, has explored the functional and symbolic possibilities of tents more than Dutch artist/designer Dré Wapenaar. Wapenaar has produced tents for reading newspapers, playing pianos, hanging off trees, and, in this exhibition, for giving birth and for memorializing the dead.

Ready to Wear

Trained as a fashion designer, Lucy Orta develops conceptual and functional projects that extend and perpetuate her socially engaged aesthetic. She produces nomadic architecture as well as nomadic clothing. In Orta's oeuvre, clothes become tools that activate the body as a locus for politics. Among many of her radical fashion creations, she has developed architectural clothing lines that make literal the symbols of Wodiczko's *Homeless Vehicle*. Her Refuge Wear series (1992-1998), which she produced in response to the Gulf War, won Orta international attention. The work is most distilled in the early piece *Habitent* (1992-93): a tent/jacket with whistle, lantern, and transport bag. Here we see yet another example of clothing making visible and assisting the situation of global refugees. Her clothes are spaces of refuge at the most intimate of levels.[20] Her fashion is of resistance and survival.

Fashion also acts as camouflage. As the Center for Tactical Magic (CTM) writes, "Disguise is the power to conceal, to hide away in the shadows of another's misperception. The appropriation of signifiers in the minds of onlookers, keyed in to their signal decoders along hacked bandwidths."[21] Going "under cover" is not so much an entertaining game (although fun does play a part); it is often a necessary survival tactic when trespassing. Influenced by various schools of concealment and espionage (private detective, magician, ninja), the CTM produced *The Ultimate Jacket* (2004) as a means to augment the ability to act in various situations. The jacket contains over 50 secret pockets and allows an intrepid interventionist to segue from the identity of a worker, for example, to ninja.

The art of undercover finds perhaps its greatest example in the work of the collective, the Yes Men. Although their name contains the word "Men," it doesn't describe who they are; it describes what they do. Yes Men use any means necessary to agree their way into the fortified compounds of commerce, ask questions, and then smuggle out the stories of their undercover escapades to provide a public glimpse at the behind-the-scenes world of business.[22]

Their project stems from the strange opportunities made available when the group took control of the website www.gatt.org. The site copied the official site for the General Agreement of Trades and Tariffs, with a few critical modifications. The collective has a history of producing these sites, such as their previous web creation www.GWBush.org. Treating these domains as public terrain, the collective created its own version of these various political entities. While they expected some people to confuse their site with the official one, they did not expect visitors to actually invite them to speak as official representatives of these organizations. Their charade became increasingly complex.

In October 2000, the Yes Men found themselves in the confounding situation of agreeing to speak in Salzburg, Austria, on behalf of the World Trade Organization (WTO) at a conference of international trade lawyers. The Yes Men wrote that unfortunately the General Director of the WTO, Michael Moore, would be unable to attend but they would happily send a substitute representative, Dr. Andreas Bichlbaum. Dr. Bichlbaum arrived with a security guard and cameraman and proceeded to give an audacious Powerpoint presentation on the need to streamline voting in the United States by selling votes on-line and the need to ban siestas as an inefficient holiday. After the talk, the cameraman claimed Dr. Bichlbaum received a pie in the face from an angry anti-WTO protester.

Since their first foray into speaking, the Yes Men have given several talks, with increasing absurdity, as representatives of the WTO. The gold leotard with a three-foot phallus on display here is the result of one of the Yes Men's most bizarre forays in Tampere, Finland. The group, represented this time by Hank Hardy Unruh, presented a lecture to a group of Finnish college students on the inefficiency of the Civil War. Slavery, Unruh argued, would have inevitably been replaced by the much cheaper economic solution of sweatshops. At the end of his lecture, Unruh's assistant ripped off the lecturer's clothes. Underneath his suit, Unruh wore a golden "Management Leisure Suit" which came equipped with a large, inflating phallus. At the head of the phallus, Unruh explained to the astonished students, a satellite-fed monitor allowed the manager to monitor workers across the globe while retaining the management's requisite level of comfort.

The Experimental University

Although the Experimental University is a departure from the more literal forms of intervention, it also points to a critical departure in thinking about what art is and how art can be used. In the Experimental University (Nicholas Mirzoeff's manifesto speaks to this in spirited terms),

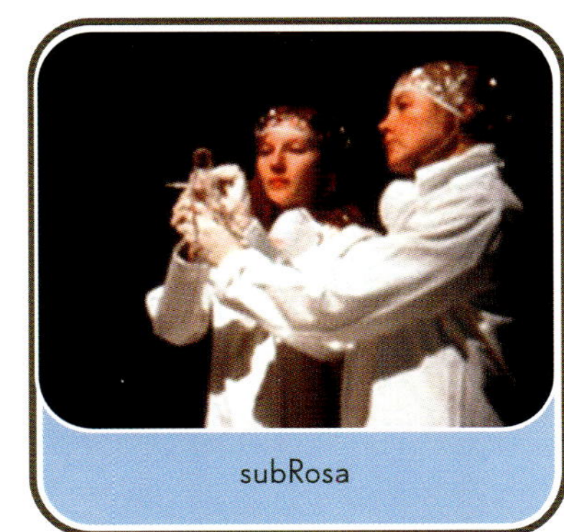

subRosa

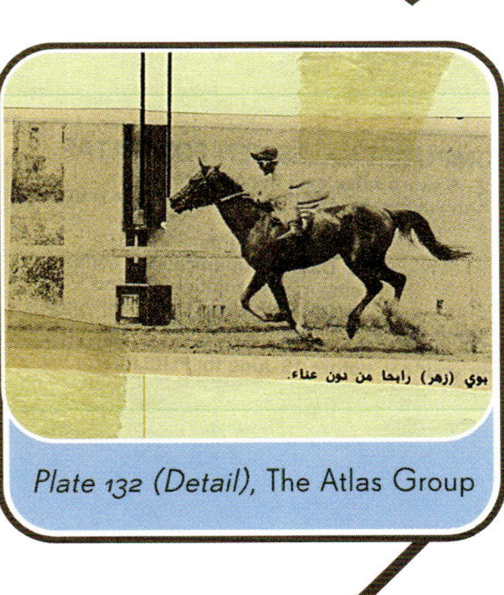

Plate 132 (Detail), The Atlas Group

Continue →

artists interrupt a particular field of study (whether this is urban studies, biotechnology, anthropology, or ethnography) in order to present alternative critical perspectives. We can recognize these practices as "art-inspired" because they manipulate visual and spatial codes in order to produce criticality.

In their *Can You See US Now? Ya Nos Pueden Ver?* (2004) project at MASS MoCA, the cyber-feminist collective subRosa produced research here in North Adams on spaces of refuge for women. This study took a number of forms including assistance from both an engineering and feminist studies class at Smith College. The collective set out to "uncover and map the intersections of women's material and affective labor in cultures of production in North Adams and Ciudad Juarez, Mexico." Their interest in Ciudad relates to the fact that the jobs once held at Sprague Electric — the capacitor manufacturing company that previously existed at the MASS MoCA site for 50 years and closed in 1986 — migrated there. Their installation includes a series of trap doors hidden in a "forensic floor" that can be opened by visitors to reveal points of associations (also marked on large satellite surveillance maps on the walls) between women's lives and labor conditions in factories in North Adams and Ciudad Juarez, as well as a series of kiosks placed at local places of refuge. This web of interconnections links theoretical constructs of globalization and real aspects of local life.

While subRosa produces factual correlations, the Atlas Group presents imaginary findings. In its archival display titled *The Truth Will Be Known When The Last Witness Is Dead: Documents from the Fakhouri File at the Atlas Group Archive*. The Atlas Group investigates the contemporary landscape of Lebanon, with particular focus on the history of the Lebanese Civil War (1975-1991). If the term "imaginary research" doesn't immediately make sense, there is a good reason. The "imaginary" part of the Atlas Group research is that it is culled from its collective imaginations. That is to say, the facts are not necessarily "true," but then again, as the project implicitly asks, whose perspective is?

This project, like many projects in the Experimental University, problematizes truth claims. As the title says, the truth will be known when the last witness is dead. So what, then, does research look like if it doesn't trust assertions of truth? The installation is open-ended and lets viewers make up their own minds. In particular, when investigating the imagery and history of the Middle East, the Atlas Group is careful to not repeat the use of neocolonial techniques. It does not assert. It does not define. Yet, this technique also does not slip into the postmodern relativism of which many rigorous scientists accuse cultural studies. The research is ultimately grounded in the history of the Lebanese wars.

The research conducted in the Experimental University possesses an urgency that aligns it with traditional activism. The seductive visual displays highlight a dramatically changing political landscape, whether in the lives of women, the technologies of race, the biotechnology of agro-business, or the politics of Arab visual representation. These interventionists manipulate the visual field to create a learning environment in which we, as viewers, participate. It is, in the end, a form of pedagogy, but of radically shifted perspectives.

But these experiments can only become transformative in the open, evolving context of a social movement, outside the cliques and clienteles of the artistic game. - Brian Holmes, "Liars Poker" [23]

While tactics are a useful place to begin, they are not necessarily a satisfactory place to end. While it is true that many of these projects gain resonance by dancing within the dominant systems, some prefer to operate more strategically to change these systems as well. As the French theorist Michel De Certeau defines it, tactics depend on a dominant system.[24] For De Certeau, tactics constituted small subversions, such as lazy work ethics and meandering walks through the city. He was not particularly interested in whether or not these tactics added up.

However, political artists are constantly concerned with — to use De Certeau's term — strategies. They want results beyond aesthetic pleasure (and some practitioners have no interest at all in aesthetic pleasure). Frustrated with political irrelevance, they operate in many different social games, from the art world to political activism to biotechnology. They understand their work means different things to different people. With this in mind, we can sidestep the argument about whether these practices, in and of themselves, are politically effective. Their connection to a robust array of audiences and methods — such as activists, publishers, or people on the street — allows their specific interests to come into light. The documentary *Disobbedienti* (2002) by Oliver Ressler and Dario Azzellini demonstrates the extent to which tactics used by interventionists have been availed in the global justice movement (and vice versa). To say there is a connection between experimental interventionist practices and the collective protest actions of today would be putting it lightly. Interventionist practices do not work in isolation and, in fact, are part of a larger movement.

That is why New York-based art collective 16 Beaver has been included in this show as both a signpost and metaphor for social connection. It would be difficult to say that what this constantly shifting collective does constitutes "art," yet its centrality to interventionist practice should not be underestimated. 16 Beaver is, at heart, a reading group that has met every Monday since 1999. Over the course of five years, it has produced projects reacting to war and has connected various intellectuals, artists, and activists. This connectivity — and there are countless examples of it in action — blurs the distinctions between those who produce art and those who produce political results.

There is no political consensus among interventionists. Interventionism is not a political movement disguised as art. Practices and ideologies among interventionists vary greatly. Nor should this exhibition be misinterpreted as a "greatest hits" of interventionist practices. This assortment of artists / activists / reading groups/designers presented here points to new forms of resistance in the age of an increasingly privatized and visualized cultural sphere. They represent methods of protest and public education integrally connected to larger social movements. And while there are extraordinary differences of opinion regarding how and what social changes should be brought about, it is also true that many artists seem to agree that the current political climate is dangerous. The artists in the exhibition are not telling us what to do about that perceived danger, but are providing tools for engagement. In short, the interventionists provide, as William Pope.L's *Black Factory* explicitly advertises, "opportunity."

Notes

1. From a lecture given at the *Rethinking Marxism* conference, UMASS, Amherst, Nov. 21, 2003.
2. This is not to say that there haven't been informative and important exhibitions of political art in the 1990s. In 1994, the Boston ICA produced the exhibition *Public Interventions* curated by Eleanor Heartney and then ICA director Milena Kalinovska. In 1993, Mary Jane Jacob produced the critical exhibition *Culture In Action: New Public Art in Chicago*, sponsored by Sculpture Chicago.
3. See Nicolas Mirzoeff's *Visual Culture Reader* (London and New York, Routledge, 1998).
4. Thomas Frank, *Conquest of Cool*, (Chicago: University of Chicago Press, 1997), p. 235.
5. Michael Hardt and Antonio Negri, *Empire*, (Cambridge, Massachusetts, and London: Harvard University Press, 2000), p. 275.
6. Naomi Klein, *No Logo* (New York, Picador, 1999), p. 30.
7. Elizabeth Jackson, *The World Today*, Tuesday, 7 October, 2003.
8. James B Twitchel, "Plop, Plop, Fizz, Fizz," *Signs of Life*, eds. Sonia Maasik and Jack Solomon. (3rd. eds Boston: Bedford/ St. Martins, 2000) p. 202-221.
9. Saskia Sassen, *Globalization and its Discontents* (New York: New Press, 1999).
10. Rosalyn Deutsche, *Evictions: Art and Spatial Politics* (Cambridge, Massachusetts, MIT Press, 1998), p. 151.
11. Brian Wallis, "Public Funding and Alternative Spaces," *Alternative Art in New York, 1965-1985*, ed. Julie Ault. (Minneapolis - London: University of Minnesota Press, 2002) p. 178.
12. For more information, see the burgeoning field of critical geography spearheaded by the writings of David Harvey, Mike Davis, Edward Soja, Neil Smith, and the art writings of Rosalyne Deutsche and Miwon Kwon.
13. Definition found at www.angelfire.com/ar/corei/SI/SIsecc.htm
14. Jerry Rubin, *Do It! Scenarios of the Revolution* (New York: Ballantine Books, 1970), p. 108.
15. According to Alix Kates Shulman in "Dances with Feminists" *Women's Review of Books*, Vol. IX, no. 3, December 1991, Emma Goldman never actually said the above quote. This popular quote paraphrased a much longer quote from Emma Goldman's book *Living My Life*.
16. Bill Talen quoted in Jason Grote's "The God that people who do not believe in God believe in: taking a bust with Reverend Billy", in *Cultural Resistance Reader*, ed. Stephen Duncombe (London: Verso, 2002), p. 366.
17. Rene Gabri, personal interview, 18 Nov. 2003.
18. Krzysztof Wodiczko, "Interrogative Design", *Critical Vehicles*, (Cambridge, Massachusetts: MIT Press, 1999), p. 17.
19. Ibid.
20. subRosa's project, *Can You See Us now? Ya Nos Pueden Ver?*, (2004), investigates sites of refuge for women. The prominence in the exhibition of the term "refuge" correlates directly to larger social conditions such as the shrinkage of social services and the increasing displacement of global populations.
21. From the website, www.tacticalmagic.org
22. From the Yes Men website, www.gatt.org
23. Brian Holmes, "Liar's Poker: Representation of Politics: Politics of Representation", *Springerin* (Vienna, Austria: January, 2003: http://www.springerin.at/en/
24. Michel De Certeau, *The Practice of Everyday Life*, trans. Steven Rendall (Berkeley and Los Angeles, California, and London: University of California Press, Ltd., 1988), p. 37.

Michel De Certeau, in his 1984 book *The Practice of Everyday Life*, made a useful distinction between "strategies" and "tactics." "I call strategy", he writes, "the calculation (or manipulation) of power relation ships that become possible as soon as a subject with will and power (a business, an army, a city, a scientific institution) can be isolated." That is to say, a strategy is a plan made by those who have the power to predict and change the lived landscape. On the other hand, a tactic "operates in isolated actions, blow by blow. It takes advantage of 'opportunities' and depends on them, being without any base where it could stockpile its winnings, build up its own position, and plan raids." "In short, the tactic is the art of the weak."

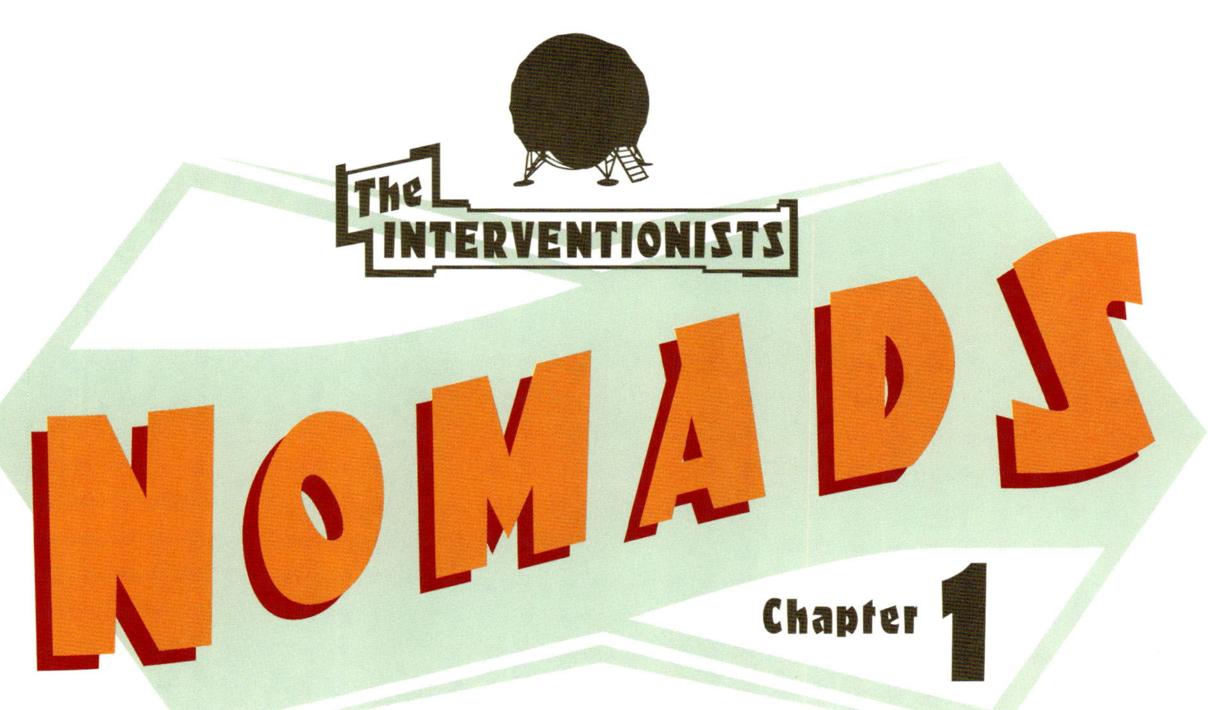

The INTERVENTIONISTS
NOMADS
Chapter 1

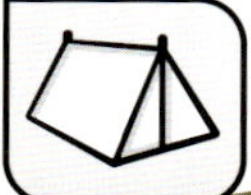

New York, NY & Boston, MA, USA
Krzysztof ★ Wodiczko
Born 1943

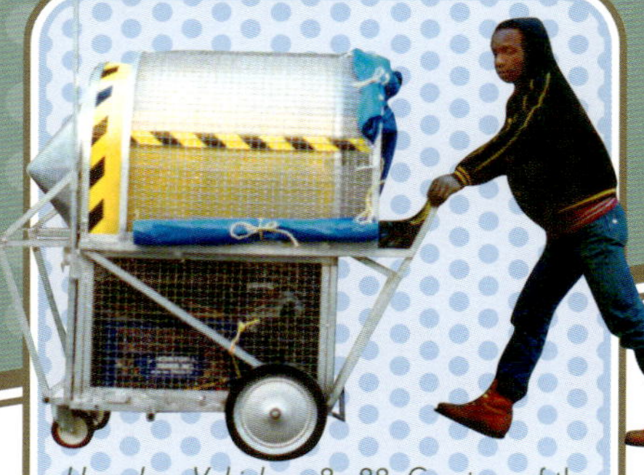

Homeless Vehicle, 1987-88. Courtesy of the artist and Galerie Lelong, New York.

Biographical Info:

Krzysztof Wodiczko is renowned for his large-scale slide and video projections on architectural facades and monuments. Since the late 1980s, he has developed nomadic instruments for both homeless and immigrant operators that function as implements for survival, communication and empowerment. Wodiczko coined the term "Interrogative Design" to describe these works which identify and heal social injuries. He compares them to bandages, because they not only draw attention to a wound (in this case a social wound), but also work towards healing it. Wodiczko earned his MFA in 1968 from the Academy of Fine Arts in Warsaw, Poland, where he studied architecture, industrial design, and the visual arts. His work has been exhibited in Documenta, the Paris Biennale, the Sydney Biennale, the Lyon Biennale, the Venice Biennale and other major international art festivals and exhibitions.

In 1998, Wodiczko was awarded the Hiroshima Prize for his contribution as an artist to world peace. He is the acting director of the Center for Advanced Visual Studies at the Massachusetts Institute of Technology, where he has taught since 1991.

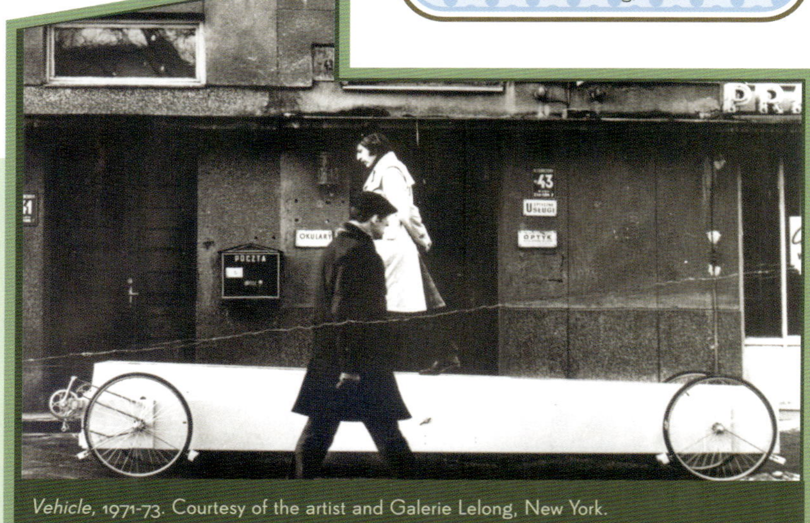

Vehicle, 1971-73. Courtesy of the artist and Galerie Lelong, New York.

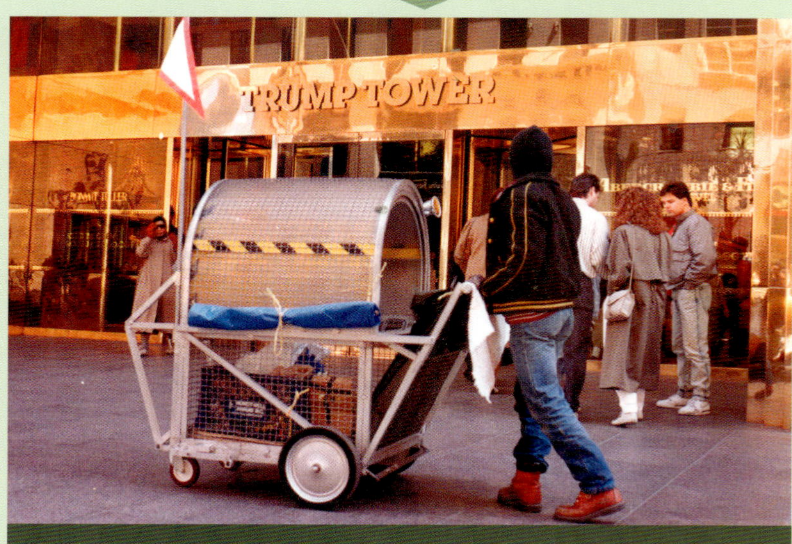

Homeless Vehicle, 1987-88. Courtesy of the artist and Galerie Lelong, New York.

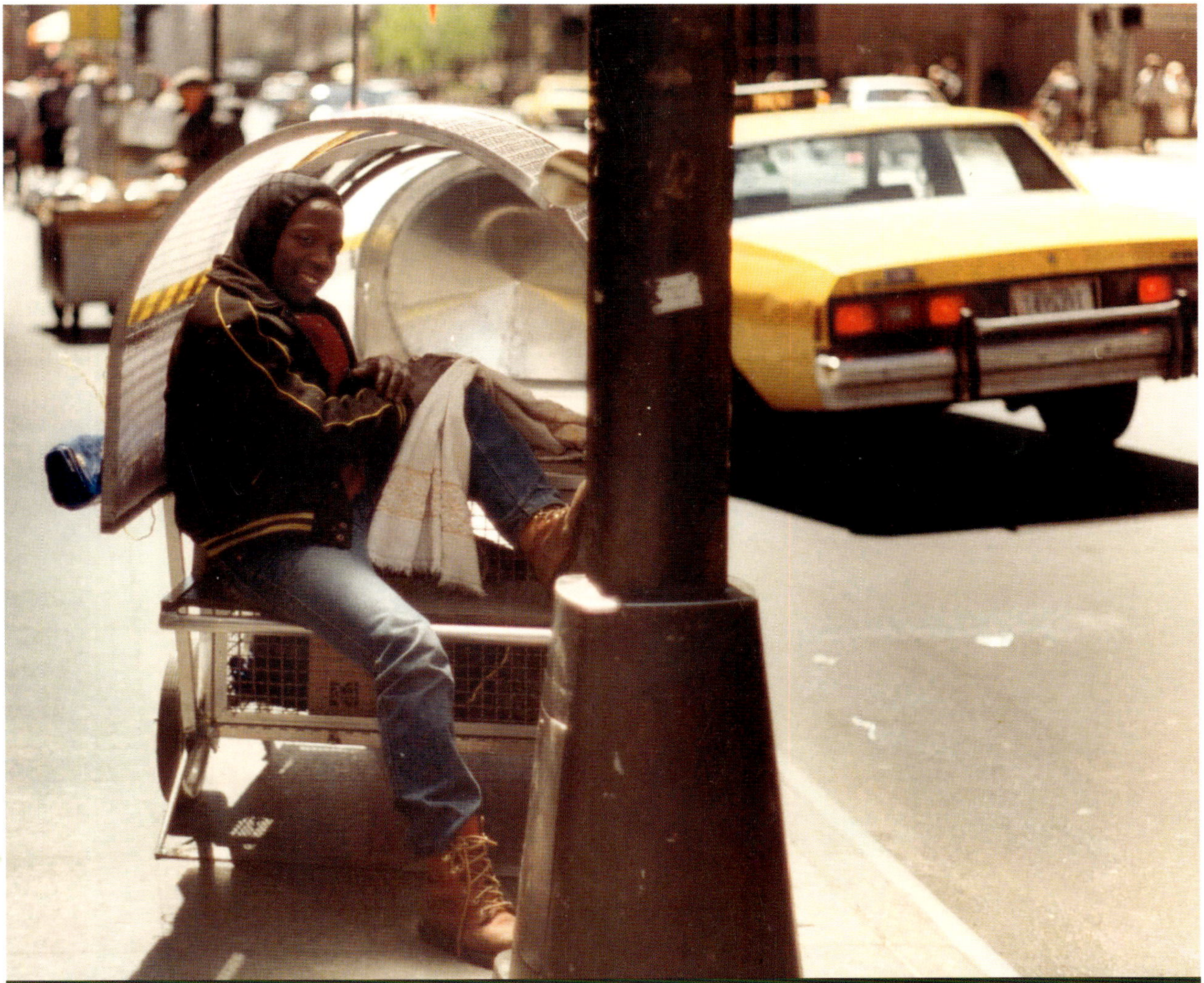

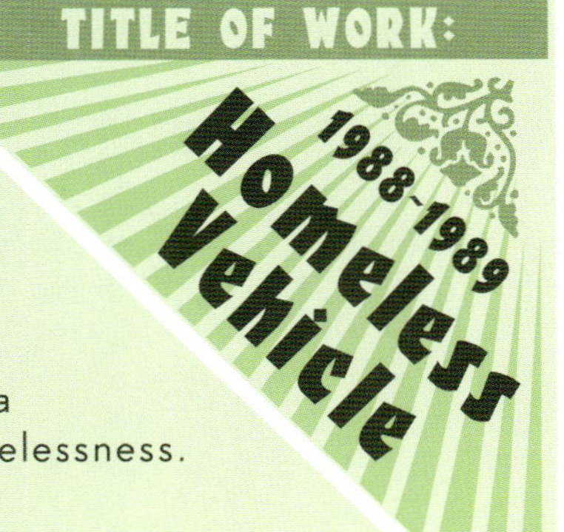

Homeless Vehicle, 1987-88. Courtesy of the artist and Galerie Lelong, New York.

Project Description: Together with a group of homeless New Yorkers, Wodiczko constructed the *Homeless Vehicle* as an instrument of survival for urban nomads. A modified shopping cart that facilitates refundable bottle and can collection, it also provides temporary shelter. As a house on wheels intended for New York City sidewalks, the *Homeless Vehicle* embodies Wodiczko's practice of "Interrogative Design." It provides sturdy refuge for the homeless and becomes a sidewalk intervention that draws attention to the condition of homelessness.

Krzysztof Wodiczko

Interview with C. Ondine Chavoya
March 19, 2004

Which practices and/or movements associated with the visual culture of the 1980s were you most engaged by, influenced by, or active in?

Among the precedents, I could cite artists' participation in urban struggle against the effects of Reaganomics, like uneven urban redevelopment, revitalization ('gentrification'), and the production of homelessness; the critique of the city as an image produced by real-estate action groups (the image of 'well-managed' city); the British contribution to urban geography; the Birmingham school of cultural studies; the feminist critique of representation as related to the image of the city and urban life; the British film journal *Screen* and *ZG Magazine* (in particular the writings of Rosetta Brooks, Sylvia Kolbowski, and Brian Hutton); The New Museum exhibition *Difference and Sexuality*, as seen in the context of writings by Rosalyn Deutsche on public art and Neil Smith on uneven development; and the activism of Act-Up, the intellectual interventions of Douglas Crimp, the activism and survival of East Village squatters' collectives, the Bullit Group, the projects of Group Material, and others.

When the viewer experiences your work, what type(s) of relationships do you hope to establish?

In my work from the 1990s, I focus more on the experience of the participants, my 'co-artists,' in each project. They are the initial, most important, 'viewers,' and the primary subjects in my instrumentation projects (as in the case of the user-performer in *Dis-Armor*, and less so but still important, in the case of the user-performer of the *Homeless Vehicle*), as well as in my participatory projections (as in the case of Tijuana Projection's testimonial-artist and monument-animator). The participants/co-artists are the ones who truly 'experience' the projects. Furthermore, all the preparatory stages of recording and re-recording by participants before the actual projections-animations or the public performance with my instruments are essential to the development of the work, and parallel the 'interior' development of the participants, and of their ability to use the work as a 'speech-act' of their own. The 'experience' (strictly speaking, here one should use the word 'perception') on the part of the so-called public is important but not primary. Its presence is indispensable as a witness representing the larger social and political world. This witnessing by the public also bears the possibility and potential for the public co-agency and dissemination or re-transmission of the speaking projections and instruments.

What are the different fields or networks that you operate in (not just aesthetically but specifically)? How do you view these various facets of your activity?

My work operates within an extremely wide range of institutional and organizational contexts: from festivals that incorporate public-art projects (for example, *InSite 2000*, across the U.S.-Mexico border between San Diego and Tijuana, where I did a projection in collaboration with the workers' rights and self-help agency El Grupo Factor X, along with other social work agencies and social research groups, without whom I would never succeed in building the contacts and confidence required) to the research components of university structures (I am the director of the Center for Advanced Visual Studies at the Massachusetts Institute of Technology). But these examples only map out the terrain (I could also add museums, and municipalities, among others). In fact, my work always requires operating with and at several personal and institutional levels simultaneously, most often with entities that propose a form of resistance as their reason for being. Sometimes it takes being useful to make oneself an artist. This is the distinction I have tried to uphold throughout my entire artistic past. And being useful has many facets.

How do you use preexisting visual forms or discourses in your work? To what end(s) do you use them?

My work often 'adopts' existing symbolic structures of city architecture, and — often with the help of specially designed instruments — attempts to offer them as transitional objects to participants and to the public (as well as to the media, activists and others). All the preparatory stages of recording and re-recording by participants (before the projections and performances with my instruments) constitute a developmental holding zone in which my work, along with architectural forms and the organizing cultural institutions, are transitional phenomena. This is designed to foster a developmental process that leads to the possibility of an enhanced confidence in our engagement with an often unfriendly and risky world, both the outside world and the fearful, often frozen and discouraged, inner world. It is clear, of course, that this approach goes against any 'modernist' notion of the art object based on a utopian ideal of discovering a 'good' (that is, not just 'good enough,' but perfect) form — by a perhaps 'too-good-to-be-true' avant-garde — as essential elements in transforming our care for — and cure for — the world.

How does technology function in your work? In general, what is your relationship to technology?

The question is how to find a place for technology in the explosion of communications technologies during a time of breakdown in cultural communication — a search for a new interface, an artistic, not just an industrial, interface. Technology, as communicative artifice, is needed to operate between alienated subjects. Using the concept proposed by psychoanalyst D. W. Winnicot, technology is also needed as a 'transitional object,' as a potential space located between the inner and outer world, between reality and fantasy. Such a communicative, transitional technological effort can protect and encourage a developmental process through the use of the designed or adopted object, a vehicle from the inner 'me-world' towards the 'not-me-world' of others, from posttraumatic hopelessness and silence, to the use of words and gestures directed toward both the conscious self and others. What I have done is design special speech-act equipment, even to the extent of taking up, on a grand scale, one's fantasy of becoming powerful, 'cyborg,' or a 'speaking monument.'

The concept "intervention" is key in the exhibition: what constitutes an intervention for you?

I try to contribute to the process of transformation of the fearful silence of the invisible and unheard city residents (the participants) and of the deaf ear of those who are visible and heard (the public) into agonistic public discourse of 'fearless' speaking and listening. My artistic method has consisted of creating a socio-aesthetic situation that allows, inspires, and protects a process where others may become (if only briefly) artists themselves. In this way my art may be used as a transition in the development of their lives and the lives of others. An articulation of the city silences and transmission of the regained inhabitant voices — a newly developed 'response-ability,' practiced with a sense of responsibility is, in my opinion, an intervention.

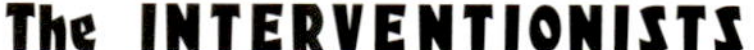

London, England
Lucy Orta
Born 1966

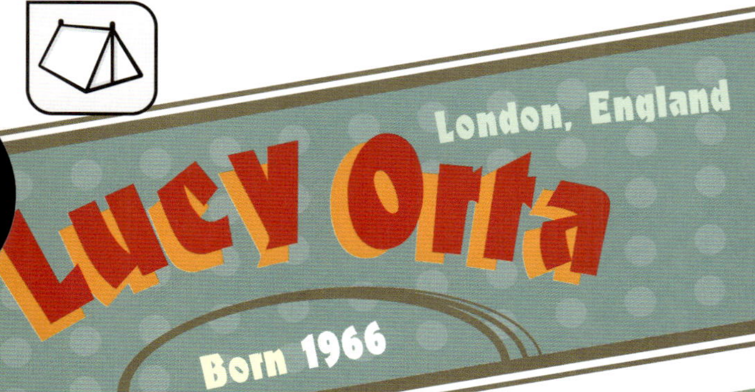

Nexus Architecture x 50 – Nexus Intervention Köln 2001, 2001
Photo: Peter Guenzel

Biographical Info:

Lucy Orta is trained as a fashion/textile designer whose artwork ranges from sculpture to performances to dinner parties. Disillusioned with the consumerism of the fashion industry, in 1994 she installed her *Refuge Wear* (1992-1998) intervention under the Louvre Pyramid during Paris Fashion Week. The clothes combined fashion with portable architecture. Conceived as a response to the Gulf War, Refuge Wear highlighted notions of survivalism and refuge. During this period, Orta also collaborated with the collective *Casa Moda*, whose work investigated links between textile research and experimental design.

Her *Collective Wear* sculptures, in the form of tent domes with protruding appendages, were situated in decidedly urban contexts such as public housing projects and subway stations. *Collective Wear* was exhibited at the ARC Musée d'art Moderne in Paris in 1994. Orta's work has been presented in site-specific performances at the Venice Biennale in 1995, Johannesburg Biennale in 1997 and Museum of Contemporary Art, Sydney, in 1998, as well as Bolivia, Berlin, New York, and Mexico City. She is the Rootstein Hopkins Chair at the London College of Fashion at the London Institute.

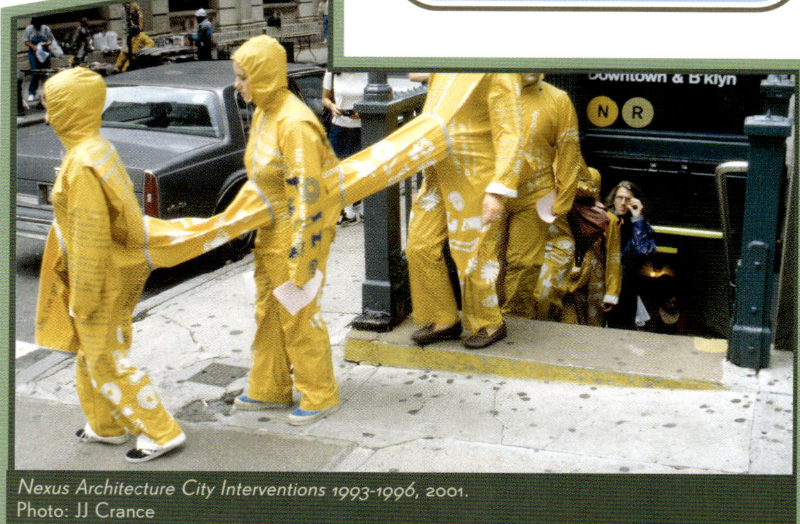

Nexus Architecture City Interventions 1993-1996, 2001.
Photo: JJ Crance

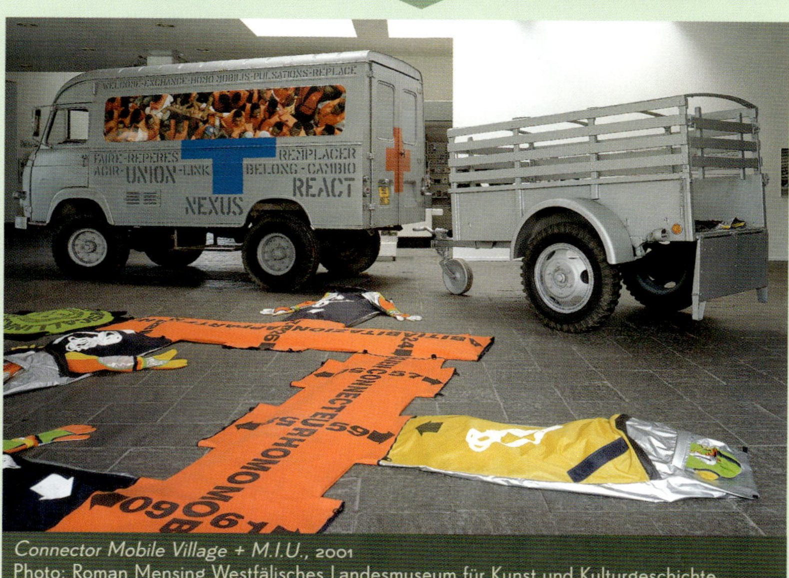

Connector Mobile Village + M.I.U., 2001
Photo: Roman Mensing Westfälisches Landesmuseum für Kunst und Kulturgeschichte

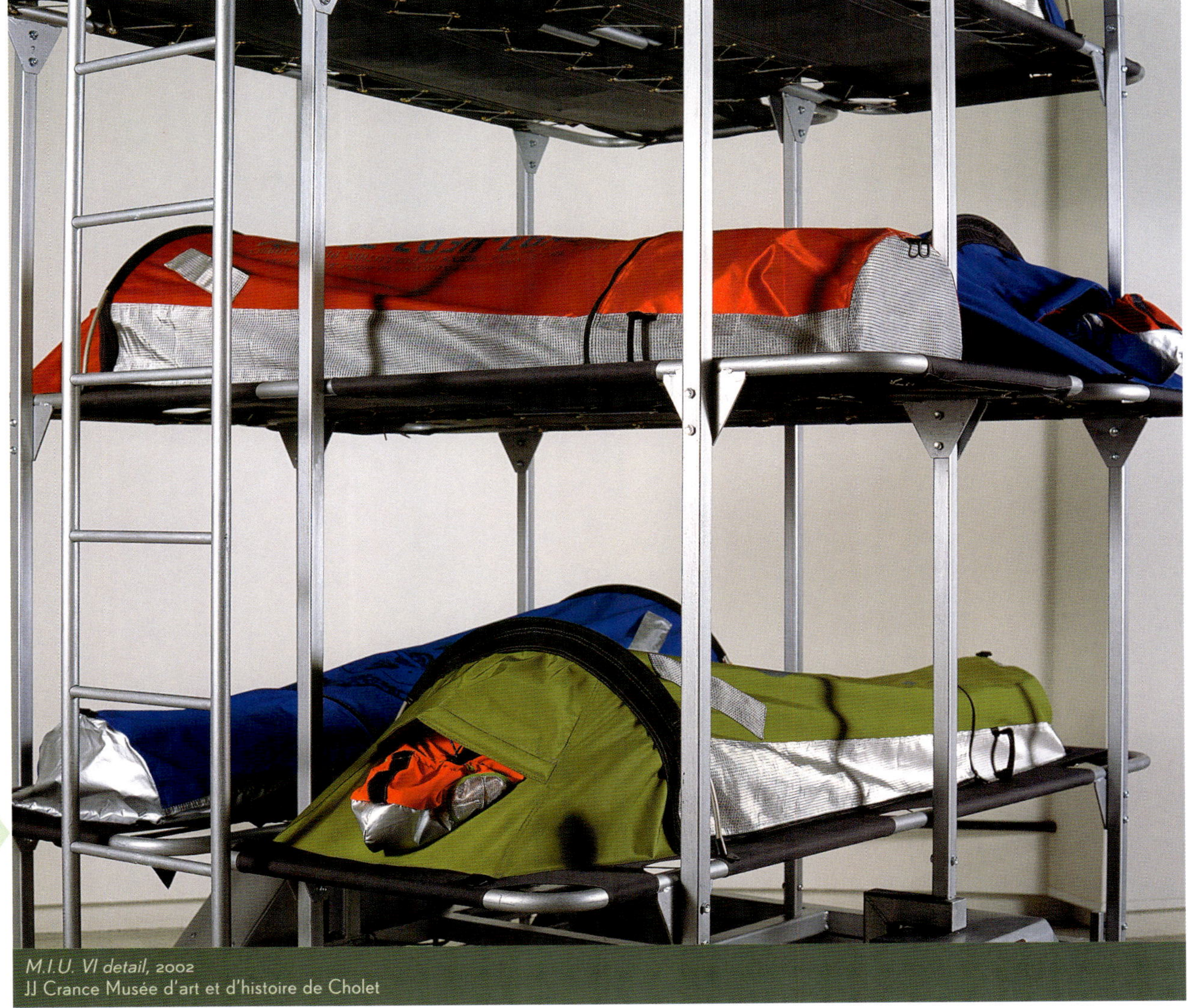

M.I.U. VI detail, 2002
JJ Crance Musée d'art et d'histoire de Cholet

Project Description: *The Mobile Intervention Unit (M.I.U.)* is a single-person module built onto a lightweight trailer made from composite aluminum parts, which was originally placed in front of civic buildings for the G8 Environment Summit in Trieste, Italy. When assembled, the *M.I.U.* produces temporary sleeping quarters for several people, a type of nomadic dormitory. Orta produced this series as part of a larger work from 2001, in which she adorned two Red Cross ambulances with the faces of cows, referring to mad cow disease, and dressed a crowd of people wearing life jackets, an image that referred to Rwandan refugees.

TITLE OF WORK:

M.I.U. VI
2002

Lucy Orta

Interview with C. Ondine Chavoya
February 3, 2004

Which practices and/or movements associated with the visual culture of the 1980s were you most engaged by, influenced by, or active in?

I began art school in 1985, so my cultural references were fairly reduced before that date. My father was an Impressionist fanatic and my great-aunt was a prominent Surrealist painter, so you could say that I was confronted with two ends of the modernist spectrum at an early age. My mother's activist goings-on were far more dominant in the 1980s: protests, social work, campaigns, political rallies, she stood as candidate for the Independent Party.

During art school in the late '80s, my cultural references obviously expanded. I studied fashion and was interested in the radical fashion concepts of Japanese design, Commes des Garçons, Issey Miyake, etc. Also, designers like Donna Karan and Jil Sander were promoting collections for the "new corporate women." It was an era that created a tremendous clash of opinions and styles. My fine art friends were looking at alternative European cinema and at pop art. I remember running an errand for a friend who wanted some information for his dissertation; I was an intern in New York at the time, and I turned up at a SoHo gallery show to get a few posters signed by Keith Haring.

New York City and the cultural multiplicity — East Village, street culture, homelessness, art, fashion, independence, and fear — were all powerful forces on a naive English fashion student. One of the most memorable museum experiences was the contemporary section of the MoMA; it bowled me over. The most powerful influence on any British art student at the time was Maggie Thatcher. The context for the development of my artistic career was the encounter with my partner Jorge Orta, an Argentine artist who had lived through the dictatorship, and the terrible economic recession in the early 1990s, caused by the repercussions of the first Gulf War and the stock market crash. Meeting Paul Virilio in 1994 was also instrumental in the development of my art practice.

When the viewer experiences your work, what type(s) of relationships do you hope to establish?

Multiple

What are the different fields or networks that you operate in (not just aesthetically but specifically)? How do you view these various facets of your activity?

I was recently nominated as head of a new graduate program "Man & Humanity" at the Design Academy Eindhoven in The Netherlands, so I am constantly developing and implementing a high-level pedagogic program for students who wish to confront design with new social, ethical, and critical standards. My networks expand to the master level student population, art education teaching institutions worldwide, non-governmental organizations, Fair Trade agencies, crisis agencies, independent funding agencies, local government representatives, etc. etc. My academic research post as Chair and Professor at London College of Fashion has brought me into contact with theorists and practitioners working within the fashion sphere, and also the wider academic circle of the five art schools that belong to The University of the Arts, London. Through the research projects conducted at LCF, I hope to broaden the perception of fashion as an academic subject and a multi-disciplinary creative industry and help to establish a rigorous, cross-disciplinary dialogue between art, architecture, fashion, and design, broadly, in an effort to forge a discourse uniquely relevant to the current social and economic situation. My practice creates opportunities to engage and reflect upon situations arising from urban dislocation making the invisible visible. Because the work I do is sculptural and represents tactile and spatial expression of society, it moves beyond the ability to provide just protection or assume identities. Projects such as the Sciart research award or the RSA Art for Architecture will amplify a power to communicate with other disciplines, negotiating social bonds and uniting members of a community.

What spheres do you find appropriate for your work?

All that make space for critical comment.

How do you see your work operating in larger social movements?

As a catalyst for ideas that can improve society and human relations. The Man & Humanity students will be implementing these projects in the future.

How does your work situate the local and the global?

I work closely with both communities, as much as possible. We need to understand local problems in global communities; work on site to live and play with the populations; sense and understand the emotions and the differences. These problems can be social, environmental, or political. We also need to be aware of the problems in our local community: understanding the needs of even our closest neighbors, however small or large the scale.

I think that one major battle that has to be fought is the loss of cultural identity and the resistance to an overriding dominant aesthetic, and these are the fundaments of my postgraduate program Man & Humanity. The first assignment for our students is the development of a new "global" awareness devised around an eight-week design period in a developing country. Here we coach our students to apprehend the experience of working together with local population, artists and artisans, before even considering what aesthetic could be "exported" for Western consumption. The students gradually re-define their notion of beauty by discovering the people they are living with, their skills, images, textures, gestures, smells, taste, and, most importantly, exchanges of emotions. As in all new discoveries, the difficulty is bringing these sensations in the form of ideas back to the West. When re-situating or re-enacting that special circumstantial experience in a totally different context, the viewer, or in the case of my students, the customer, is not attuned with a capacity to project into the original situation and often does not even have the time, or the will. There is a great need to discuss, but also to act, through the education of a new awareness of choice and by opening windows to other cultures, becoming aware of the poverty of spirit in our own lives, through the beauty of experiencing others.

How do you use preexisting visual forms or discourses in your work? To what end(s) do you use them?

Together with my partner Jorge, we have devised five levels of visual signifiers (a sign system or lexicon). Each artwork is the pretext to create new signs on any one of these levels. Site visits and encounters with different cultures are important occasions where we "gather" contextual indicators for transcription, re-interpretation, transformation, categorization, and re-use.

Ideogram Signs:
Transcriptions of a global legacy collected from various sources:
Natural, such as rocks, stones, erosive formations, silhouettes, geological faults, roots, branches, leaves, bark, fruit, flowers, feathers, colors, and "sensations."
Cultural, such as rock carvings, museum archives, found objects, idiosyncratic designs and graphics, marks inscribed in architecture and contemporary life.
Metasocial Signs:
Images that interpret the contradictions and clashing forces within the reality of our contemporary society.
Object Signs:
Beyond their formal aspect, they are the living proof of a community, and homage to memories and cultures.
Textual Signs:
Transcriptions of community memory in the form of words, phrases, oral expressions, and written fragments. Assembled together, they constitute a new layer of writing, which are "global and interchangeable."
Sound Signs:
An archive of natural murmurs, spoken accounts, and inter views specific to each site. They can be transformed into image through digital trans-coding, and vice versa into sound through the analysis of the morphological structure. This experiment challenges the correlation system; it is an intense fusion between the sound space and the visual space.

What do you consider the advantages and/or disadvantages to collaboration, compared to individualized forms of art production?

The advantages outweigh the disadvantages: research can be thorough in specialist fields, more ideas generated on any one subject, competencies divided. Projects tend to take longer when discrepancies arise, as they inevitably do!

How do you see humor as functioning in your art? What about delight and pleasure in your work?

I do not consider my work to be humorous, but many people do!

Why is movement necessary in your work?
What do we gain from movement?

Art has no meaning if it does not move beyond traditional assumptions of art.

How does technology function in your work? In general, what is your relationship to technology?

I embrace it quite happily, but it would take too long to talk about all the projects and developments I have put into place.

In the past two decades, public space has become increasingly privatized as private space (and private lives) have become increasingly subject to the expanded structures and technologies of surveillance. How might your work respond to or demonstrate this scenario?

The city is a vital space for interaction and a hub for social activity, a vector for exchange and an ever-changing scenario in which I "intervene," employing new formats. In my early investigations, such as the *Refuge Wear/Nexus Architecture* interventions, I utilized the street in an investigative manner, questioning the individual's right to occupy public space rather than becoming subsumed by the architecture. By reclaiming public space, these projects sought to empower marginalized individuals and render them more visible. In more recent public works such as the open-air fetes, meals, and picnics, I use the urban geography as a powerful tool to mediate dialogues between different social groups. The buffet of surplus produce served up at the openings of All in One Basket and Hortirecycling Enterprise are a result of my dismay during the French agricultural demonstrations. Each year tons of fruit are dumped onto the highways to protest against imported goods. Living in a city, my reaction was to act locally, and direct my demonstration of empowerment towards the tons of edible leftover produce, utilizing the urban fabric of the Parisian street markets: vendors, clients, passersby, and gleaners to create microcommunity gatherings and discussion forums. The tasty dishes of surplus food prepared by a famous French chef in the public space lead quite naturally to the larger-scale public picnics and open-air dinners. The 70' x 7' Meal in the rural town of Dieuze in the East of France with its snake-like table setting 300 meters along the main street, cannot go amiss in the public space. To prepare such a setting, the whole town was informed and involved: all age, social, and religious groups share a meal, which here assumes the role of social space.

The concept "intervention" is key in the exhibition: what constitutes an intervention for you?

Answered above.

Can there be revolutionary art without a revolution?

We need to find a new word for revolution.

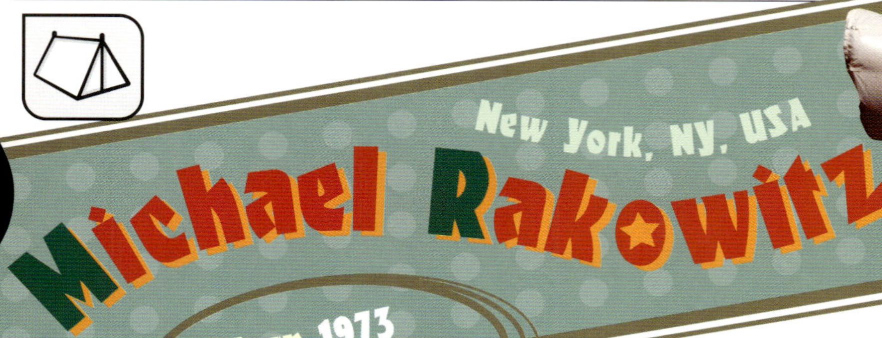

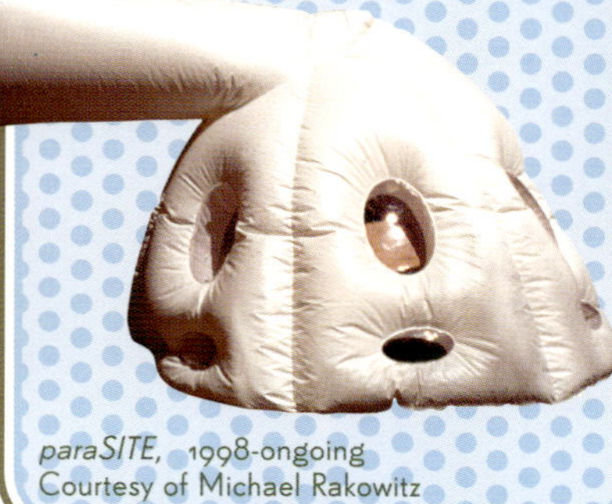

paraSITE, 1998-ongoing
Courtesy of Michael Rakowitz

Biographical Info:

Michael Rakowitz, a former student of Krzysztof Wodiczko, expands on Wodiczko's notion of "Interrogative Design." In the 2000-01 project *Climate Control*, Rakowitz tapped into the existing heating system at P.S.1 Contemporary Art Museum in New York with an elaborate network of ducts and fans. This extraordinary arrangement of pipes filled the gallery space as an exaggerated climate-control system. His interest in duct work continued in his 2001 project, *Rise*, in which he extended an oven duct of a Chinese bakery into a 9th-floor gallery space. Upon entering the gallery, visitors were overwhelmed by the smell of fresh pastries. *Rise* was an olfactory incursion into the exhibition space, referring to the neighborhood of Chinatown and its relationship to an encroaching gallery development.

In addition to P.S.1, Rakowitz's work has appeared at the Queens Museum of Art, the Storefront for Art and Architecture, the Cooper-Hewitt Design Museum, and the Fabric Workshop in Philadelphia. He is Professor of Sculpture at the Maryland Institute College of Art in Baltimore.

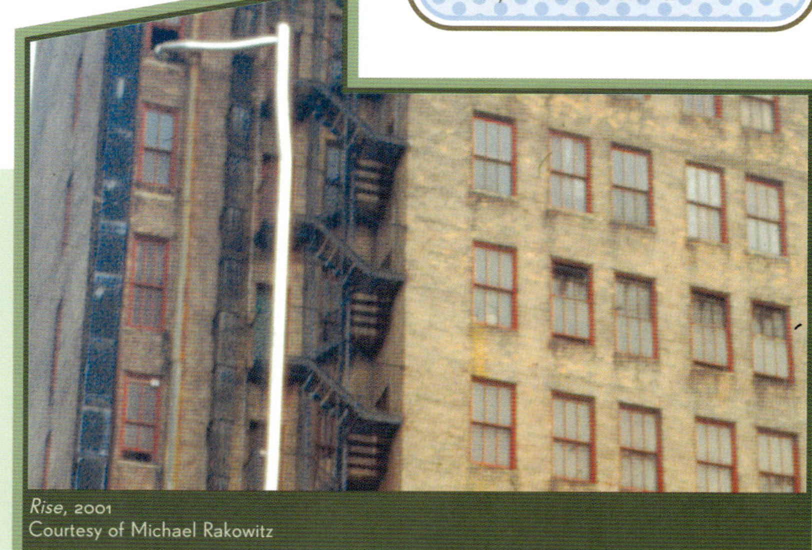

Rise, 2001
Courtesy of Michael Rakowitz

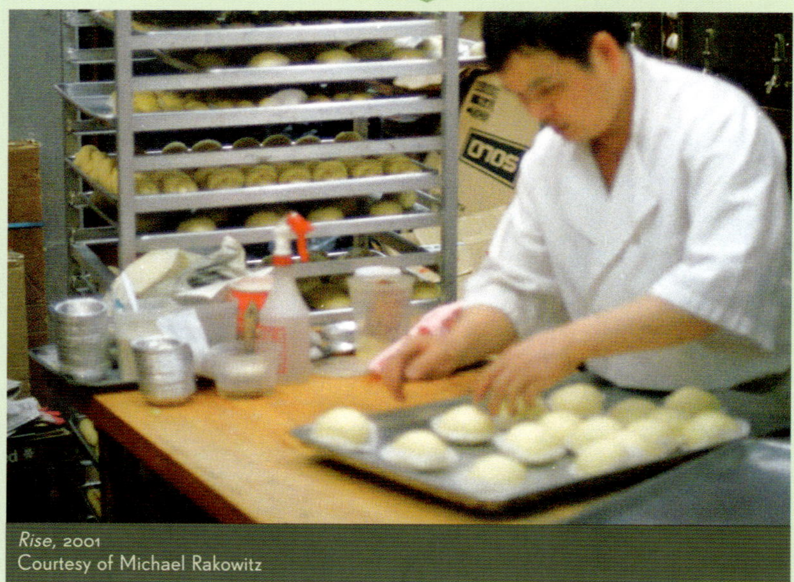

Rise, 2001
Courtesy of Michael Rakowitz

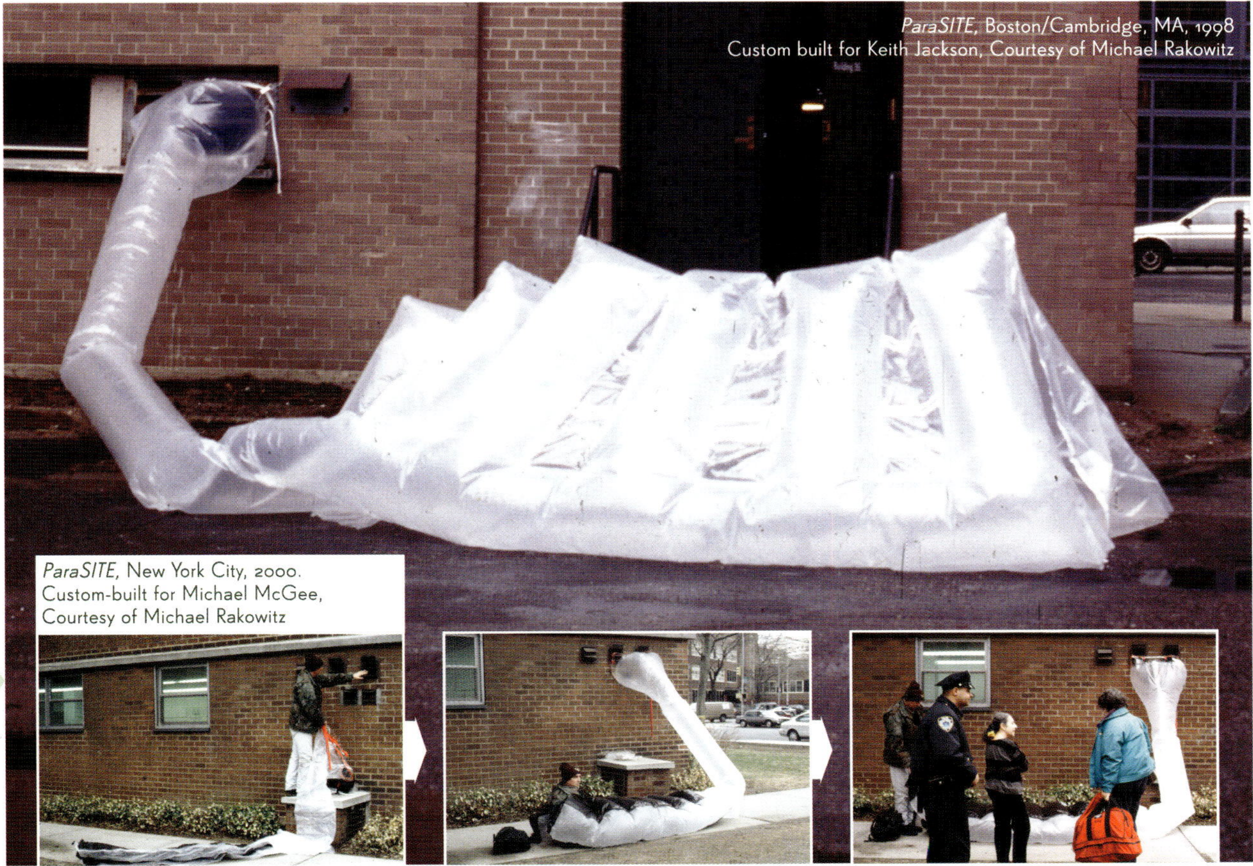

ParaSITE, Boston/Cambridge, MA, 1998
Custom built for Keith Jackson, Courtesy of Michael Rakowitz

ParaSITE, New York City, 2000.
Custom-built for Michael McGee,
Courtesy of Michael Rakowitz

TITLE OF WORK:

1998–ongoing
paraSITE

Project Description: *paraSITE* is an inflatable shelter for homeless people. Produced from plastic bags and tape and attached to air vents on buildings, these one-person shelters are quite portable and put a wasted resource — the warm air expelled from an HVAC system — to beneficial use.

Between February and April 1998, as a graduate student at MIT, Rakowitz developed and circulated seven prototypes for this project. Working with homeless people in Boston, including Bill Stone, George Livingston, and Freddie Flynn, Rakowitz modified his designs to better fit their needs. Since 1998, Rakowitz has custom-built and distributed more than 30 *paraSITE* shelters in Boston, Cambridge, New York City, and Baltimore. As Rakowitz states, "The visibly parasitic relationship of these devices to the buildings — appropriating a readily available situation with readily available materials — elicited immediate speculation about the future of the city: would these things completely take over, given the enormous number of homeless in our society? Could we wake up one morning to find these encampments engulfing buildings like ivy?"(1)

1. Email from Michael Rakowitz to Nato Thompson, December 10, 2003.

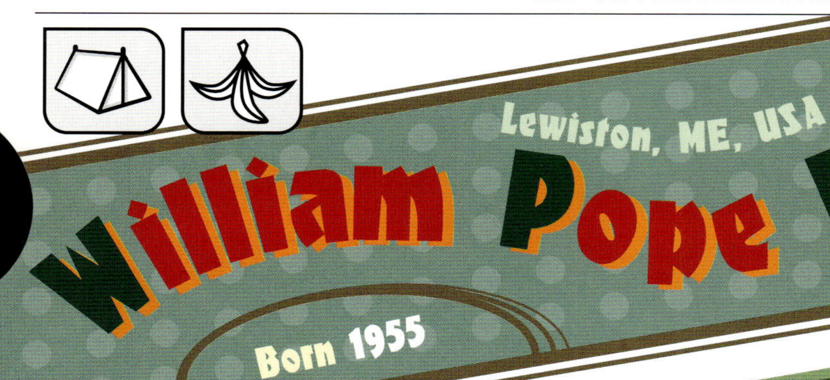

Biographical Info:

William Pope.L's work defies conventional expectations while dealing with familiar issues of class, race, and consumerism. He migrates fluidly between studio work and outdoor public actions, such as his famous "crawl" pieces. In those projects, Pope.L literally crawls across cityscapes dressed in costumes, including a six-foot pelvic prosthesis in *Member a.k.a. Schlong Journey* (1996) and a business suit with plants in its arms in *Tompkins Square Crawl* (1991). His art installations and performances use unconventional materials ranging from peanut butter to dollar bills. In his 2000 performance *Eating the Wall Street Journal*, Pope L. literalized the notions of financial and information consumption, literally digesting the newspaper regarded as the seminal purveyor of news about American economics.

William Pope.L (the L stands for Lancaster, abbreviated by his mother), has been a member of the Department of Theatre and Rhetoric at Bates College for 13 years. In Summer 2002, William Pope.L's 25-year retrospective, *eRacism*, opened at the ICA in Portland, Maine, and traveled to Diverse Works in Houston and Artist Space in New York City.

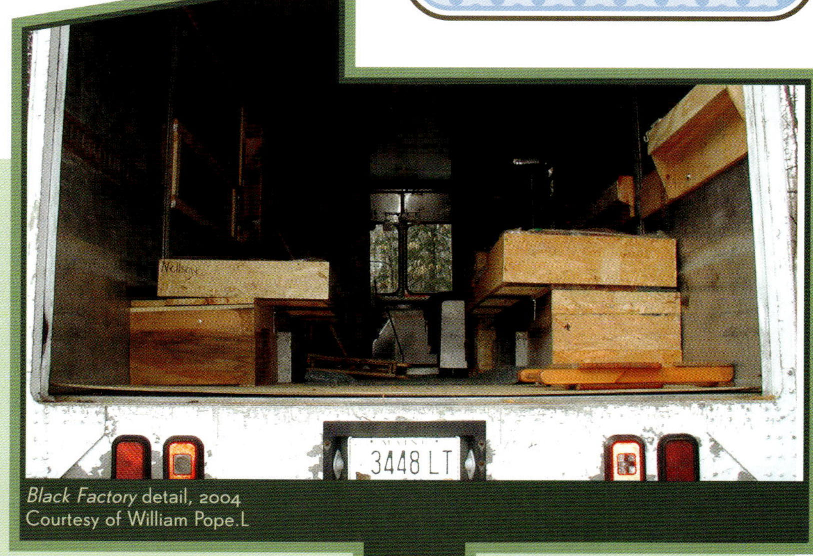

Black Factory detail, 2004
Courtesy of William Pope.L

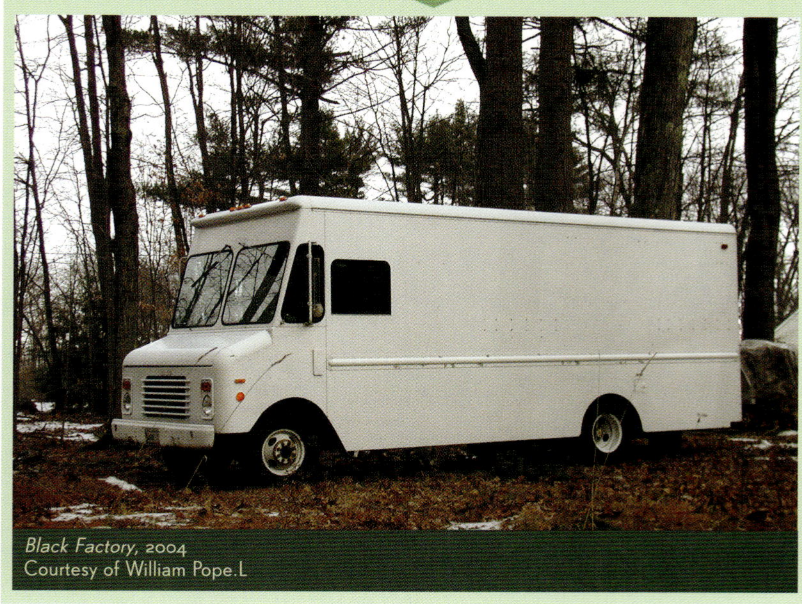

Black Factory, 2004
Courtesy of William Pope.L

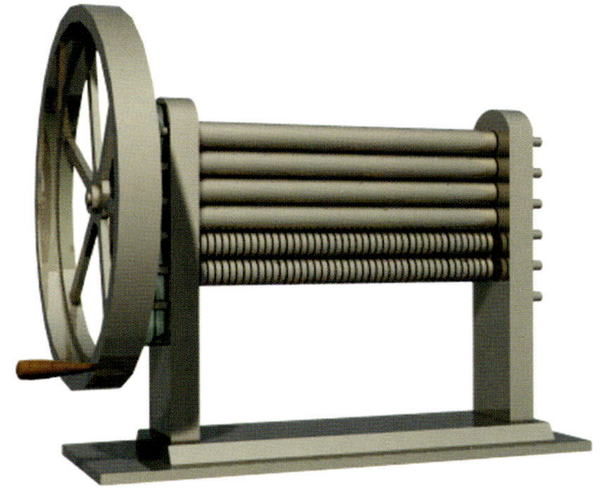

Black Factory detail, 2004
Computer Modeling by Studio Mnemosyne, courtesy of William Pope.L

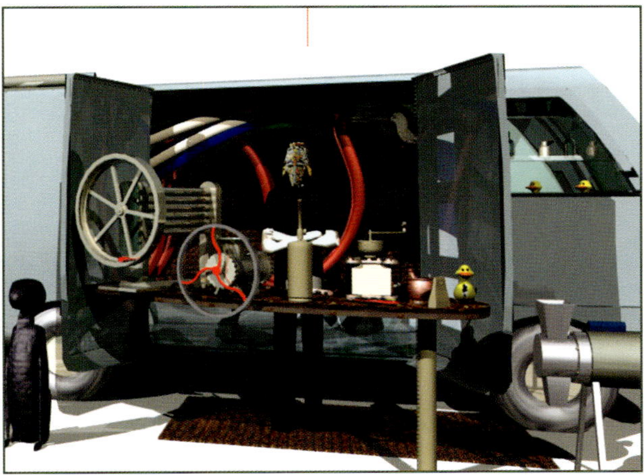

Black Factory detail, 2004
Computer Modeling by Studio Mnemosyne, courtesy of William Pope.L

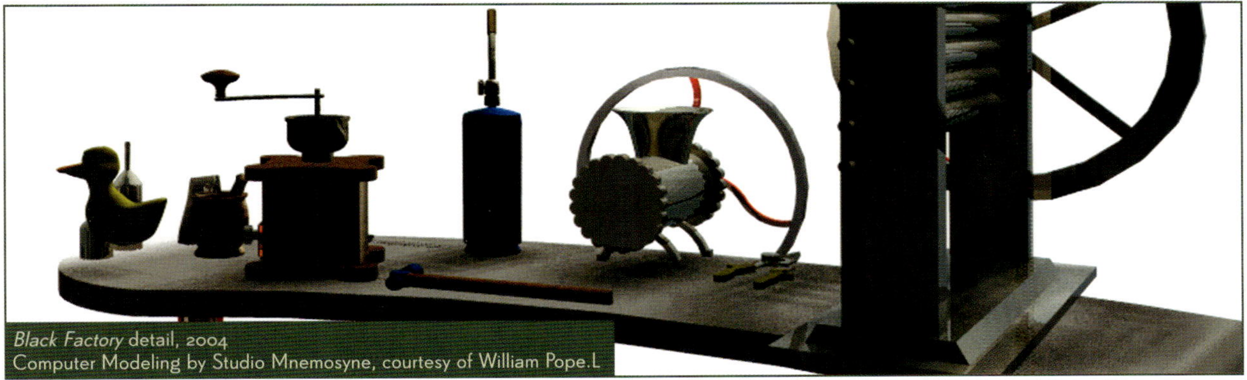

Black Factory detail, 2004
Computer Modeling by Studio Mnemosyne, courtesy of William Pope.L

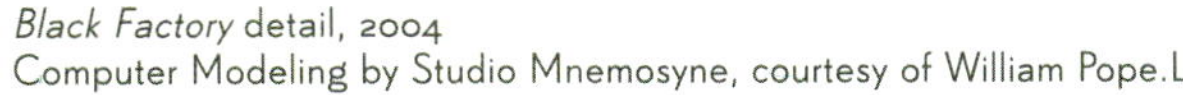

Project Description: The *Black Factory* is a large panel truck that travels to museums and other public places and serves as a stage and prop for a collaborative public event. According to Pope.L, the *Black Factory* "brings the contradictions of difference where they are needed most. A visit from the *Black Factory* provides more than thought-provoking entertainment and exploration; it presents opportunity." the *Black Factory* truck, designed in collaboration with Spurse, is equipped with a pulverizing center and gift shop. It will be parked outside MASS MoCA after it completes a tour throughout New England. From its rear, a giant inflatable igloo will expand to the museum's second floor, through a window, and into the gallery. Inside the igloo, visitors will see items of "blackness" that were collected during the tour.

During the *Black Factory*'s tour, which included stops at the Tang Teaching Museum and Bard College, its visitors had the option to take part in "Check Days," a term that Pope.L says refers to both the idea of checking in with someone and "the day of celebration in working-class culture when the check arrives." "Check Day" participants are encouraged to bring to the *Black Factory* site between three and ten objects that speak to them of blackness. Visitors participate in one of two ways: their items can either be photographed and published in an archive on the World Wide Web or donated outright. Some of the donated objects will continue to tour with the *Black Factory*, while others are ground up and pulverized to be molded into new products offered for sale in the Factory's gift shop (including rubber ducks, among other interesting items). The *Black Factory* is "aimed at anyone interested in issues of what makes us different," explains Pope.L. "Calling it the 'Black' Factory is just a way of making it concrete. It's not specifically for black people; it's using the black experience as a funnel to talk about difference."

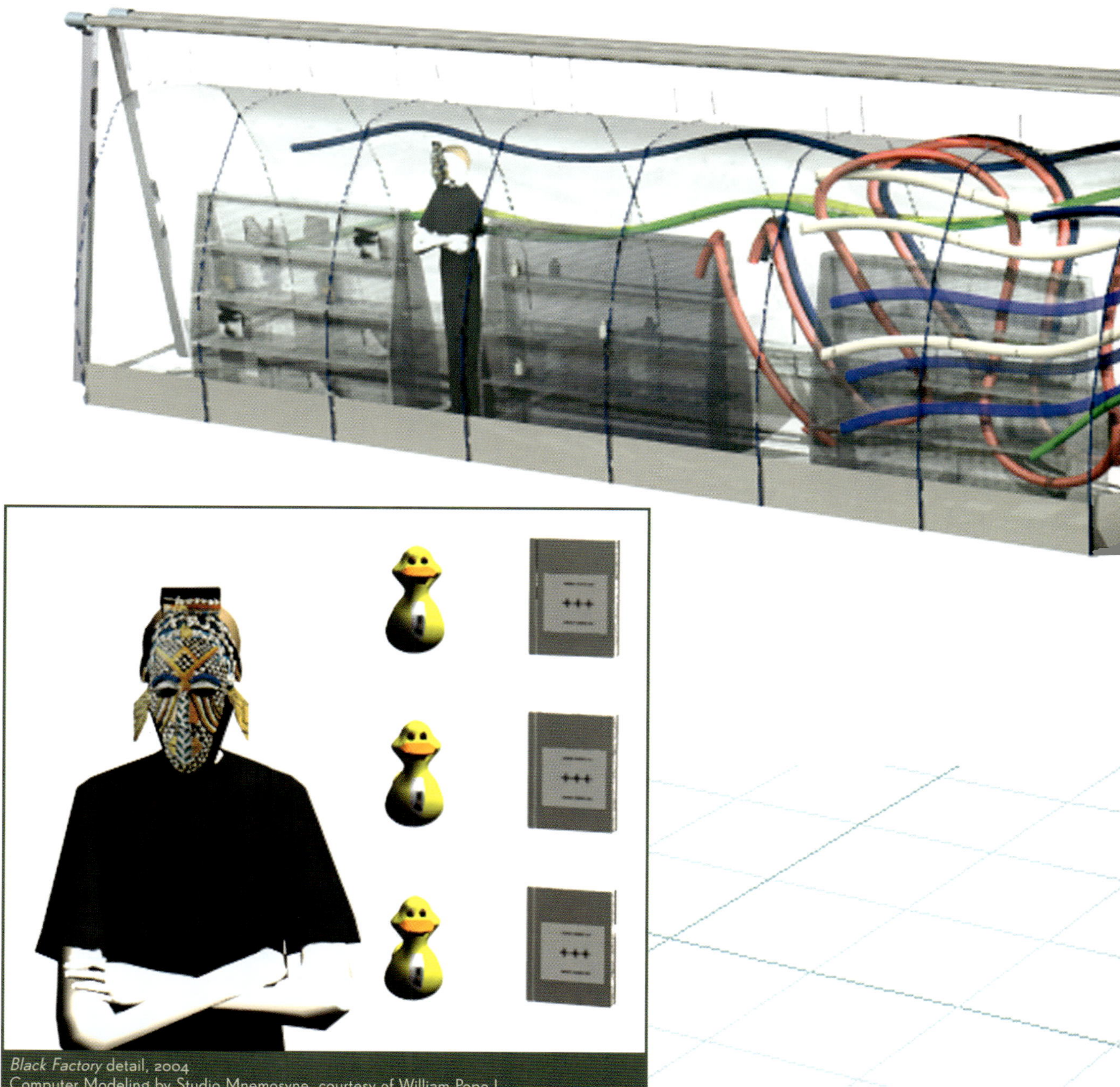

Black Factory detail, 2004
Computer Modeling by Studio Mnemosyne, courtesy of William Pope.L

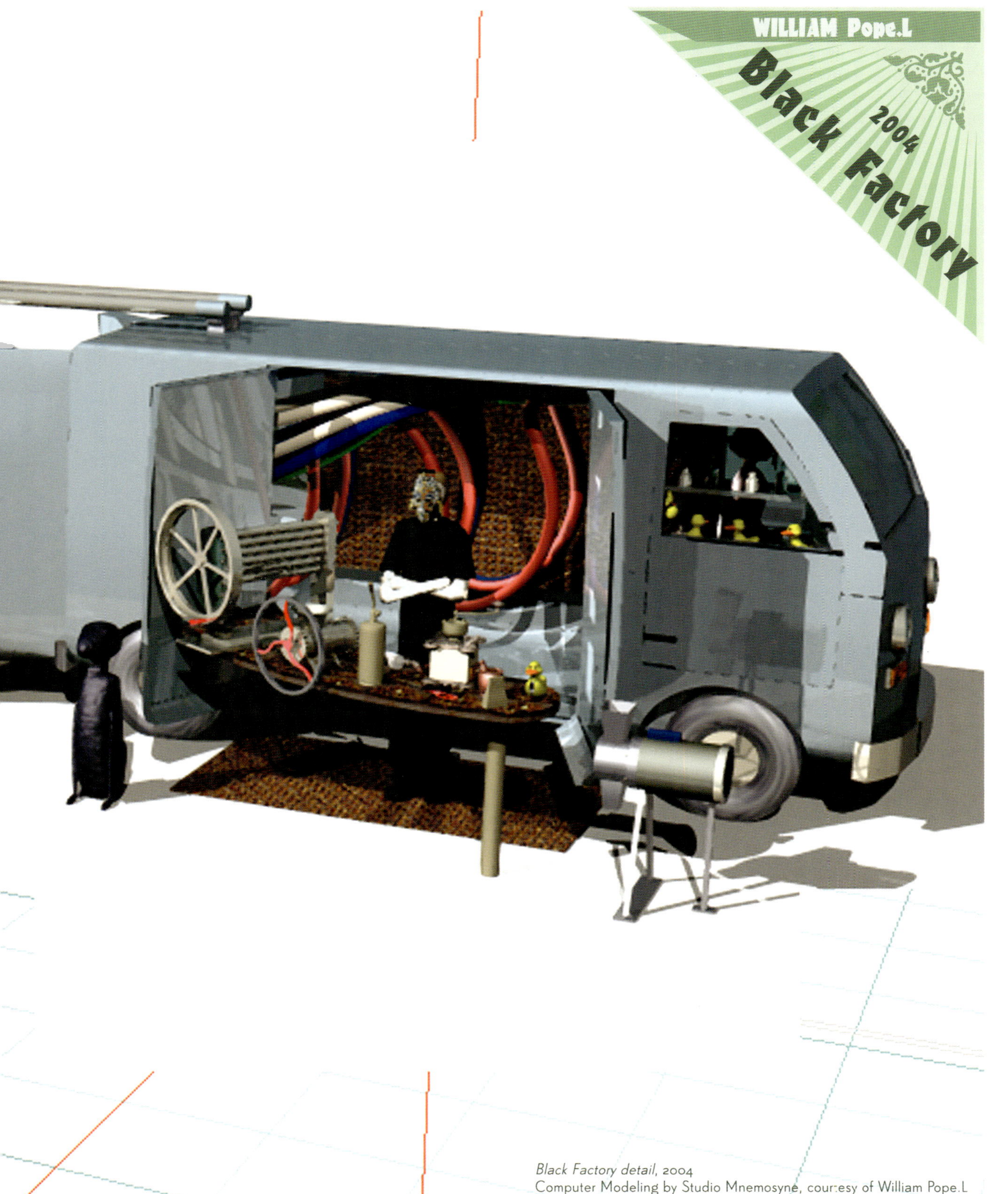

Black Factory detail, 2004
Computer Modeling by Studio Mnemosyne, courtesy of William Pope.L

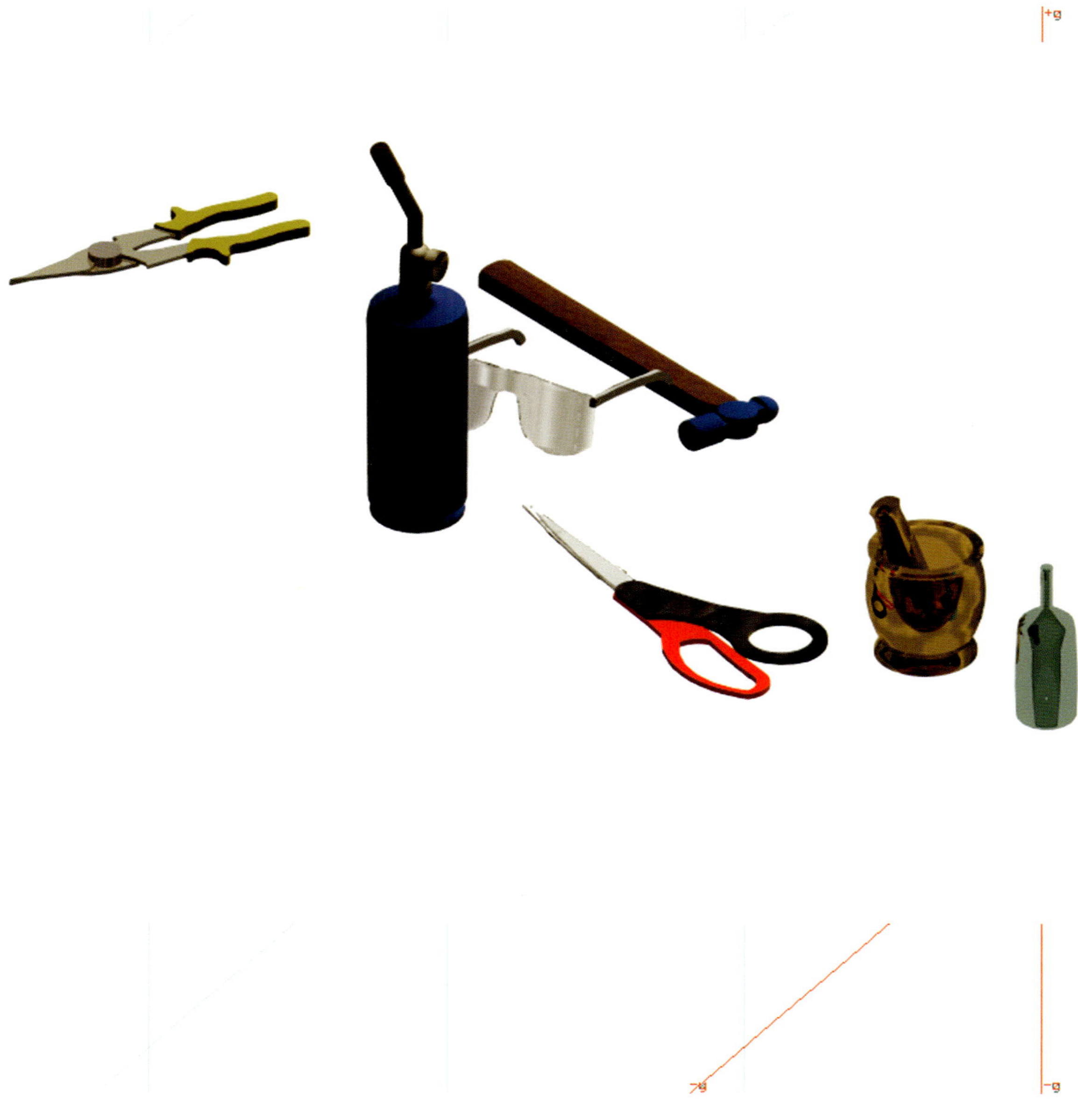

Tools / Black Factory detail, 2004
Computer Modeling by Studio Mnemosyne, courtesy of William Pope.L

William Pope.L

Interview with C. Ondine Chavoya
March 2, 2004

> Which practices and/or movements associated with the
> visual culture of the 1980s were you most engaged by,
> influenced by, or active in?

The idea of collapsing all germinative experience into "practices
and/or movements associated with visual culture of the 1980s"
runs the risk of excluding knowledge equally helpful to creating
fresh culture but, perhaps, not so neatly categorized. For example,
here is a little story: during a mite chunk of the '80s, I made my
way doing construction work, or what I liked to call construction
work. My real name for this work was spaghetti carpentry. I worked
primarily in the Lower East Side and Harlem in New York City.
There was also this building on 116th Street. People said Babe Ruth
once lived there. The building had seen its glory days but was still
beautiful in a dilapidated sort of way. Time, poverty, drugs, and
dog feces were destroying it. It had ten floors. On the ninth,
spaced apart every ten feet or so, chained to this huge mar-
ble and tile landing were eight Doberman pinchers guarding
the gates to nothing...

I got my first construction job via an experimental theater
buddy. Started out as a laborer. Hauling things. In time, I
became a taper. I made the seams between things disappear; for example, between pieces of sheetrock. In those
days, a lot of visual artists did construction. Most of them
worked in galleries or for other artists. My situation was more
— *Merlin*. That was the name of the company I worked for —
Merlin. They had an office on 2nd Avenue near the Bowery.
At first I thought they were landlords, but they were actually
real estate speculators. They bought brownstones all over
Manhattan, sometimes renovated them, sometimes not, and
then re-sold these properties at incredibly inflated prices. Merlin's
relationship to its employees, meaning folks like me, was equally
open-ended. Merlin liked it that way. I thought I did too, until I fell
off a ladder and landed right on my knees like I was Mary or
Joseph or one of the disciples. Yes, I was praying 'cause I knew I
didn't have any insurance and I thought: Yes, yes, lord, surely I am
screwed. But lucky me. The floor was old and over the years had
been covered with twenty or so layers of linoleum. Looking down,
I could see the imprint of my knees in its pattern...

Merlin treated its employees like its buildings. Each was expend-
able and individual. Each functioned as its own "company." They
said this was to protect us so we would pay less tax. In fact, it was
only in the best interest of Merlin because it meant they could
avoid paying our health insurance, worker's compensation, etc.
etc. Of course, at the time most of us, meaning people like me,
did not get the subtleties of the arrangement...

Merlin was sweet to its tenants. This does not mean they treated
them well. Land speculation requires empty buildings, not happy

buildings. Even so, Merlin wanted happy tenants as well.
Unfortunately, this meant cheating most of them. You see, most of
Merlin's tenants were poor, elderly or very young, uneducated,
Spanish-speaking folk unschooled in the workings of real estate
maneuvering. Many of these people had lived in their rent-con-
trolled apartments for years. Market-wise they paid very little. Of
course, to them even a little was a lot, but compared to a rabid
'80s real estate market, which inflated the potential rental price of
their cribs to maybe 3 or 4 or 5 times their value, they were living
in gold mines. Most did not know this. However, Merlin did. Their
strategy was simple: empty the buildings in any way possible. By
hook or crook. A last ditch hook, when nothing else worked, was
to offer each tenant a shit-load of money to move out. Then reno-
vate (or not), re-sell, and make a big-ass profit. Initially, the tenant thought they were getting over, at least until they actually had
to move out and realized how expensive a new apartment costs.
Even so, if Merlin could make the tenants happy, they could
change the world. And so they did in their own way and... with my
help...

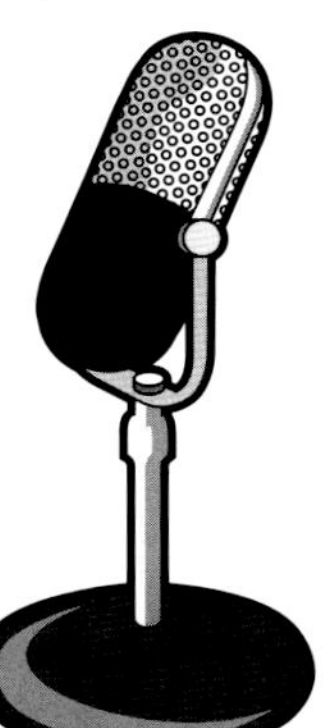

To sum up: I don't mean to create the idea that my
understanding of Merlin's activities or my complicity
with them was achieved without effort. On a certain
level, I did not want to grasp it at all. Part of my
"refusal" was driven by my will to succeed. It is difficult to succeed as an artist in our country today if you
are not willing to look the other way — even if only for
a little while. Another part of my blindness was not
necessarily willed but determined by fear — fear of
the landlord. That is why I initially mistook Merlin for
a landlord. The idea of property and money, I understand at a very basic level. Part of the reason for this
kindergarten understanding is determined by how I
grew up. All my life, landlords had a great impact on
the geographical fate of my family. My mother's
motto was: when you move, you lose. And we moved a lot. In a
certain way coming from my background, homelessness made
more sense than a condo. The idea that home and hearth could
be something other than one thing after another, and that one
thing after another might not just be a puddle, was a radical idea
to me. Indeed, Capitalism seemed to suggest a fresh alternative
to me. Imagine: If I focused only on myself, my own well-being and
ignored the world around me, I might flourish. To me, this was a
radical idea. One I hadn't really thought much about before. In
addition, growing up poor with a fear of poverty made it difficult
for me to admit my identification with the misfortunes of the tenants. Identification was too threatening. I was a fucking company,
goddamnit! Merlin said so!! If I identified, I might actually have to
do something, and then what?

Eventually I quit Merlin. Or I was fired. It got hard to tell the difference. I wasn't happy. I did not like cheating people in order to
cheat myself. Plus I was in pain most of the time. My joints. After
I quit, the doctor told me it was all the white powders I was working with that were killing me. It wasn't my conscience; it was the
powders that were doing it.

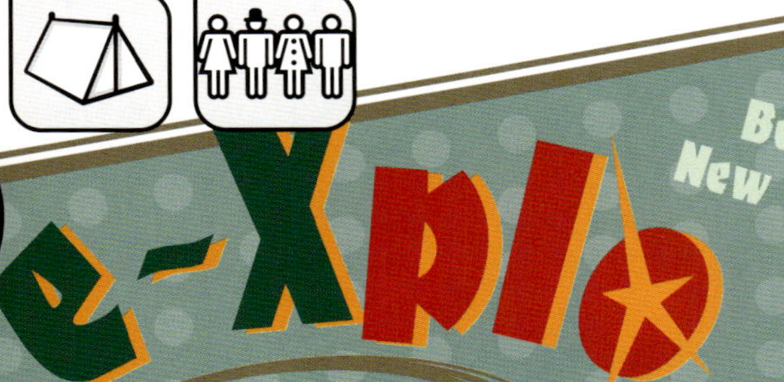

Berlin, Germany &
New York, NY, USA

Founded 1999

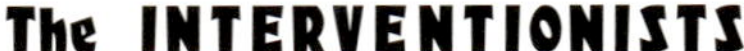

Biographical Info:

Based in Berlin and New York City, the collective **e-Xplo** includes Heimo Lattner, Rene Gabri, and Erin McGonigle. The collective's practice involves sonic explorations of cities: the group develops audio tours that include local interviews, field recordings, sound archives from local libraries, and other sound sources which are then scored to accompany carefully choreographed bus routes. In December 2000, e-Xplo developed its first bus tour for Williamsburg, Brooklyn. In May 2001, they produced *65 MPH* which traversed the bridges and highways of New York City. More recently, e-Xplo has worked with an on-board computer and Global Positioning Systems that use the location, heading, and speed of the bus to determine which sounds will be triggered based on a programmed score. Since developing their tours for New York City, they have produced projects for Turin, Berlin, Rotterdam, and London.

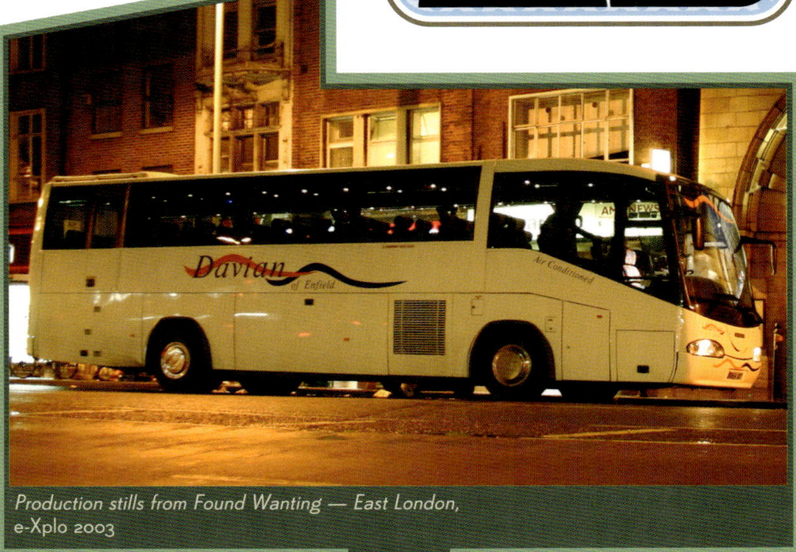

Production stills from Found Wanting — East London,
e-Xplo 2003

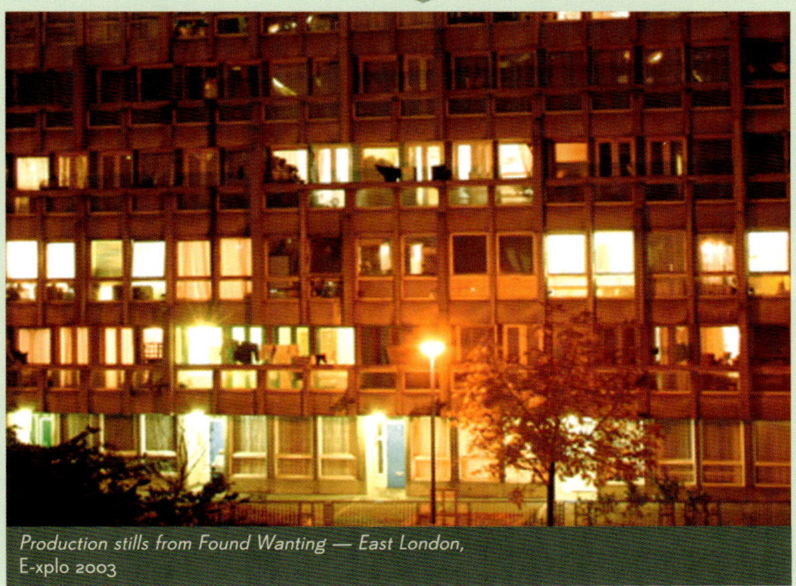

Production stills from Found Wanting — East London,
E-xplo 2003

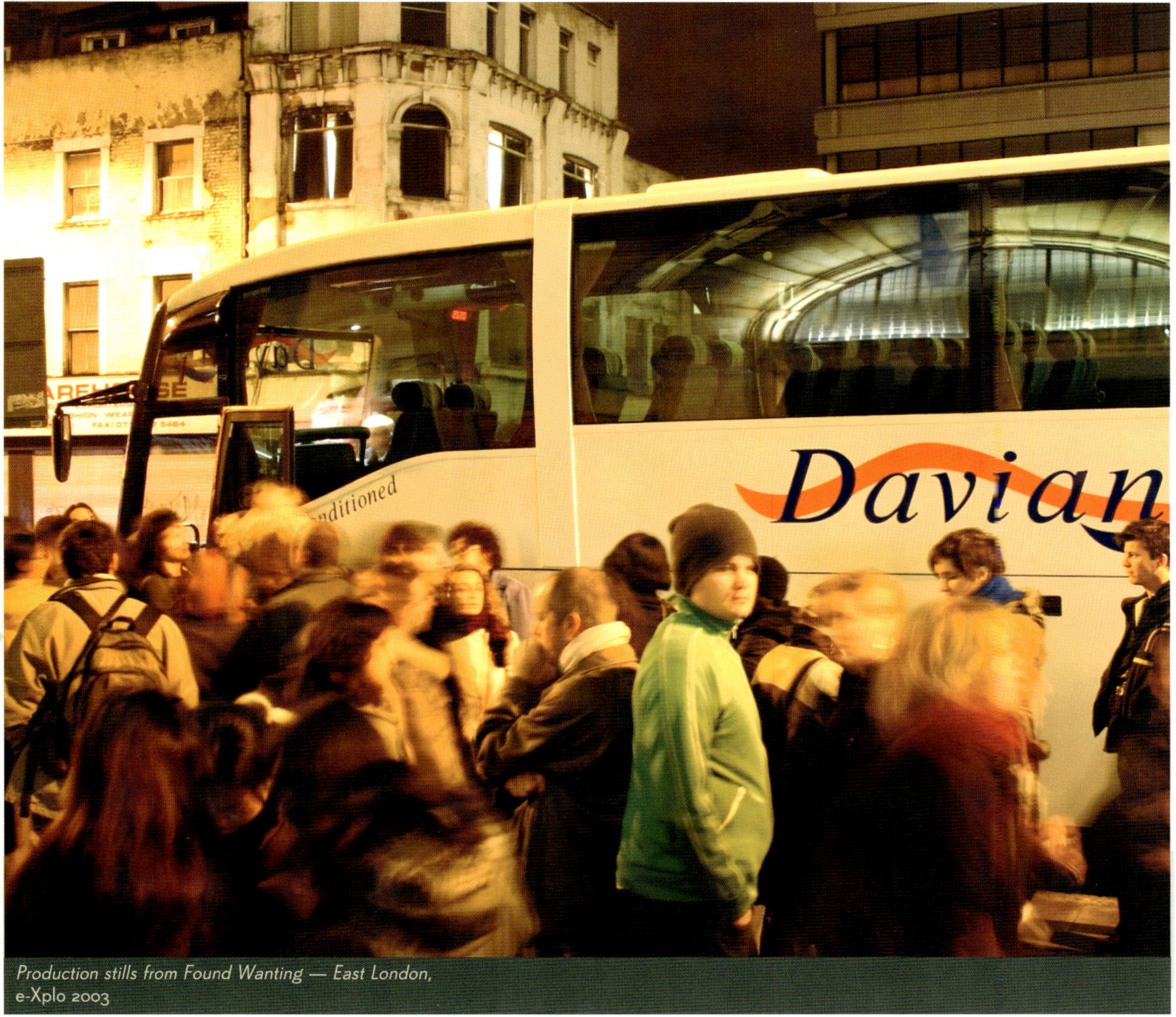

Production stills from Found Wanting — East London,
e-Xplo 2003

Project Description: e-Xplo's bus tour for
The Interventionists runs between the Clark Art Institute, in
Williamstown, Massachusetts, and MASS MoCA, in the neighboring
city of North Adams. These two communities have contrasting socioeconomic and geographical characteristics. The former is a wealthy
college town in a valley, the latter — home to MASS MoCA — is a recover-
ing post-industrial city rising on the steep slopes of the Berkshire Mountains.
e-Xplo's bus travels along an indirect route back and forth between the two communities, offering a recorded tour with speech, music, and other "found" sound drawn
from a database of sounds that are triggered by the bus's location, poetically articulating
the things that bind and divide them.

TITLE OF WORK:

2004
Roundabout
Love at Leisure:
Help Me Stranger

e-Xplo (Heimo Lattner, Rene Gabri, and Erin McGonigle)
Interview with C. Ondine Chavoya
March 2, 2004

Which practices and/or movements associated with the visual culture of the 1980s were you most engaged by, influenced by, or active in?

R: I would say in visual art the work of Group Material, and in performance the Wooster Group could be said to be influential for me, but more so after the fact than during the 1980s. If we stay in the past tense, then, at least for my part, the '80s were a sort of decade of transition, leaving Iran, the Revolution, living in Athens, and then moving with my family to Los Angeles, learning how to forget. Bad pop music, the valley, heavy metal, early hip hop and what was then termed "postmodern" rock, helped in this process, as did Hollywood movies. But I guess in relation to e-Xplo, figures like Antonioni, Godard, Tarkovsky, Kubrick, Brecht, Beckett, Burroughs, Joyce probably have more influence on our work than any practices or movements specifically produced in the '80s.

H: In the '80s a big euphoria swashed over to Europe from the States. These mystical figures surrounding Warhol's factory, the Velvets and all these crazy stories about money, sex, parties, market—politics and superstarism. I have to say, by all naivete, that this was impressive for an art student at that time. There was not much tolerance for discussions outside beaux-arts for a painter at the Art Academy in Vienna in the early '90s. But I remember a performance I attended in New York in '92. It was John Zorn's Cobra. In this work, he instructed musicians by using little signs. He was composing music in real-time based on visual codes. From this moment on until now, the New York '80s downtown music scene had a big impact on my work. Perhaps, I should add the Viennese Actionists - Nitsch, Schwarzkogler, Brus, and Muehl — to this list.

When the viewer experiences your work, what type(s) of relationships do you hope to establish?

R: Well, this is a nice question for several reasons. First, it underlines one of the key concerns in our work. If — as Hannah Arendt argues in The Life of the Mind — that from its outset, in formal philosophy, "thinking has been thought in terms of seeing," our work tries to foreground this problem. By problem here, we mean question. Rather than privilege the audible over the visual, many of our projects, particularly the bus tours, have worked to consciously create tensions between what one is hearing and what one is seeing.

I think our works often produce a heightened sensual awareness, a conscious listening (vs. hearing) and looking (vs. seeing) which often results in a physical as well as mental response. The responsibility falls on the passenger to actively construct a narrative, choosing what to look at, when to listen attentively, when to seek out meaning, and when to feel emotion. So all this hopefully produces a more attentive, active, and critical subject.

Now what exactly does this critical subject do? Well, you hope the work you create generates questions, but questions for questions' sake are also not enough. I think this is a problem today. I have this feeling that many artists feel that it is enough to just generate questions, but I am not sure if that is enough, particularly now; this moment seems to require more. In a recent talk by Alain Badiou in New York, he argued that the contemporary artist represents one of the last figures still capable of proposing or discovering an alternative to Empire.

Raising questions is a critical element in arriving at solutions or alternatives, so don't misunderstand me. As Deleuze notes, it is in the formulation and construction of problems that "humanity makes its own history." I am with him here, but I am also with him when he states: "...nor is it a case of saying that only the problems count. On the contrary, it is the solution that counts..." So the question remains: how to generate the most questions while also encouraging a critical position that reflects your own views?

So you want your work to be grounded enough in its own politics, in its own positions, that the questions you generate are also somewhat directed.

H: There is no bright light of revelation given to the scenes. Rather, they are seen in an obscure or uncertain light. And, there is always enough room for the passengers, the audience, to sit back and have an afterthought or two, to stay within a scene, the site, the sounds and the narration. Most of our works engage in a struggle over ownership of memory. The experience of seeing is itself subject to the forces of forgetting, and the labor of reading traces is equivalent to coming to terms with the past. Walter Benjamin's warning comes to mind: not even the dead are safe when only the victors tell the story.

R: I recall "Picnolepsy," our bus tour in Manhattan in the spring following September 11, 2001. In it, we included fragments from an article by Robert Fisk reporting on the massacres in Sabra and Chatila. So, although we were physically passing by the site of the former World Trade Center, the only text relating to tragedy was of another event, one with a similar number of dead and missing, but with little or no resolution or "justice" carried out. Among other questions in this tour, we wanted to foreground questions related to memory, how and what gets remembered, transmitted. We wanted to transplant a tragedy that involved another city, Beirut, into the context of post 9-11 New York, but for many, I think, the weight of what had just transpired in the city, as well as our own shortcomings, prevented this from occurring successfully with most of our audience. One reviewer failed to even note that the only reference to "an event" involved physical descriptions (e.g., the separation of the men from the women or soldiers sitting on tank turrets) which in no way could be mistaken for a description of September 11.

What are the different fields or networks that you operate in (not just aesthetically but specifically)? How do you view these various facets of your activity?

H: I am still standing with one foot in the experimental music scene.

And, sometimes, I perform my work in rather conventional settings like concerts. Besides that, I have always tried to tie knots with radio stations no matter where I have lived. In Berlin, I am part of a network called Originafassung (original version), organizing talks and discussions based on an understanding of collaboration rather than competition, motivated by the curiosity of strangers or visitors to tap into different fields, such as science, music, architecture, art, dance, choreography, theater, film, politics, design, media, economics, journalism.

R: My main network of activity has really been 16 Beaver, an open platform that a group of us has been developing since 1999. We have organized readings, discussions, presentations, panels, walks, lunches and dinners, grounded by our everyday interests and concerns. In fact, I first met Heimo at 16 Beaver at an informal event we held at the space to discuss the then recent election of Haider in Austria. So that has been a critical part of my creative, political, and social being.

In that sense, my work within e-Xplo seems to me at times an autistic practice, because we are often working in the solitude of the night, driving, researching, looking at maps, and trying to make recordings when things are most quiet. But I guess the main protagonists in e-Xplo's world would consist of night watchmen, nightwalkers, security guards, tour & bus operators, bus drivers, sound engineers, mechanics, programmers, prostitutes, drug dealers, scavengers, tourists, journalists, illegal garbage dumpers, musicians, taxi drivers, "voice talents," police, architects, geographers, garbage men and women (but usually men), those who take to or live on the streets, protesters, activists, road workers, wanderers, passersby, insomniacs.

H: Curators.

What spheres do you find appropriate for your work?

H: We have always tried to create situations of concentration and silence, something we did most often not find inside galleries or concert venues. We created with e-Xplo a sphere that challenged us and one that would provide us and the audience with the circumstances we consider important. In terms of reaching an audience, the decision to take our performances onto the streets was significant. The widespread — in terms of interests, professions and expectations — is larger than ever imaginable by staying, let's say, exclusively within the art world. We always tried to attract a wide audience by promoting the tours not only in art- or music-related media but also by pushing tourist magazines to write about them.

Our latest review was in a British car magazine!

R: One of the strengths of our projects utilizing the "bus tour" genre is the incredible diversity of our public. Longtime residents, visitors and tourists, urban planners and architects, artists, musicians, political and apolitical-minded individuals, club kids, and curious elderly all find their way into our work.

The format itself is familiar, yet unique enough that a wide sphere of individuals has found interest in us. Obviously, when you organize a tour on your own, as we have done in the past, you tend to attract a more diverse audience than when it is part of an art,

music, or new media festival/exhibition. But even in those circumstances, we have developed strategies (e.g. the location of the bus before the tours, listings or articles in local papers) for attracting a more general public.

I don't think any of us ever thought the tours would appeal to as diverse an audience as they have.

How do you see your work operating in larger social movements?

R: Well, this is ultimately a question that will be answered more with time, and in time, I think. Because really our work is in the midst of a great many social movements. At least as of yet, there is no e-Xplo manifesto or political platform. However, there are individuals who are working to transform the ways in which people relate to or experience the places they occupy; or there are other artists who utilize the very mechanisms of capitalism or the culture industry to open up to divergent or resistant views, positions. But then again, I would hate to overstate what we are doing.

The term "larger social movements" could stand for anti-war, anti-WTO, anti-Zionism, anti-power plants in poor neighborhoods, anti-Fascism, anti-racism, anti-eurocentrism, but in an explicit sense our work often remains under the radar of such movements. In fact, one of the strengths of our work may be that it never feels "preachy" or "educational" or "pedantic." This does not mean that the politics are hidden either; this is a fine line to tow, but we attempt it to greater or lesser success. Our work is informed by our political positions and theoretical interests, and, in that sense, it does have some relation to "larger social movements."

If I think about it, the question may also mislead some to think that thought, that thinking, is not a central part of larger social movements, or larger social movements are not also being informed by thinking. Culture, art, philosophy, and politics in time do inform one another whether explicitly or implicitly. If Foucault interrogates Bentham to underline issues of power and control within vision, if Derrida resuscitates the specter of Marx in order to question our relation to the past, to question resurrection inheritance, or if Zizek resurrects Lenin for the purposes of rethinking the present and of the revolutionary moment, or if Negri and Hardt resurrect Spinoza in order to resurface with a concept of the multitudes, it ties directly or indirectly to these movements, and in some cases to our methods, the issues we deal with, or how we deal with them.

I don't know if this question has been answered.

How does your work situate the local and the global?

R: Each tour we develop in a particular city takes on very local issues, issues of representation of the city, the particular histories, the specific contestations (past, present, future), the particular intersection of politics, memory, and history with geography, architecture, and landscape. But, at the same time, there are elements in our tours that often repeat: the night as a

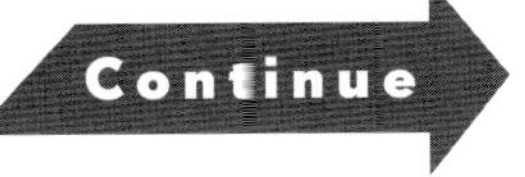

figure, as a unique time-space; the highway, as a place of movement, departure; and then there is, of course, our penchant for industrial sites which have fallen into disuse, prisons, new and old housing projects, cemeteries, and sewage and trash facilities lying at the peripheries of cities. These latter elements are integral parts of most cities, and they help form what is a general vocabulary for cities. And then there are the larger dynamics related to economic changes, globalization, the "migration of labor," and how they affect the city. The same can occur with questions we may raise in relation to the expansive category of "tourism." There are some themes that remain general or global, and others that are local, more specific. In our work, the local and global issues are sometimes fused and sometimes confronted with one another.

What do you consider the advantages and/or disadvantages to collaboration, compared to individualized forms of art production?

R: It is harder, more time, more discussions, more personalities, more questions, more opportunities for misunderstanding, but when it works well, the work you produce is greater than the sum of its parts. And I'd like to think that the work we have produced is above what any of us could produce on our own. We each bring something unique to the table, not just technically, but our interests, backgrounds, and education are so different, it gives depth to our work together.
Sometimes, with time also, the differences can also take their toll. The paradox of enablement, the very things that enable you to make interesting work can also take away from it. I am purposely weaving the positives with the negatives, because this is how I have always experienced collaboration. It has never been easy for me, collaboration, but it has given more than it has taken away. And can you imagine doing the work we do alone?
H: As I am still digesting what Rene said, it becomes clear that an itinerary and a journey are the recipe for this work together. An integral element in the way I approached my work has always been through collaboration with others. When attempting to create art within the context of collaboration, the artists are obliged to express more than just their own emotions and ideas. This doesn't mean compromising one's artistic vision. Rather, it means being flexible and aware of the language of others. Furthermore, one must work out a balance as a unity, without losing the richness of diversity.

How do you see humor as functioning in your art?
What about delight and pleasure in your work?

R: Humor is not easy, but it is definitely a part of the puzzle. Pleasure, on the other hand, is a tricky thing, particularly when you are dealing with a tourist-like medium such as our "bus tour." Having said that, I think we take risks with pleasure, we let it creep in and we also take it away, or call it into question. But, I could not imagine submitting people to a one- or two-hour bus ride without elements of pleasure (or delight or humor). Moreover, I think it is important to note that pleasure does not have to stand for mindless entertainment; pleasure can come from encountering feelings or states you

have never known. Pleasure can come from discovery; pleasure can come from being introduced to new questions or thoughts. One element that exists in our work is a sort of management of these multiple pleasures.
The way we map the route, work with the sounds, texts, and music, we attempt to pace our audience, combining the pleasures of looking and listening with the space for critical distance, reflection, and questioning.

Why is movement necessary in your work?
What do we gain from movement?

R: Personally, I am not so sure if "necessary" is the best term to use here. There are a great deal of interesting and important artists, filmmakers, and scholars writing about the city, or working with issues we are interested in that do not employ our specific strategies in relation to movement. I do think that we can speak about specific dynamics related to movement, however, that are unique to our work.

As Elizabeth Grosz notes, architecture (and I would say art, particularly public art) has often faced time through the questions posed by history, and through its response to the ravages of that history has posited itself as something that overcomes time, freezing it, transcending it, memorializing it. I think our "bus tours" resist this impulse, and instead approach time via the circuit of duration. In other words, time less as something to resist or to fix, but instead something to live through, witness its unfolding, experience, interpret, and possibly learn from.

In moving through the city, highway, or even countryside with this altered sensibility toward time, one can create a unique relation to even the most familiar places. Furthermore, rather than become something fixed or homogenous, the experiences of time and space in a city, for example, are allowed to be heterogeneous, full of minute-by-minute alterations, contestations, ever-changing, dividing, surprising us.

In other words, by moving in this manner, we are not just commuting or even "touring" in the ordinary sense. One could say it is a movement more akin to "cruising," in which time is no longer something to overcome, and there are no known "sights" to arrive to. In this movement, every turn or pause is significant not for what it may be keeping you from getting to, but rather what new experience it might present you with. It is a movement intrinsically locked into a different relation to time, a relation linked to experience, passage, and emergence.

How does technology function in your work?
In general, what is your relationship to technology?

R: Sometimes as an object of inquiry, but most often it is a means to an end. We have worked with some technologies and software that in and of themselves are interesting to programmers and those working within the realm of new media and technology, but for us, I think, we remain pretty weary of technology for technology's sake. H: We prefer analog strategies. Analogy poetry resides in finding possible correspondences and connections between mutually exclusive modes of otherness.

But, of course, we are using the GPS system and Korin. And we are aware that we open an entire new can of worms the moment we start contextualizing these technologies. The computer program has been developed to move our performances onto a new level. The duration of a performance does not depend on our physical and mental capacities any longer. That was the original consideration. The politics of mobility were an issue for us before we started making use of the GPS. Perhaps we use the satellite, which might sound paradoxical, as tactile connection, an interactive tool. And by doing so we stress the common assumption that satellites are merely little relay stations in outer space. For decades, satellites have been used not only to relay images but also to monitor activities on earth.

In the past two decades, public space has become increasingly privatized as private space (and private lives) have become increasingly subject to the expanded structures and technologies of surveillance. How might your work respond to or demonstrate this scenario?

H: When the idea for the bus tours appeared in 1999-2000, Erin had already developed several projects for and within abandoned sites in Brooklyn. That's how we actually met. It was rather easy at this point to get access to the empty lots and warehouses. Nobody seemed to care, and the questions of ownership were not clear in many cases. With the increasing gentrification in these areas, things changed rapidly. We found ourselves confronted with an entirely new situation. Putting our performances on board buses was a reaction to these circumstances. Neither did we have to ask for permission, nor did we have to compromise ourselves.

Where do you find support for your work?

H: We have received great support from universities lately. The Technical University in Eindhoven invited us to develop Korin, the software we are using to control and trigger the data in the GPS-based tours like the one we are working on for the project at MASS MoCA right now. But, more importantly, several teachers in London, California, Vienna, and New York have introduced their students to e-Xplo's work, and we have received great feedback from them. In the end, that weighs more than financial support. But, I do not want to downplay the importance of money for our projects Getting a bus onto the streets, hosting us for several weeks, letting us do all the research and stepping out with a little profit at the end, taking all of that into account, well, it isn't an inexpensive enterprise we are trying to maintain. I guess we should thank at this point all the curators, festivals, and museums that had the courage to take on an e-Xplo project in the last four years.

Can there be revolutionary art without a revolution?

H: What came first: the hen or the egg?
R: The question of revolution is an interesting one, because when you deal with social and political subject matter, you are confronted with questions of change, social transformation, and possibly "revolution." But what is revolution really? Julia Kristeva has recently argued for a reappraisal of the term. She suggests that politics has a stranglehold on the term, and her project involves freeing it from its grips. Instead, she advocates a renewed relationship to revolt, one in which revolution would involve a critical relationship with oneself, intrinsically tied to memory and to anxious thinking. This concept of "anxious thinking" is interesting; revolution, revolver, a return, an eternal return (Sanskrit root) that is always in process, always reappraising, reasserting and then questioning one's ways, methods, approaches. Although some elements of her narrative may sound reactionary and somehow conservative, what is useful in the context of our discussion is rethinking what we mean by revolution. By revolution, do we want to project something that is a break, a pure rupture, a solution, or something that involves a process, a method?

Ha·ha

Chicago, IL & Cambridge, MA, USA

Founded 1988

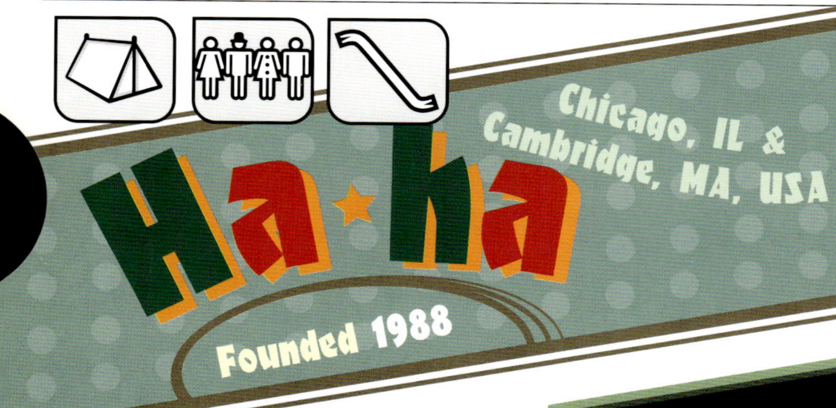

Taxi, Chicago, 2003
Courtesy of Haha

Biographical Info:

Haha consists of Wendy Jacob, Laurie Palmer, and John Ploof. Sharing an interest in community participation, the collective formed in Chicago in 1988. In 1993, as part of the exhibition Culture-in-Action curated by Mary Jane Jacob, Haha produced *FLOOD*, a project that focused on the AIDS crisis. For *FLOOD*, Haha created a hydroponic community garden that grew vegetables and herbs for AIDS patients. The garden serviced as a practical vehicle for discussing issues of mutual interest. In addition to their collaborative work with Haha, each artist works individually as well. Wendy Jacob is currently a professor at the Massachusetts Institute of Technology, and Laurie Palmer and John Ploof teach at the School of the Art Institute of Chicago. Haha has exhibited widely, including exhibitions at the New Museum of Contemporary Art, the Venice Biennale and the David and Alfred Smart Museum of Art in Chicago.

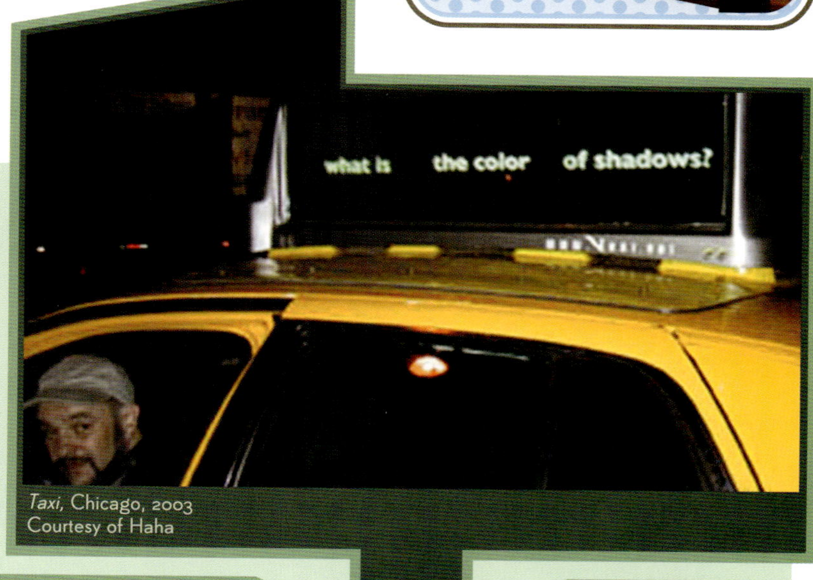

Taxi, Chicago, 2003
Courtesy of Haha

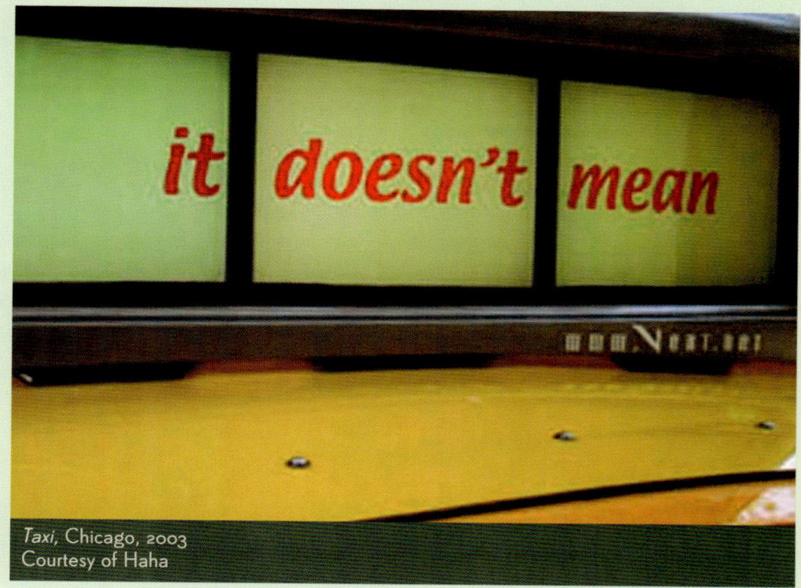

Taxi, Chicago, 2003
Courtesy of Haha

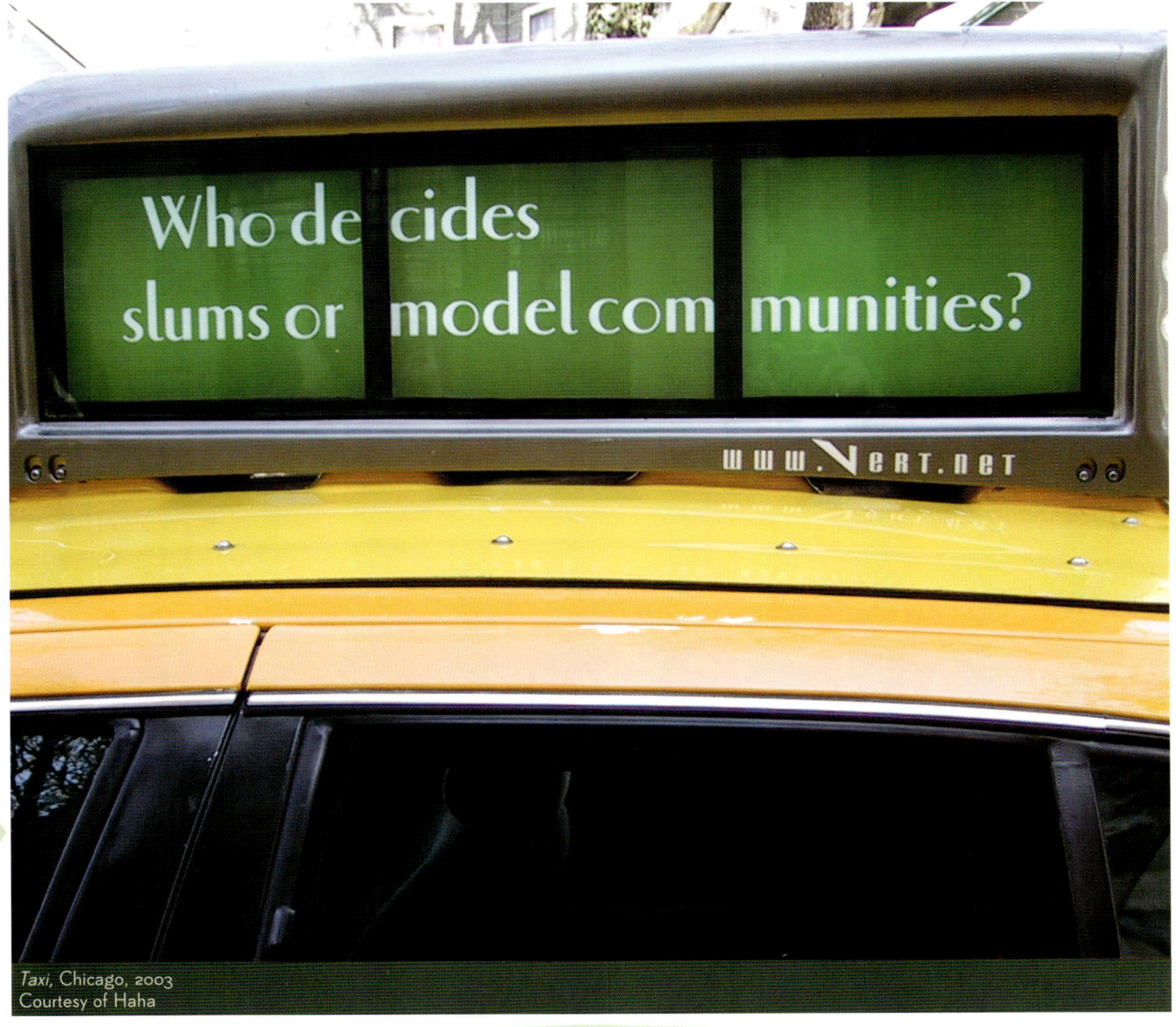

Taxi, Chicago, 2003
Courtesy of Haha

Project Description: *Taxi* had its debut performance in Chicago in 2003. With the assistance of location-sensitive signage equipment mounted on the roof of a taxi cab, the work presents flash-animated messages keyed to particular sites as the taxi moves throughout the city. For the North Adams version of *Taxi*, members of Haha spent time in various community centers, ranging from a seniors' aerobics class to a YMCA after-school program, interviewing people and seeking short statements about specific places in North Adams. Transforming a medium originally intended for advertising, Haha's project provides a lithe and inventive vehicle for community members to speak to their city. Messages include "This is my second home" as the car drives by the Holiday Inn and "Court-appointed lawyers should be free" as the car drives by the local courthouse, to such strange and impenetrable thoughts such as "Check Out Lane 2."

TITLE OF WORK:

2004
Taxi,
North Adams

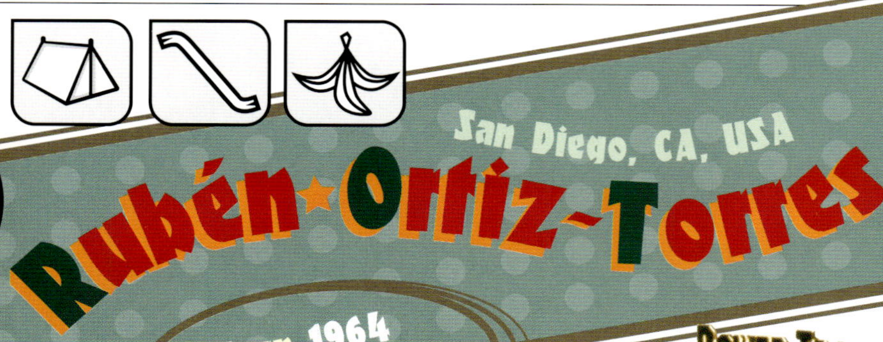

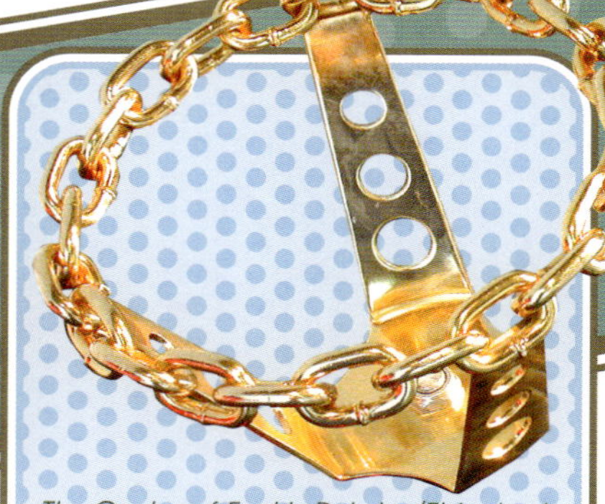
The Garden of Earthly Delights/El Jardín de las Delicias detail, 2002. Photo by Patrick Miller. Courtesy of Rubén Ortiz-Torres

Biographical Info:

Rubén Ortiz-Torres works in a variety of non-traditional media to explore cultural collisions, often with comic effect. In particular, Ortiz-Torres focuses on the migrations of meanings and forms as they apply to Latin America and the United States. He has produced photographs, paintings, hats, trucks, and even leaf-blowers to investigate signature materials and images of this changing cultural landscape.

The son of Latin American folk musicians, Ortiz-Torres was born in Mexico City. He trained in architecture at the Harvard Graduate School of Design and studied art at the Academy of San Carlos in Mexico City and the California Institute of Arts in Valencia, California.

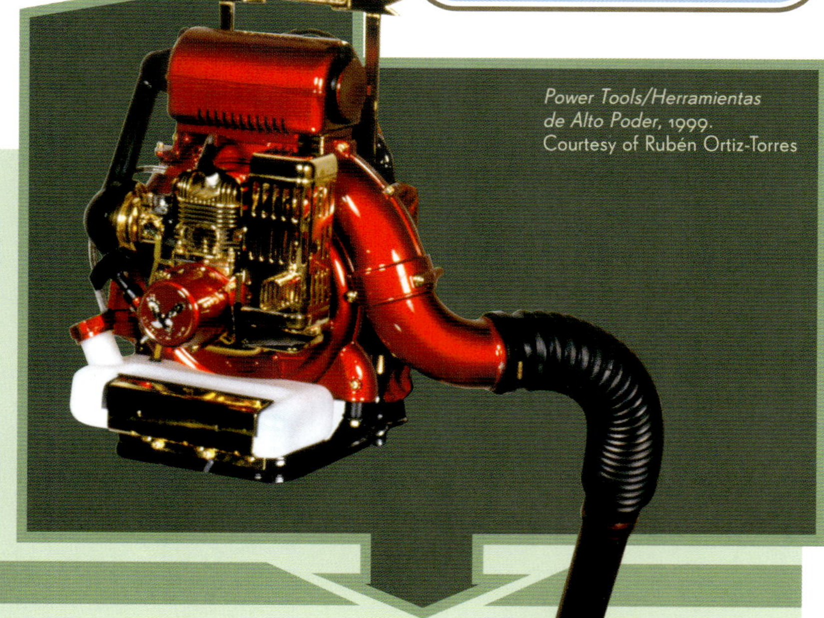

Power Tools/Herramientas de Alto Poder, 1999. Courtesy of Rubén Ortiz-Torres

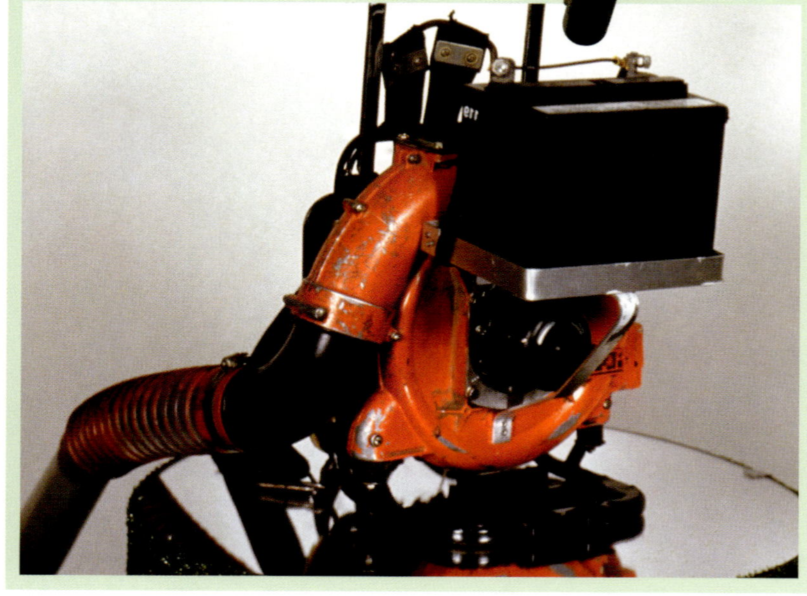

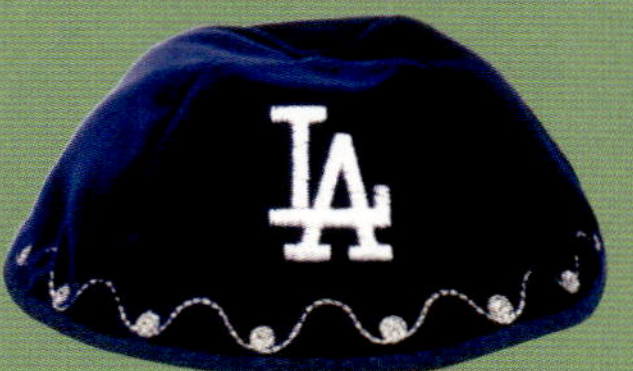
Dodger Yarmulke/A Lefty's Legacy
Courtesy of Rubén Ortiz-Torres

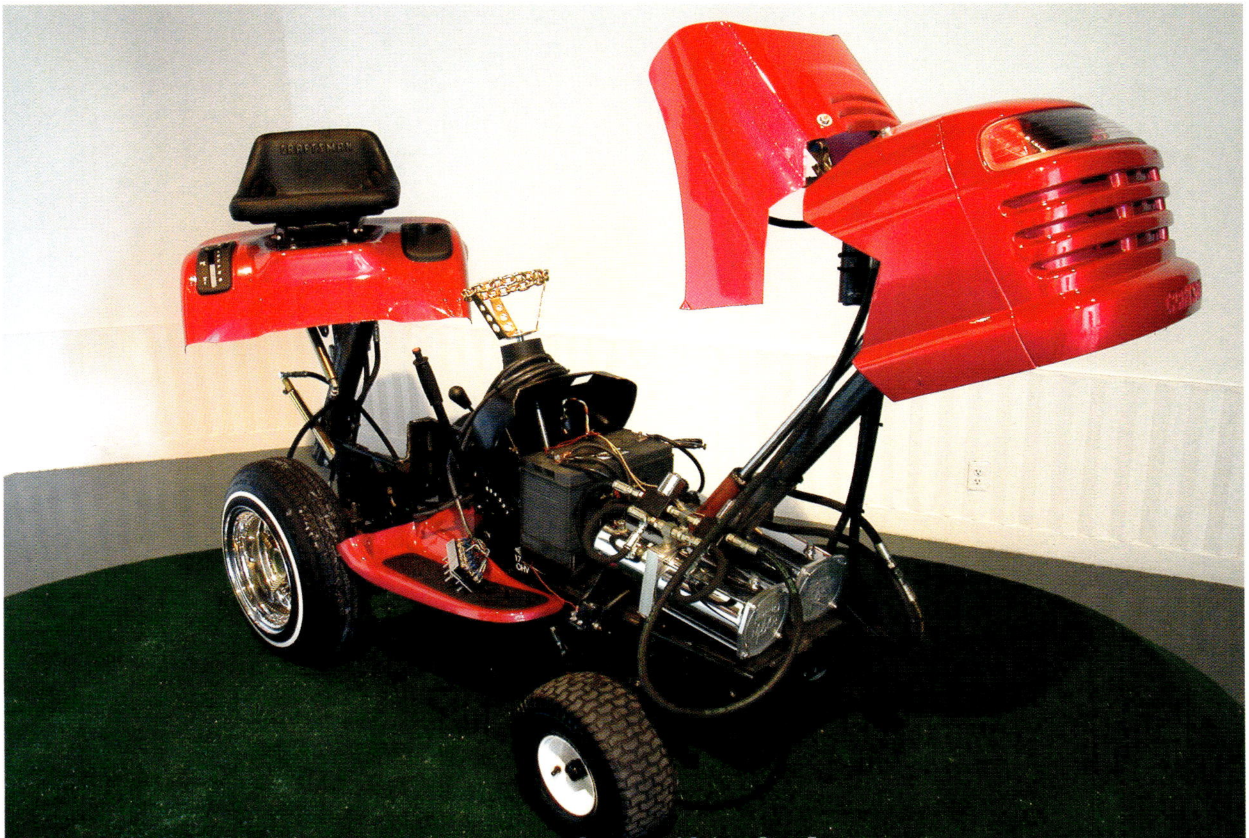

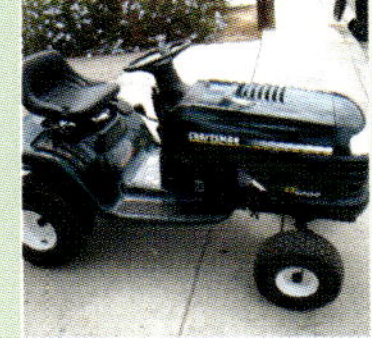

Garden of Earthly Delights/ El jardín de las delicias, 2003. Courtesy of Rubén Ortiz-Torres

Project Description: For Ortiz-Torres, who lives in southern California, yard work is emblematic of the everyday labor of Latin American immigrants in California. Playing their trade as grounds-keepers, Latino gardeners are perhaps the most visible part of the informal economy that connects culture and class in southern California. In *Garden of Earthly Delights*, Ortiz-Torres has reworked a piece of vernacular machinery, the lawn mower, infusing it with Chicano low-rider aesthetics: hydraulics, flashy paint, and shining chrome in a wry recasting of tools and stylized fashion. Also on display is a series of Ortiz-Torres' baseball hats, for which the artist designed minor customizations to familiar sports and corporate logos, changing their meanings entirely. Ortiz-Torres often works with a wide range of collaborators to realize his work. See the following interview for a description of his often complex work process.

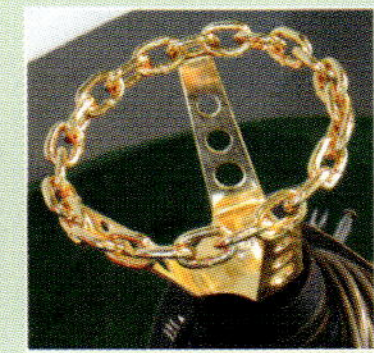
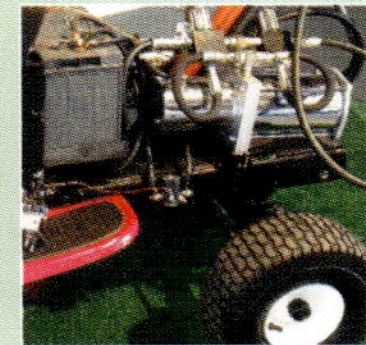
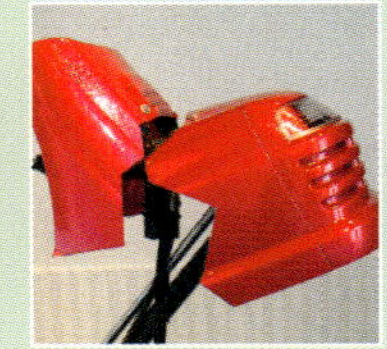
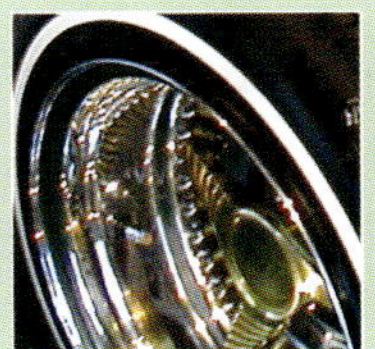
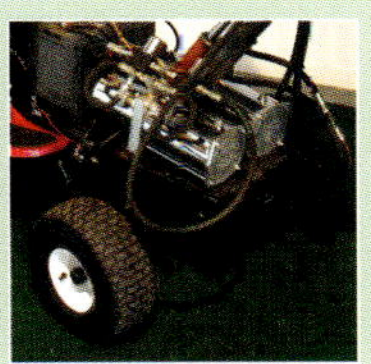

The Garden of Earthly Delights/El Jardín de las Delicias detail, 2002. Photo by Patrick Miller. Courtesy of Rubén Ortiz-Torres

The INTERVENTIONISTS

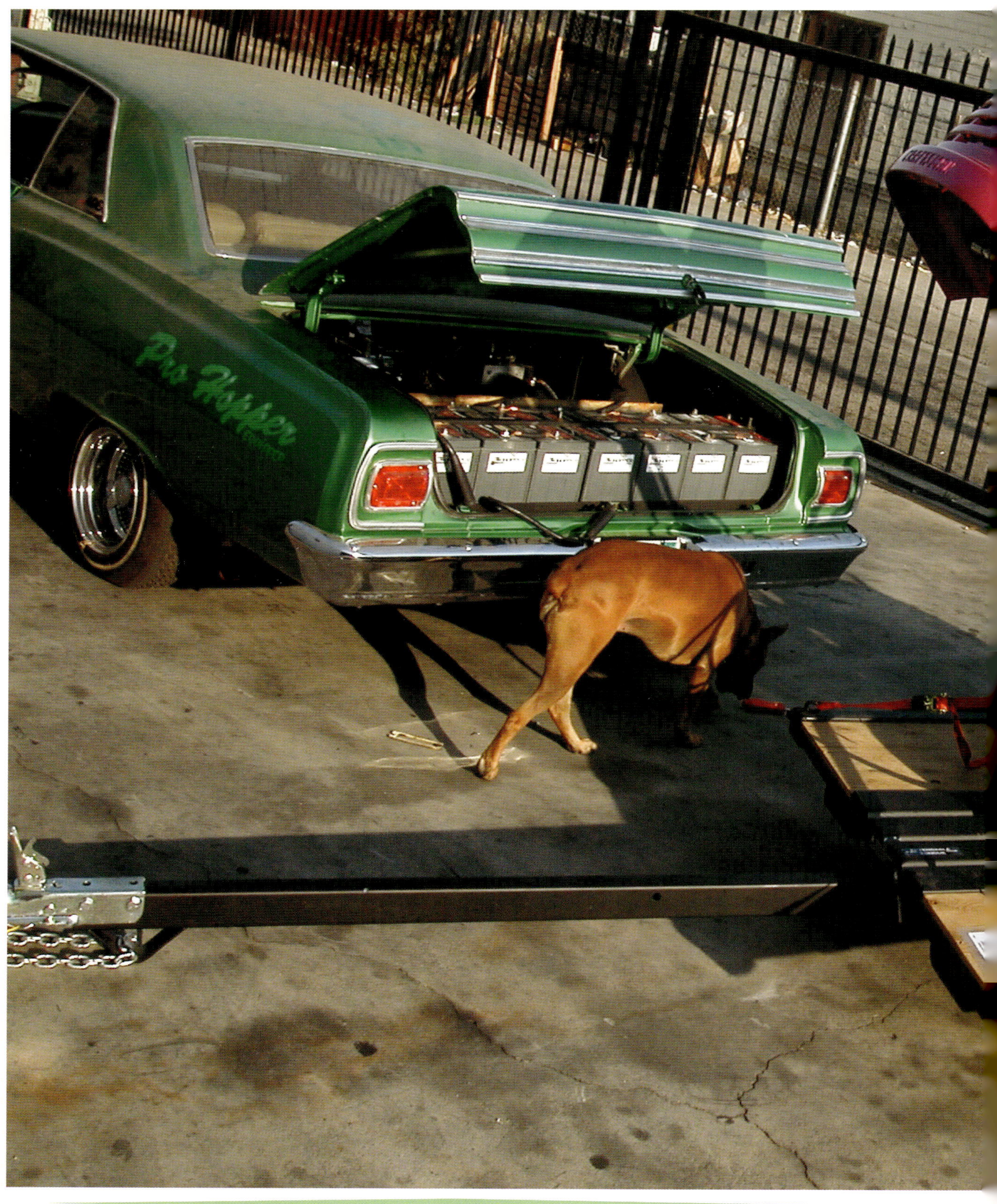

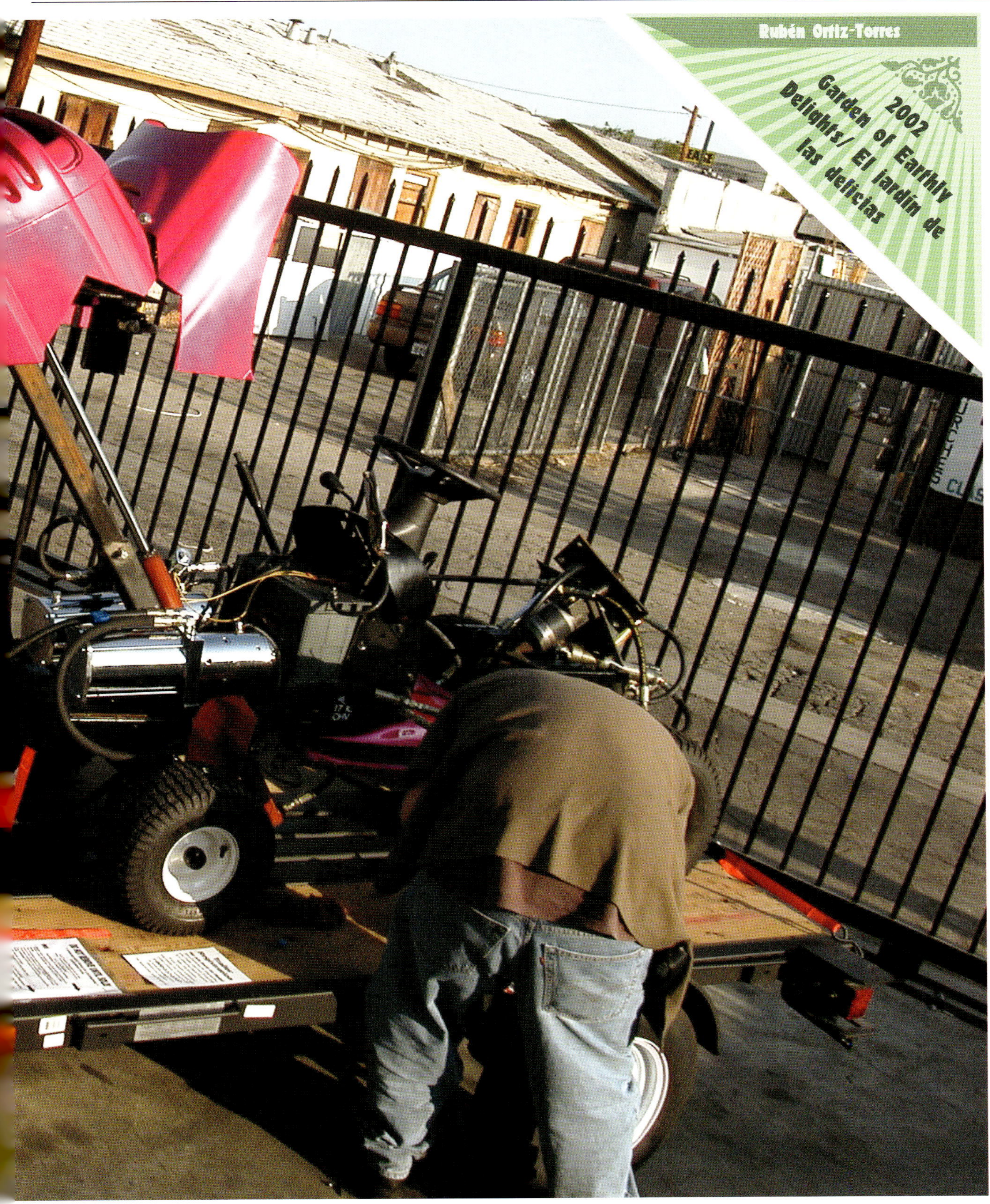
Rubén Ortiz-Torres
2002
Garden of Earthly
Delights/ El Jardín de
las delicias

Rubén Ortiz-Torres

Interview with C. Ondine Chavoya
March 24, 2004

C. Ondine Chavoya: What aspects of popular culture were you most involved in during the period of the 1980s?

Rubén Ortiz-Torres: This is an interesting question to consider in light of the work I do now. At some point in the 1980s, I became very interested in the power and ambivalence of cultural hierarchies, and these questions eventually led to the art I make today. When we speak of popular culture, high culture, and folk culture, certain hierarchies are necessarily implied. At the time, however, these distinctions were in the process of collapsing, or had already collapsed, in Mexico as in parts of the globe. As any trip to the public markets in Mexico City demonstrates, the distinction between folk and popular culture has always been confused in Mexico; rather than being clearly delineated, they coexist.

O: That attention to ambivalence and coexistence is certainly evident in your work and visually amplified in your photographs. I am also interested in your own personal affiliations, if you will, or involvement with youth culture in the 1980s, since I have seen your "rock star" photographs from the 1980s. Would you care to speak about that?

R: In my personal case, my parents were folklorists and I rebelled against that. I could not identify with the folk songs about "condors soaring the Andes," when I was living in this fucked up, polluted, overcrowded, earthquake-prone, industrialized, third-world concoction. So I started listening to punk music. It's always curious how people initially become involved in art and aesthetics, but, in my case, it was through rock and roll - collecting records, looking at the cover art and photographs, and then all the culture that was built around that, including shows and the cineclubs. Punk music came to me at a time when I was trying to define what I was going to do, and beginning to think about the issues of making art and culture. And, even though I identified with punk, it was also very alienating, perhaps even schizophrenic, because all the information about it was coming from abroad - so these things always seemed to exist out of context. I remember a friend from that period we called El Gordito Lafontaine, who was this punk musician who played in the scene with his band Las Toronjas. He was this gothic kid who was convinced that if Siouxsie and the Banshees showed up in Mexico, or if he landed in London, he would be able to communicate with Siouxsie Sioux, even if he did not speak English, because he was wearing all the proper icons.

Punk culture was obviously very attractive visually, and, originally, I was just trying to make, or maybe "recreate," documentary punk photographs in black in white. The first award I ever received for my art was for a series of photographs featuring my eccentric punk friends [Bienal de Fotografía, I.N.B.A, Mexico City, 1984]. These photographs did not look like the photographs of The Clash, such as those taken by Kate Simon or Sheila Rock; instead, they looked like "The Clash" in a third-world country. I came to realize that the most interesting aspect of these photographs was precisely this "schizophrenic" situation where everything and everyone was apparently always out of context.

This idea led me to examine other local icons, and I became increasingly interested in the cultural clashes, visually and socially, that emerged. Certain local icons were also being mutated by various modern and postmodern transformations, and, in the process, taken out of context. This was particularly evident with regard to religious iconography. For example, there was an annual contest to honor the best shrine to the virgin in a particular neighborhood in Mexico City, and these shrines were crazy, totally unconventional; I mean this was not even Catholicism anymore. The virgins and saints were placed in shrines alongside neon lights, disco balls, fountains and figures in stylized Aztec neon suits, and I started documenting these manifestations. Since then, my photographs have continued to investigate and document these elements of crossover eccentricity or displacement without context. But, the original impetus for this interest in regional reflection and transformation, heterogeneity and disjuncture, came from my punk experience.

O: The next question I wanted to ask concerns the viewer. When a viewer experiences your work, what types of relationships do you hope to establish?

R: When I first started developing a response to this question, the tone was very generic, almost manifesto-like. It said something like, "I would hope that my work would engage, would give the viewer the opportunity to embrace a different perspective of the cultural, social, artistic, and political mechanisms that define the aesthetic experience." Basically, I am interested in making art that can somehow play with or create various levels of engagement. Aesthetics occur in the art world, of course, but they also happen outside the art world, and, ultimately, they might not be that different. For example, aesthetics are at play when you identify with a sports team or a certain kind of music; just as aesthetics inform the way you dress, or the car you drive, and so on and so forth. Now, I am not suggesting that consumerism or purchasing and driving a car is exactly the same as making art. Instead, I want to suggest that the art I make can exist and operate in different circuits and often does so in unpredictable ways.

In certain contexts, people assume I am simply a photographer; in other contexts, I am known more as a sculptor, and sometimes just as someone who works with cars. Following the La Zamba del Chevy installation and performance, made in collaboration with Salvador "Chava" Muñoz and Tony Ortiz for the J. Paul Getty Museum in 2000, the project received a lot of attention, and yet it was not necessarily the kind of attention an artist would traditionally seek. For example, several car magazines reviewed the piece. [The installation and accompanying 3-D video blend the traditions of low-rider car culture with the memory of Ernesto "Che" Guevara, whose prized possession was a 1960 Chevy Impala.] And, I was invited to discuss cars and customizing on the radio a couple of times and once specifically to talk about the song - also titled La Zamba del Chevy composed by my father in 1967 - its history and the new version. Every once in a while I will turn on the radio, and certain programs on NPR or Pacifica continue to play the song! The song had been distributed in a circuit that is not necessarily an art circuit, and, therefore, its audience has expanded.

After I exhibited the *Power Tools* installation in New York, some collectors were interested in it. But, since it played a role in the history of the city and the labor movement in Los Angeles, I thought it would be better if the piece stayed here, where the gardeners and the people involved in the struggle over the leaf-blower ban could see it. When the Los Angeles County Museum of Art acquired it, I was definitely pleased since I believe the sculpture and the issues it represents truly belong to the city. However, this also prompted a certain kind of "reality check" concerning the impact that art can and cannot have. Although I am interested in making political art, we should not confuse political art with politics, which often happens.

In the case of the *Power Tools*, the point is this: while teaching at Otis College of Art, a student approached me and asked, "Hey, Mr. Ortiz, you did the leaf-blowers at LACMA, right?" "Yes," I replied. He then said, "Oh, those are cool. We have photographs of them in our living room." I had to ask, "What do you mean?" It turns out that his father was a gardener, and he and his family went to LACMA specifically to see the leaf-blower installation. Of course, not every gardener in Los Angeles will ever see the sculpture or even care to. But, just the fact that this piece could foster this type of connection between a father and his son enrolled in art school, it made me think that maybe I was not complete bullshit (laughter). Maybe these connections are made in certain circuitous ways sometimes.

O: You often use different models for collaboration in the production of your work; for example, the installation projects and the film and video works. How would you characterize the process for collaboration in the works that will be on view at MASS MoCA?

R: Well, first of all, I come from a somewhat anarchist educational background that really fosters team effort. Thus, I have a hard time adjusting to certain notions that determine how we judge or think about art as an exclusively individual experience. The idea that an artwork is the work of "an individual," or an individual effort of intentionality, is an illusion. In addition to an artist, you need a curator, gallery, collector, and all sorts of networks and situations. To a certain degree, we could even make the case that meaning and authorship in contemporary art today depends more on the curator than the artist. Regardless, art is the result of a process of negotiation and collaboration on all sorts of different levels.

I enjoy working with people, so usually I work with people. There are multiple examples in my work where the role of authorship has been negotiated and shared. In the case of the customized baseball caps

that will be exhibited at MASS MoCA, many different processes were involved in their production. Often, different icons were added or layered on to already existing ones, but there are very few examples where I was the one that physically produced the intervention. A computer was used to design and produce some; for others I took them to various shops with embroidery machines where the work was completed as I requested. In many instances, they were handmade. Sometimes I knew who did them; sometimes I did not. Several were commissioned and produced in places around the world, such as Guatemala, Minnesota and Sweden, using very different regional styles of embroidery, which I hope is apparent. Some of the embroiderers in Guatemala actually requested to be compensated with licensed, wool American baseball caps, which are high-priced and popular commodities in Guatemala. The baseball caps made there are very curious, and I have collected some of them: you can find a New York Yankees cap in the market but it might be bright pink cotton with a Yankees logo on the front, "Lakers" on one side, and on the other side "Mexico."

In Minneapolis, I commissioned Terry Bright Nose to alter a cap using a traditional Ojibwa style of embroidery. When I first presented her with the Chicago Black Hawks cap, she was hesitant and questioned my motivations. She clearly found the hockey team mascot and emblem problematic. I showed her examples of other completed sports caps from the series, and she recognized that this would be a critical commentary on what she, in fact, found so problematic. Contrasting different forms of representation could provide a method to address the issue. In a way, the final version, Ojibwa Black Hawks, provides the opportunity to compete with that logo and to represent another aesthetic point of view.

In the case of *The Garden of Earthly Delights*, Salvador "Chava" Muñoz developed the hydraulics and my sister produced the sound. She composed the soundtrack using recordings she made of landscaping, recording the sounds of the labor and equipment of urban gardeners.

O: *The Garden of Earthly Delights* seems somehow distinct from the earlier Alien Toy or Power Tools installations. In the previous works, the process involved re-customizing already existing customized objects for museum installation. A history of low-rider automobiles, pickup trucks, and hydraulic lifts preceded them. Salvador Muñoz had already customized the pickup truck, *Wicked Bed*, which was then re-customized to produce Alien Toy. Gody Sanchez had begun to produce customized prototypes for more efficient leaf-blowers, which inspired and were then incorporated into the *Power Tools* installation. But were there previous models for customized tractor mowers?

R: In the case of the tractor lawn mower, no, there was not a pre-existing model. I made some initial designs and drawings, and then Salvador "Chava" Muñoz

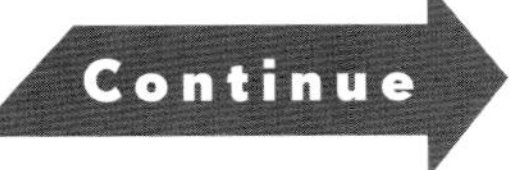

made multiple adjustments and improvements. The other two pieces, Alien Toy also made with Salvador "Chava" Muñoz and Power Tools made with Gody Sanchez, are more complex. The piece with Gody was produced in the fashion of a dialogue: he made one, I made another, and then they were displayed together for exhibition. The two leaf-blowers are very different aesthetically and they have different functions. I was interested in this contrast and together they accomplish something different.

In the case of *Alien Toy* with "Chava," the process of collaboration was very complicated and, at the same time, very problematic. And I will not deny the fact that it is problematic. It raises some questions that I hope people consider concerning the readymade and strategies of appropriation. In the art world, these strategies are still generally perceived as innovative and legitimate, whereas in the case of low-rider competitions, if I showed up with a car with a hydraulic system that I did not work on, "authorship" would be seriously questioned. In the case of *Alien Toy*, I created and added several things, including a video that is projected from the body of the truck, and inserted the truck into a narrative that was not originally there. However, for certain people those elements are not even relevant; they might simply be interested in the object.

These are questions that I thought were important to engage and are complex, political questions. Collaboration can provide new methods of production and propose different modes of address. There is not a single point of view; there are at least two points of view, if not several more. And, thus, contradiction and ambivalence will always exist. In the case of the film *Frontierland/Fronterilandia*, made in collaboration with Jesse Lerner, that was the main thesis: to create a movie that does not present a single point of view but rather presents several positions and points of view simultaneously.

Other models for collaboration relate to specialized responsibilities, which might more closely resemble a model associated with filmmaking. I actually respect the Hollywood system for the way they credit labor and responsibility. At least in a movie it is generally clear who did what. In an art piece, on the other hand, this is often thoroughly obscured.

In the case of *Alien Toy* and certainly in the piece with Gody Sanchez, the whole notion of authorship is put in question. At this point, the problematic part is that what ultimately defines authorship is the legitimization of the object by the art world or in an art context.

O: An institution might not always provide all the details the catalogue, but you have provided all this information in the video component.

R: Yes, that is all detailed in both the *Alien Toy* video and publication, and I thought this was very important. The process adds another layer of meaning to the work, as does the history of the pickup

truck, *Wicked Bed*, itself, since it won titles in car show competitions four years in a row.

I mean, who decides when and where authorship begins? Because the way we value... not just art, but almost everything... let's face it, this is fundamentally a capitalist issue because it is about property and rights. Society often refuses to accept an object without those rights or that property, or where they are unclear, since it might prevent the seamless transfer of property or title.

O: The registration stickers from the multiple car shows and competitions the truck entered are still on it, right?

R: Yes, they are. For "Chava" this is sometimes difficult because when the truck was in the car show circuit, he would get all the attention and credit. Now, when we go to a museum, it's a different story. He gets part of the credit, but it is shared.

Low-rider automobiles are sort of like Aztec pyramids! You work on a car, win some contests, and then sell it to someone who continues to add to it or build on top of what was there before. The car may keep the original name, but the author changes, and the new owner gets the credit because, in this case, it is the owner who is valued more than the designer or mechanic. And, quite often, this process involves a group effort: one person paints, another does the upholstery, and yet another the hydraulics. Personally, I am most familiar with the process of painting and design. I am not too good at welding. I know the basics, but other people are better at it.

O: One of the things that has really interested me about your work over the years is that, although you often use collaborative methods, you have not developed a collaborative model. Rather, when collaboration is appropriate, it seems to develop based on the kind of object or project before you. That is to say, that collaboration has not been codified in your practice.

R: Yes, each collaboration is absolutely different from the other, just as each collection of individuals is unique.

O: How does humor function in your work?

R: Well, obviously, humor often allows one to address certain issues in a way that enables people to identify with the issues without confrontation. Humor can function as a space for critique; like the tradition of the carnivalesque and the jester, humor can open a palpable space for forms of critique that might otherwise be deemed unacceptable. In my work, I see humor as an aesthetic strategy involved with several others. Humor is not an end in itself for either entertainment or lamentation. Although I have utilized these forms, I do not have that puritanical, situationist point of view where, if you make something spectacular, then that becomes the end in itself and thus disables any potential for critique. On the contrary, these are things that we can play with, and in the process perhaps broaden our audiences and involve and engage them. Of course, there is an argument that can be made against this. It could be said that this process might banalize or neutralize the content and ultimately make the audience immune. Then again, my work does not only engage humor: parts are humorous and other parts are not.

Humor is a way to sugarcoat the pill, to provide a point of entry, and to make what I do interesting for someone else. I guess the beauty of art is that if you know how to say the things you want to say, you can transcend boundaries. If you have the skills and the craft, you can make people interested in what you have to say.

O: So, for you, what might constitute an intervention? How do you understand or maybe even practice the term?

R: I am interested in the process. We have spoken about different strategies to question authorship, but I want to expand beyond that, because I think we have also been discussing different ways to make culture - not just making a critique of culture - but making culture. And, making culture is not something that one person can accomplish. I think this notion of intervention is a way to participate in social processes at large. However, in order to intervene, something must already exist, something must precede the intervention. That is precisely why I am interested in the process of customizing. For me, customizing is an interesting and powerful model for democratic cultural dialogue.

The traditions of customizing demonstrate how an object can be adapted to both individual and social circumstances in a particular context. In customizing, you activate a process of adaptation and transformation, and move from passive consumer to active participant. The process involves dialogue and negotiation, participation and activation, which can produce forms of interventions. These are the types of interventions I am interested in because there are other forms of intervention, like the one we are currently witnessing in Iraq, that I have no interest in participating in.

So that is why I am interested in the process of customization, since it is not about passive consumption and it is not a situationist-style negation: "I'm going to mess the whole thing up." Intervention is a very heavy, loaded word, by the way.

O: Your work certainly takes up the non-nihilist interventionist stance within the trajectory you outlined. One could take the more nihilist interventionist position quite easily.

R: Yes, like "culture jamming," where you mess up the system because it's fucked up. I am interested in that, too (laughing), but it's not really the way I practice these things. You know, in Mexico we have a Museum of Interventions.

O: Is that a historical museum?

R: It is a historical museum about the French intervention in Mexico, the Mexican-American war, etc. It's the nationalist monument to victimization. (They laugh).

O: One final question, for now, that builds off one of the essays included in the exhibition catalogue: "Can there be revolutionary art without a revolution?"

R: Unfortunately, I think that is the only revolutionary art we have seen. I suppose, we would have to define "revolution." Call the central committee and find out (laughing)! But, seriously, can there be revolutionary art without the revolution? Yes, I suppose, since I believe the voice of an individual can exist in a revolutionary way. That does not necessarily mean, however, that a single voice can change society. Nevertheless, I do believe that there can be some sort of individual effort that can transcend, or at least change, the way we see things. Call me a romantic or utopian. For me, revolutionary art or political art... we are talking about representations, and that is not "reality" per se but language, systems of representation. I don't know, Ondine. I mean, what kind of question is that?

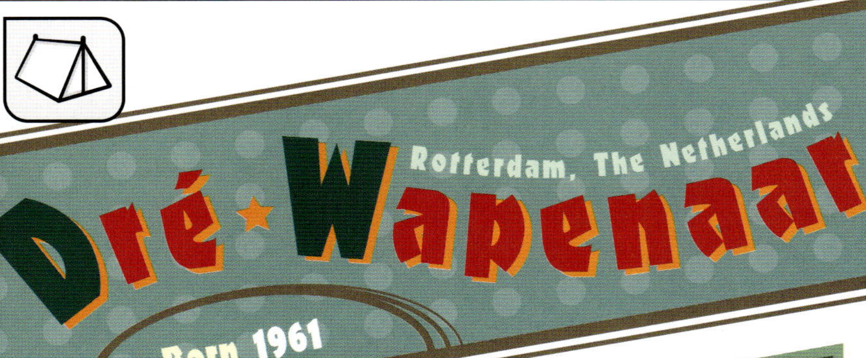

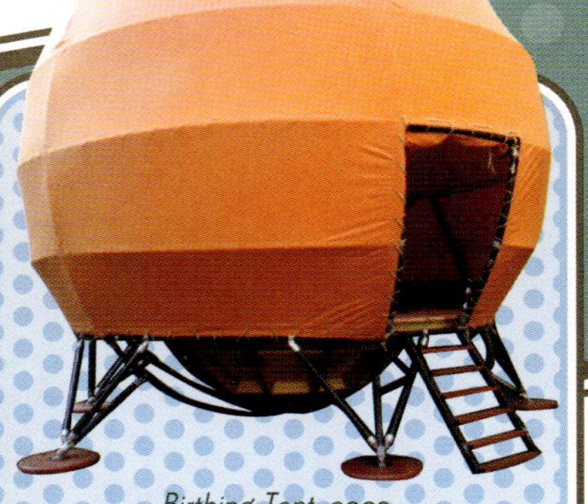

Birthing Tent, 2003.
Courtesy of Museum Boijmans Van Beuningen, Stadscollectie, Rotterdam, Photo: Robbert Roos

Biographical Info:

Dré Wapenaar is a designer and sculptor predominantly known for his inventive use of tents. He believes that a properly designed tent alters human behavior. Wapenaar has produced tents for selling flowers, playing piano, sleeping in trees and, in the exhibition at MASS MoCA, giving birth and paying respects to the dead.

His work has been exhibited in the Netherlands, Italy, England, Japan, France, and the United States.

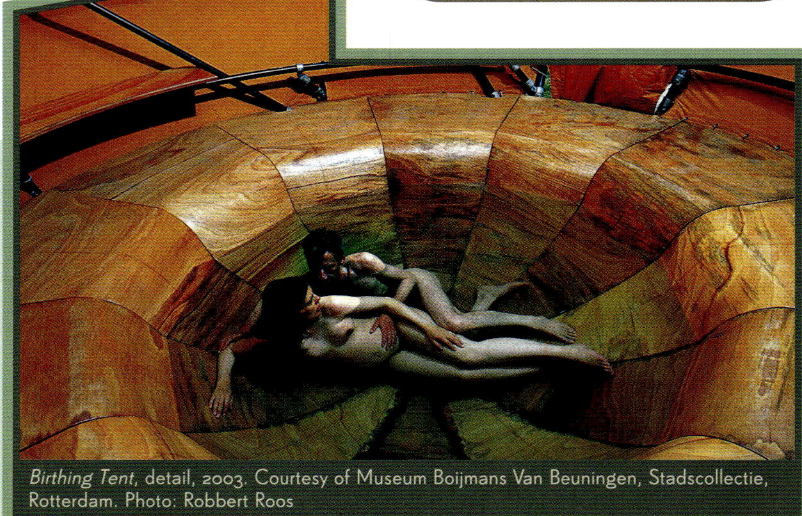

Birthing Tent, detail, 2003. Courtesy of Museum Boijmans Van Beuningen, Stadscollectie, Rotterdam. Photo: Robbert Roos

Project Description: The *Birthing Tent* is a large spherical structure designed for giving birth and celebrating a baby's arrival. A large opening in the ceiling provides a view to the stars. The tent is equipped with benches for family, friends, nurses and co-parents. Wapenaar sees his work as a more "familiar" alternative to the hospital environment, a place that is both intimate and open, sheltering and expansive.

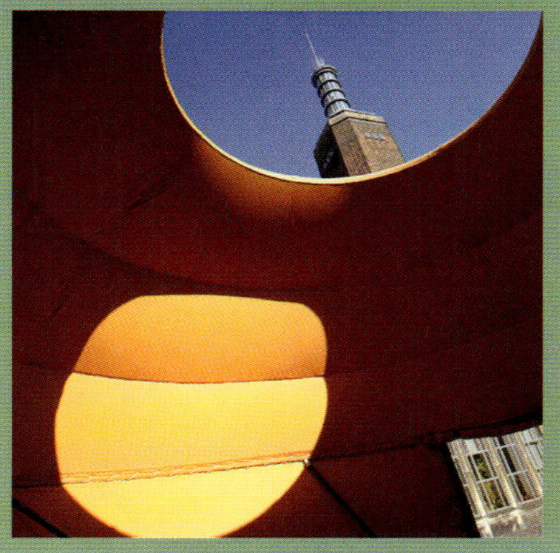

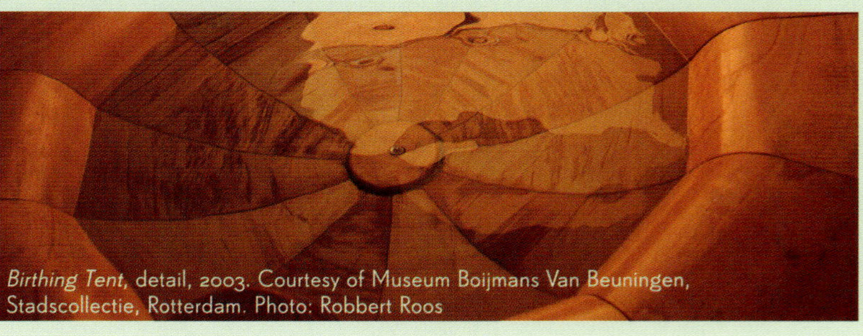

Birthing Tent, detail, 2003. Courtesy of Museum Boijmans Van Beuningen, Stadscollectie, Rotterdam. Photo: Robbert Roos

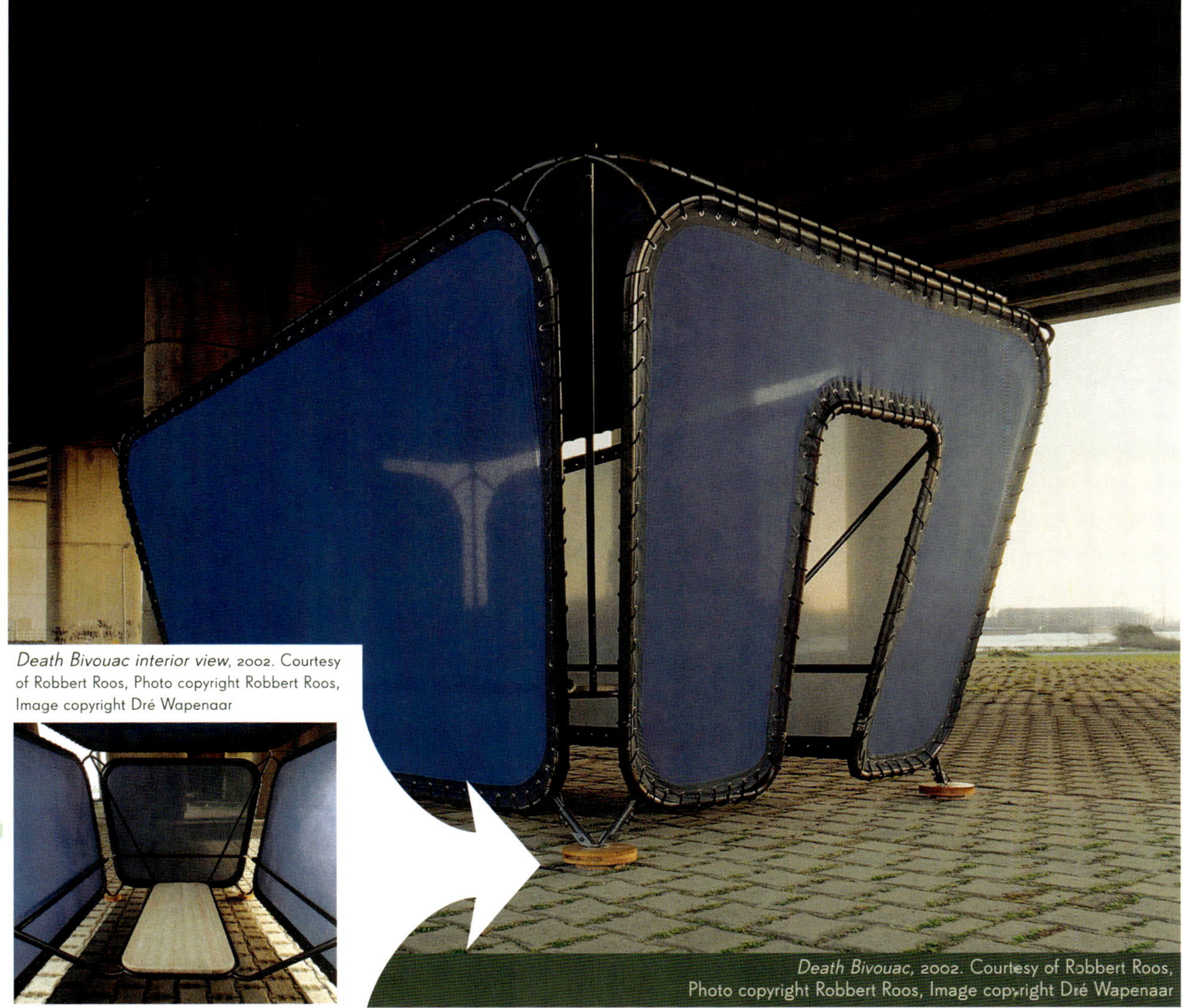

Death Bivouac interior view, 2002. Courtesy of Robbert Roos, Photo copyright Robbert Roos, Image copyright Dré Wapenaar

Death Bivouac, 2002. Courtesy of Robbert Roos, Photo copyright Robbert Roos, Image copyright Dré Wapenaar

Project Description: "In protestant Holland I experienced many death 'ceremonies,' taking 1-1/2 hours of your time, with one cup of coffee and piece of cake at the end, and then you may go. The machines are left to cover the grave. No emotions, individually or shared. I see some changes, but only in individual cases. The public 'death ceremony' is still left with the idea of a commercial activity." The *Death Bivouac* is a tent for memorializing the dead. Wapenaar incorporated the physical and spiritual elements of death into the design by balancing a sense of heaviness and lightness in the structure. Wapenaar sees the moments of birth and death as benefiting from a particular kind of privacy that can extend past the "borderlines" of an individual person.

(1)Email from Dré Wapenaar to Nato Thompson, December 2, 2003.

TITLE OF WORK:

2002
Death Bivouac

N55

Copenhagen, Denmark

Founded 1994

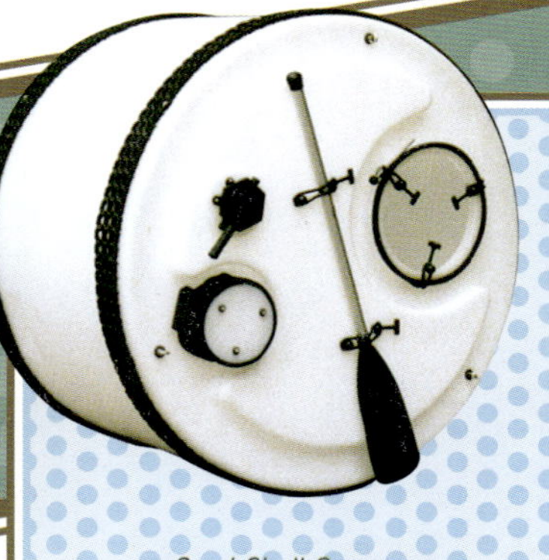

Snail Shell System, 2001
Courtesy of N55

Biographical Info:

Based in a city long known for good design, **N55** has four members/designers: Ingvil Aarbakke, Jon Sørvin, Rikke Luther and Cecilia Wendt. N55's projects — including vehicles, furniture, and buildings— are intended for actual use and occupation. The integration of aesthetics and ethics is the guiding principle of their designs. The group's work includes a Spaceframe (in which they live), a home hydroponic unit, chairs, compost machines, and bizarre public address systems. Their theoretical project *Land* proposes to "liberate" land across the globe. In short, the project requires purchasing sections of land — acreage has already been acquired in Denmark, Switzerland, Rumania, Chicago, and San Diego — and placing a "cairn" on each parcel. A booklet accompanies each cairn and specifies qualified public uses for the land where it sits.

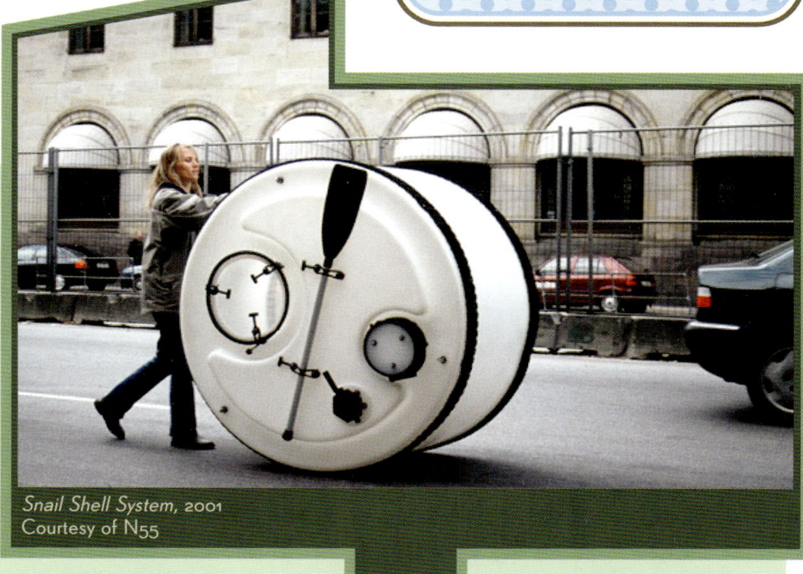

Snail Shell System, 2001
Courtesy of N55

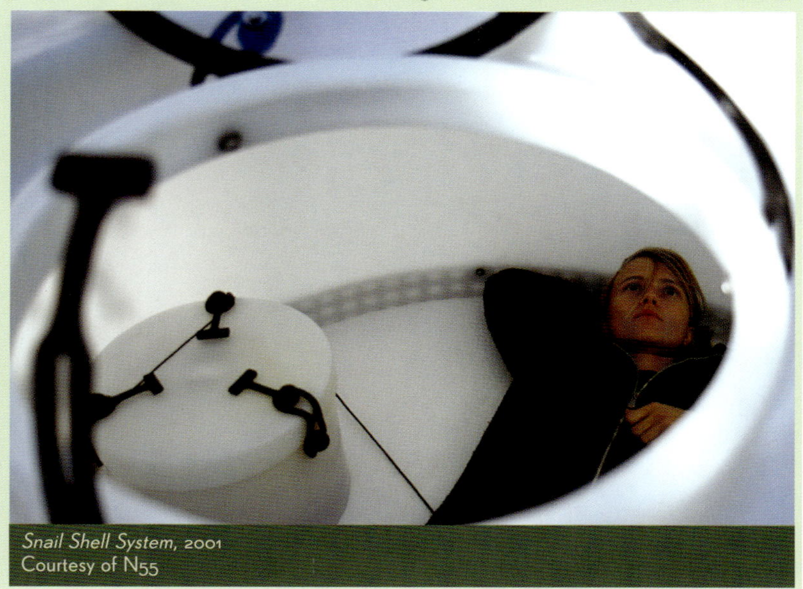

Snail Shell System, 2001
Courtesy of N55

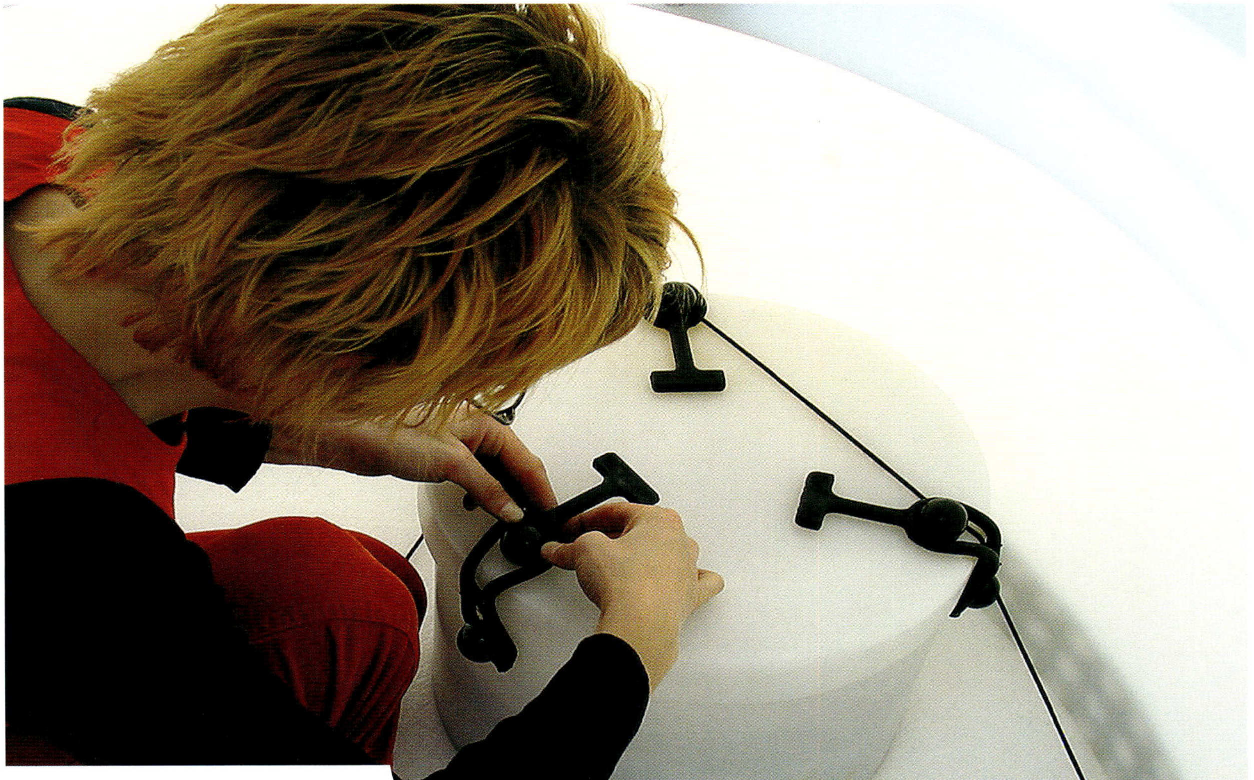

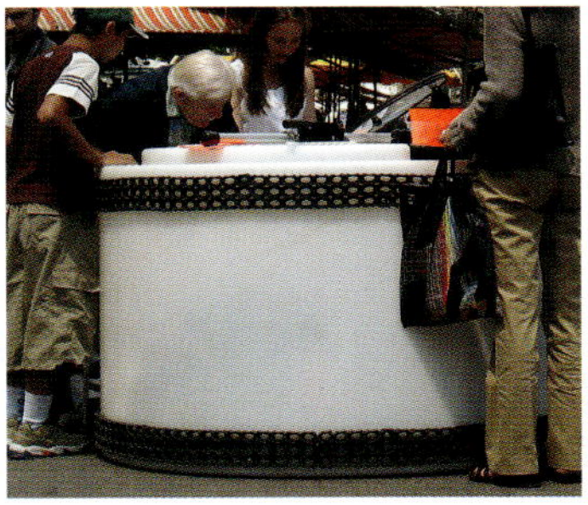

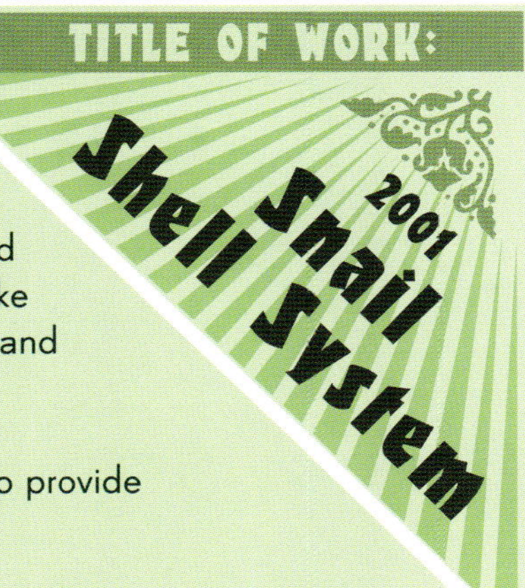

Snail Shell System, 2001
Courtesy of N55

Project Description: The *Snail Shell System* is a low-cost mobile home. — A swishy European answer to Wodiczko's *Homeless Vehicle.* Shaped like a wheel, the *Snail Shell System* is covered with rubber caterpillar tracks to facilitate movement through city streets. The system is designed for one person and works on both land and water (on water it can be rowed). The home comes equipped with air intake valves, an equipment box containing a kitchen pan, kettle, alcohol burner and plastic bags, a bilge pump and a toilet.

N55 suggest that *Snail Shell System* could be used to transport items or to provide protection from violence during demonstrations.

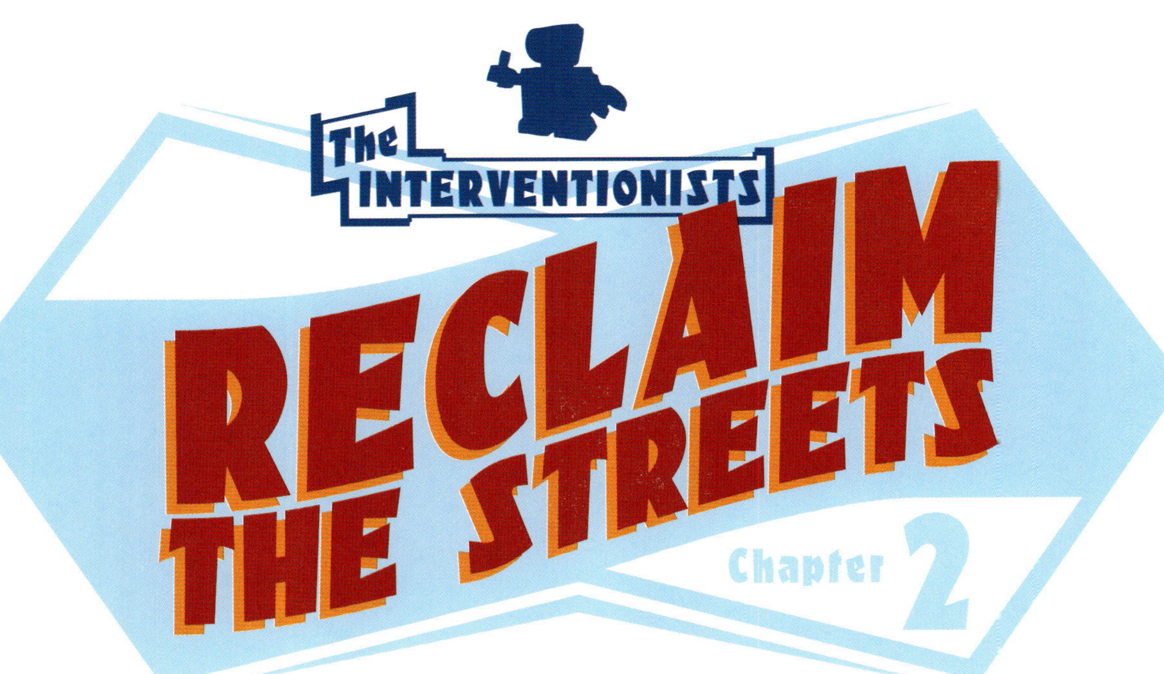
The INTERVENTIONISTS
RECLAIM THE STREETS
Chapter 2

Craig Baldwin's San Francisco, CA, USA
Billboard Outlaws

Born 1952

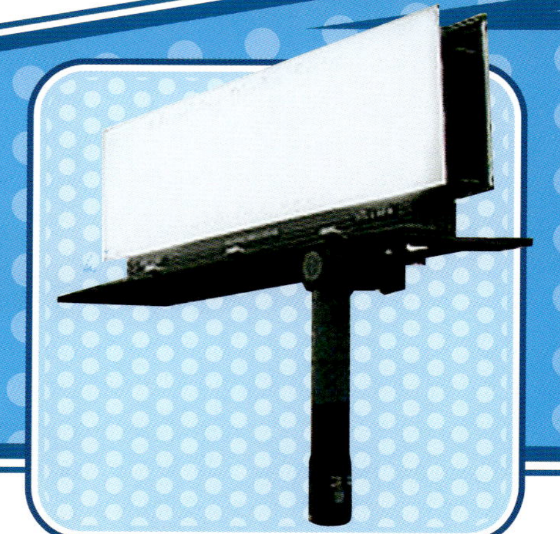

Biographical Info:

Craig Baldwin is a pioneer independent filmmaker who has produced numerous politically satirical films including *Tribulation 99: Alien Anomalies under America*, 1991; *O No Coronado!*, 1992; *Sonic Outlaws*, 1995; and *Specters of the Spectrum*, 1999.

His film *Sonic Outlaws* chronicles the early period of culture jamming featuring the work of the renegade band Negativeland.

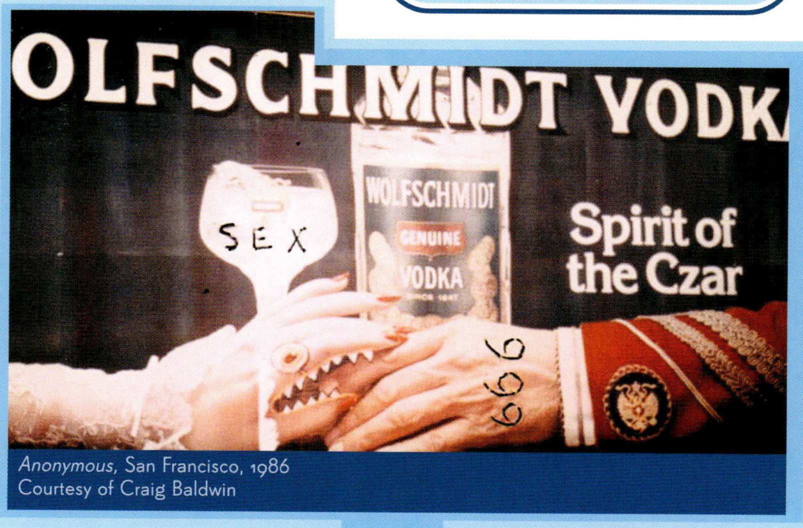

Anonymous, San Francisco, 1986
Courtesy of Craig Baldwin

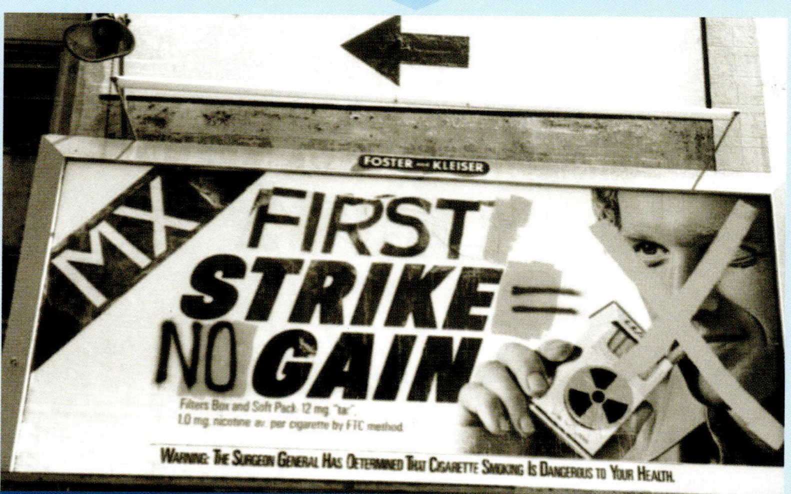

Joel Katz, Pad McLaughlin & Jeff Skoller, San Francisco, 1987
Courtesy of Craig Baldwin

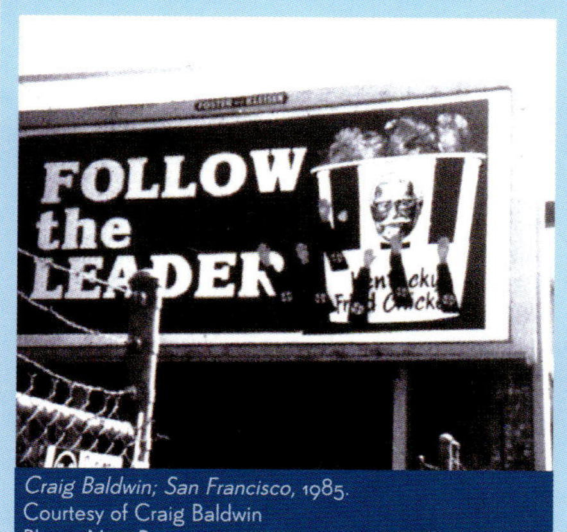

Craig Baldwin; San Francisco, 1985.
Courtesy of Craig Baldwin
Photo: Nina Peters

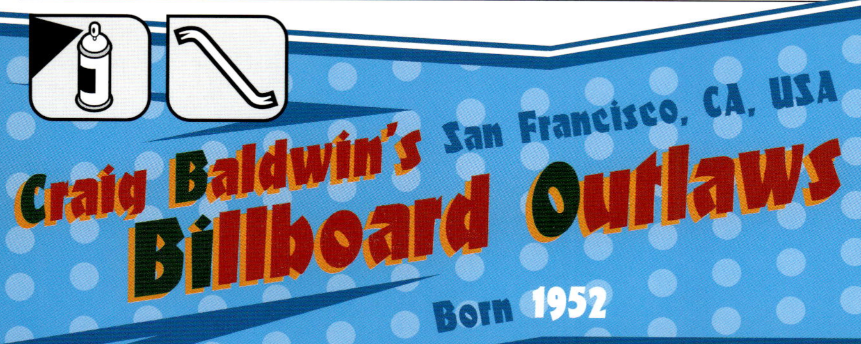

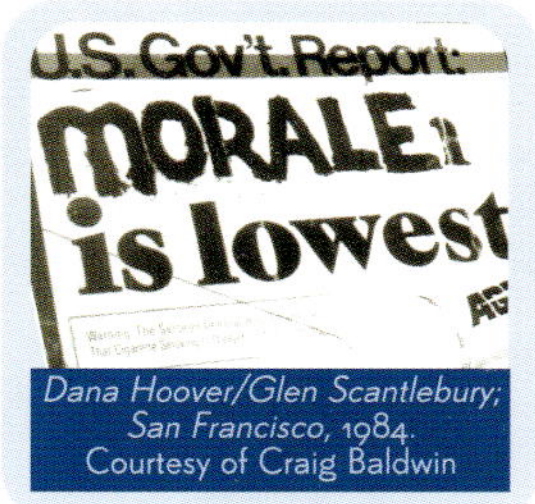

Dana Hoover/Glen Scantlebury; San Francisco, 1984. Courtesy of Craig Baldwin

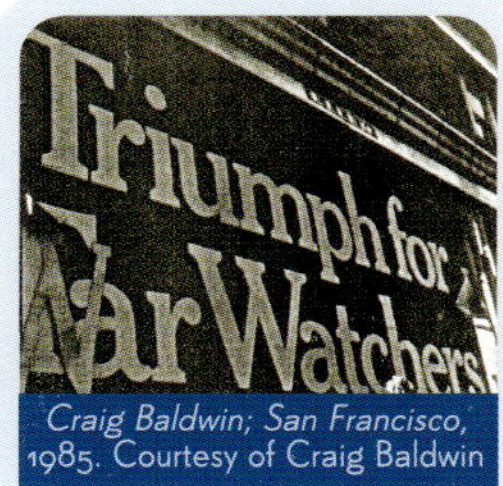

Craig Baldwin; San Francisco, 1985. Courtesy of Craig Baldwin

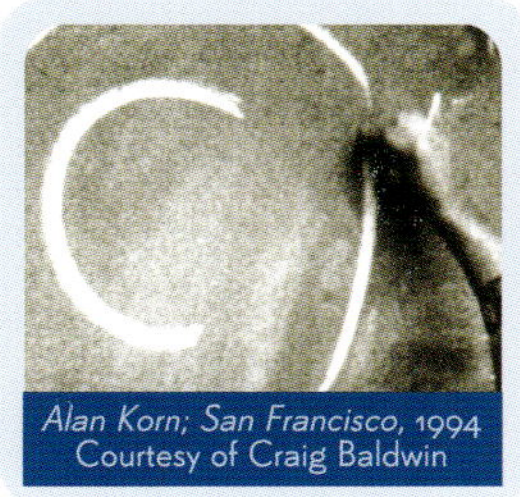

Alan Korn; San Francisco, 1994 Courtesy of Craig Baldwin

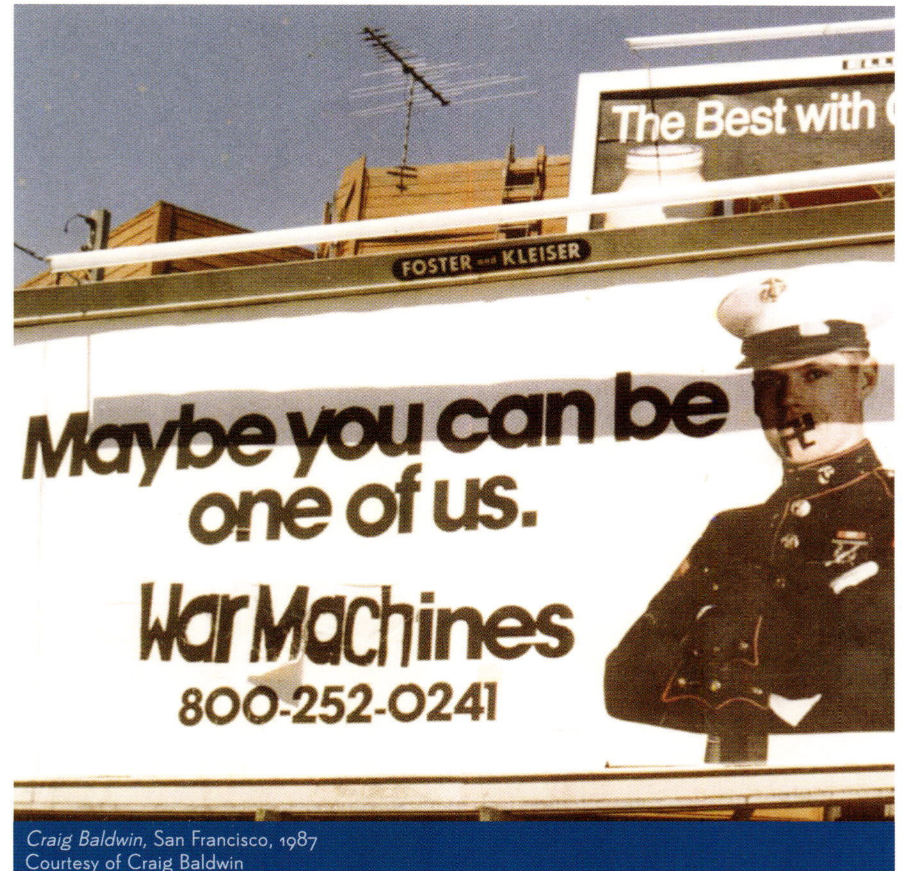

Craig Baldwin, San Francisco, 1987 Courtesy of Craig Baldwin

Project Description: Craig Baldwin has amassed a collection of slides documenting billboards whose originally intended message —usually an advertisement— have been altered or subverted. The slides will be projected in the gallery.

Baldwin changed some of the billboards himself, but most of the interventions were undertaken by others, including the so-called California Department of Corrections, Billboard Liberation Front, Mary Fortuna, Dana Hoover, Joel Katz, and Nina Peters. Many were done anonymously, working the thin lines between graffiti, art, vandalism and civil disobedience.

TITLE OF WORK:

2004 Billboard Outlaws

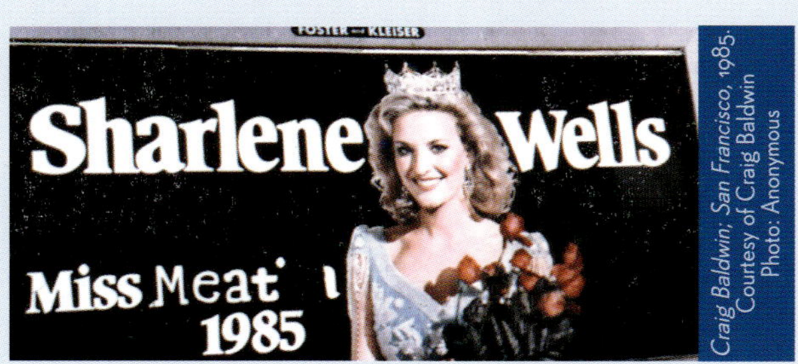

Craig Baldwin; San Francisco, 1985. Courtesy of Craig Baldwin Photo: Anonymous

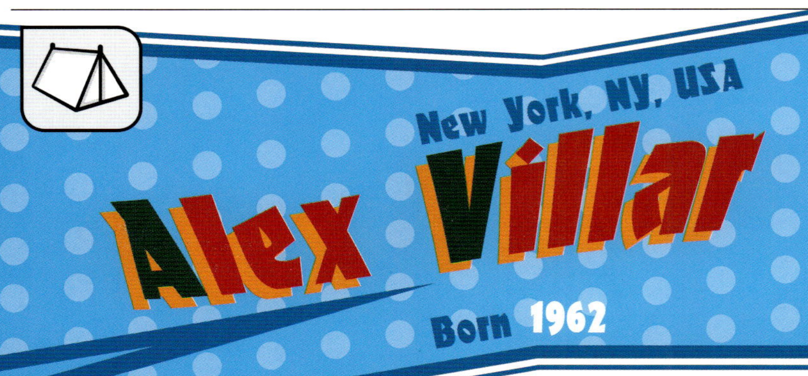

New York, NY, USA

Alex Villar

Born 1962

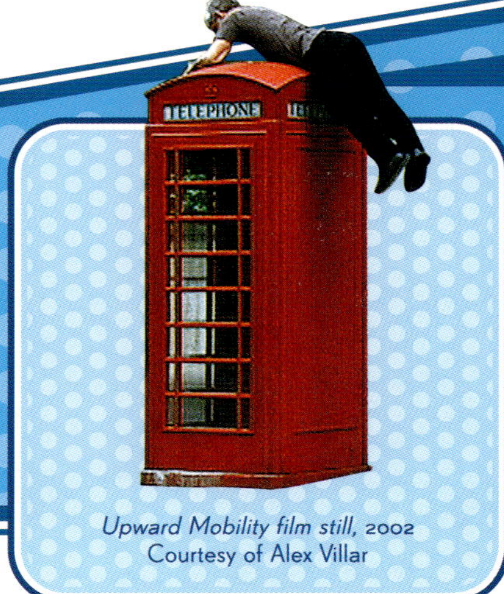

Upward Mobility film still, 2002
Courtesy of Alex Villar

Biographical Info:

"Drawing from interdisciplinary theoretical sources and employing video-performance, installation and photography, I have developed a practice that concentrates on matters of social space. My interventions are done primarily in public spaces. They consist of positioning the body of the performer in situations where the codes that regulate everyday activity can be made explicit." (1)

The focus of **Alex Villar**'s photo and video work is the social use of space. For example, in his *Irrational Intervals* (2002), Villar projected video onto a window at One World Financial Center that overlooked the reconstruction at Ground Zero. The video, depicting designated smoking zones in public places, marked a distinction of spaces in terms of work versus leisure, private versus public, and interior verses exterior.

Villar was a studio fellow at the Whitney Independent Studies Program. Past U.S. exhibitions include presentations at the Art Container, Highbridge Park and Vacancy Gallery in New York, Bona Fide Gallery in Chicago, the New Art Center in Boston and the Jacksonville Museum of Contemporary Art.

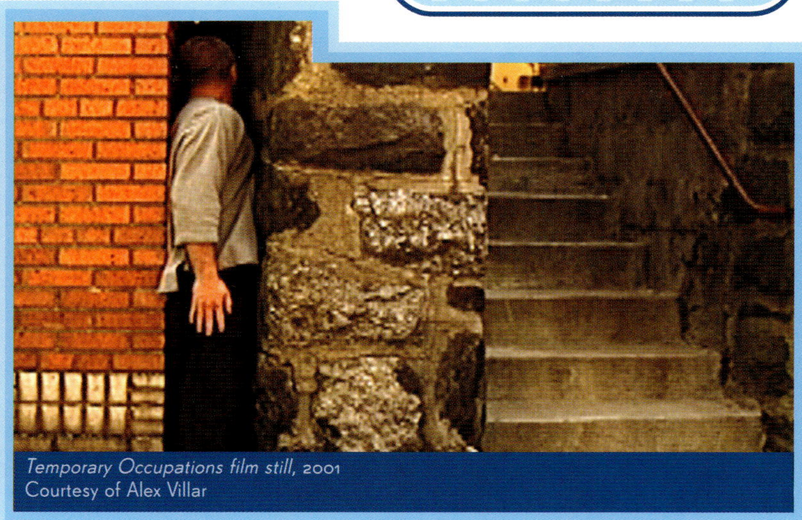

Temporary Occupations film still, 2001
Courtesy of Alex Villar

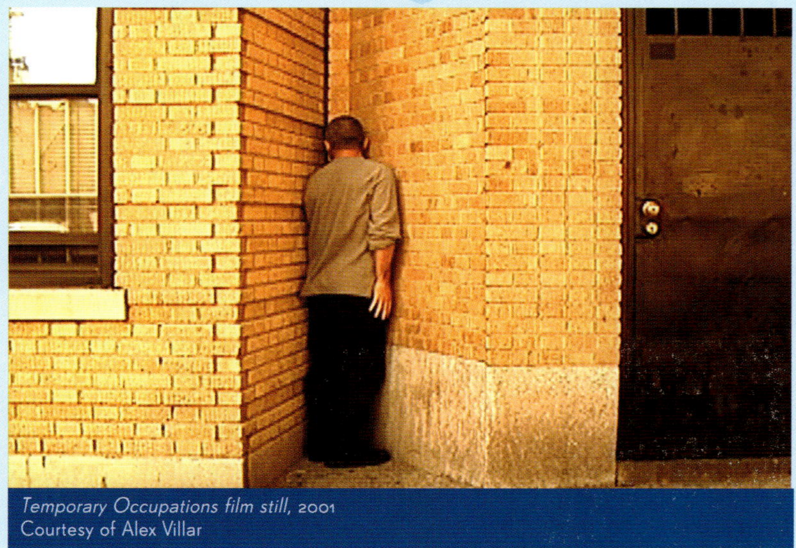

Temporary Occupations film still, 2001
Courtesy of Alex Villar

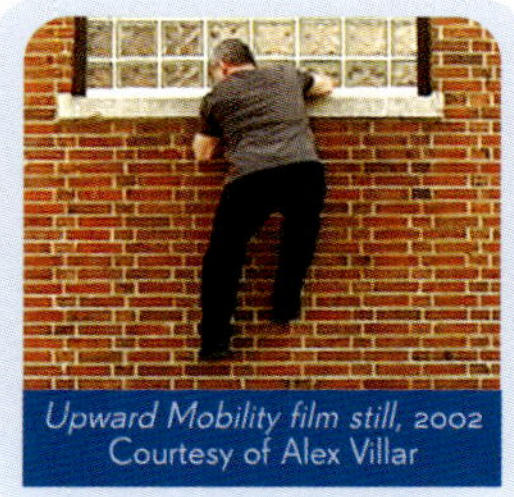

Upward Mobility film still, 2002
Courtesy of Alex Villar

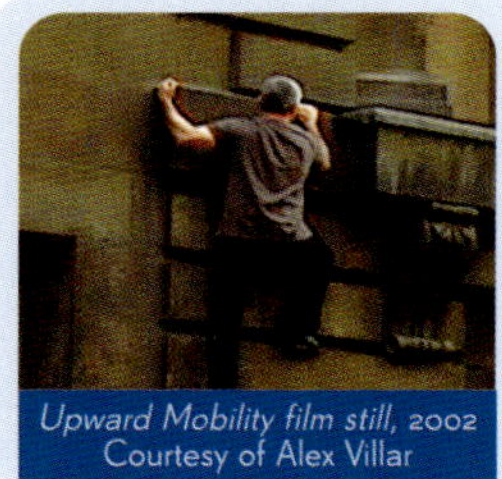

Upward Mobility film still, 2002
Courtesy of Alex Villar

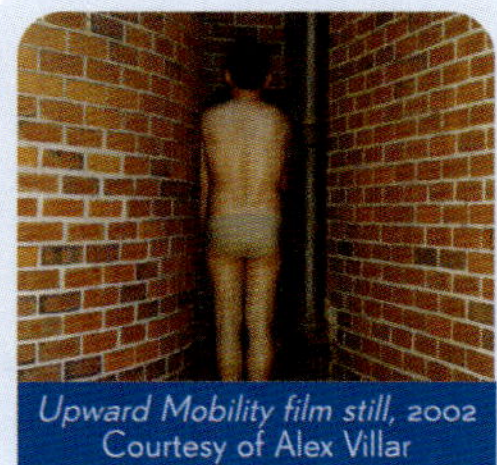

Upward Mobility film still, 2002
Courtesy of Alex Villar

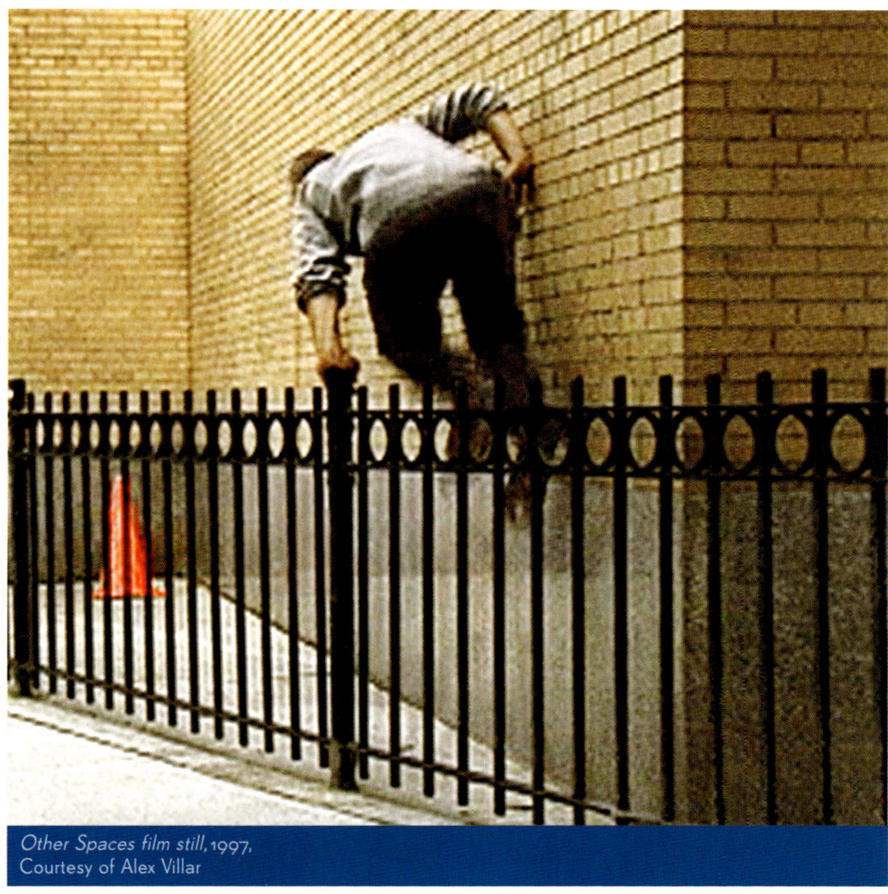

Other Spaces film still, 1997,
Courtesy of Alex Villar

Project Description: In his video *Temporary Occupations*, Villar makes visible the "uses" of public space. The video shows Villar ignoring the city's spatial codes and therefore resisting their effects upon the organization of everyday experience. He jumps fences, slides between railings, and squeezes into the corners of buildings.

As an extended series of trespasses, both subtle and substantial, his antics at first appear outlandish, but his meandering route ultimately makes visible the organization of otherwise invisible and forbidden spaces that might be productively re-configured in the public sphere.

1. Taken from Alex Villar's artist statement.
Danger Museum Newsletter #13 "Report #1: Alex Villar with DM at Iniva, London 4.
September 6, 2002

Alex Villar

Interview with C. Ondine Chavoya
February 6, 2004

Which practices and/or movements associated with the
visual culture of the 1980s were you most engaged by,
influenced by, or active in?

I was in Brazil in the 1980s, where regrettably the only noticeable
event in the visual arts was the return to painting, which was often
reported as a return to pleasure. I reached for the previous decade,
when there were many examples of art engaging the social realm —
Hélio Oiticica and Cildo Meireles are the most well-known cases. I
moved to New York at the end of the '80s and again reached for
previous decades in search of works that I felt were pertinent to my
education. The work of Gordon Matta-Clark and the multiple practices of the Situationists were particularly formative in my education.
I spent most of the '90s in school, where I dealt quite a lot with critical practices from the '80s. But looking back, what I feel was the
most striking and indeed remarkable event in the '80s was how
activist practices efficiently deployed aesthetics to gain
media visibility.

When the viewer experiences your work, what
type(s) of relationships do you hope to establish?

There are several instances in which viewers experience my
work. The first type is a circumstantial audience that occa-
sionally forms around the sites where I perform the actions.
There are also audiences that experience my pieces in a
screening environment. And, finally, there are audiences that
experience the work in an installation or single projection situation. I know very little about the first instance and would
rather not generalize on such contingent terrain. About the
second instance, I would speculate that the viewer would be more
inclined to evaluate the piece in relation to the other projects presented in the same screening rather than on its own. The viewer in
this case is someone who compares, relates, and associates, in sum,
someone who might come to an intellectual understanding about
what is being presented. The third type is a situation upon which I
have the most relative control. And, therefore, it is the one case
about which I would attempt to better formulate my position. What I
seek to establish is a relationship of equivalence between, on the
one hand, the depicted space and the actual one, and, on the other
hand, between the body that appears in the video and the body of
the viewer. Through such conflation of virtuality and actuality, I
attempt to defer the piece's immediate intelligibility in the hope that
the viewer's entire body, not only her/his mind, will experience the
interventions that I perform.

What are the different fields or networks that you operate in
(not just aesthetically but specifically)? How do you view these
various facets of your activity?

I have, more or less, from the beginning of my productive career,
been involved in a loose network of cultural producers who share
similar progressive views. More tangibly, this association has manifested itself as collaborations in various projects, going from art
pieces to discussion groups to the production of text. One recent
example was a week-long discussion about the intersection between
power and representation that took place in Helsinki. I think it is
absolutely necessary to find multiple channels of engagement, especially since the established channels of circulation and reception are
limited and tend to fit snugly within the established cultural sphere.

What spheres do you find appropriate for your work?

I have sought to produce my work mostly in the general public
sphere. I have also, in some instances, presented the work in the
same context of its production. But, mostly, the work has been shown
in art spaces of some sort. I like the idea of reacting or activating a
given situation instead of postulating an ideal setting.

How do you see your work operating in larger social
movements?

I have not had any experience of direct, instrumental use
of my work in a particular struggle. I do think that this can
be a valuable alternative, especially when the work possesses a very direct and clear position. Communication
usually functions better when the signs are unambiguous.
I think my work clearly is in solidarity with progressive
social movements. But I see it working in parallel to them,
countering the same forces, yet operating at another junc-
ture of the hegemonic order.

How does your work situate the local and the
global?

I have usually occupied myself with practically microscopic everyday
situations. One could say that such situations might even be severe-
ly local. Nevertheless, I perceive the instances of resistance that I
represent to be general potentialities that are significant precisely
because they indicate nodal points that can exist anywhere in the
global context.

How do you use preexisting visual forms or discourses in
your work? To what end(s) do you use them?

I have taken the idea of the *dérive* from the Situationists and
employed it outside the bohemian context in which they deployed it.
I have considerably narrowed its range and often use it to propose
very slight detours in behavior, which are really more like performative slippages.

What do you consider the advantages and/or
disadvantages to collaboration, compared to
individualized forms of art production?

Collaborations are wonderful opportunities to negotiate personal idiosyncrasies. Having said that, I would not go on to polarize individual and collective ways of producing. The problem, as I see it, does not reside solely in the organizational form. There are productive possibilities in both models. I enjoy both. Generally speaking, one can advance an idea further while working individually or with the help of a constant collaborator, while larger groups tend to bring strength and energy, which can be used to accomplish larger tasks.

How do you see humor as functioning in your art?
What about delight and pleasure in your work?

Humor is absolutely necessary in my work. Growing up during a "serious" dictatorship in Brazil, humor was often the strongest weapon. I've undoubtedly extended that notion to my work. Although, in my case, I do not use humor as a weapon, but rather as a means to disarm the viewer and clear the way for reflection. I would subsume delight and pleasure into humor.

Why is movement necessary in your work?
What do we gain from movement?

Although I have done a good number of consecutive video pieces, I normally work between photography and video without prioritizing one over the other. For instance, while emphasizing containment or immobility, I found it to be more appropriate to use photography. In other cases, when the quest was to propose a deviation of normative procedures that are accomplished through cumulative uniformity, video appeared to me to be the natural choice.

How does technology function in your work?
In general, what is your relationship to technology?

I am not involved in furthering technological research but am generally very curious about its possibilities. Although largely controlled by capital, changes in technology often create shifts in certain aspects of the overall mode of production and that sometimes presents opportunities for counter-action. I have kept my critical self tuned in.

In the past two decades, public space has become
increasingly privatized as private space and private
lives have become increasingly subject to the expanded
structures and technologies of surveillance. How might
your work respond to or demonstrate this scenario?

It is certainly true that we have seen a sharp increase in the surveillance of the average individual. It is also accurate to qualify as escalating the privatization of the public sphere. It appears as if the private and public sphere would have collapsed. But, rather than complete fluidity, what we experience is a high degree of control over the borders of these two spheres. Although this situation is more tangibly experienced today, its conditions of possibility have been theorized for some time now. Therefore, I think

that this problematic has already been rendered very clearly. In my work, I try instead to imagine resistant possibilities located at the very threshold where these segregated spheres meet.

The concept "intervention" is key in the exhibition:
what constitutes an intervention for you?

An intervention is a diagonal force that bursts through a given field. It can cause a disruption, a shaking-up, a rearrangement of plateaus.

Where do you find support for your work?

Financially, it comes from mixed sources: small grants, production fees, and self-support. But the most significant type of support is the one that comes in the form of appreciation from peers and audiences.

Can there be revolutionary art without a revolution?

I think it is absolutely necessary to sustain goals irrespective of imminent possibilities. Without a radical argument to expand the spectrum of public debates, the democratic range of possibilities contracts to an unbearable degree.

The Biotic Baking Brigade

New York, NY, USA

Founded Late 20th Century

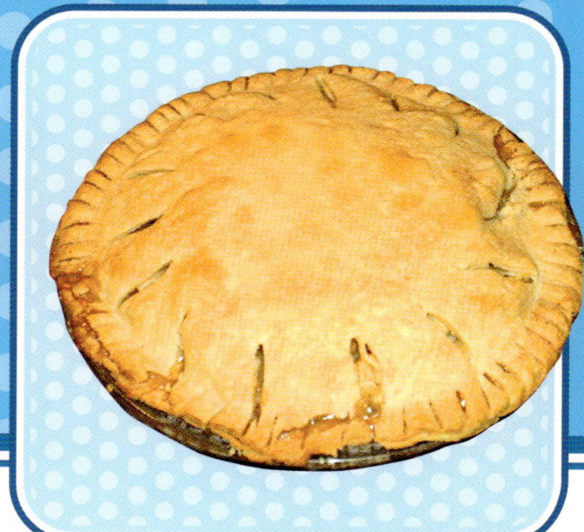

Biographical Info:

Based around the world, **The Biotic Baking Brigade**'s members are often seasoned activists in ecology, social justice, feminist, and animal rights movements. To protect themselves, their 'agents' take on pseudonyms such as Agent Apple, Agent Salmonberry or Agent Chocolate Supreme. Their book *Pie Any Means Necessary: The Biotic Baking Brigade Cookbook* is available from AK Press.

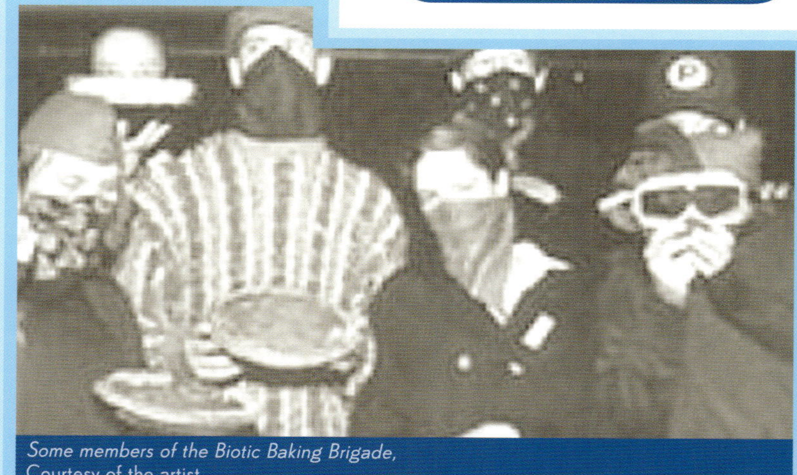

Some members of the Biotic Baking Brigade,
Courtesy of the artist

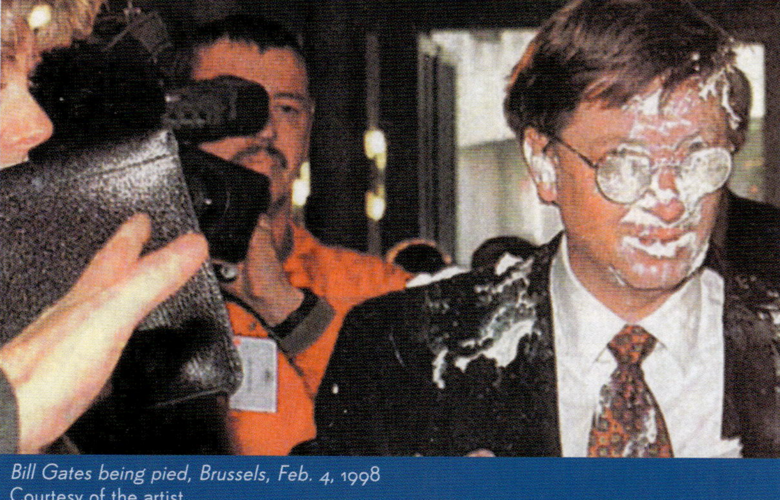

Bill Gates being pied, Brussels, Feb. 4, 1998
Courtesy of the artist

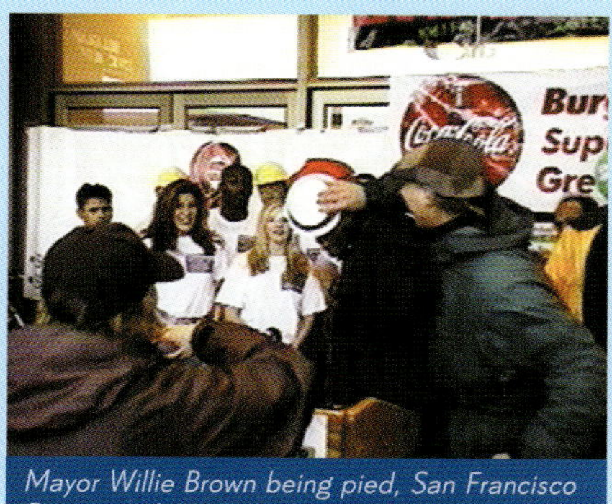

Mayor Willie Brown being pied, San Francisco
Courtesy of the artist

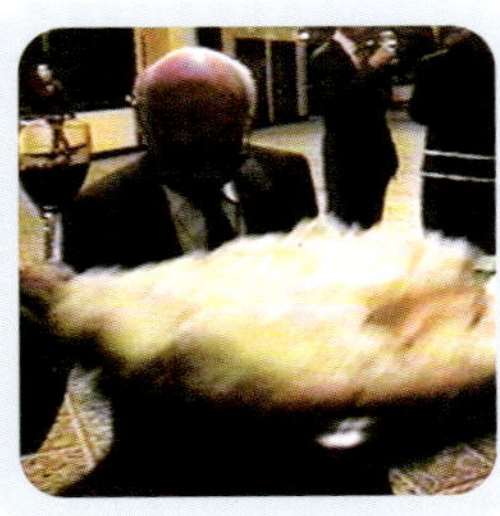

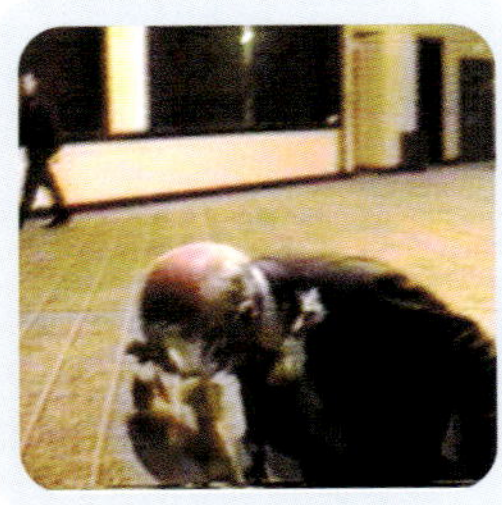

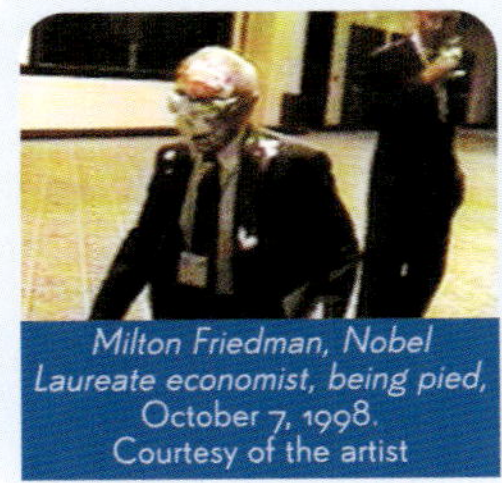

Milton Friedman, Nobel Laureate economist, being pied, October 7, 1998. Courtesy of the artist

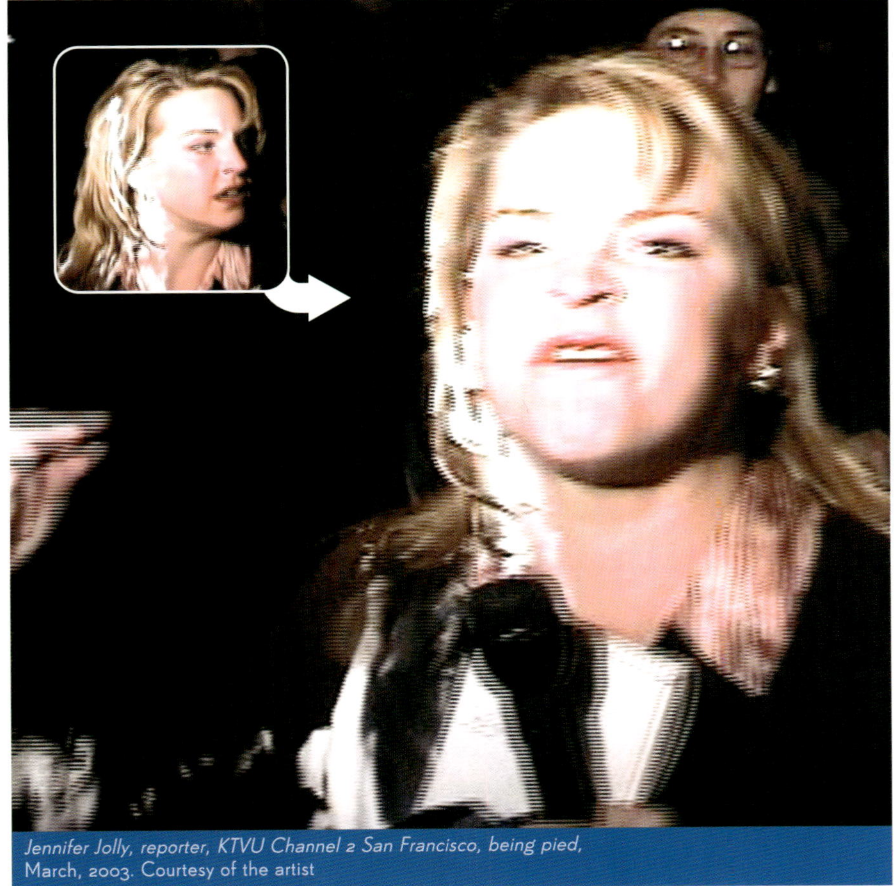

Jennifer Jolly, reporter, KTVU Channel 2 San Francisco, being pied, March, 2003. Courtesy of the artist

TITLE OF WORK:

The Pie is the Limit
(28 minutes) edited and directed by A. Mark Liiv and Jeff Taylor, produced by Whispered Media
1999

Project Description: "The Biotic Baking Brigade (BBB) believes that under neoliberalism, we all can throw a pie in the face of economic fascism." (1)

The Pie is the Limit is a video that documents the Biotic Baking Brigade, an amorphous, international organization. According to the BBB, the group's members are often seasoned activists in ecology, social justice, feminist, and animal rights movements. With the assistance of slapstick comedy's most enduring prop — the pie — the BBB has managed to throw pie in the face of some of the most powerful figures in the world. Targets of their pie-throwing antics include: Microsoft founder Bill Gates, San Francisco Mayor Willie Brown, Canadian Prime Minister Jean Chrétien, ex-president of the World Trade Organization Renaldo Ruggiero, and Hilmar Kabas of Vienna's Freedom Party.

Our reactions are complex. If the act is embarrassing — either by its effect on the victim, or for its juvenile tactics — it also humanizes the target. We empathize with the victims, who in many cases operate in a powerful world with which it is difficult to connect. And in other instances we might celebrate the prank.

1. From the BBB website: www.bioticbakingbrigade.org.

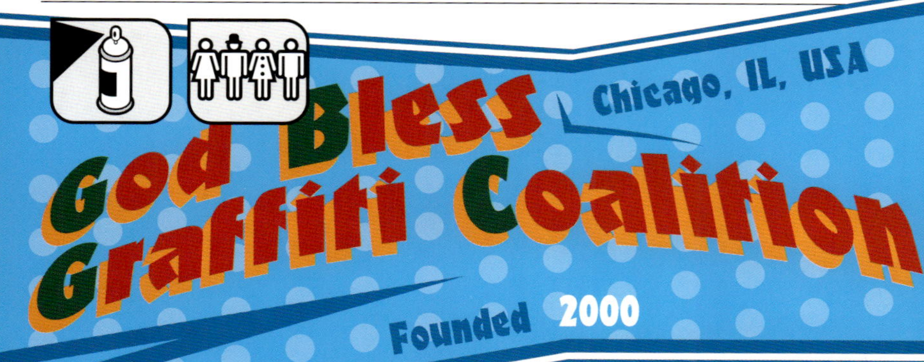

Courtesy of God Bless Graffiti Coalition

Biographical Info:

Artists include: 108 (Alessandria, Italy), Abe Lincoln Jr. (New York), Aerosolarts (La Jolla, CA), Raji Ajl (Amherst, MA), ANT (Vienna, Austria), APE7 (Sydney), Jason Archer & Paul Beck (Austin, TX), Arigo (Salt Lake City), Arrrgh! (Hannover, Germany), Bask (Detroit), Brandon Bauer (Milwaukee), Bo130 (Milan, Italy), BOB215 (NJ), Bongout (Kuttolsheim, France), Buffmonster (LA), Calma (Brazil), Ceet (France), Etta Cetera (Pittsburgh), Alex Costa (Sao Paulo, Brazil), Michael De Feo (New York), Downey (New York), Dr. Blade (Atlanta), Dub Syndicate (Houston), Shepard Fairey (LA), Jerome G (Paris), Give Em Hell (NJ), Lord Hao (Paris), HECZ (Chicago), Height Lab (Los Angeles), Hubert One (Brooklyn), INK 76 (New York), Insane Fame (New York), Jet-Pac (York, UK), JS04 (Chicago), Kempt (Boston), Klutch (Portland, OR), Ladybug (Italy), Nicolas Lampert (Milwaukee), Charlene K. Lau (Toronto), Mike Ley (Bloomington, IN), MAD One (Tempe, AZ), Magic Propaganda Mill (New York), MAKE (Los Angeles), Markron103 (Phillipines), Minigraff (Sydney), Claude Moller (San Francisco), Most Ghost (Halifax, Canada), Mr. Mad (Lanesville, IN), Open Your Eyes (Paris), Roger Peet (Tucson, AZ), Cody Pickrodt (Levittown, NY), POCH (France), RB827 (Brooklyn), REVISE CMW (Chicago), RikCat (Secaucus, NJ), Erik Ruin (Detroit), Schhh (Barcelona), Scout (Albany, NY), Sevenist (Chicago), Shiro (Los Angeles), Skewville (New York), Skumskullz (Germany), Slowpoke (Pheonix, AZ), Olivier Stak (Paris), Sunkist (Netherlands), Super-Mega (Japan), Swoon (Brooklyn), Rocky Tobey (Toronto), Toyshop Collective (New York), Beth Tub (Urbana, IL), TXMX (Hamburg), Nick Walker (UK), W/REMOTE (Minneapolis).

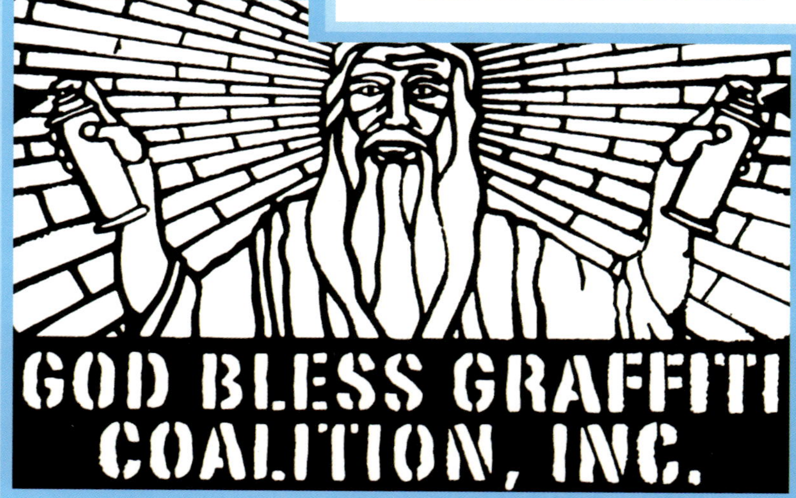

Courtesy of God Bless Graffiti Coalition

The God Bless Graffiti Coalition, Inc. was founded in Chicago "to combat growing national and international anti-graffiti trends." The collective first published its brochure, "*Give Graffiti the Thumbs Up,*" in 2001 to help educate the public regarding their perspective on graffiti. This small brochure was distributed on the streets by way of co-opting newspaper boxes in Chicago, Columbus, San Francisco, and Los Angeles. It has also been distributed by an underground network of street artists. The success of the initial brochure led the collective to expand its activities to include subway ads and its latest endeavor, graffiti bible tracts.

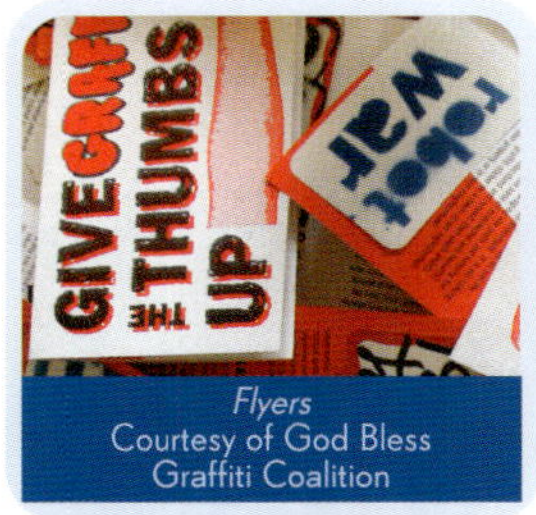

Flyers
Courtesy of God Bless
Graffiti Coalition

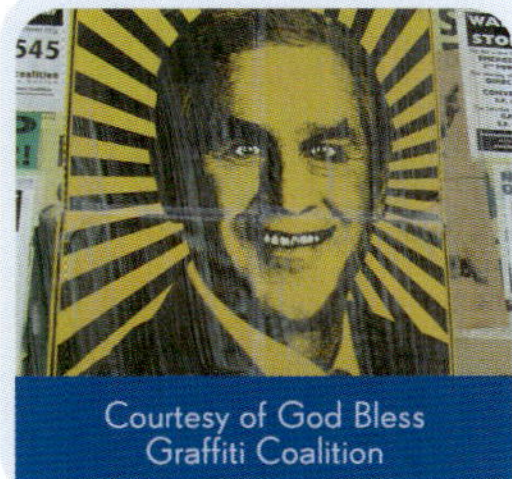

Courtesy of God Bless
Graffiti Coalition

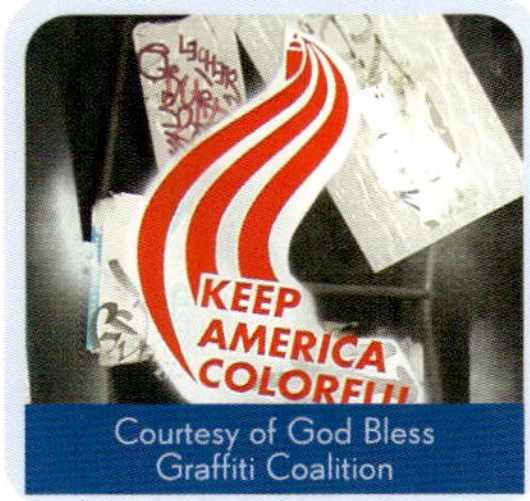

Courtesy of God Bless
Graffiti Coalition

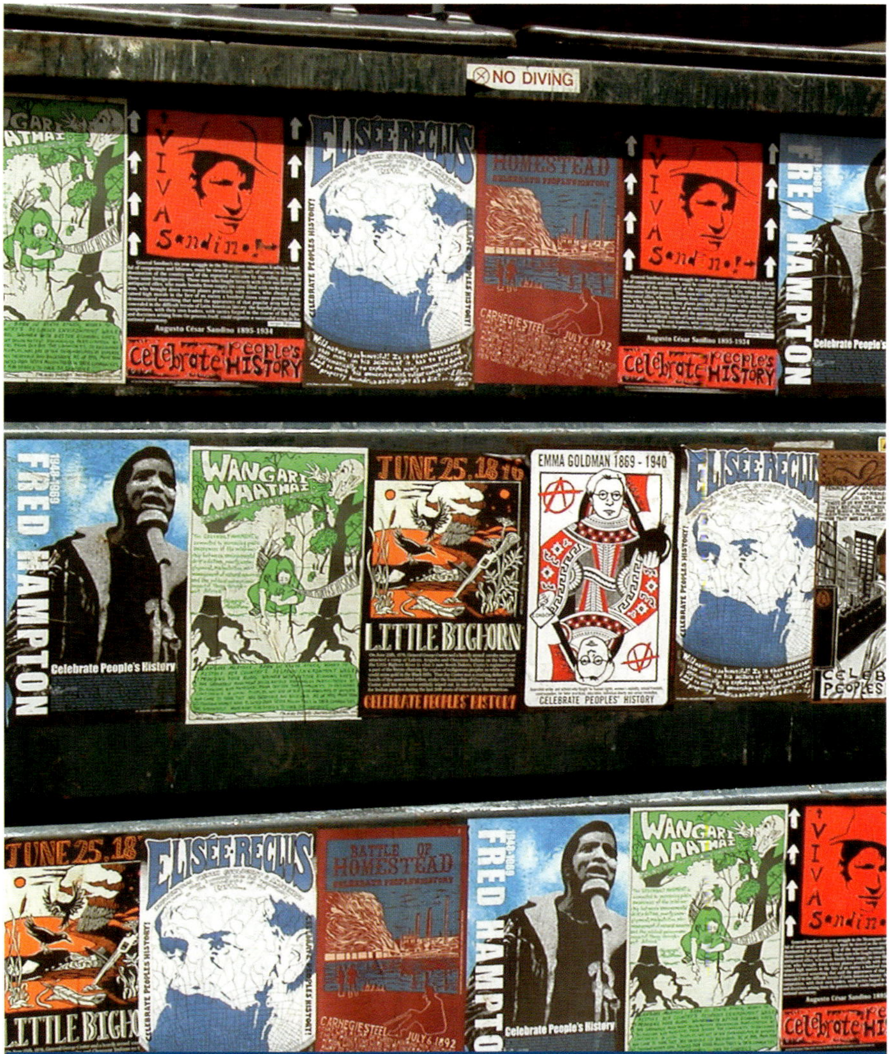

People's History Posters, Nashville, TN
Courtesy of God Bless Graffiti Coalition

Project Description: God Bless Graffiti Coalition, Inc. has curated and assembled a collection of over 200 wheatpaste posters from artists around the globe (listed above). These posters, which generally adorn the streets of major cities, present one of the most common and compelling forms of interventionist practices.

While many might view graffiti as vandalism, or petty crime, the Coalition argues that graffiti, like advertising, is simply a message delivery in public space. Unlike ads, however, which use public space to encourage consumption, graffiti is simply a form of personal expression.

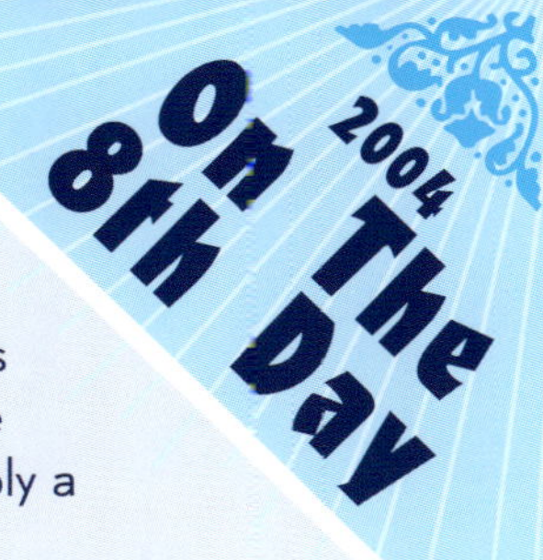

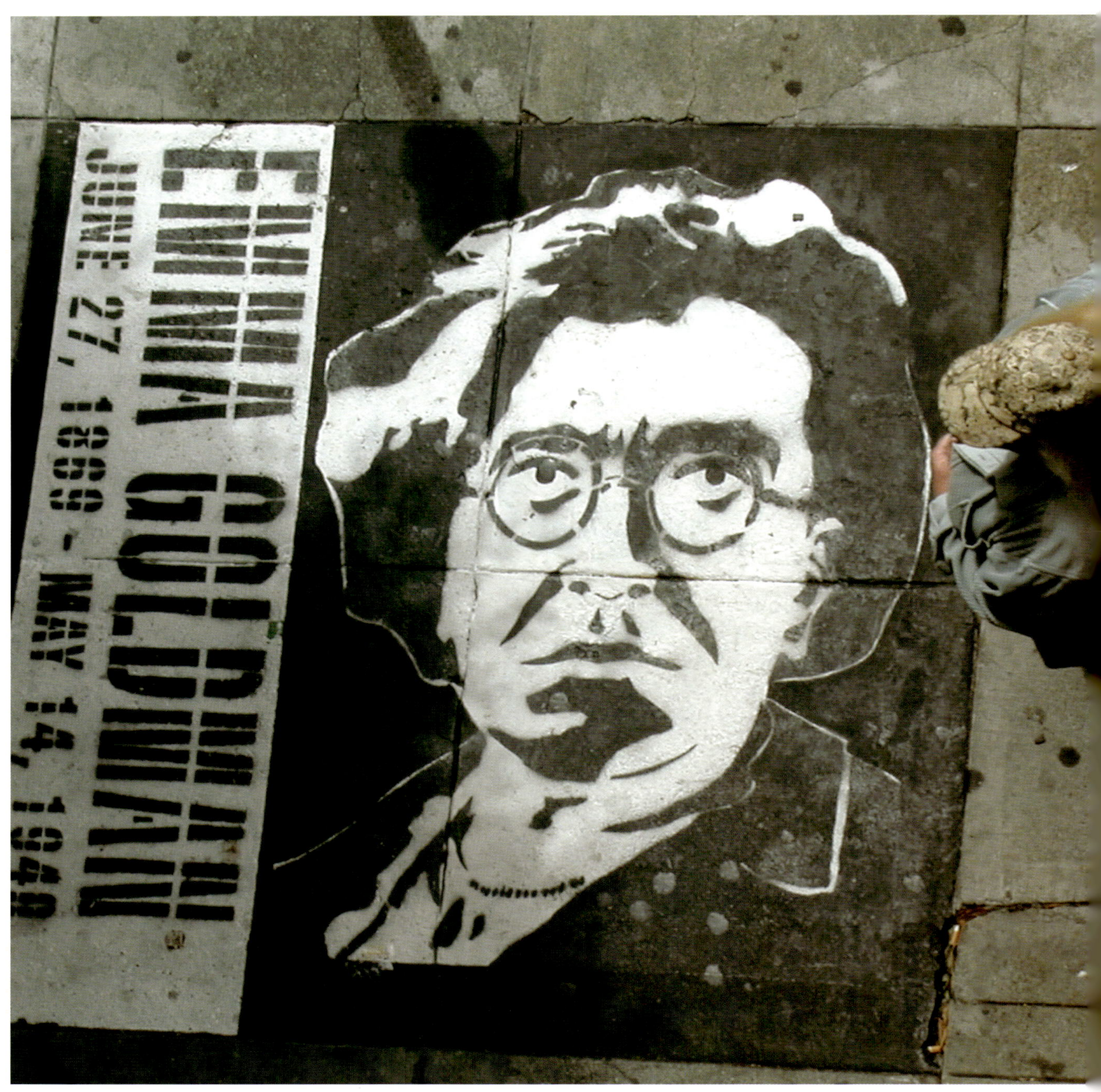

Emma Goldman stencil, San Francisco by "Claude Moller"

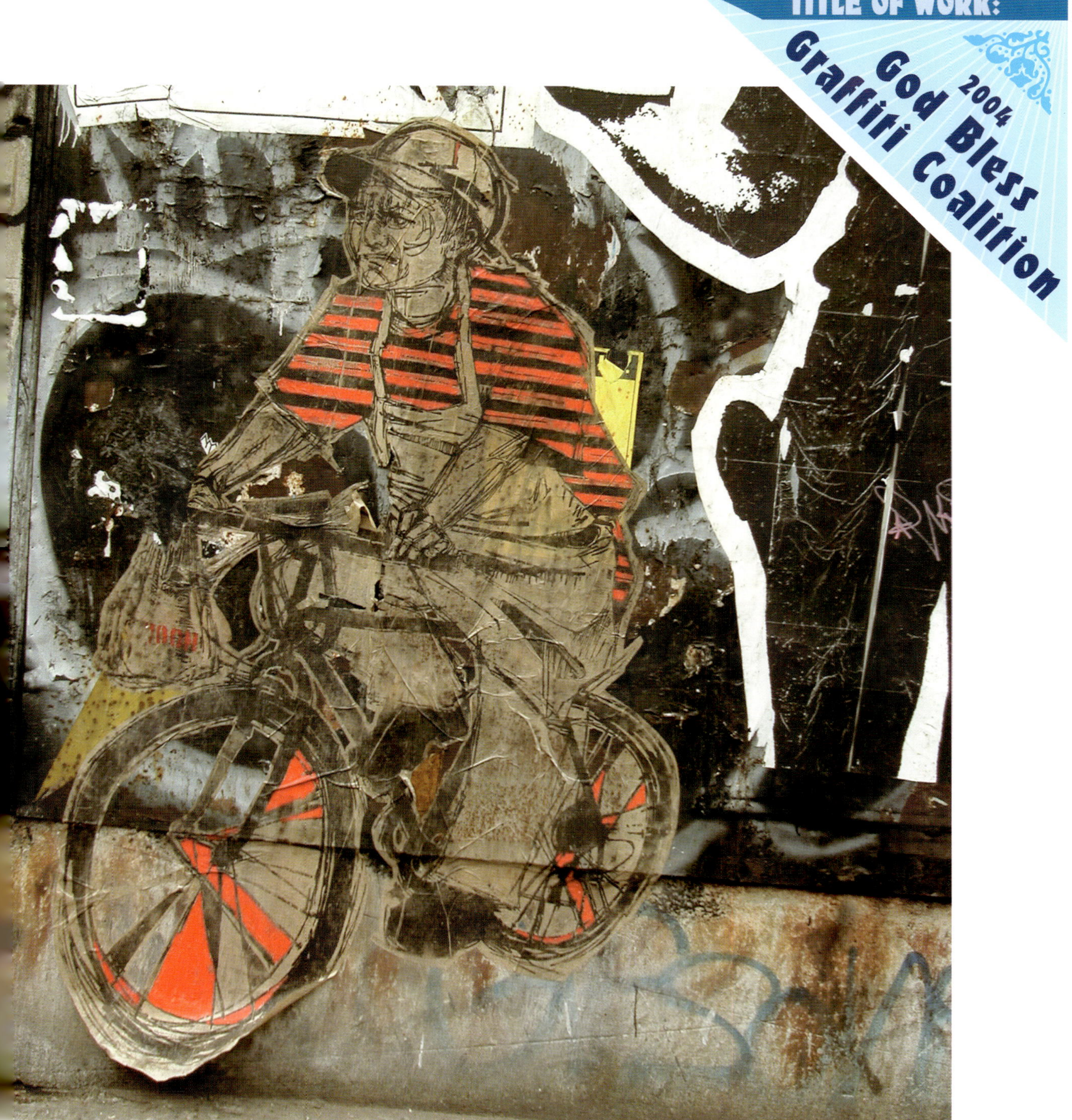

...g bike, New York City by "Swoon"

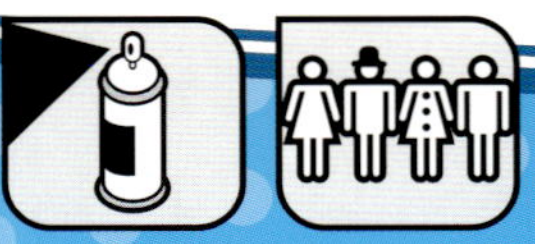

Institute for Applied Autonomy (IAA)

New York, NY, USA

Founded 1998

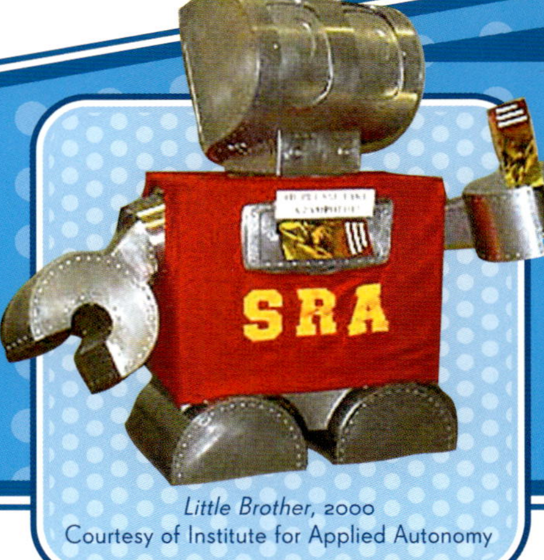

Little Brother, 2000
Courtesy of Institute for Applied Autonomy

Biographical Info:

The Institute for Applied Autonomy (IAA) was founded as a technological research and development organization concerned with individual and collective self-determination. Its mission is to study the forces and structures that affect self-determination, and to develop and utilize technologies that serve social and human needs.

An anonymous collective of critically engaged artists, engineers, and researchers, the IAA has exhibited and lectured widely since its founding in 1998 at such diverse venues as the Zentrum fur Kunst und Medientechnologie (ZKM), Hackers on Planet Earth (HOPE), and the IEEE International Conference of Robotics and Automation.

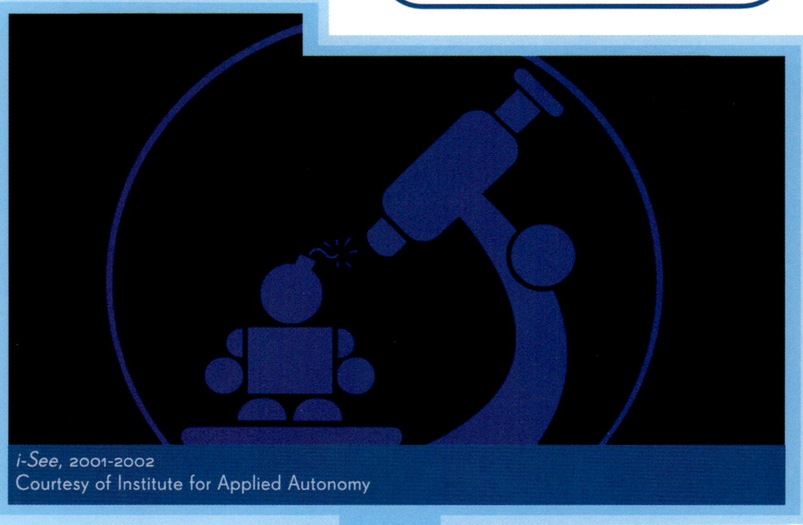

i-See, 2001-2002
Courtesy of Institute for Applied Autonomy

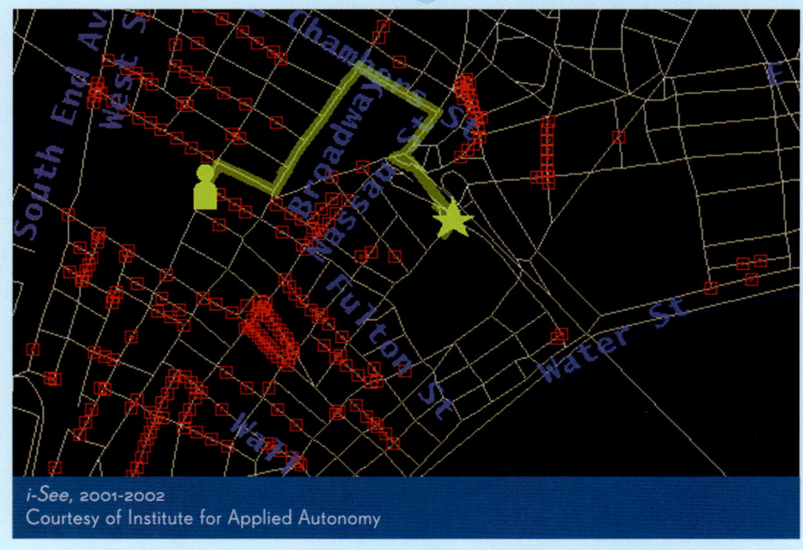

i-See, 2001-2002
Courtesy of Institute for Applied Autonomy

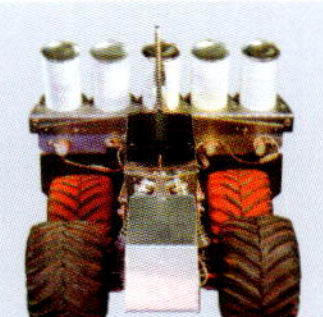

Graffiti Writer, Back 1999
Courtesy of Institute for
Applied Autonomy

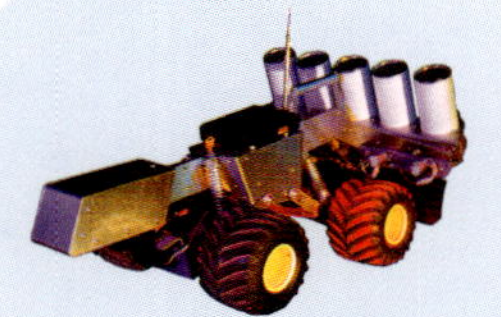

Graffiti Writer, 3/4 View, 1999
Courtesy of Institute for
Applied Autonomy

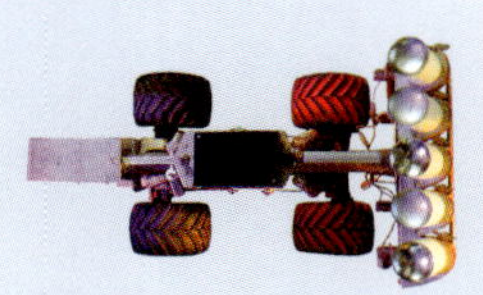

Graffiti Writer, Top 1999
Courtesy of Institute for
Applied Autonomy

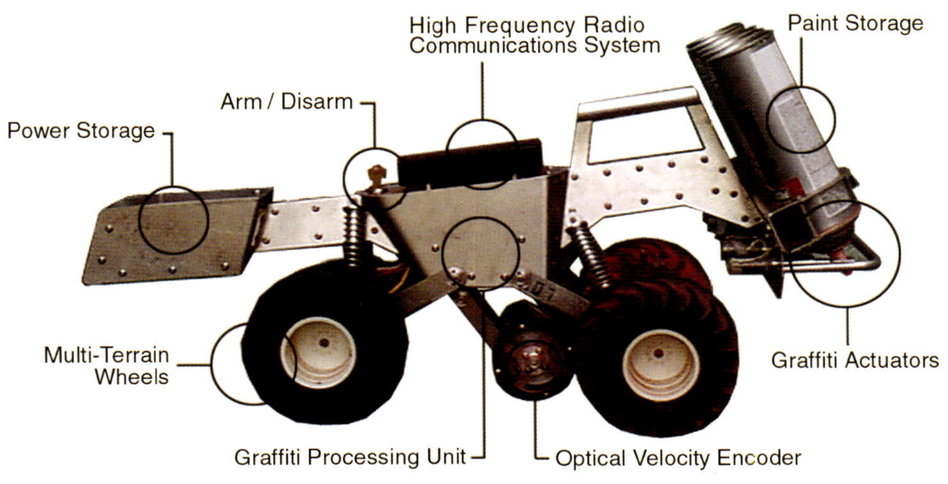

Graffiti Writer, 1999
Courtesy of Institute for Applied Autonomy

Project Description: *The Institute for Applied Autonomy* video showcases three Contestational Robotics projects and one project from IAA's Inverse Surveillance Program. *Little Brother, GraffitiWriter,* and *StreetWriter* are examples of Contestational Robotics, an IAA research initiative to develop technologies that meet the needs of street protesters. Contestational robots, or Robotic Objectors, are intended to support or replace human activists in environments that are hostile to acts of public dissent. For example, *StreetWriter* is a graffiti-writing robot disguised as a 1986 Ford extended-body cargo van, capable of writing stealthy text messages that are hundreds of yards in length.

iSee, developed under the IAA's Inverse Surveillance program, enables citizens to monitor state and corporate surveillance networks and agents. The iSee software tools for mapping and avoiding surveillance cameras run in web-browsers and in the public sphere, and were developed with the support of the ZKM, Rhizome.org, and Eyebeam Atelier. It debuted in the fall of 2001, and was optimized for use during the 2002 World Economic Forum meeting in New York. iSee has also been deployed in Amsterdam and Ljubljana, Slovenia.

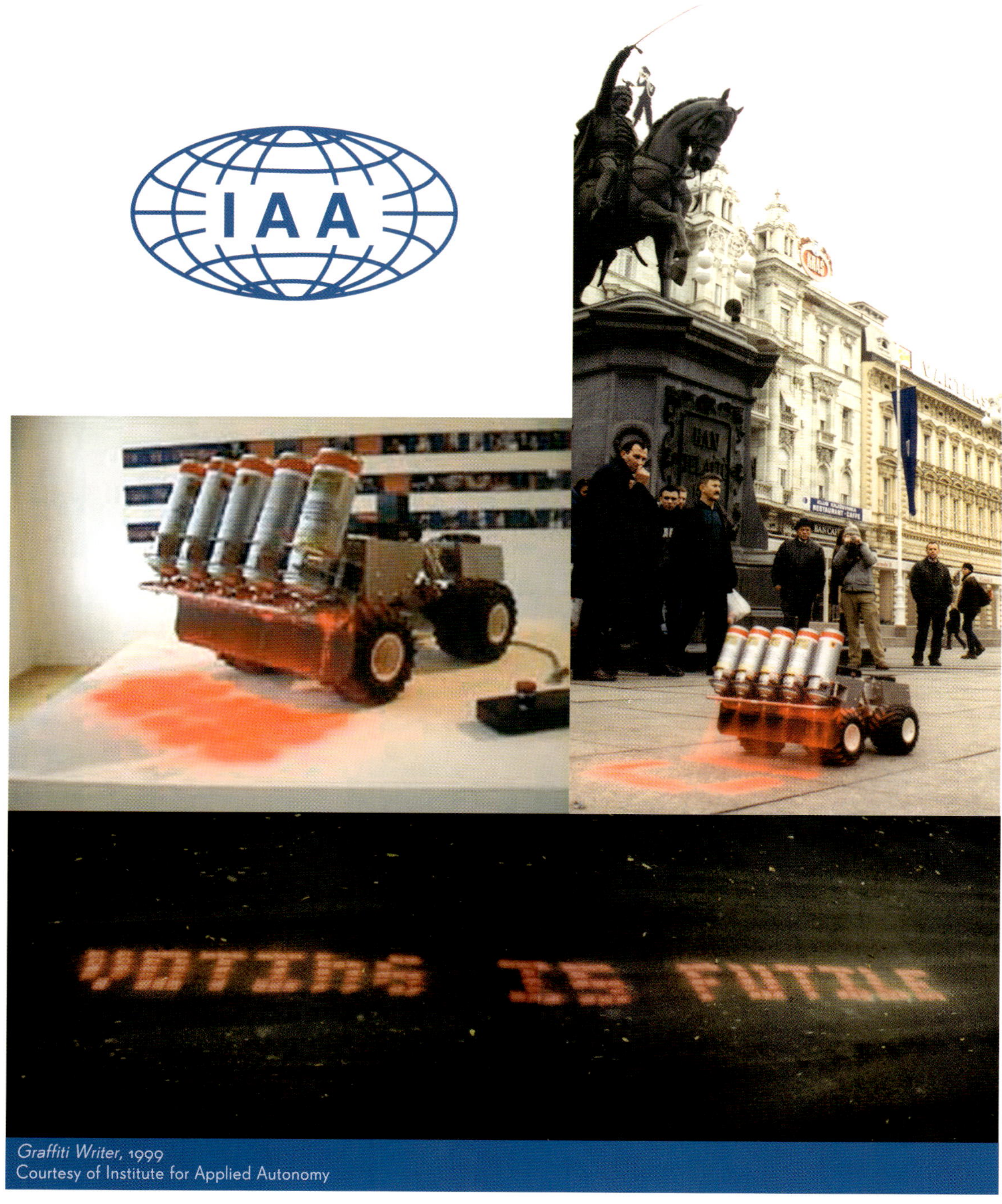

Graffiti Writer, 1999
Courtesy of Institute for Applied Autonomy

Institute for Applied Autonomy

Interview with C. Ondine Chavoya
February 11, 2004

Which practices and/or movements associated with the visual culture of the 1980s were you most engaged by, influenced by, or active in?

Hardcore punk and Saturday morning cartoons.

What are the different fields or networks that you operate in (not just aesthetically but specifically)? How do you view these various facets of your activity?

The members of our collective have proficiencies and professional associations in the arts, humanities, social sciences, and engineering, as well as ongoing involvement with grassroots activism.

What spheres do you find appropriate for your work?

We operate in public places, trade shows, and research institutions, as well as in the mass media. Because our work thrives on unscripted interaction with an audience, we're less interested in "cultural" institutions, which tend to suppress spontaneous experience and critical thought - simply put, through their self-conscious attempts to create "experiences," most museums make it impossible to have one. So, we tend to avoid the art establishment unless, of course, we think we can get paid.

How do you see your work operating in larger social movements?

Both as symbolic and tactical resistances. Our projects are functional artifacts intended for use in political resistance, and at the same time, they function as reference points for discourses about relationships between technology, democracy, and culture.

How do you use preexisting visual forms or discourses in your work? To what end(s) do you use them?

Much of our work is inspired by ongoing social discourse. Generally speaking, we reject the usual dialectics of right/left, privacy/security, public/private. We accept the existing circumstances as our playing field, and design appropriate interventions that empower individuals and highlight contradictions. Whenever useful we use aesthetic forms that people are familiar with. For instance, if we want a project to be viewed as coming from an institution, we make it shiny and complicated looking. If we want it to fade into the urban background, we will paint it black and call it a day. It all depends whether you are flying above or below the radar.

What do you consider the advantages and/or disadvantages to collaboration, compared to individualized forms of art production?

In a collaboration there are many more people who can point out

that something is a bad idea and thus save you and everyone else valuable time and money. It is also much more fun to go to the bar with your collaborators than to drink alone in your studio.

How do you see humor as functioning in your art? What about delight and pleasure in your work?

Humor is a good way to make people pay attention, who might otherwise tune you out. Absurdity can be an effective means for changing the parameters of a debate.

Why is movement necessary in your work? What do we gain from movement?

We once tried to stay still for as long as possible, but our legs fell asleep and we soon got hungry. Movement aids in blood circulation.

How does technology function in your work? In general, what is your relationship to technology?

We use technology as a means to an end to point out problems with the way power utilizes technology for its own ends. Our critiques are rarely levied at the technology itself, but at the agendas that drive it.

In the past two decades, public space has become increasingly privatized as private space and private lives have become increasingly subject to the expanded structures and technologies of surveillance. How might your work respond to or demonstrate this scenario?

In your question, there is a romanticization of public space that strikes us as both naive and historically inaccurate. Urban space is a social construction, the use and meaning of which is determined by ever-shifting relations between public and private actors. Whether the players in this game are governments, corporations, or private citizens, the central issue is and always has been one of power: who has it, who wields it, and how it is manifest in the daily experience of the city. Our work gives voice to radicals, subversives, and youth — groups with limited ability to shape urban space.

The concept "intervention" is key in the exhibition: what constitutes an intervention for you?

Interventions change the behavior of a system in a way that the system is not prepared to deal with.

Where do you find support for your work?

In the sofa, pockets of old winter clothes, and the occasional guilty liberal.

Can there be revolutionary art without a revolution?

Why not? There's plenty of conceptual art without a clue.

Oliver Ressler & Dario Azzellini

Vienna, Austria
Berlin, Germany

Born 1970, 1967

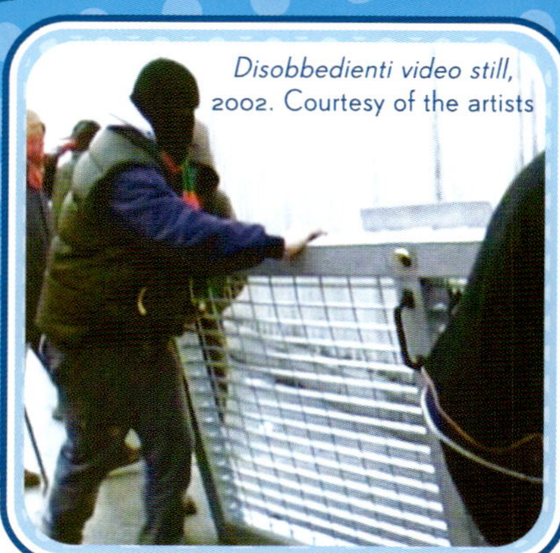
Disobbedienti video still, 2002. Courtesy of the artists

Biographical Info:

Since 1994 **Oliver Ressler** has worked in video, installation, and web-based formats to document pressing political issues. He has recently produced several widely screened documentaries including *This is What Democracy Looks Like*, 2002 and *Rote Zora*, 2000. Some of his topics include corporate culture, racism, and ecology, all in the context of the global protest movement. Ressler's work has been exhibited at the Centre for Contemporary Art, Calgary, Kunsthalle Wien, Vienna and the Center for Contemporary Art, Linz.

Dario N. Azzellini, a frequent collaborator of Ressler, is a free-lance journalist for print media, radio and TV. He has published numerous articles and books with a focus on Latin America. His film projects include *Autonomy* (Nicaragua 1993) and Interview with Paco Ignacio *Taibo II* (Mexico 1997) and *al norte* (Mexico 1998).

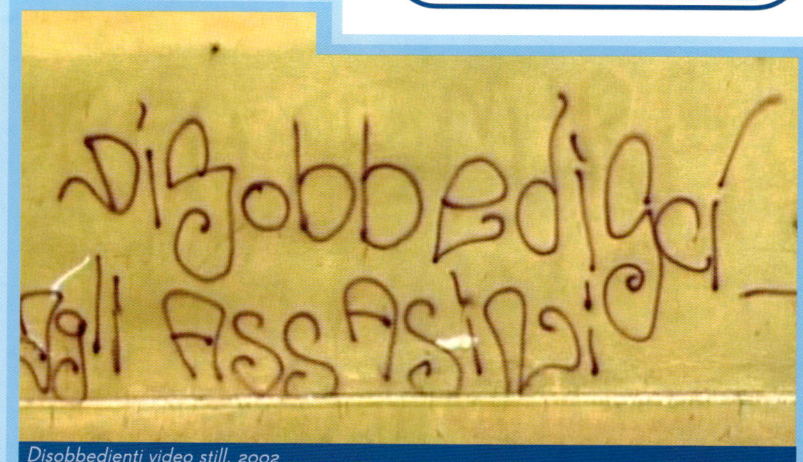
Disobbedienti video still, 2002
Courtesy of the artists

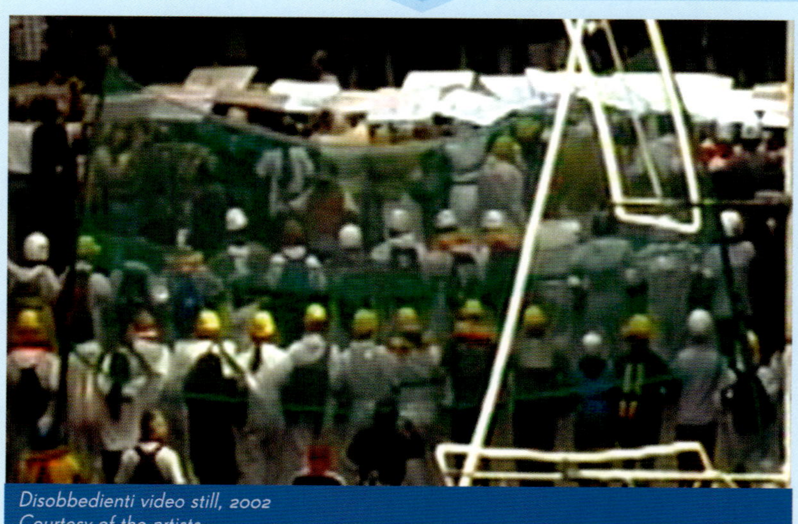
Disobbedienti video still, 2002
Courtesy of the artists

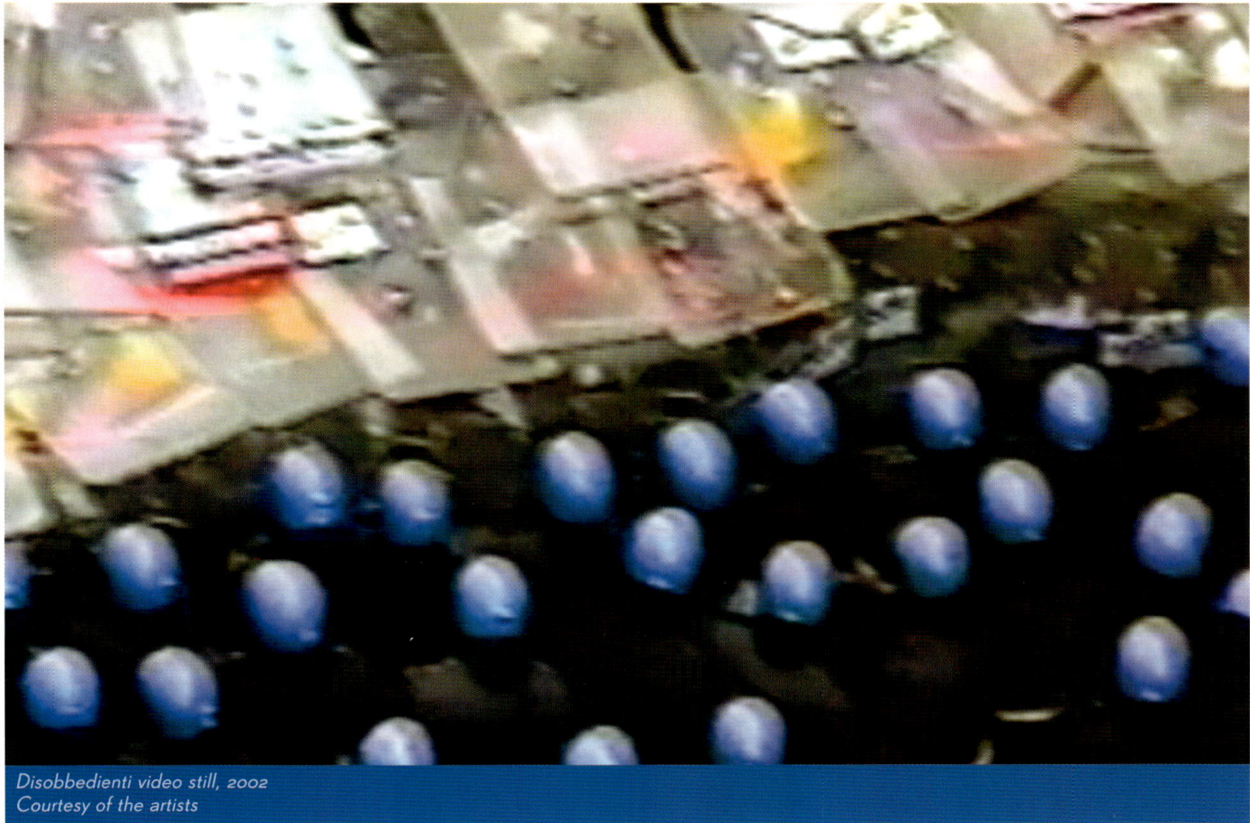

Disobbedienti video still, 2002
Courtesy of the artists

Project Description: The video *Disobbedienti* documents a group of Italian activists who participated in many of the major global-justice protests that punctuated the late 1990s. An outgrowth of a group calling themselves the Tutte Bianche, Disobbedienti emerged during the demonstrations against the G8 summit in Genoa in July 2001. For many activists, the Tutte Bianche were seen as among the most visible, effective, and radical activist groups, making a specialty of the large-scale street protests. The Tutte Bianche were known for wearing white coveralls and cladding their bodies from head to toe in padding, helmets, gas masks and shields.

After the G8 summit (where the street protests took a more dramatic and violent turn, including one fatality), the Tutte Bianche disbanded, reorganizing as Disobbedienti. Instead of focusing on "civil disobedience," their energy turned toward "social disobedience." Whereas civil disobedience utilizes law-breaking as a form of social protest (such as crossing a police line during a rally), social disobedience takes aim at oppressive social codes. The subtle differences between these two terms are explored in this film and, in short, represent a growing interest in longer-term strategies and a willingness to address more difficult, if diffuse, issues within the global protest movement.

TITLE OF WORK:
Disobbedienti
2002

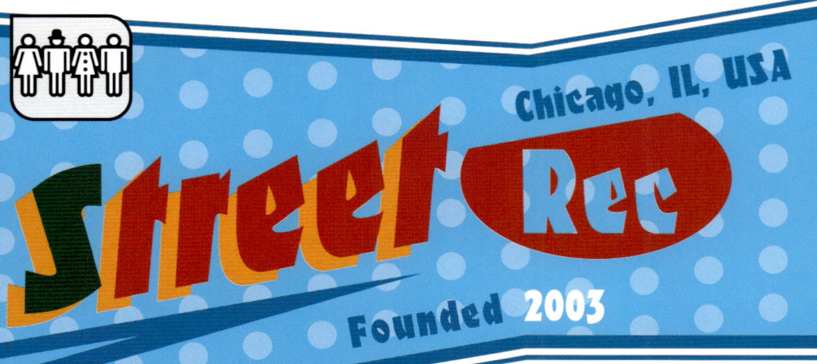

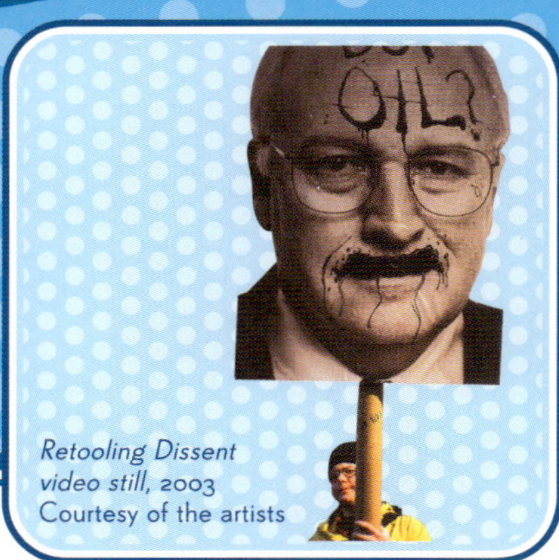
Retooling Dissent
video still, 2003
Courtesy of the artists

Biographical Info:

Street Rec was a short-lived radical arts collective born out of the protests against the World Economic Forum in New York City in 2002. The collective consisted of members of several radical arts organizations in Chicago including Temporary Services, the God Bless Graffiti Coalition, the Department of Space and Land Reclamation and the anarchist collective, the A-Zone.

The temporary collective focused primarily on developing and documenting tools for creative resistance, with particular emphasis on the global protest movement. They have since disbanded.

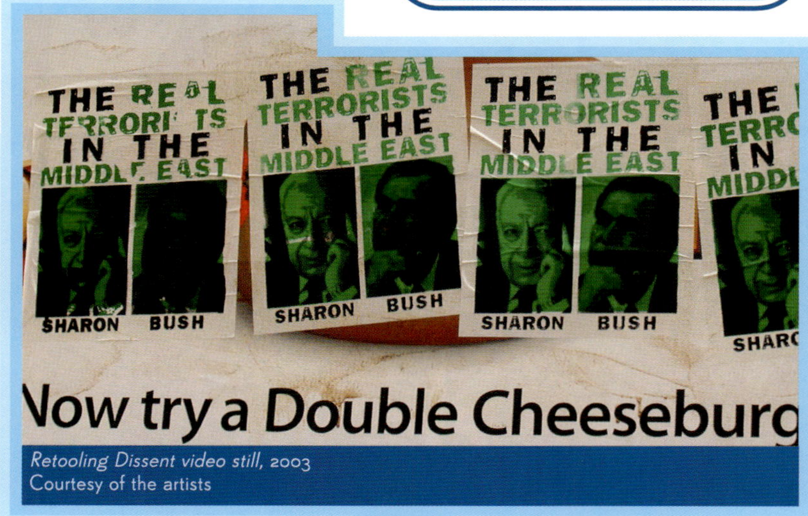

Retooling Dissent video still, 2003
Courtesy of the artists

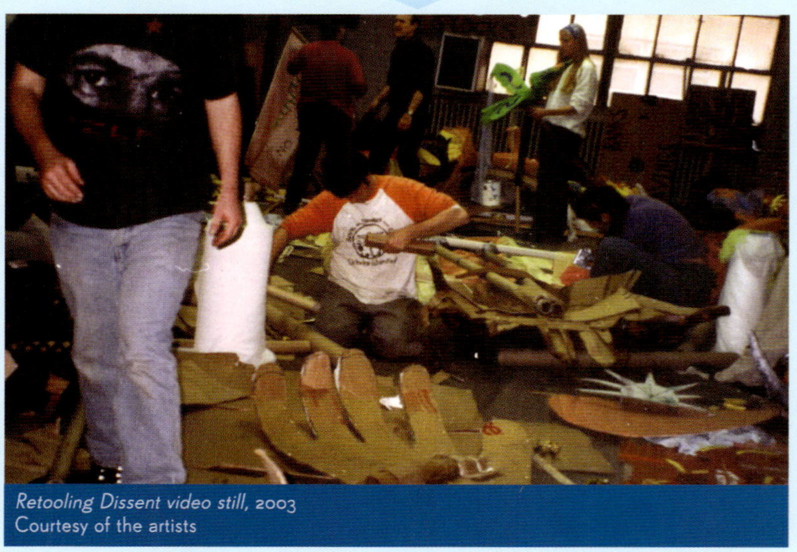
Retooling Dissent video still, 2003
Courtesy of the artists

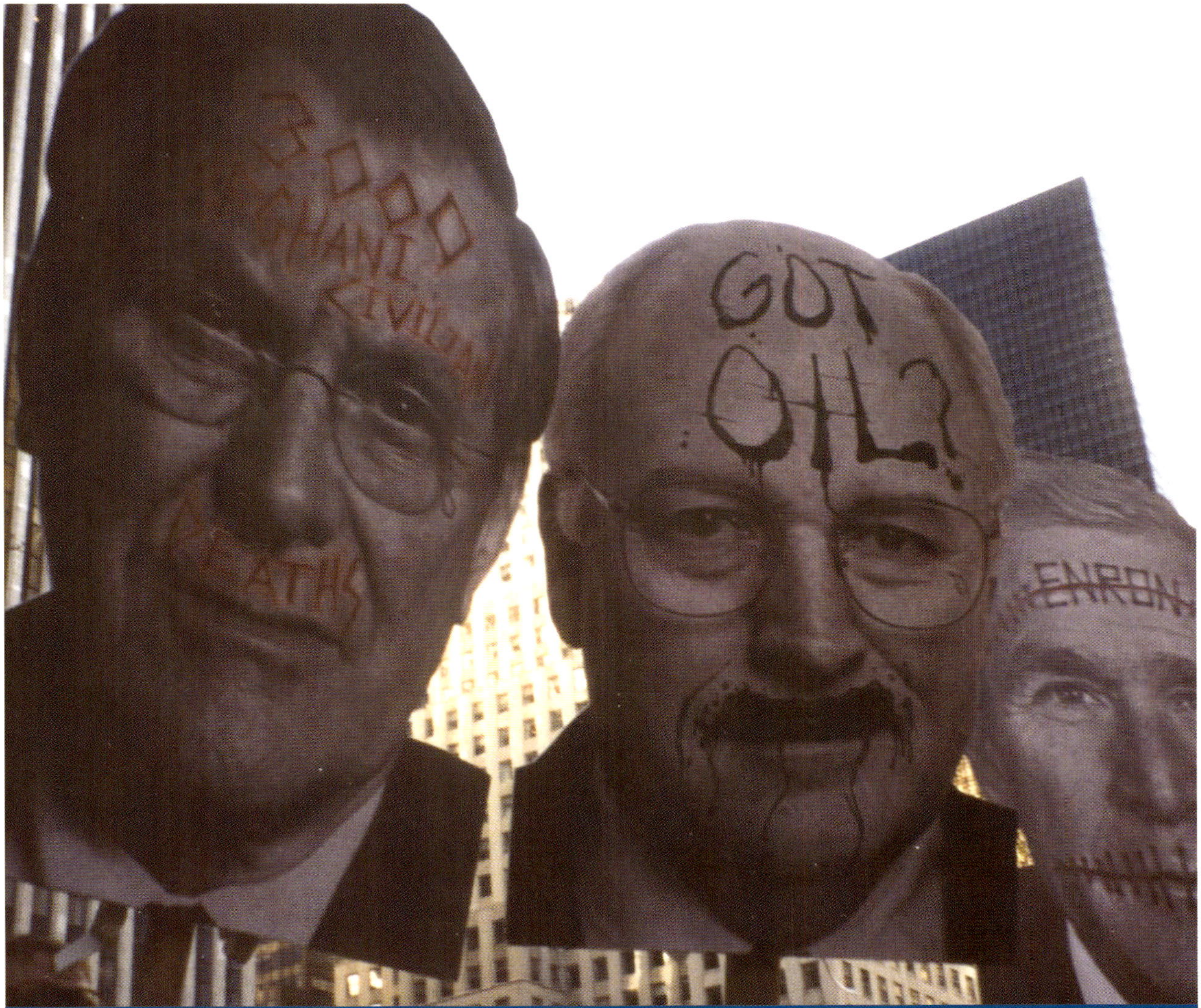

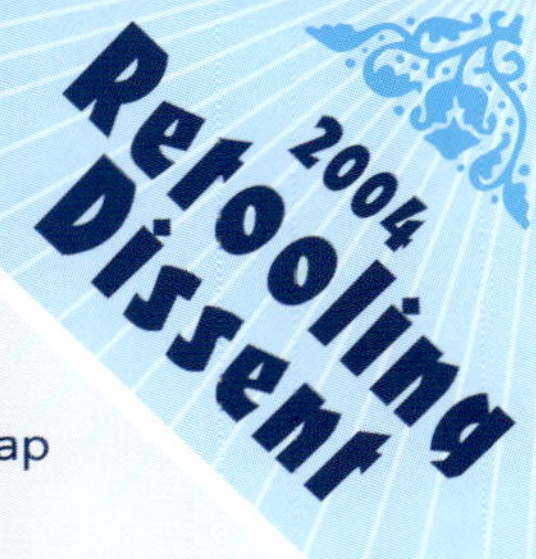

Retooling Dissent video still, 2003
Courtesy of the artists

Project Description: The video *Retooling Dissent* documents protest events produced during the World Economic Forum protests in New York City in February 2002. Included in the documentary are the large-scale heads of political figures like Dick Cheney and Donald Rumsfeld produced by Street Rec, the *iSee* program developed by the Institute for Applied Autonomy (see page 75), the *New Kids on the Black Block* by the Spanish anarchist collective Las Agencias and *the bicycle rider* produced by Affectech. *Retooling Dissent* highlights the coordination and overlap between art-inspired interventionist techniques and on-the-ground protest actions.

TITLE OF WORK:

2004
Retooling Dissent

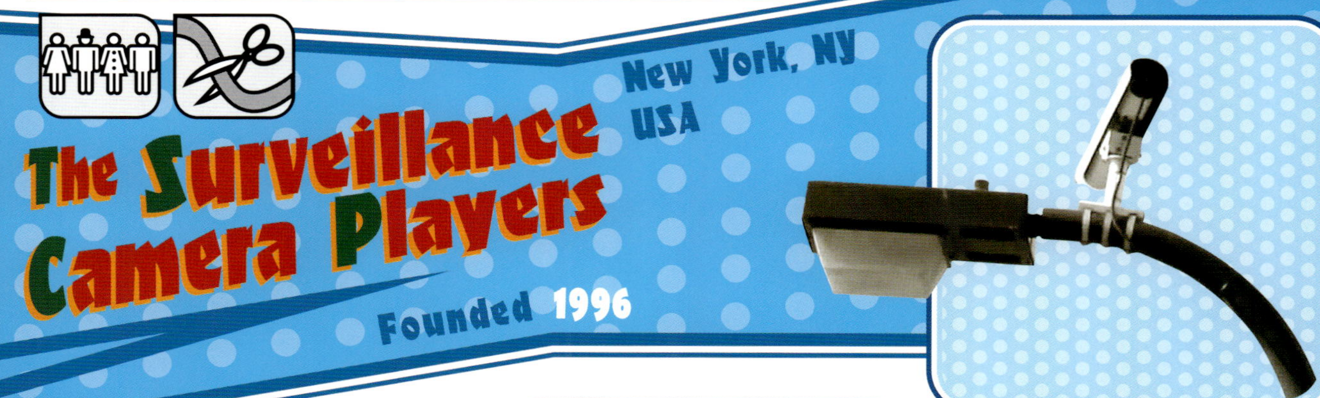

Biographical Info:

The Surveillance Camera Players' (SCP) debut performance was a rendition of Alfred Jarry's play *Ubu Roi* performed in front of a surveillance camera in Manhattan's Union Square on December 10, 1996. At that time, SCP consisted of six members, led by Bill Brown. Brown — a Fulbright Scholar with a doctorate in American literature — taught at the Rhode Island School of Design before turning his full attention to performance. The SCP protest the use of surveillance cameras in public places in the belief that these cameras violate a constitutionally protected right of privacy and free movement. In addition to performances, Bill Brown conducts free walking tours of heavily surveilled neighborhoods in New York City and publishes *Not Bored!*, an on-line Situationist magazine founded in 1983.

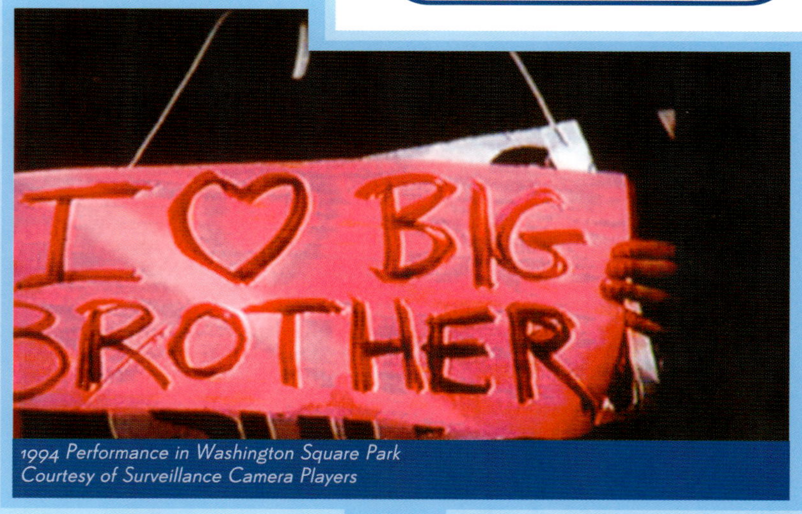

1994 Performance in Washington Square Park
Courtesy of Surveillance Camera Players

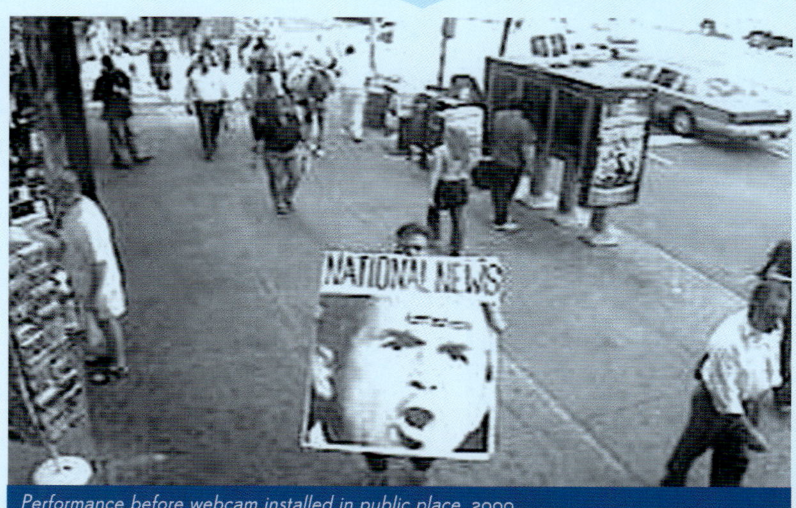

Performance before webcam installed in public place, 2000
Courtesy of Surveillance Camera Players

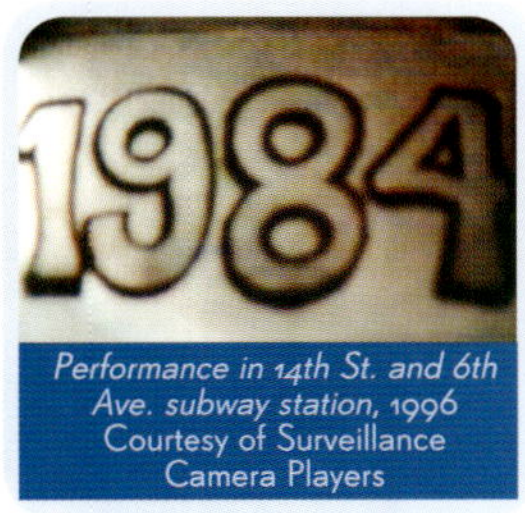

Performance in 14th St. and 6th Ave. subway station, 1996 Courtesy of Surveillance Camera Players

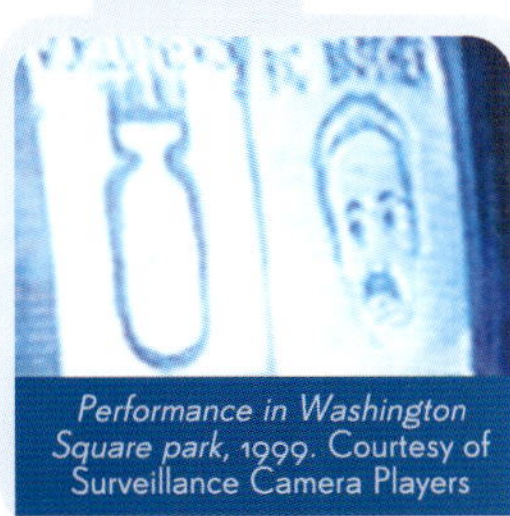

Performance in Washington Square park, 1999. Courtesy of Surveillance Camera Players

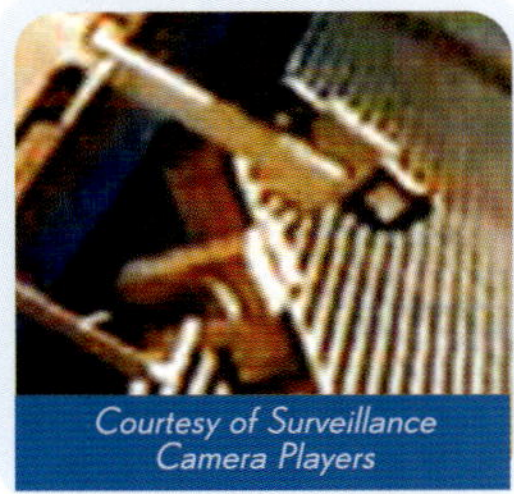

Courtesy of Surveillance Camera Players

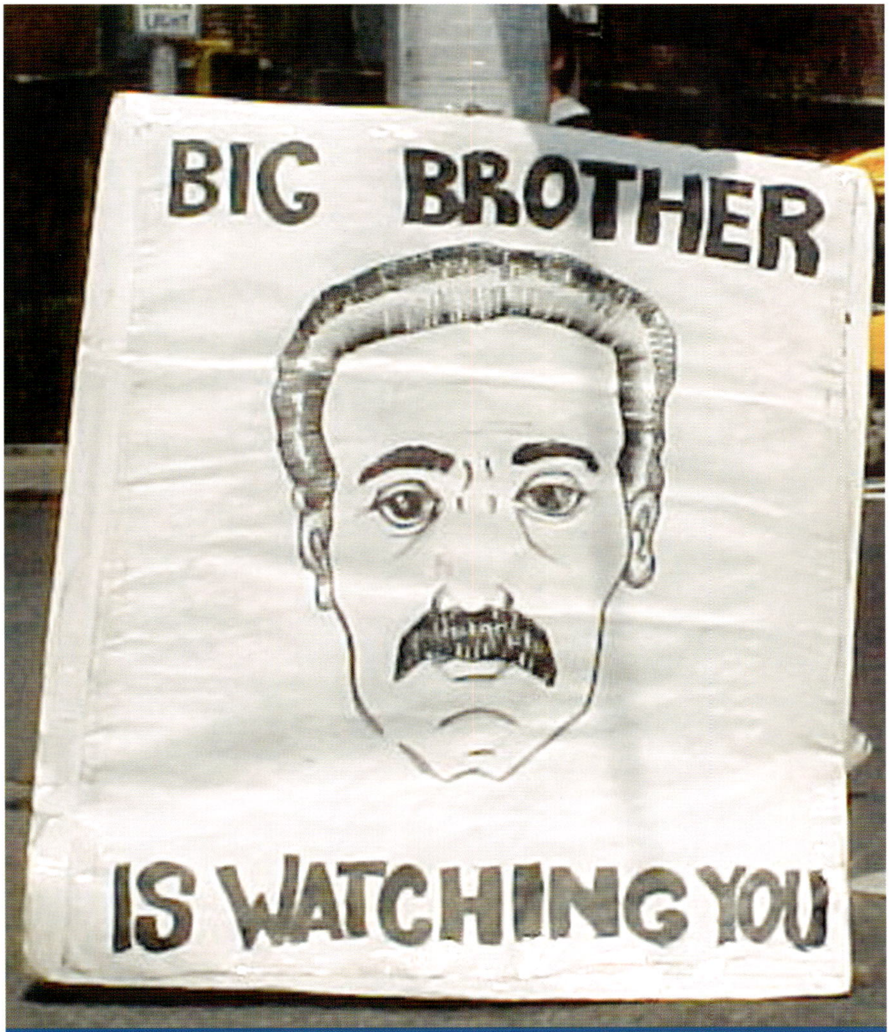

*Performance in Washington Square Park, 1999
Courtesy of Surveillance Camera Players*

Project Description: The video documents a performance by the SCP of George Orwell's *1984* inside the 14th Street and 6th Avenue subway station in New York City. The sound of commuters can be heard in the background as the video captures the players displaying posters of "Big Brother" to the surveillance monitors. Eventually, their performance is cut short by confused police officers.

TITLE OF WORK:

**1996
Surveillance
Camera Players**

The Surveillance Camera Players

Interview with C. Ondine Chavoya
January 29, 2004

Which practices and/or movements associated with the visual culture of the 1980s were you most engaged by, influenced by, or active in?

DIY ("do it yourself") punk bands, fanzines and wheat-pasted ("fly") posters. My own zine *NOT BORED!* (punk/Situationist) was founded in 1983 and is still active to this day.

When the viewer experiences your work, what type(s) of relationships do you hope to establish?

A relationship of inspiration and autonomy: "I could do that."

What are the different fields or networks that you operate in (not just aesthetically but specifically)? How do you view these various facets of your activity?

Street-theatre groups (especially The Living Theatre), privacy advocates, Internet devotees, mass-media whores, and fighters for "the molecular revolution" (Felix Guattari), a.k.a. "the revolution of everyday life" (Raoul Vaneigem).

What spheres do you find appropriate for your work?

See above.

How do you see your work operating in larger social movements?

As a model for, or example of, autonomous, networked activity.

How does your work situate the local and the global?

Vaneigem: "Think globally, act locally"

How do you use preexisting visual forms or discourses in your work? To what end(s) do you use them?

We *detourn* the pre-existing "theatre" created by the placement of surveillance cameras in public places to create a theatre of rebellion and trust, rather than a theatre of conformity and fear.

What do you consider the advantages and/or disadvantages to collaboration, compared to individualized forms of art production?

There are no individualized forms of art production. All artists are collaborators ("thieves").

How do you see humor as functioning in your art? What about delight and pleasure in your work?

Essential, especially given the despair and paranoia usually associated with surveillance and social control.

Why is movement necessary in your work? What do we gain from movement?

Movement is life; paralysis is death. Ubu Roi: "I am constantly in motion, even when I'm sitting down."

How does technology function in your work? In general, what is your relationship to technology?

Totally dependent on the technology of surveillance cameras. Without it, the SCP would have no reason to exist, no way of expressing itself directly. When the cameras are taken down (one day!), the SCP will disappear.

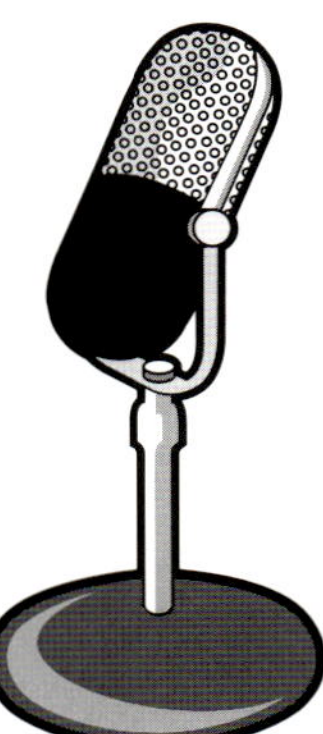

In the past two decades, public space has become increasingly privatized as private space and private lives have become increasingly subject to the expanded structures and technologies of surveillance. How might your work respond to or demonstrate this scenario?

Privatization isn't simply a spatial phenomenon. It is also functional (private entities taking on public functions such as policing and sanitation) and socio-psychological (abandonment of public life and "politics," and retreat into a non-existent "private life"). We try to fight privatization on all three levels. (Writings of Cornelius Castoriadis are very helpful here.)

The word intervention is central to the exhibition: what constitutes an intervention?

An uncoupling of one mechanic assemblage and the creation of another (Deleuze and Guattari).

Where do you find support for your work?

Among the visionary, the depressed, the drug-addicted, the paranoid, the outcast, the homeless, the disenfranchised — i.e., everywhere.

Can there be revolutionary art without a revolution?

No.

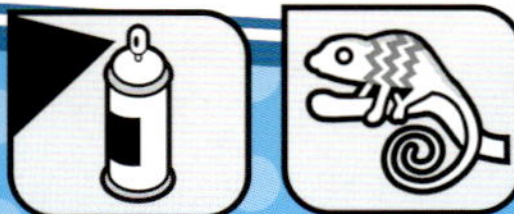

The Reverend Billy

New York, NY, USA

Born 1950

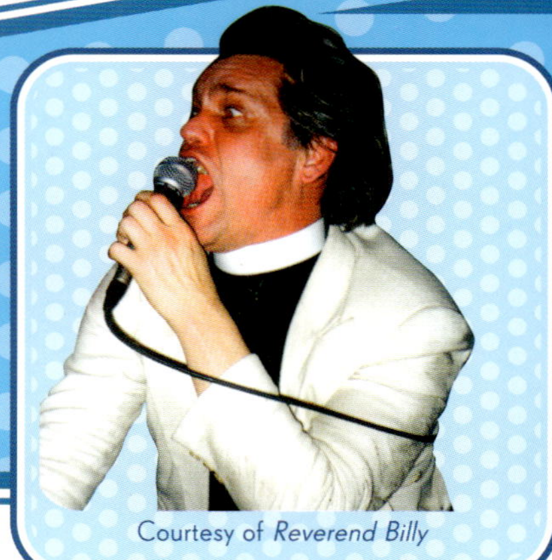

Courtesy of *Reverend Billy*

Biographical Info:

Before dawning the guise of **The Reverend Billy**, Bill Talen worked as a performance artist and managed a small theater company in San Francisco. He arrived in New York in the mid-'90s, taking a job as house manager at St. Clements Episcopel Church in Hell's Kitchen. Talen became disillusioned with the inequities of the economic development that took place in downtown New York during that period, where gentrification and homelessness were both on the rise. Sydney Lanier, a former priest at St. Clemens, encouraged Talen to voice his frustrations through sermonizing. Initially reluctant, in 1998 Talen began performing as the Reverend Billy at The Times Square Disney Store. Since then, Talen has created what might be called a church of controversy, preaching against the evils of consumerism, gentrification, and global power.

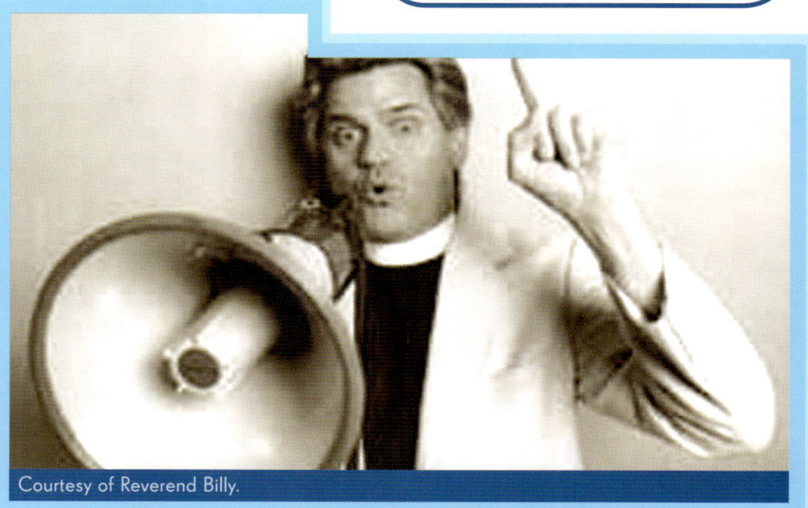

Courtesy of Reverend Billy.

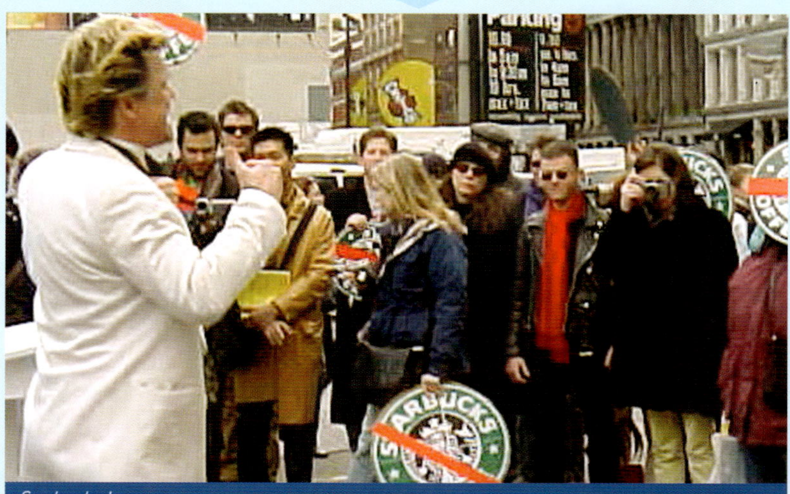

Starbucks Interventions
Courtesy of the artists

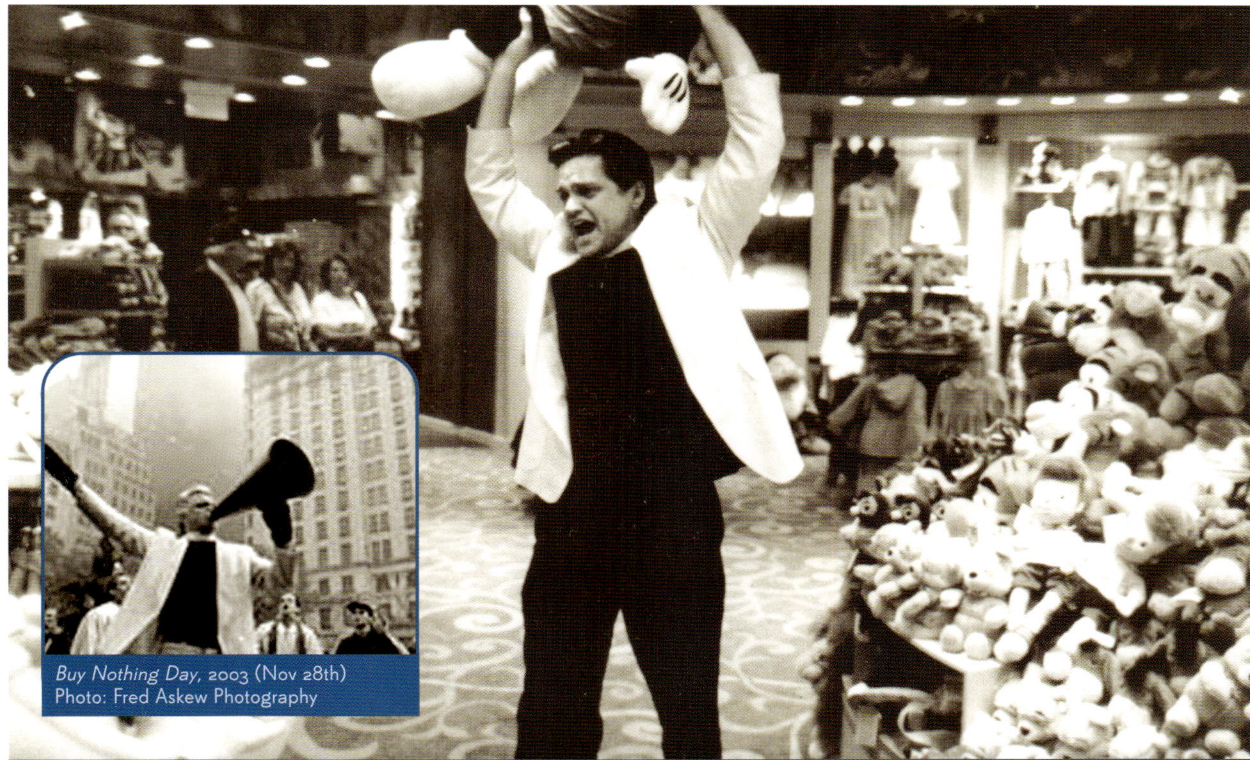

Buy Nothing Day, 2003 (Nov 28th)
Photo: Fred Askew Photography

First Disney intervention, 1997.
Courtesy of Reverend Billy.

Project Description: The video *Reverend Billy* and the Church of Stop Shopping, directed by Dietmar Post, documents Reverend Billy in action. The video documents the preacher sermonizing at Starbucks, the Disney Store, and at Edgar Allan Poe's tenement apartment — slated for occupation by New York University's Law School.

The Reverend performs rites ranging from public "credit card exorcisms" to Starbucks graduations (protesting tax breaks given to a university coffee shop). Notoriously, Starbucks circulated an in-house memo to employees, with official instructions for handling Reverend Billy's theatrical disruptions. This memo is reprinted in Talen's 2003 book *What Should I Do if Reverend Billy is in My Store?* (New Press). In 2000, Bill Talen won an Obie award for his development of the Reverend Billy character.

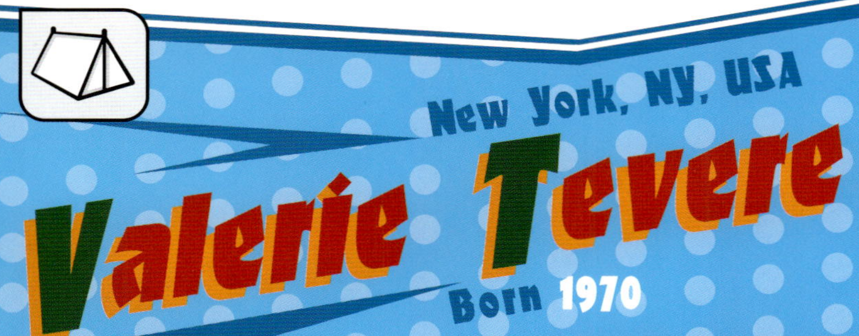

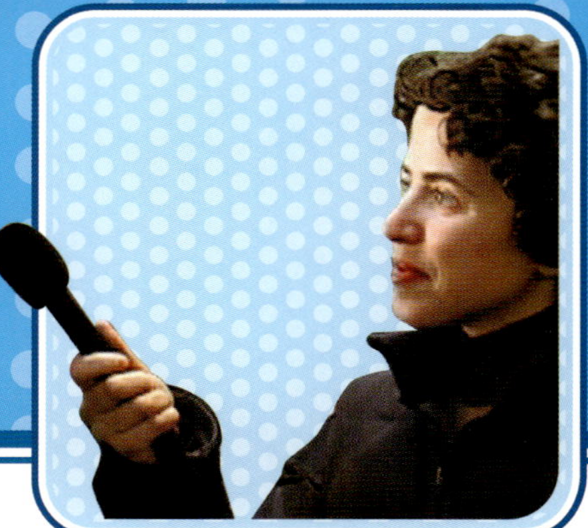

Biographical Info:

Valerie Tevere was an artist-in-residence at Smart Project Space in Amsterdam (2001), recipient of a Mellon Humanities fellowship at the City University of New York Graduate Center (2002/2003), and an artist-in-residence with the Lower Manhattan Cultural Council (2002).

Though the heart of Tevere's recent work has been the interview format, she also utilizes video, social activism and micro-radio broadcasts to produce and distribute her work.

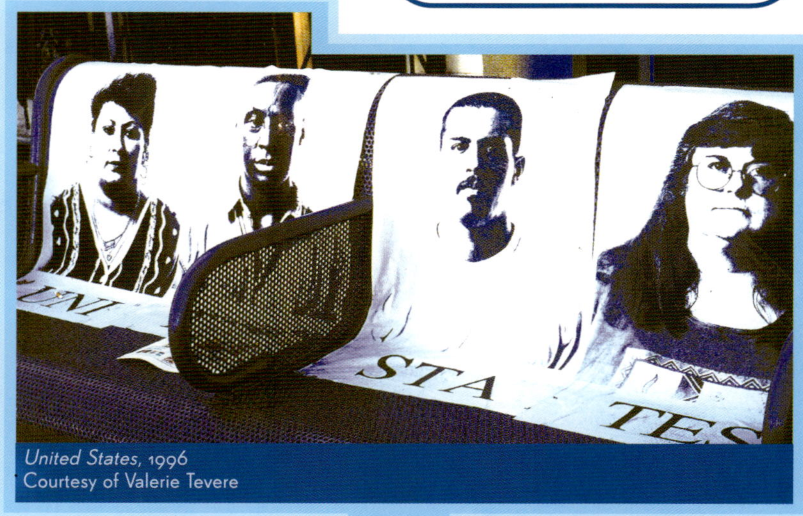

United States, 1996
Courtesy of Valerie Tevere

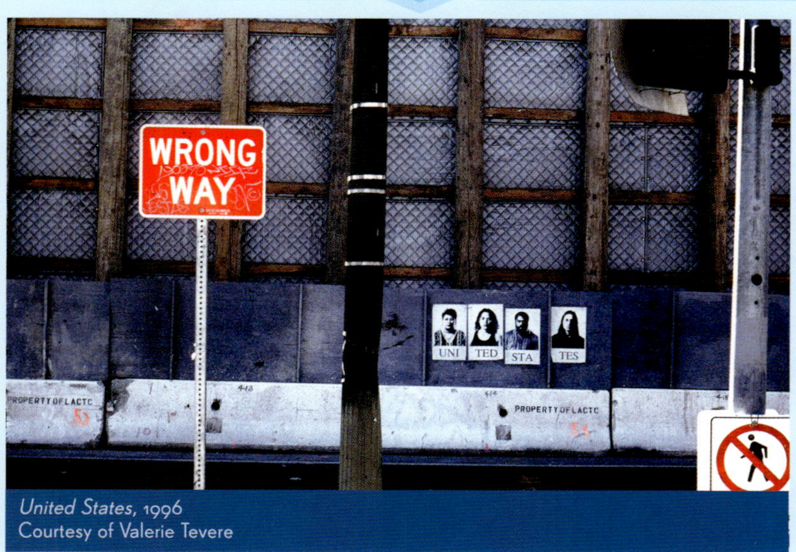

United States, 1996
Courtesy of Valerie Tevere

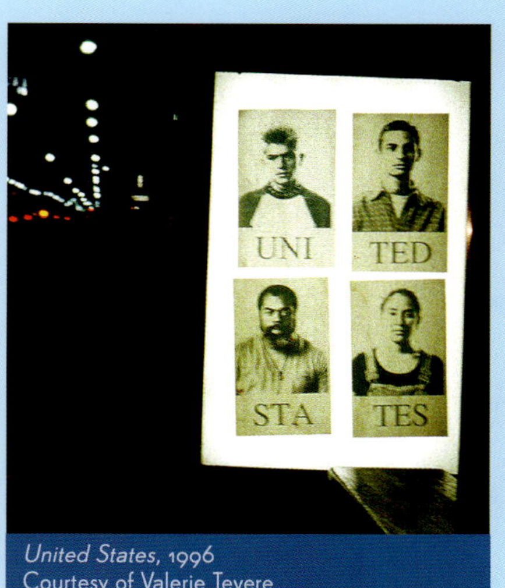

United States, 1996
Courtesy of Valerie Tevere

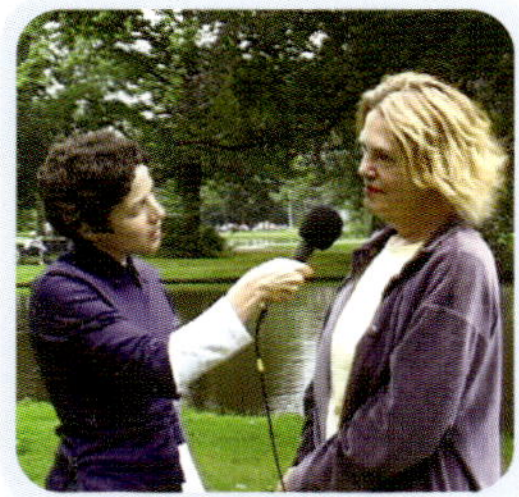

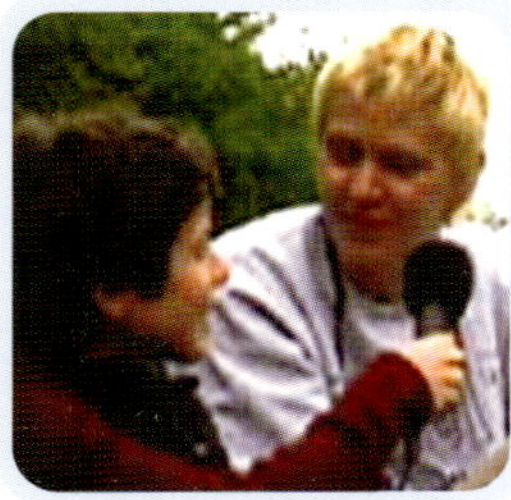

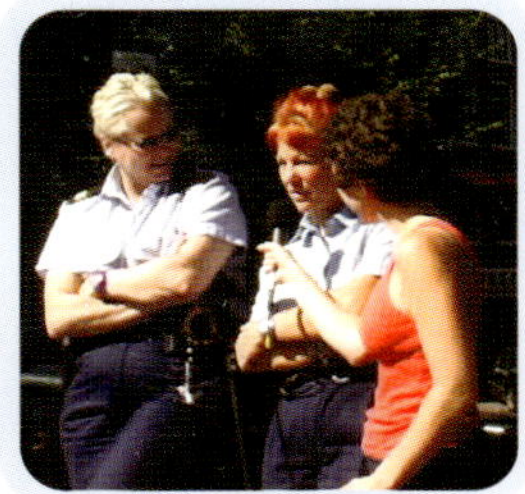

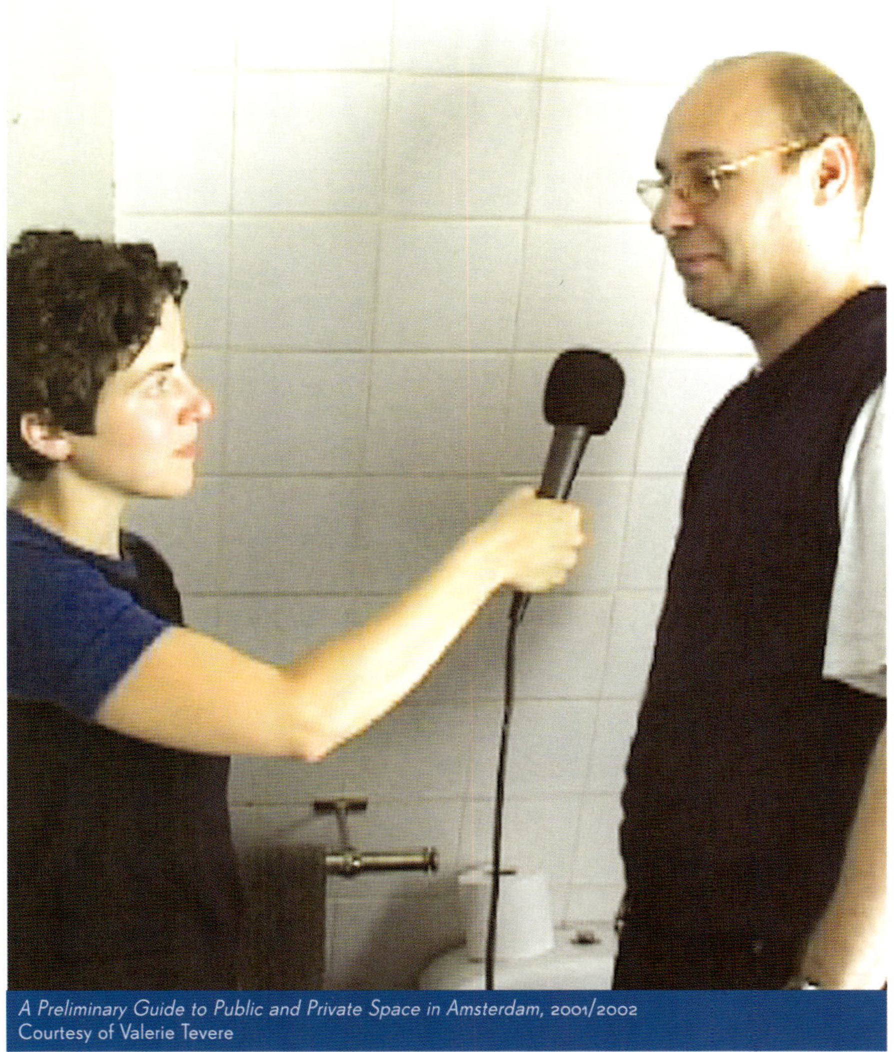

A Preliminary Guide to Public and Private Space in Amsterdam, 2001/2002
Courtesy of Valerie Tevere

Project Description: Tevere's interactive DVD project uses interviews to map public perceptions of public and private space. Tevere begins the work by asking random individuals on the streets of Amsterdam to describe one public and one private space in the city. Tevere then moves to those locations for her next interviews. As the project grows geometrically, so too does our understanding of nuance differences between public and private spaces. In essence, the DVD allows us to "walk" a geo-psychological map of Amsterdam.

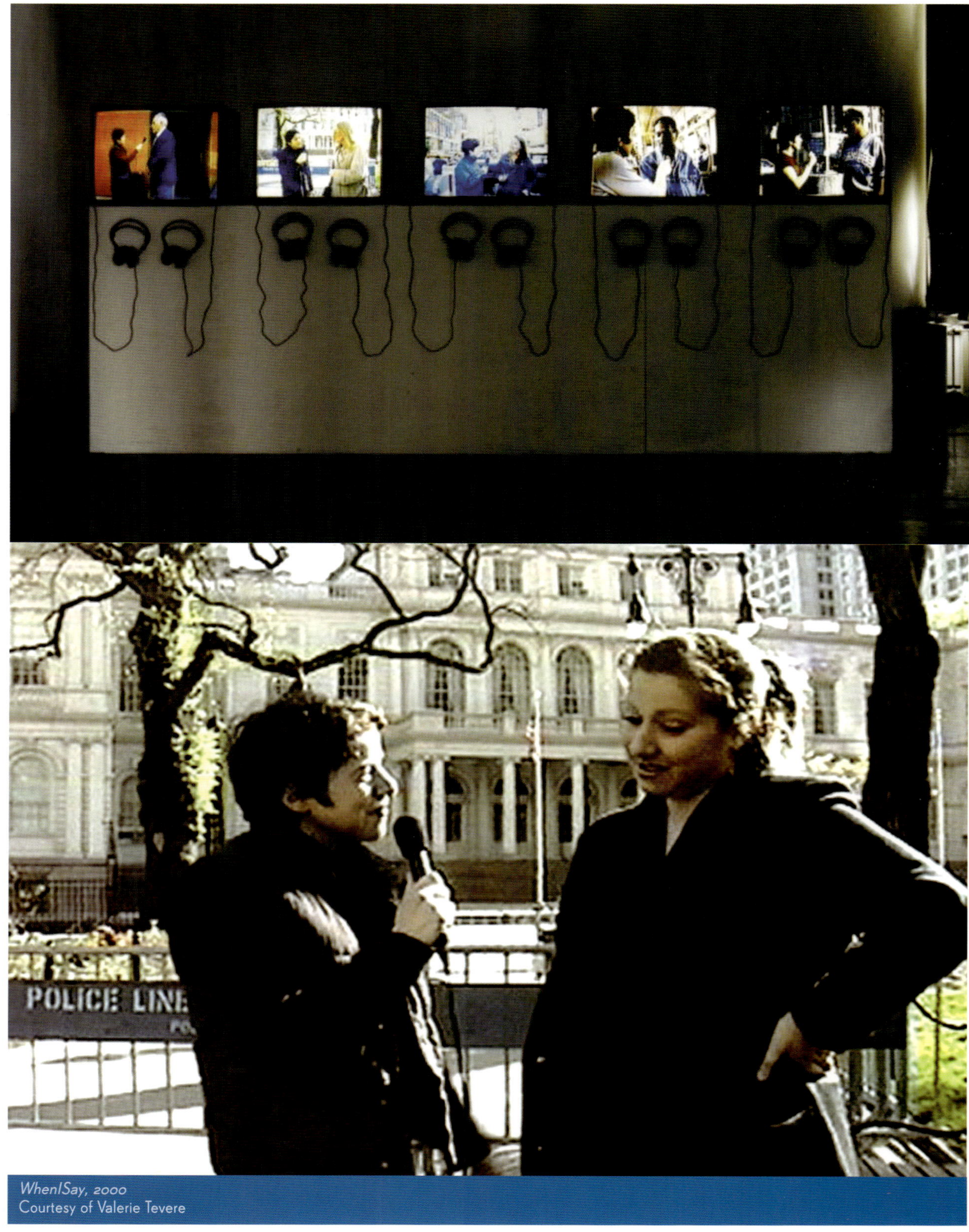

WhenISay, 2000
Courtesy of Valerie Tevere

Valerie Tevere

Interview with C. Ondine Chavoya
March 17, 2004

What do you consider the advantages and/or disadvantages to collaboration, compared to individualized forms of art production?

I think there are advantages and disadvantages within any sort of practice; however, my individual and collective work [*neuro-Transmitter*] involves different levels of collaboration. An artist doesn't work in an airtight room devoid of cultural influences; collaboration can occur through interaction, dialogue with another person or a text, among other possibilities. My individual work focuses on the idea of spontaneous or scripted interactions with city residents in public, private, and chosen locations in the urban sphere. I consider each interaction a collaborative encounter, one that activates, changes, and completes the work. The collaborative work of *neuroTransmitter* is about continuing interaction and dialogue, finding the fissures of possibility, carving collective spaces for discursivity outside of the ultra-commercialized radio broadcast spectrum.

Additional information on *neuroTransmitter* can be found at www.neurotransmitter.fm

How do you see humor as functioning in your art?

I think of humor, play, and satire as disarming and necessary tactics employed to catch power off guard. Within my practice, humor shifts the expectations of the interview process, opening up a comfortable space for revealing dialogue.

Why is movement necessary in your work?
What do we gain from movement?

When considering the larger charting of a particular work, movement is an important aspect of my process. The project *A Preliminary Guide to Public and Private Space in Amsterdam* maps the city through spontaneous interactions in previously chosen public and private spaces. Each interaction happens in a location chosen by the preceding interviewee. I continually move through and map the city based on these choices — creating a vulnerable yet alternate "tourism."

How does technology function in your work? In general, what is your relation to technology?

The collaborative work of neuroTransmitter uses technologies that interrupt and mediate ether and hyper spaces. The communicative, political, and creative potentiality of "plugging" into the airwaves is the continuing focus of our work. We have constructed a device that creates the potential for mobile broadcasting. This object is a multi-use tool for information dissemination and public broadcast, and prefaces the relationship between radio transmission, the body, and how the two — through mobile experience — can negotiate, interrupt, and sonically map the space of the city.

In the past two decades, public space has become increasingly privatized as private space and private lves have become increasingly subject to the expanded structures and technologies of surveillance. How might your work respond to or demonstrate this scenario?

Individual defining and charting of the constitution of public and private spaces are the focus of *A Preliminary Guide to Public and Private Space in Amsterdam*. The work plays with the idea of an alternate guide based on personal notions of public and private spaces in Amsterdam. One location always leads to another; my path is only, and always, determined by each resident's choices of private and public spaces in the city. Due to the increasing melding of public and private spheres, defining and marking these spaces, as such, is one difficulty revealed through the project.

What constitutes an intervention?

A disruption of normative societal values and codes.

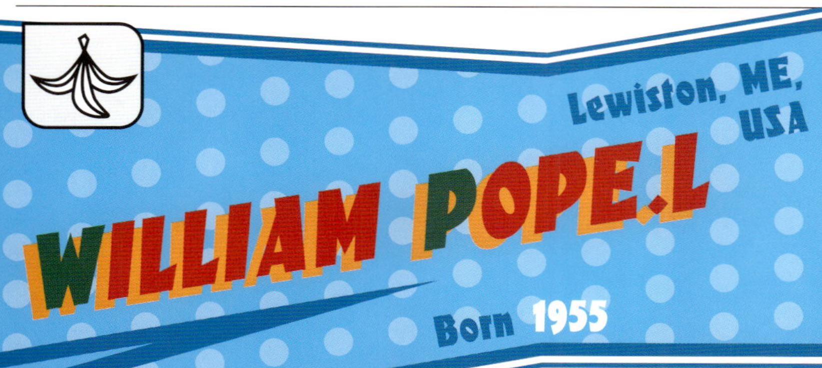

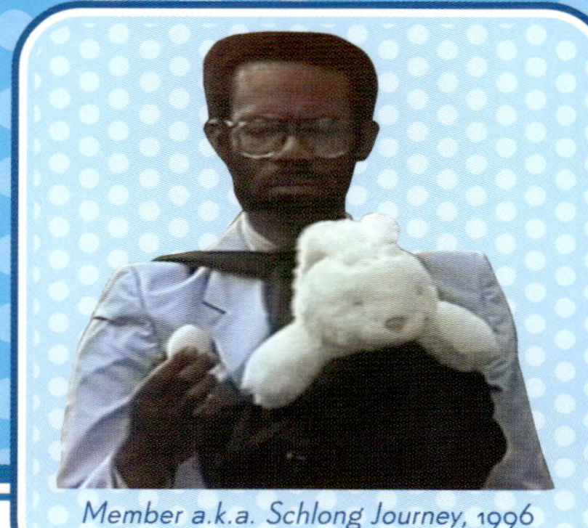

Member a.k.a. Schlong Journey, 1996
Courtesy of William Pope.L

For Biographical Info see page 35

William Pope.L is noted for his outrageous and provocative interventions in outdoor urban areas, one of which is documented in the video *Member (a.k.a. "Schlong Journey")*. On the occasion of this performance, Pope.L walked through the streets of Harlem wearing a white suit, a white bunny, a white egg, and, most visibly, a 12-foot white cardboard tube at crotch level. With his usual laconic irony, Pope.L states, "*Member* is a piece about trying to own whiteness, male whiteness, through the phallus."

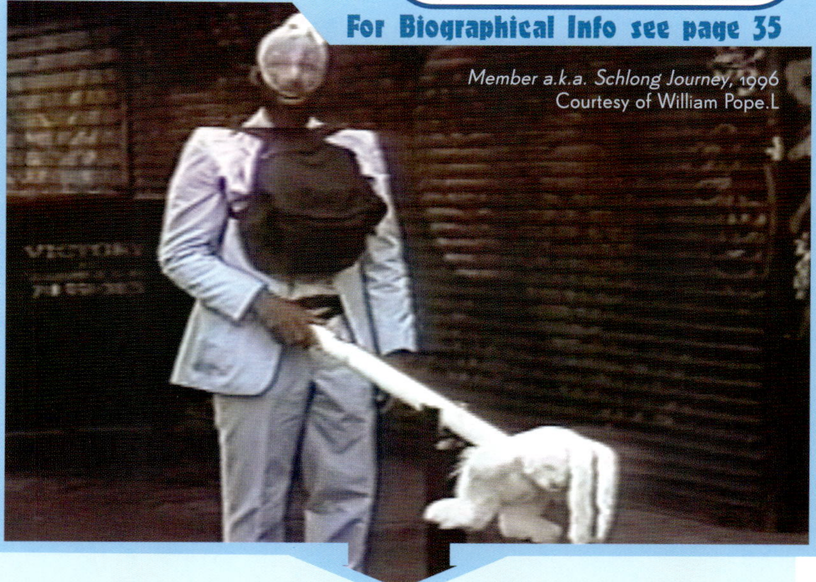

Member a.k.a. Schlong Journey, 1996
Courtesy of William Pope.L

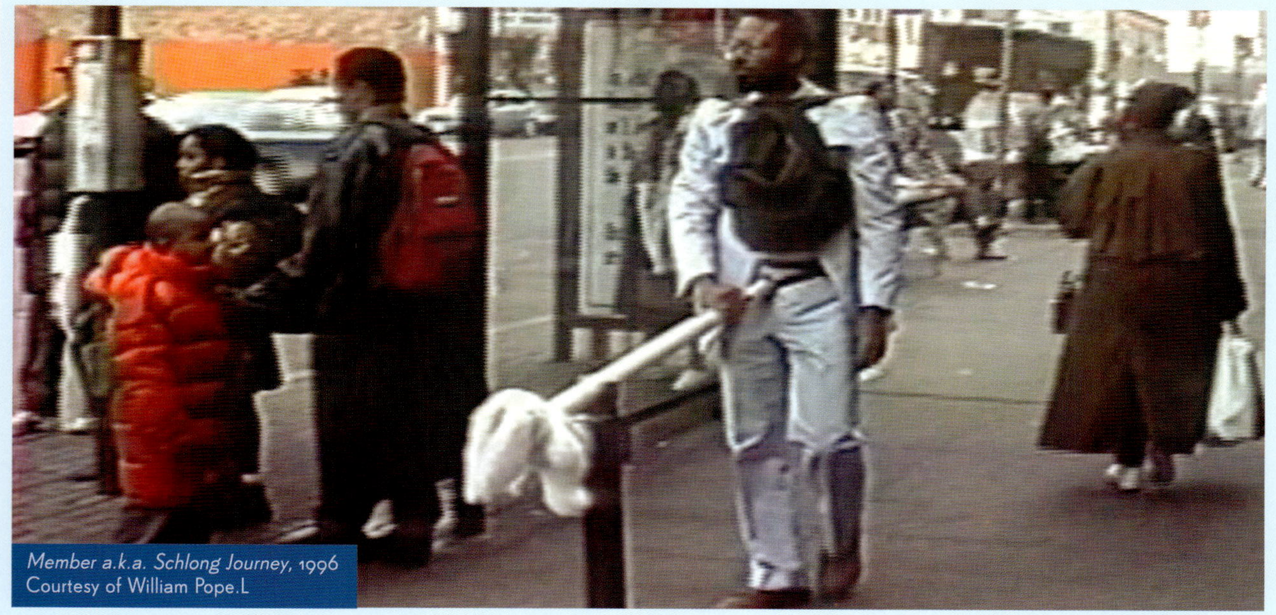

Member a.k.a. Schlong Journey, 1996
Courtesy of William Pope.L

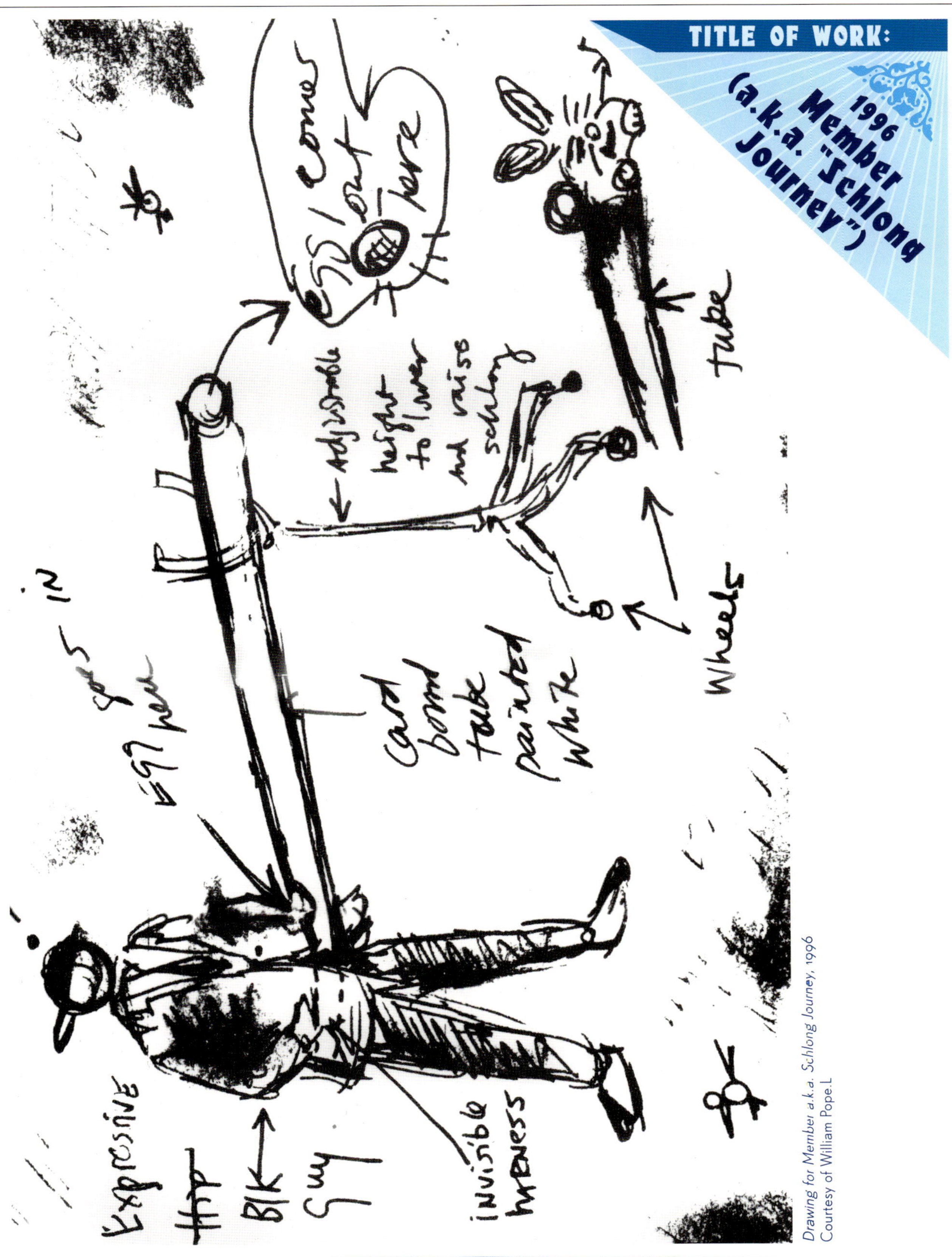

*Drawing for Member a.k.a. Schlong Journey, 1996
Courtesy of William Pope.L*

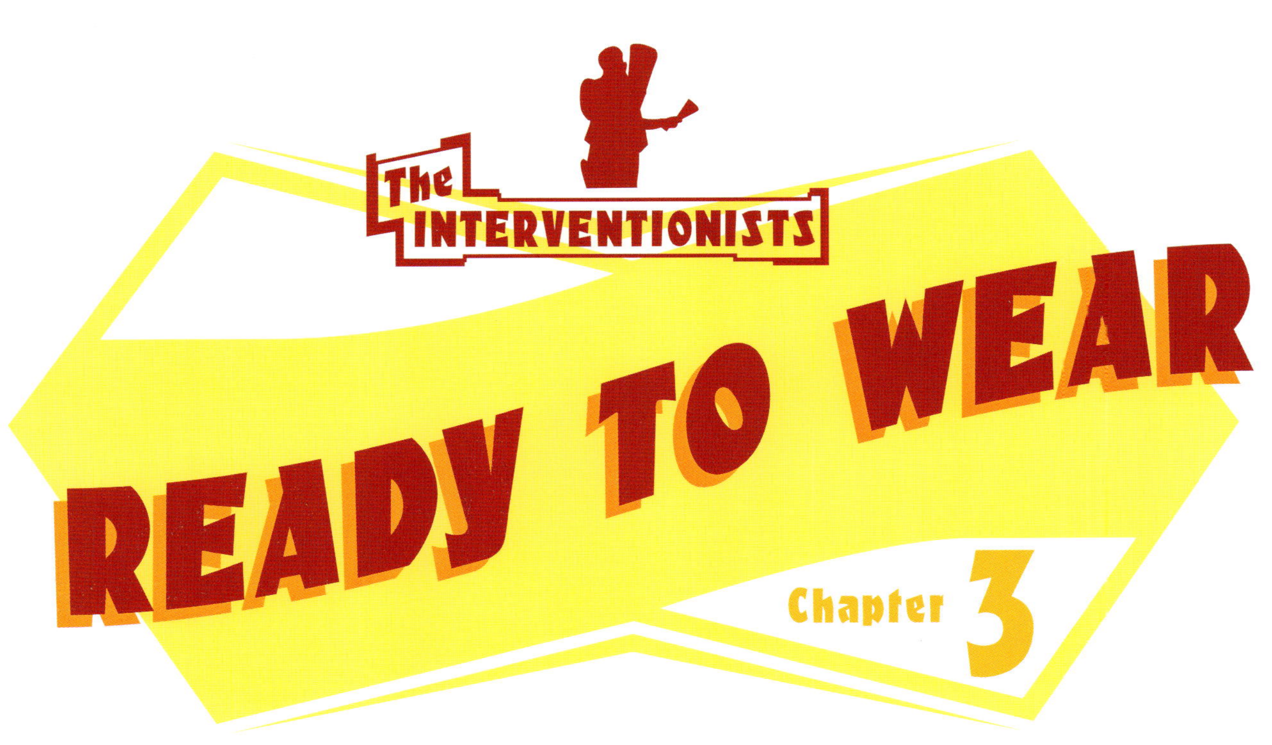

The INTERVENTIONISTS
READY TO WEAR
Chapter 3

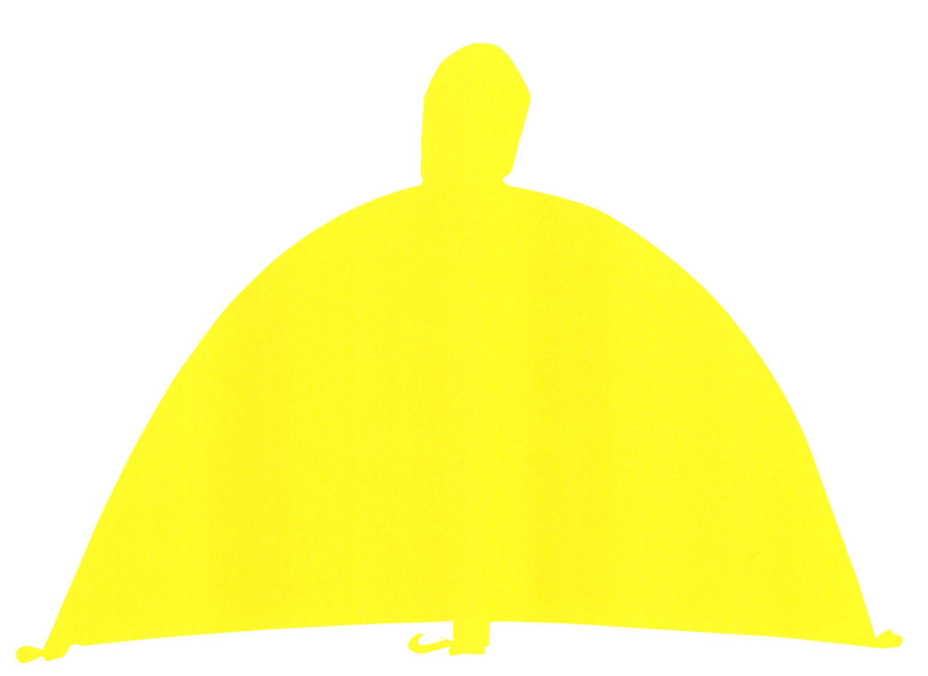

Center for Tactical Magic

Oakland, CA, USA

Founded 1997

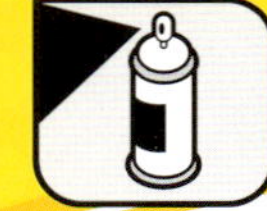
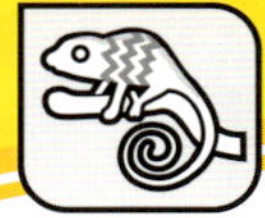
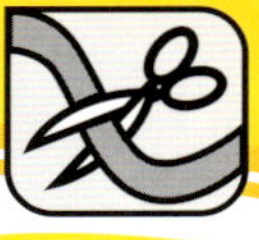

Biographical Info:

The Center for Tactical Magic (CTM), whose members are anonymous, synthesizes its practice from an unusual assortment of professions, including magician, ninja, artist, and private investigator. Conflating this apparently disconnected series of identities, the CTM defines "tactical magic" as "a fusion force derived from seemingly disparate 'art' paradigms and invoked for the purpose of activating the social imagination with notions of responsible citizenship through creative action." (1)

In 2000, the CTM produced the *Cricket Activated Defense System* in response to illegal logging in Northern California's old growth forests. The CTM proposed that when the crickets emit a distress frequency across a broad enough population, they would trigger anti-logging missiles.

In effect, the CTM proposed to arm crickets with weapons for self-defense. Rendering ambiguous the bounds of science and ethics, the work demonstrates the CTM's commitment to illusion and misdirection.

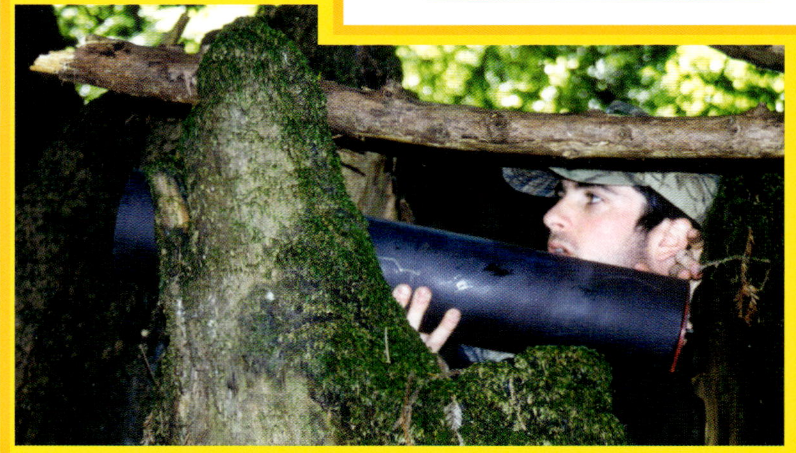

Cricket Activated Defense System, 2000
Courtesy of the Center for Tactical Magic

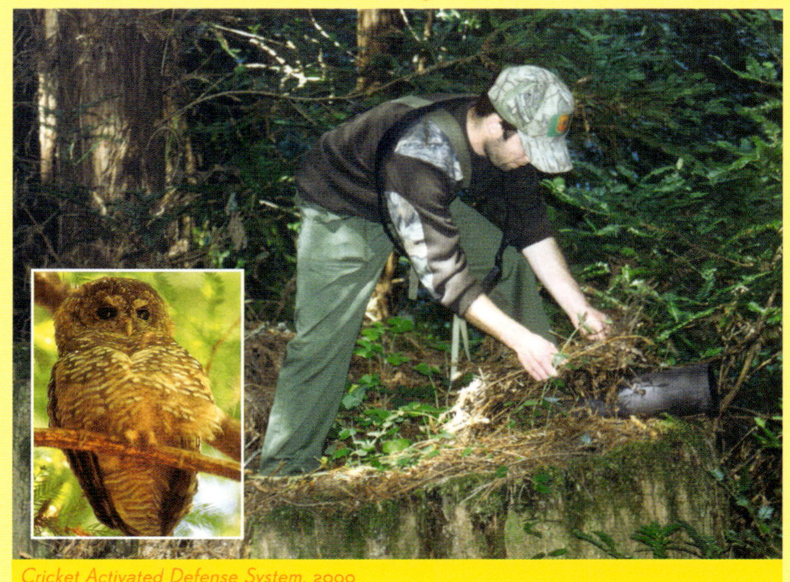

Cricket Activated Defense System, 2000
Courtesy of the Center for Tactical Magic

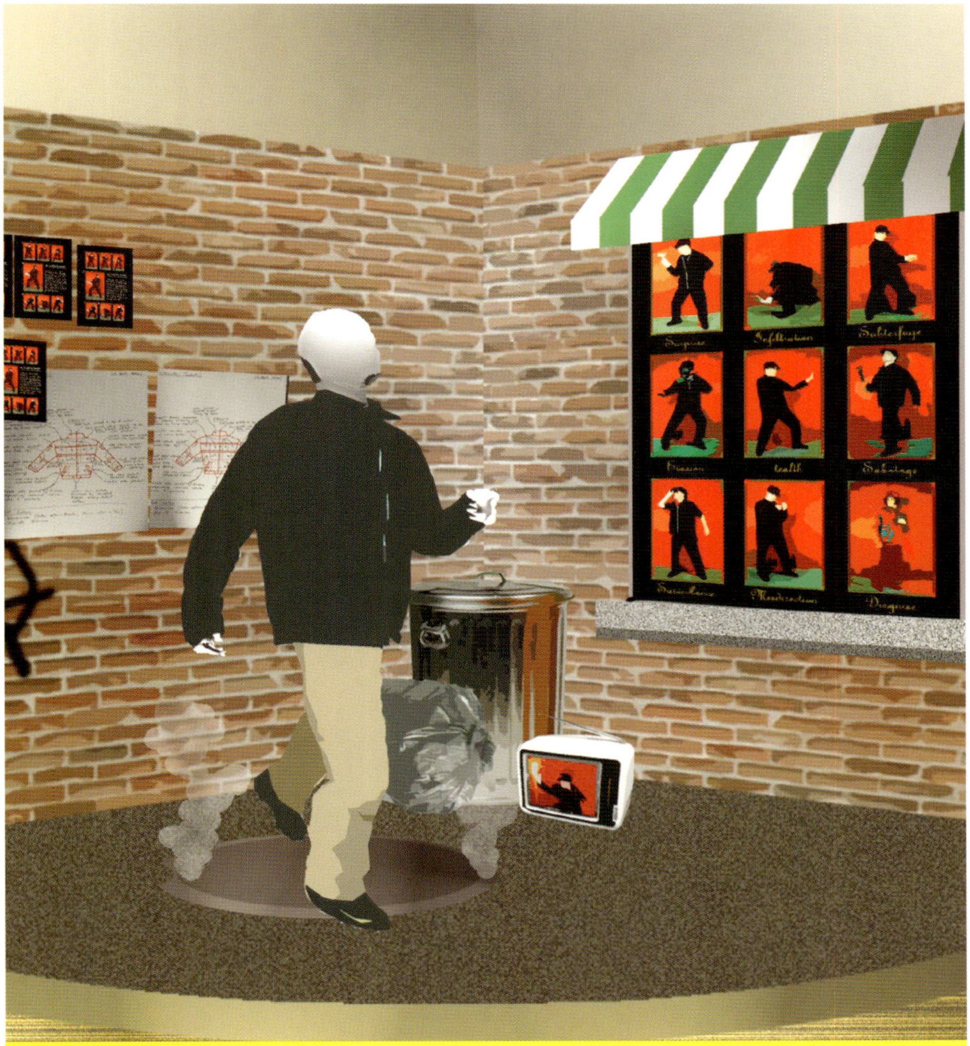

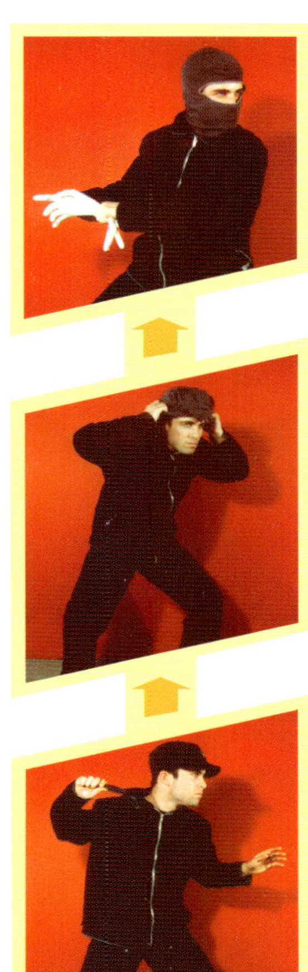

The Ultimate Jacket, 2004
Courtesy of the Center for Tactical Magic

Project Description: *The Ultimate Jacket*, through fashion and design, embodies many of the CTM's core sources. As the CTM describes this project: "At the earliest stages of research, it became apparent to us that private investigators, magicians, and ninjas all used secret pockets in their day-to-day activities." Thus, the CTM developed *The Ultimate Jacket* as "an inconspicuous yet stylish garment concealing no fewer than fifty secret pockets designed to hold a vast array of useful items for everyday interdiction." In its form and use, *The Ultimate Jacket* advocates CTM tactics of stealth, sabotage, and misdirection in "an abrasive-resistant, non-reflective, breathable, waterproof" wearable object. (2)

1. From the website: www.tacticalmagic.org.
2. Ibid

Lucy Orta
London, England
Born 1966

For biographical info see page 29

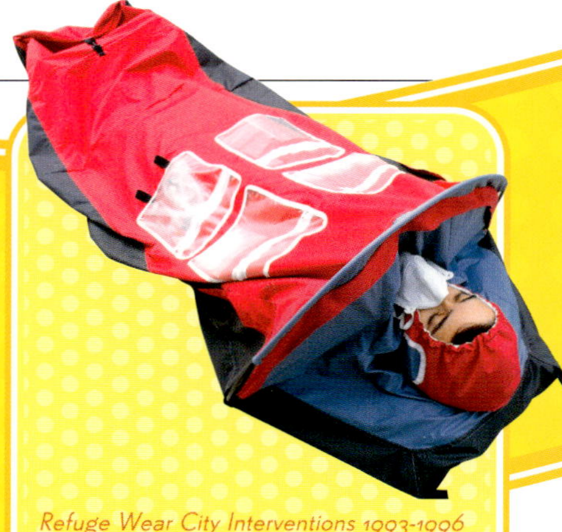

Refuge Wear City Interventions 1993-1996
2001. Photo: JJ Crance

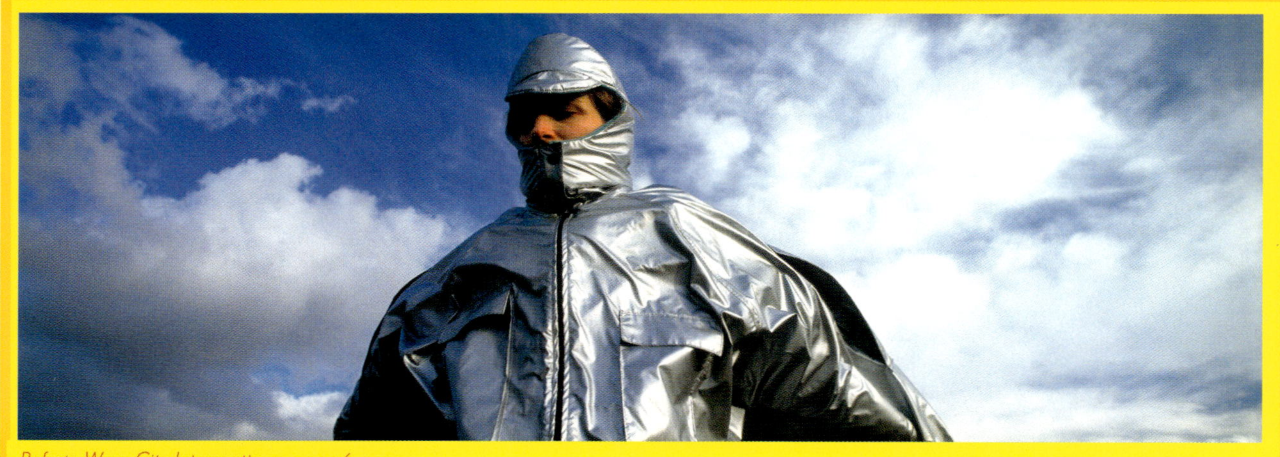

Refuge Wear City Interventions 1993-96, 2001
Photo: JJ Crance

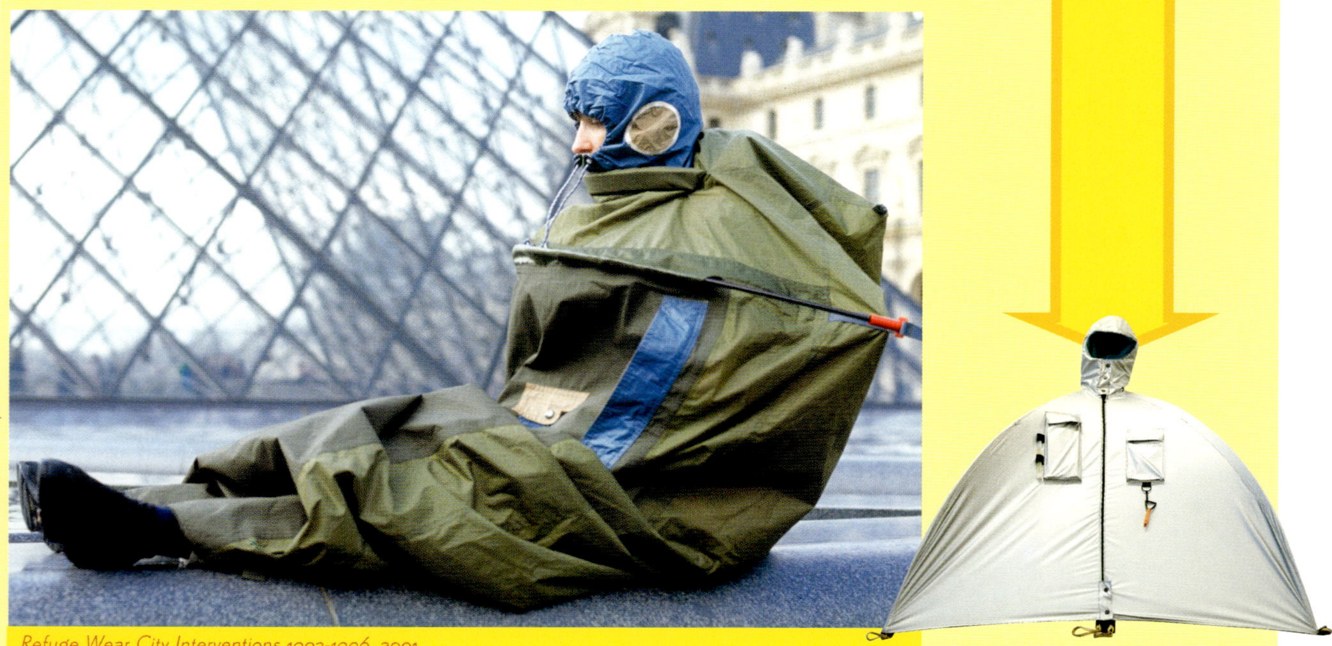

Refuge Wear City Interventions 1993-1996, 2001
Photo: JJ Crance

Refuge Wear — Habitent, 1992/1993
Galerie Anne de Villepoix

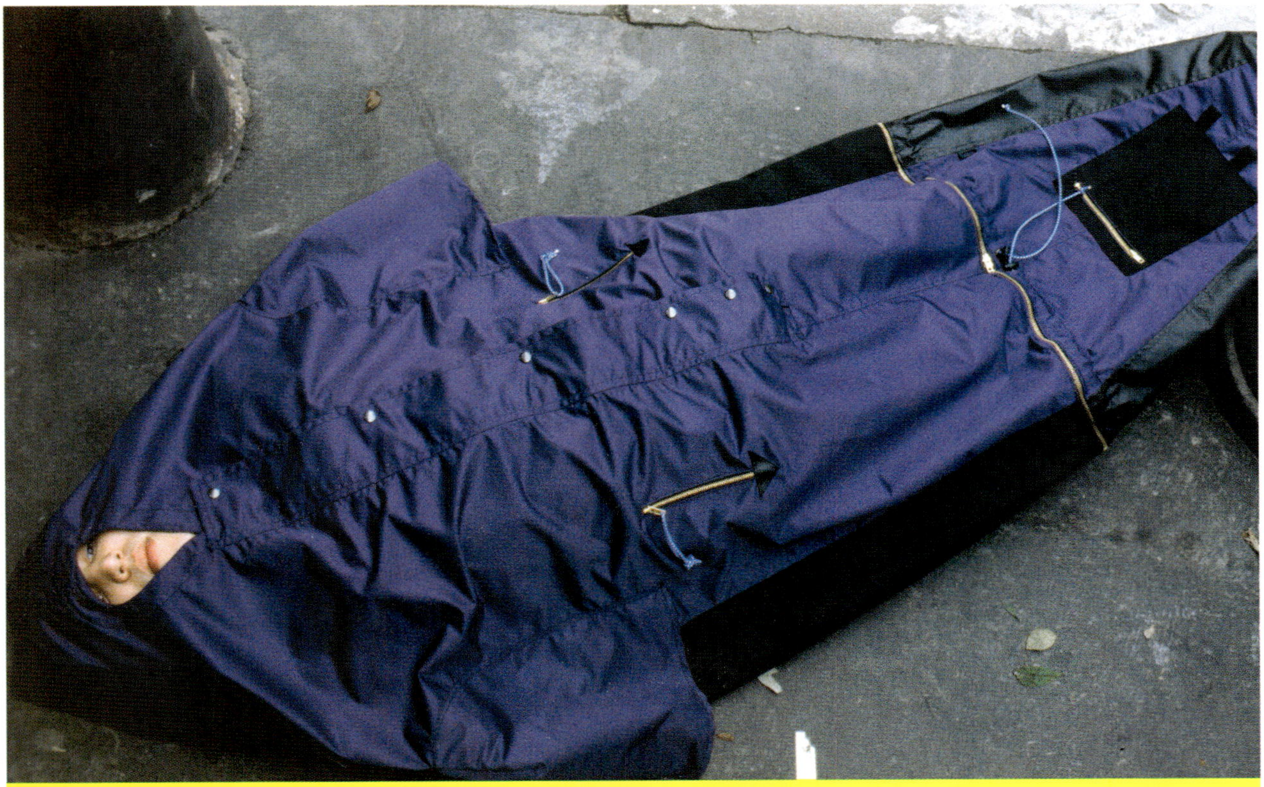

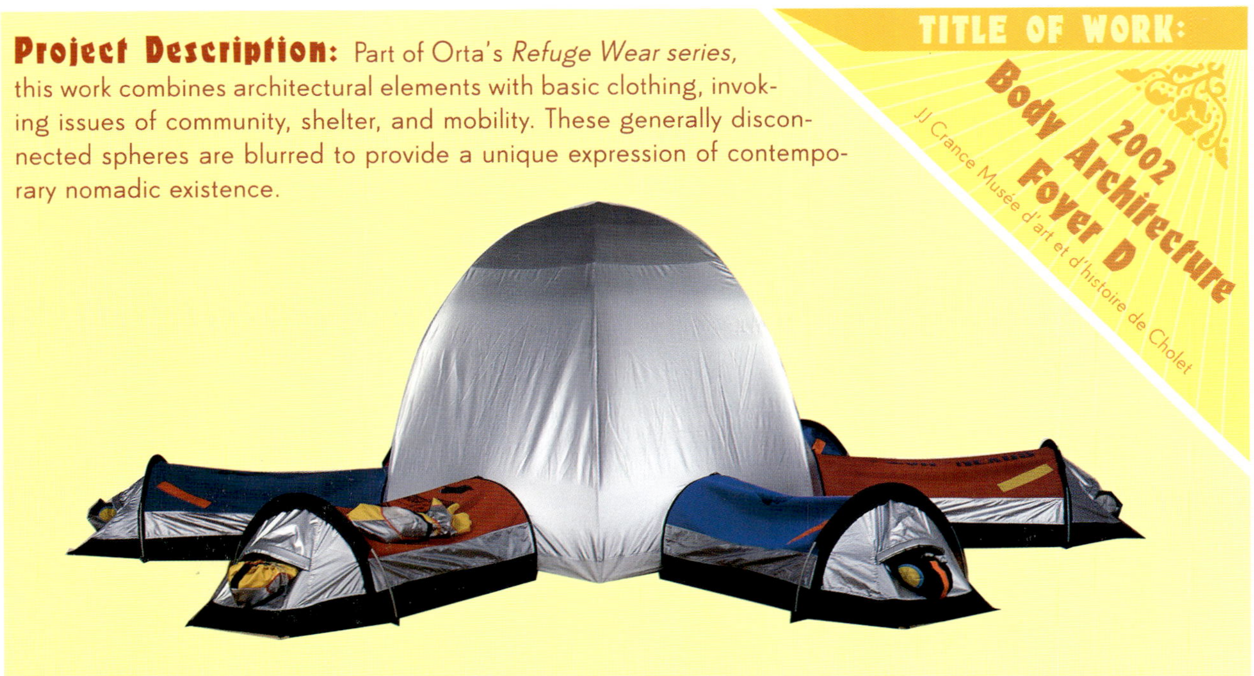

Refuge Wear City Interventions 1993-1996, 2001
Photo: JJ Crance

Project Description: Part of Orta's *Refuge Wear series*, this work combines architectural elements with basic clothing, invoking issues of community, shelter, and mobility. These generally disconnected spheres are blurred to provide a unique expression of contemporary nomadic existence.

Rubén Ortiz-Torres

San Diego, CA, USA
Born 1964

For biographical info see page 49

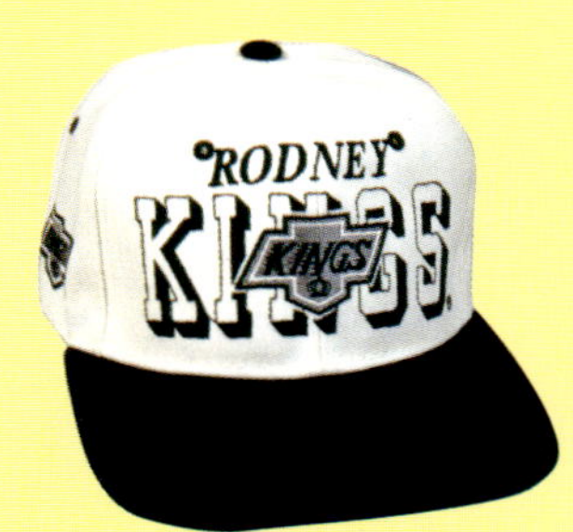

L.A. Rodney Kings (2nd Version), 1993
Courtesy of Rubén Ortiz-Torres
Collection of Museum of Contemporary Art, San Diego

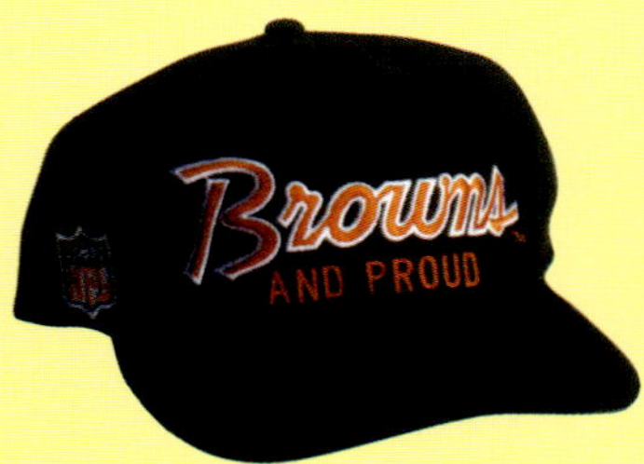

Browns and Proud, 1992
Courtesy of Rubén Ortiz-Torres

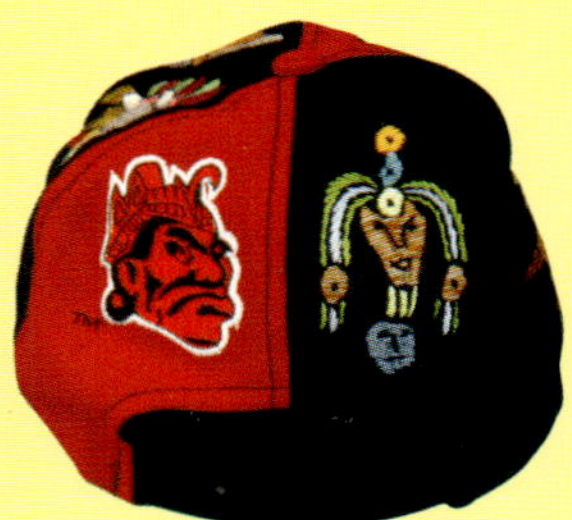

Mayan Aztecs, back, 1995
Embroidered in Guatemala by a Mayan artisan
Courtesy of Rubén Ortiz-Torres
Collection of Museum of Contemporary Art, San Diego

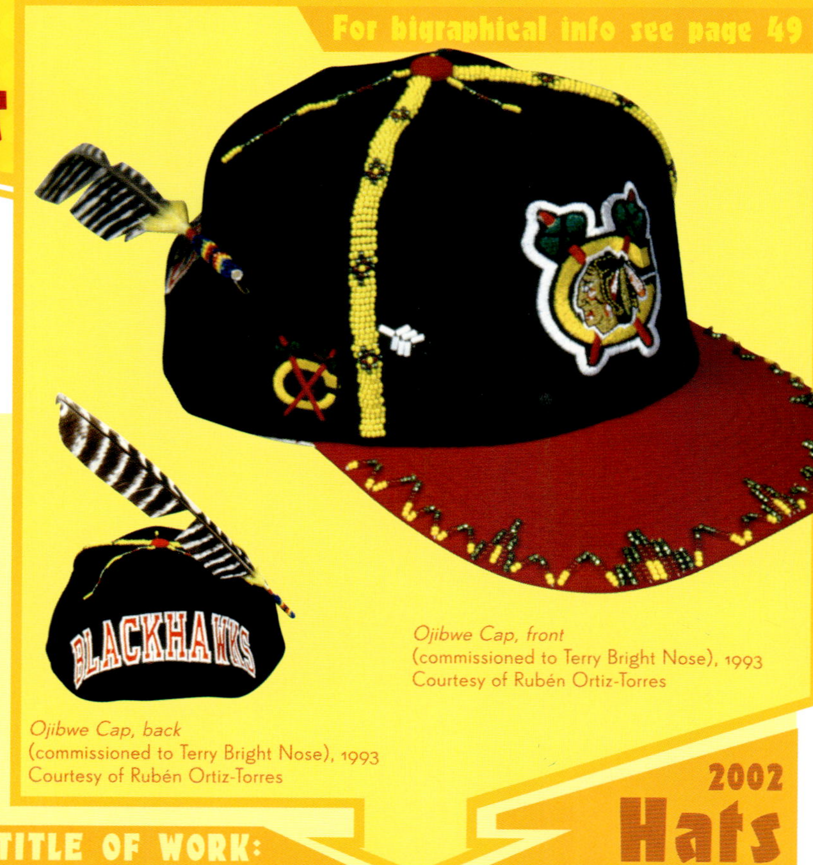

Ojibwe Cap, front
(commissioned to Terry Bright Nose), 1993
Courtesy of Rubén Ortiz-Torres

Ojibwe Cap, back
(commissioned to Terry Bright Nose), 1993
Courtesy of Rubén Ortiz-Torres

TITLE OF WORK: **Hats** 2002

Project Description: Rubén Ortiz-Torres slightly altered the well-known insignias on an array of baseball hats to produce new, culturally charged meanings.

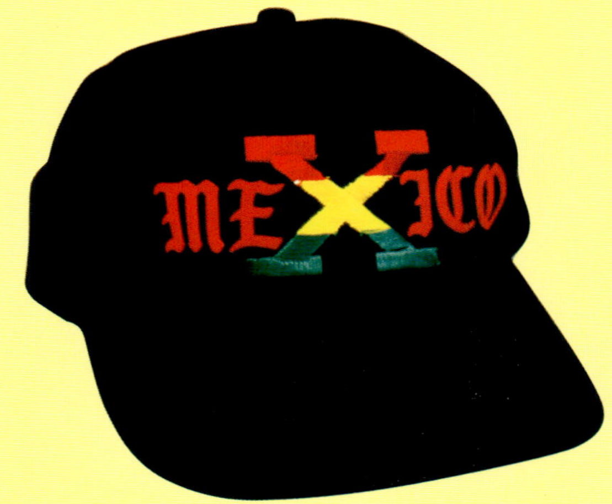

La X en la Frente/Malcolm Mex Cap, 1991
Courtesy of Rubén Ortiz-Torres

Krzysztof Wodiczko

New York, NY & Boston, MA, USA

Born 1943

For biographical info see page 25

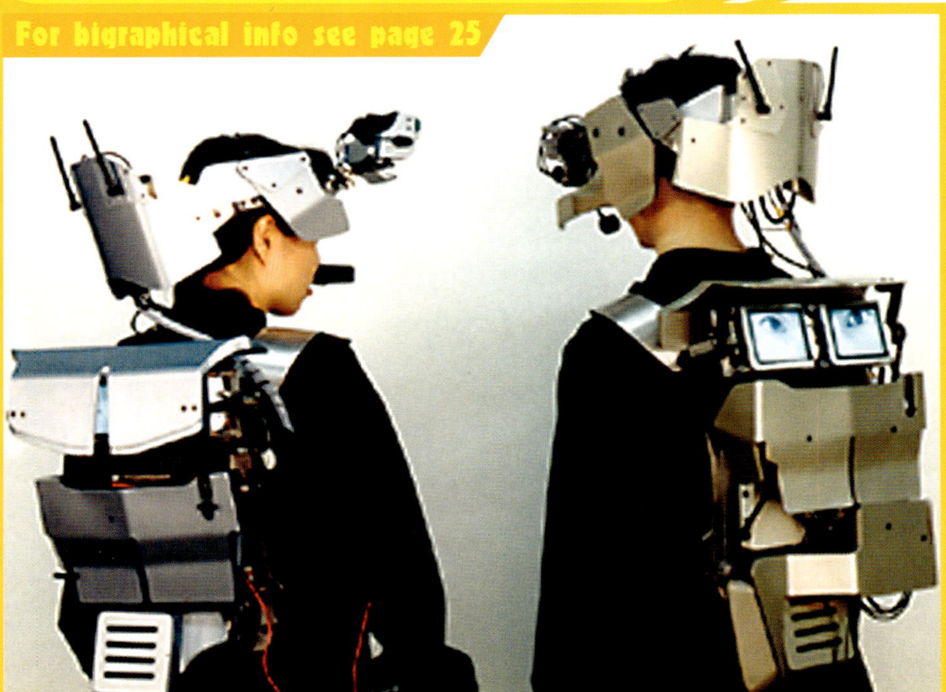

Dis-Armor, 1999-2000
Courtesy of the artist and Galerie Lelong, New York

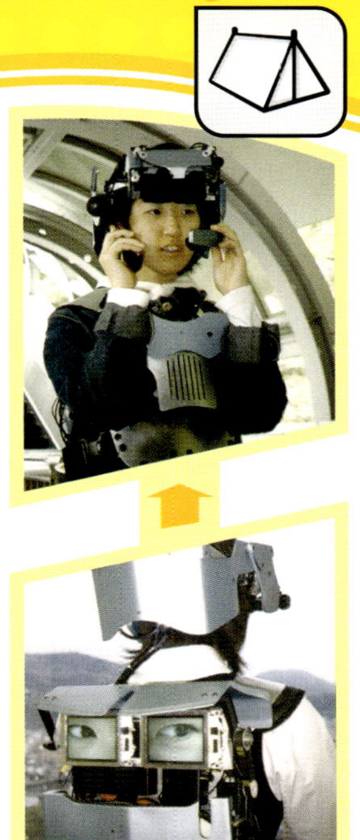

TITLE OF WORK:

Dis-Armor

2004

Project Description: *Dis-Armor* is a video backpack that projects the eyes and voice of its wearer. Through a series of video cameras and microphones, the wearer can communicate with another person standing behind him. In essence, *Dis-Armor* allows users to "face" those whom they ordinarily could not, and thus acts as a catalyst — or metaphor — for difficult dialogue. Originally created for the Hiroshima City Museum of Contemporary Art, *Dis-Armor* might be seen as a sort of technological prosthetic for communication for those otherwise alienated, traumatized, and silenced. In the manifestation for MASS MoCA, *Dis-Armor* was used to help Arab-Americans discuss their experiences since September 11th.

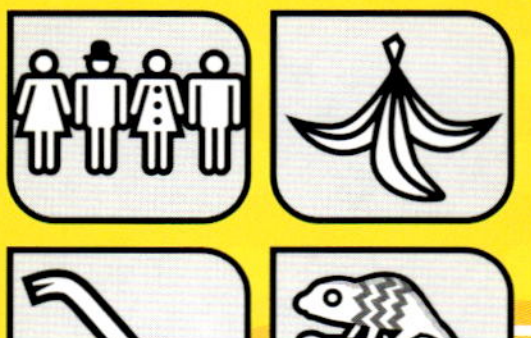

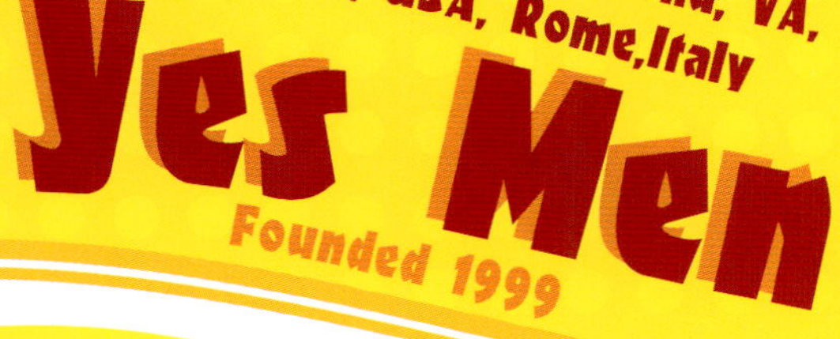

The Yes Men

Pais,NY, San Francisco,CA,, Baton Rouge, LA, Richmond, VA, Orlando, FL , USA, Rome,Italy

Founded 1999

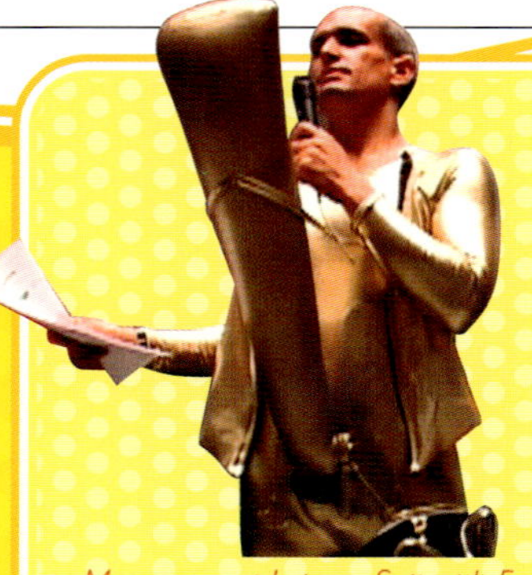

Management Leisure Suit with Employee Visualization Appendage
Courtesy of The Yes Men

Biographical Info:

The Yes Men are an ambiguous, anonymous collective with two "public" members, Mike Bonanno and Andy Bichlbaum. Bonanno and Bichlbaum previously worked on the website ®™ark and in 1999 were approached by Zack Exley, who had registered the domain www.gobush.com. ®™ark used the website to create a satirical political campaign for George W. Bush. During the 2000 presidential campaign, George W. Bush, in reference to the faux website, stated "There ought to be limits to freedom."

In 1999, as an interventionist prelude to the Seattle World Trade Organization protests, the Yes Men developed another spoof website called gatt.org. Sharing the acronym with the General Agreement on Trades and Tariffs, the site was an extended parody, similar in feeling to the *GoBush* project. Although the critique of the World Trade Organization was intended as satire, some visitors actually believed the site to be the home page for the WTO. On one occasion, the Yes Men collective was unexpectedly invited to make public presentations on behalf of the World Trade Organization. Since then, members have appeared in numerous classrooms and business conventions as parodic delegates of the WTO, using absurd Power Point presentations and costumes. The Yes Men recently produced a series of playing cards called "Try 'em," with portraits of Vice President Richard Cheney and Exxon Mobil CEO Lee. R. Raymond, as a response to the *"Most Wanted" playing cards* produced by the Pentagon during the 2002 Iraq War. A documentary about the Yes Men, by *American Movie* directors Sarah Price and Chris Smith, along with Dan Olman, is due in theaters in 2005.

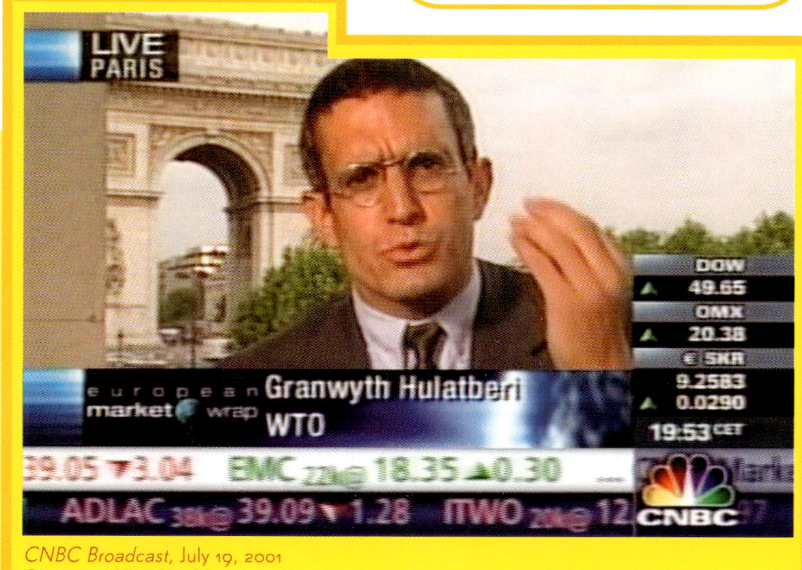

CNBC Broadcast, July 19, 2001
Courtesy of The Yes Men

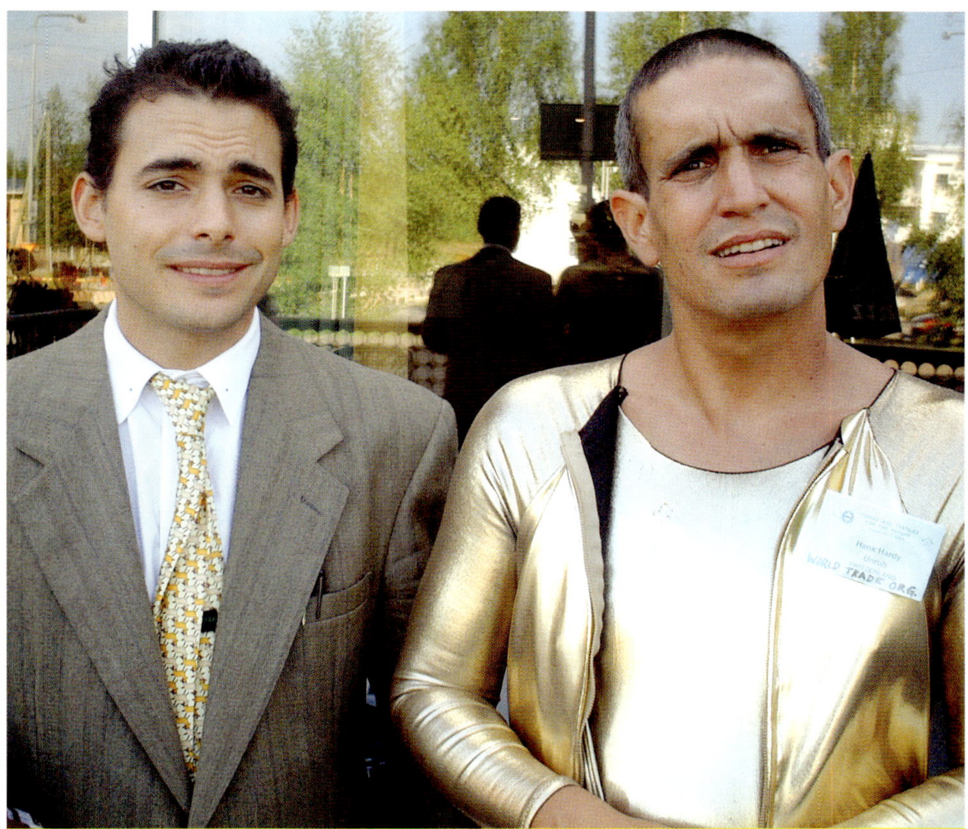

Courtesy of The Yes Men

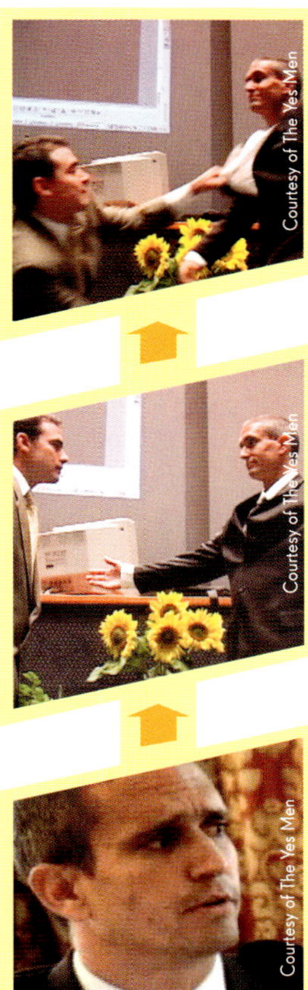

Courtesy of The Yes Men

Courtesy of The Yes Men

Courtesy of The Yes Men

TITLE OF WORK:

2001 *Management Leisure Suit and Breakaway Business Suit*

Project Description: *The Management Leisure Suit* and *Breakaway Business Suit* is a distinctive remnant from a memorable Yes Men lecture in Tampere, Finland. Mistakenly invited to speak on behalf of the World Trade Organization at a conference titled "Textile of the Future," Bichlbaum (calling himself Hank Hardy Unruh) spoke on the dangers of equating freedom with the free market. Mr. Unruh made astounding claims such as one that the U.S. Civil War (in which slavery became illegal) was a useless exercise in freedom, since slave labor then led to remote sweatshop labor.

As his over-the-top, farcical finale, Bichlbaum (as Unruh) tore off his business suit superman-like to reveal the *"Management Leisure Suit."* A golden leotard with an inflatable three-foot phallus, the suit came equipped with a video interface system that allowed surveillance of employees, and a device purported to deliver electric shocks to lax workers.

20010511-17 - May 11-17, 2001: Granwyth Hulatberi-Hulatberi-Smith instructs the Isle of Man on the several rights of sovereign nations [WTO]

Date: Fri, 11 May 2001 15:12:39 +0100
From: "Carse, Steve"
<XXXXXXXXXXXXXXXXXXXXX>
To: "'info@gatt.org'" <info@gatt.org>
Subject: Gibraltar

Could you advise me of the relationship of Gibraltar to the WTO?

Stephen Carse
Government Economic Adviser
Economic Affairs Division
The Treasury
Illiam Dhone House
2 Circular Road
Douglas
Isle of Man

XXXXXXXXXXXXXXXXXXXXX
Date: Fri, 11 May 2001 15:23:24 -0400
From: The World Trade Organization
<info@gatt.org>
To: "Carse, Steve"
<XXXXXXXXXXXXXXXXXXXXX>
Subject: Re: Gibraltar

Yes. Gibraltar is a little plot of land at the tip of Spain, right across from Morocco, under the governorship of Britain. The WTO is the World Trade Organization, which was created to allow a greater freedom for corporate entities to engage in their activities unhampered by the protective strategies of democratically elected governments.

Why do you ask?

Date: Fri, 11 May 2001 16:12:35 +0100
From: "Carse, Steve"
<XXXXXXXXXXXXXXXXXXXXX>
To: 'The World Trade Organization'
<info@gatt.org>
Subject: RE: Gibraltar

My enquiry was to do with whether Gibraltar has a relationship with WTO that was similar to the one we, the Isle of Man, has. Your response does not help me on this. Can you say anything more e.g. is it free to have its own exemptions?
Date: Fri, 11 May 2001 19:58:05 -0400
From: The World Trade Organization
<info@gatt.org>

To: "Carse, Steve"
<XXXXXXXXXXXXXXXXXXXXX>
Subject: RE: Gibraltar

No land on earth may be considered free, if freedom means to engage in activities that endanger the well-being of corporate enterprise. So long as, and only so long as, nations understand their place on earth as being in service of, and at the beck of, the driving forces of economics, so shall these nations be afforded a place at the right hand of power. But let the tiniest nation—yea, even Gibraltar, even the Isle of Man—arise upon the poop-deck of declamation... let it wield for even a moment the baton of popular power against the furnace of progress... let it stagger drunkenly into the path of the train of misguidedness... then, indeed, shall that nation see the full force of our petulance and our peevishness unleashed squarely upon its head, and all its head's heads as well.

(Sorry for that rant—we have a bug on our shoulder since the latest round of dangerous-idea circulation masquerading as protest.)

Best,
Granwyth Hulatberi-Hulatberi-Smith

Date: Sat, 12 May 2001 00:24:52 -0000
From: Jimmy Choi Kam Chuen
<XXXXXXXXXXXXXXXXXXXXX>
To: info@gatt.org

Dear Sir,
Appreciate very much if you can tell me the designation of Mr. Granwyth Hulatberi-Hulatberi-Smith in your organization.

Thanks very much
Choi Kam Chuen

Date: Sat, 12 May 2001 07:36:13 -0400
From: The World Trade Organization
<info@gatt.org>
To: Jimmy Choi Kam
Chuen<XXXXXXXXXXXXXXXXXXXXX>
Subject: Granwyth Hulatberi-Hulatberi-Smith

Dear Mr. Chuen, Mr. Hulatberi-Hulatberi-Smith is a Counselor in our Market Access Division, and often does first-level public relations assessment.
Yours, Gram Hunnerd

Date: Mon, 14 May 2001 09:24:23 +0100
From: "Carse, Steve"
<XXXXXXXXXXXXXXXXXXXXX>
To: 'The World Trade Organization'
<info@gatt.org>
Subject: RE: Gibraltar

I have absolutely no idea what your reply is all about. May I just repeat my simple request? Is Gibraltar a member of WTO in its own right or is it a member through the United Kingdom?

Date: Mon, 14 May 2001 12:19:58 -0400
From: The World Trade Organization
<info@gatt.org>
To: "Carse, Steve"
<XXXXXXXXXXXXXXXXXXXXX>
Subject: RE: Gibraltar

Now Mr. Carse, there's no reason to get uppity. We are on your side—you, the little man who plays by the rules. We are here to help you understand the exigencies of the global playground, so that you may understand the pathways through which you and your government MAY move and those through which you MAY NOT. Given this, it is hard to say why you would seek to endanger your standing through impatient words. If I were you, given the circumstances, I would question whether my nation (the Isle of Man, in your case) is really all that interested in benefitting from trade.

But to answer your question: Gibraltar's business arrangements are not the affair of other governments, either yours or those of more populous lands. Gibraltar is free and sovereign to enter into trade arrangements with the enterprises that choose it, and it would be a violation of Gibraltar—and I mean that in the full sense—to suggest that the whim of the people—its own, or those of other lands—can impede those arrangements.

With very best wishes,
Granwyth Hulatberi-Hulatberi-Smith

The Yes Men

February 2, 2004

Which practices and/or movements associated with the visual culture of the 1980s were you most engaged by, influenced by, or active in?

In the 1980s, we were heavily influenced by cannibalism. Good thing we outgrew it!

When the viewer experiences your work, what type(s) of relationships do you hope to establish?

We hope that people who see this stuff will be as shocked and outraged as we were when we experienced it ourselves. We want the viewer to come away from the experience wanting to act, needing to help effect progressive political change. We also want them to laugh... they must become laughing revolutionaries.

What spheres do you find appropriate for your work?

Every sphere we can get to is appropriate for our work. We have no weight or size limit for the moment.

How do you see your work operating in larger social movements?

Our work is a small part of a global movement that is interested in derailing the kind of no-holds-barred capitalism that is starving the world's poor and ruining the environment. Our role is a tiny one in that overall movement, where people are engaged in thousands of other approaches to the issues. It is the people doing the social organizing, legal battles, etc., that are doing the real important work, which we are trying to support.

How does your work situate the local and the global?

We operate globally because we had the opportunity to represent a global organization. Locally, we try not to shop at Wal-Mart or eat at McDonald's, and we pay our local taxes.

How do you use preexisting visual forms or discourses in your work? To what end(s) do you use them?

We have been using Microsoft PowerPoint. We do this to blend in when we are at business meetings, and because it looks like shit, which is funny.

What do you consider the advantages and/or disadvantages to collaboration, compared to individualized forms of art production?

Collaboration is great when you are having a generative time - passing things back and forth - you can work fast, do more, etc.

Collaboration is bad news if you have to collaborate with Pol Pot or Hitler.

How do you see humor as functioning in your art? What about delight and pleasure in your work?

Humor is the sugarcoating that enables us to swallow bitter pills. We delight in that.

How does technology function in your work? In general, what is your relationship to technology?

We use technology in whatever way we can, the way cops use batons and crooks use blackjacks.

In the past two decades, public space has become increasingly privatized as private space and private lives have become increasingly subject to the expanded structures and technologies of surveillance. How might your work respond to or demonstrate this scenario?

Well, when we impersonated the WTO at a textiles conference in Tampere, Finland we built a golden suit with a three-foot long golden phallus that had a mock television screen on the end of it. The premise was that managers will be able to see workers in sweatshops and manage them more efficiently... it was a new technology the WTO was introducing. I think that addresses the condition...

The word intervention is central to the exhibition: what constitutes an intervention?

We prefer the type of intervention when someone, or something, who is in a subaltern position disrupts normal flows of power and capital....

Where do you find support for your work?

Creative Capital Foundation
Herb Alpert Foundation
Our Own Wallets
Generous friends...

Can there be revolutionary art without a revolution?

Sure!

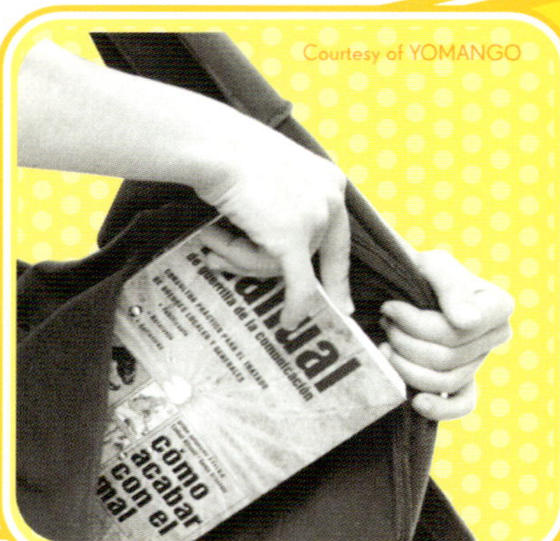

Courtesy of YOMANGO

Biographical Info:

The name **YOMANGO** is taken from fusing the name of the popular European clothing company Mango with the Spanish slang term for "I steal." The Spanish anarchist collective, with a rotating cast of members, considers its name to also be a brand name for a lifestyle. In their words, YOMANGO, "like all other major brand names, is not so much about selling as about promoting a lifestyle. In this case, the YOMANGO lifestyle consists of shoplifting as a form of social disobedience and direct action against multinational corporations."[1] In the tradition of Abbie Hoffman's *Steal This Book*, YOMANGO conflates illegality as petty theft with larger forms of civil disobedience and social change.

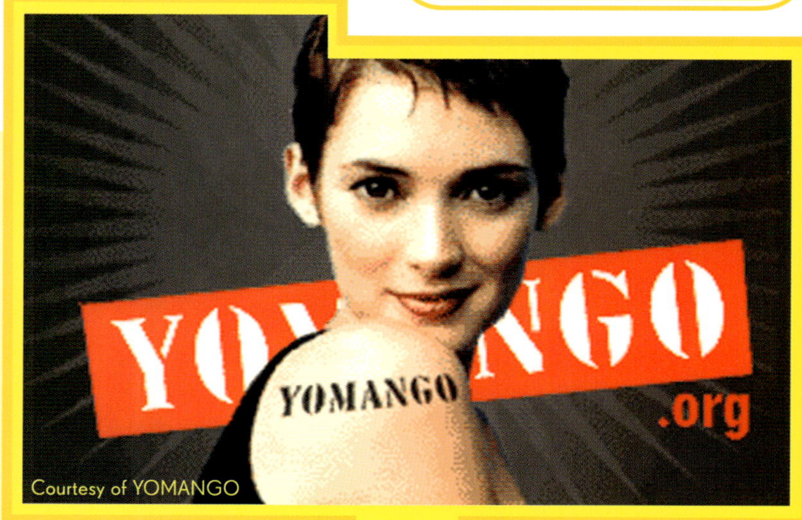

Courtesy of YOMANGO

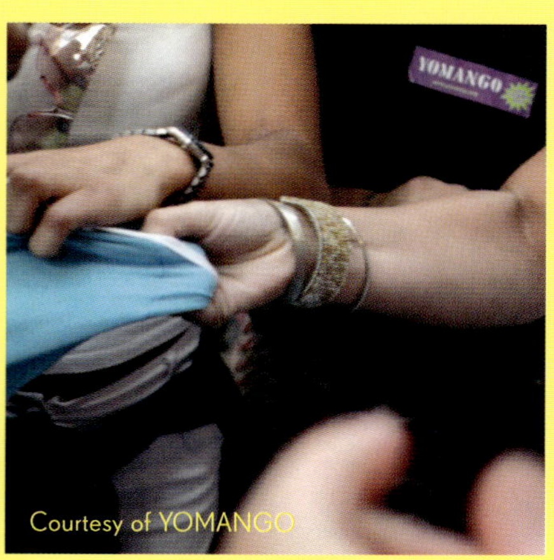

Courtesy of YOMANGO

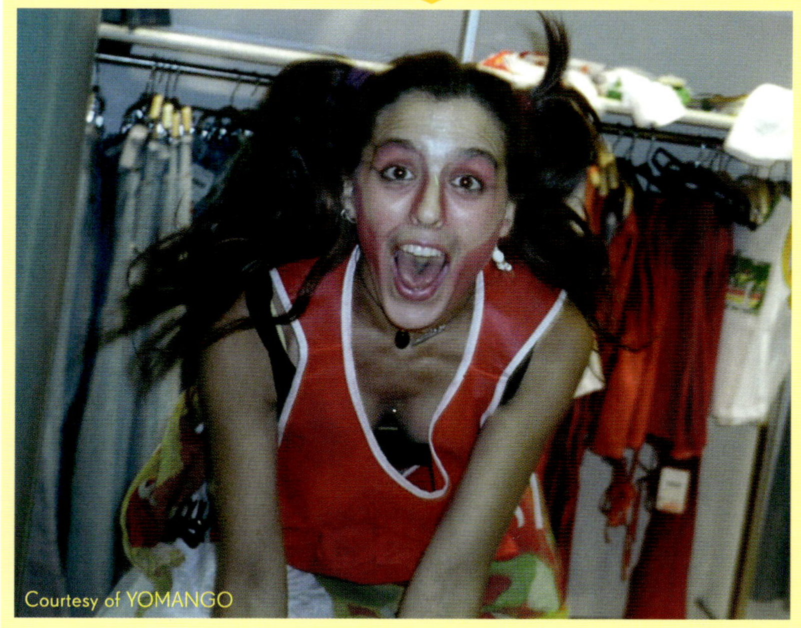

Courtesy of YOMANGO

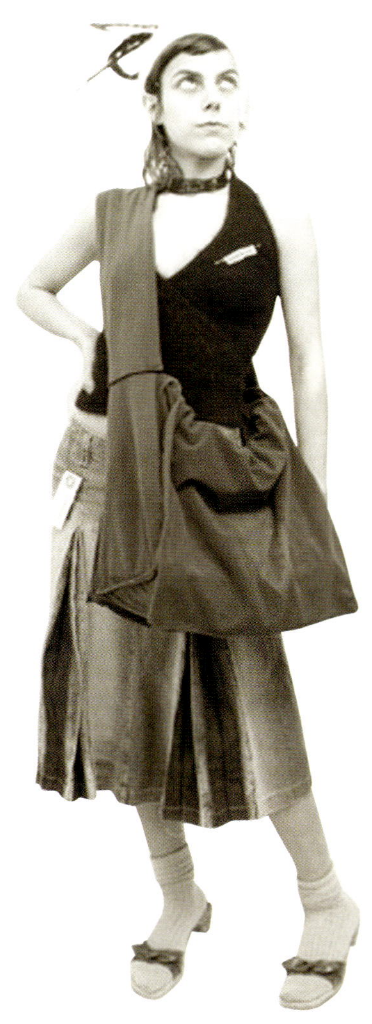

YOMANGO Bag, 2004. Courtesy of YOMANGO

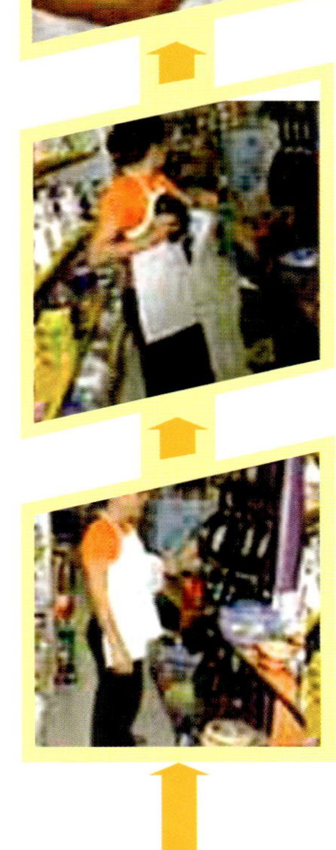

Project Description: YOMANGO has produced a shopping bag for shoplifting, offering it as a series of sewing patterns with which visitors can make their own version. YOMANGO likes to think of this work as "clothing for civil disobedience."

"This magic bag makes objects disappear. It's ergonomically designed to be the ultimate shoplifting utensil. It is simple to make and is based on the same principles as the devices used by magicians and other tricksters. YOMANGO converts going to the mall into a magical experience." (2)

1. Email from YOMANGO to Nato Thompson, Jan 3, 2004
2. Email from YOMANGO to Nato Thompson, Jan, 11, 2004

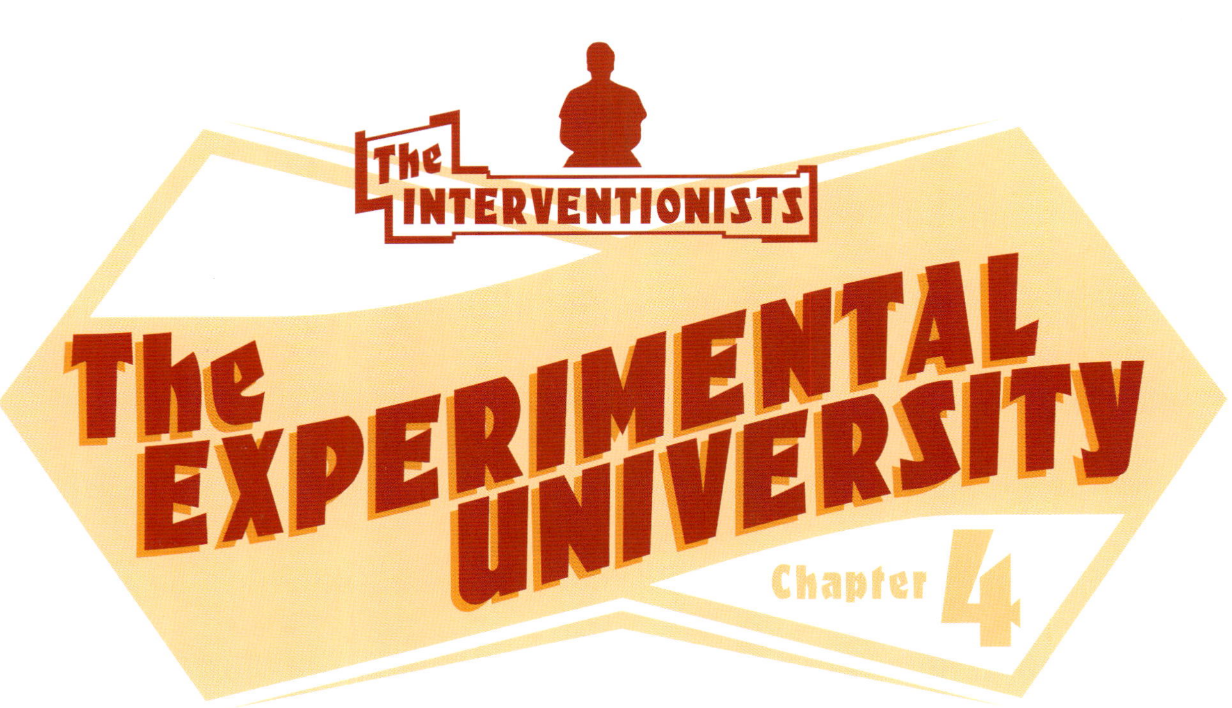

The INTERVENTIONISTS
The EXPERIMENTAL UNIVERSITY
Chapter 4

16 Beaver

New York, NY
USA

Founded 1998

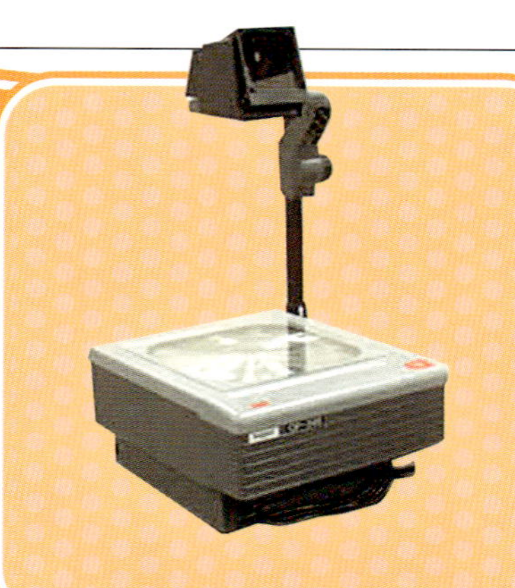

Biographical Info:

16 Beaver Street is a network of artists, curators, writers, thinkers, and activists who regularly convene on lower Manhattan to discuss issues, exchange ideas, and raise questions. Some members are "regulars" involved on a day-to-day basis, while others participate more sporadically. 16 Beaver Street's organization is flexible and open to anyone. In addition to artist presentations, political discussions, organized happenings, lunches, walks, parties, and film screenings, participants regularly share and discuss readings.

A more ambitious manifestation of the familiar book group, 16 Beaver has become a form of social sculpture that German artist Joseph Beuys referred to as an "ongoing conference."

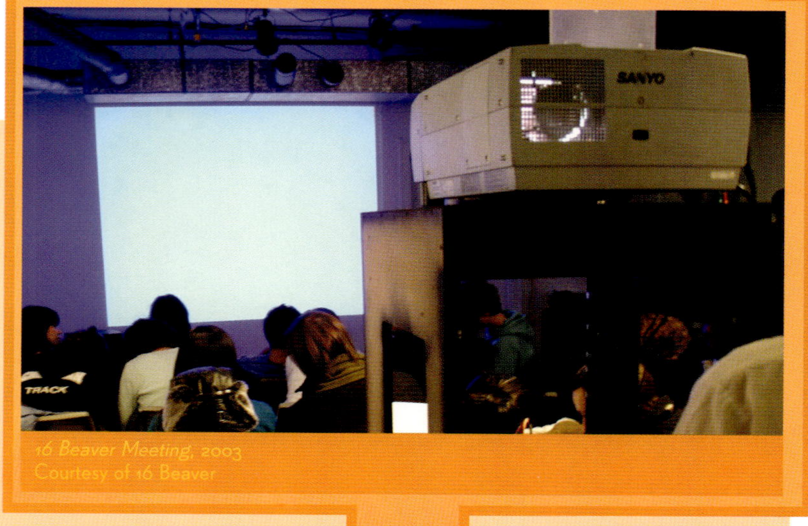

16 Beaver Meeting, 2003
Courtesy of 16 Beaver

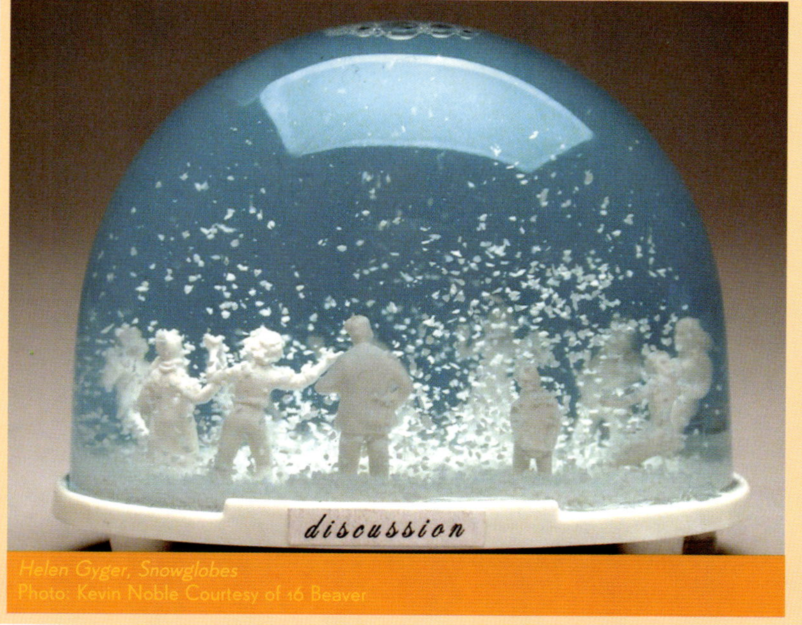

Helen Gyger, Snowglobes
Photo: Kevin Noble Courtesy of 16 Beaver

16Beavergroup*   1 Strength or continuity derived from an initial effort. **2** A directing influence or guidance, spec. (esp. in the Society of Friends) a spiritual indication of the proper course of action in any case. **3a** Strong predilection, liking, or fondness for, or devotion to something. **b** An instance of affection (now rare). Formerly also, an act of kindness. **4** The fitting moment; the momentary conjunction of circumstances, esp. as affording an opportunity. **5** 'many, much', 'having, involving, containing, etc., many' (many variously connoting 'two or more', 'three or more', 'several', or 'a large number' in different contexts) **6** The state of having time at one's own disposal. Opportunity afforded by freedom from occupations. time remaining, sufficient time. **7** The course taken by something in relation to the point towards which it is moving; the line towards anything in its relation to a given line; a point to or from which a person moves, turns, etc. the course of development of thought, effort, or action; a distinct tendency or trend; consistent progress. **8** Differing from itself in different circumstances, at different times, or in different parts; changeful; varied. **9** A deep resonant sound. **10** An index of the average level of share prices on the New York Stock Exchange at any time, based on the daily price of a selection of representative stocks. **11** He or him himself, I or me myself, it itself, she or her herself, we or us ourselves, you yourself, you yourselves, they or them themselves. **12** An engine or motor vehicle with sixteen cylinders. **13a** Move, set in motion. **b** Utter, cause (a voice or sound) to be heard. Also, make (a gesture). **c** Move (a thing) from the normal place or position; shift, displace. **14** A collection of saints'lives or similar stories. **15a** Steady or uniform in action, procedure, or occurrence; esp. recurring or repeated at fixed times, recurring at short uniform intervals. **b** Pursuing s definite course or observing a uniform principle of action or conduct. Now esp. observing fixed times for or never failing in the performance of certain actions or duties. **16** A state of supreme happiness.

*OXFORD ENGLISH DICTIONARY - THE USEFUL EDITION
 EDITED BY AYREEN ANASTAS

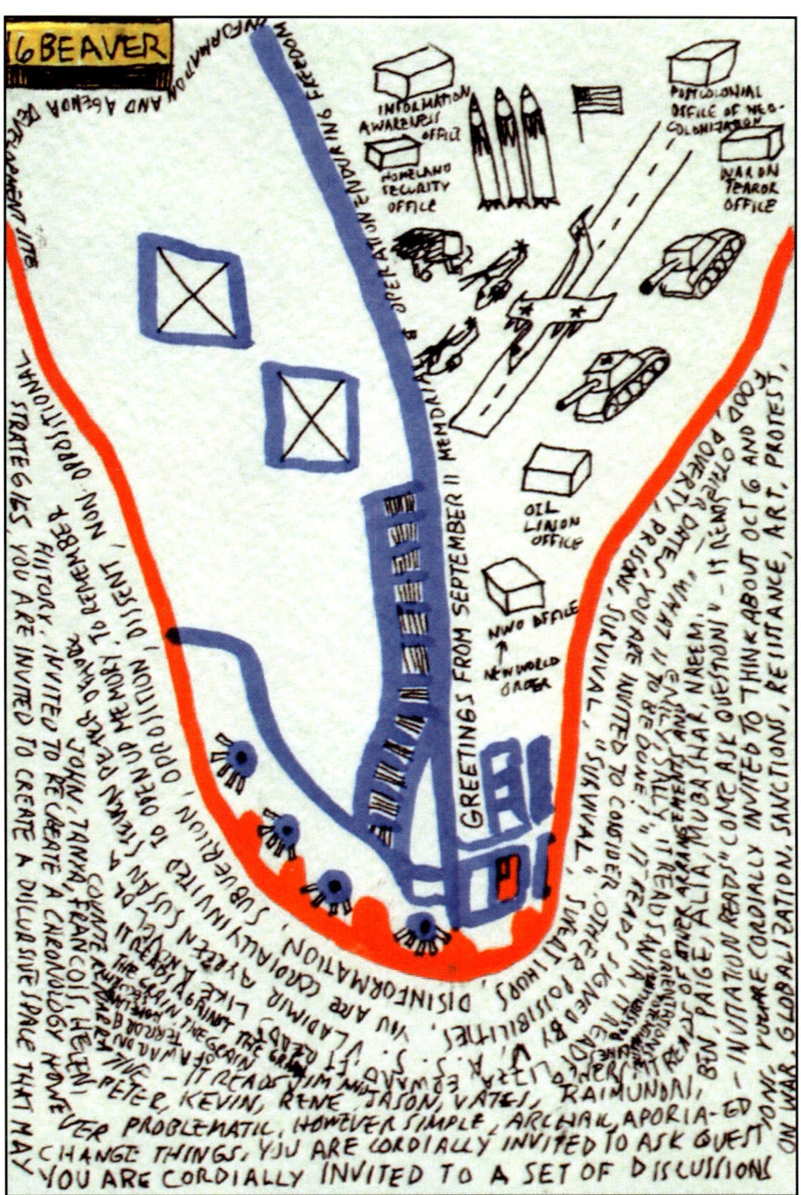

Lower Manhattan Postcard. Courtesy of 16 Beaver

Project Description: For this work 16 Beaver will act as a conversational New York satellite to MASS MoCA. During the course of this exhibition the collective will organize three talks (one of which will occur at MASS MoCA and the other two at 16 Beaver Street in New York City). The discussion at MASS MoCA will be aptly titled "Art Collectives that Don't Make Art," in which different social networks of radicals, artists, and thinkers will be invited to discuss their unique, and indefinable, process. The series at 16 Beaver will work under the heading "Yippies, Yuppies and Interventionists" to explore the diverse range of social issues raised in *The Interventionists* exhibition.

TITLE OF WORK:
2004
16Beaver
Mass MoCA Series
The Ongoing Conference

The **Atlas Group**

Founded 1999

Beiruf, Lebanon
New York, NY,
USA

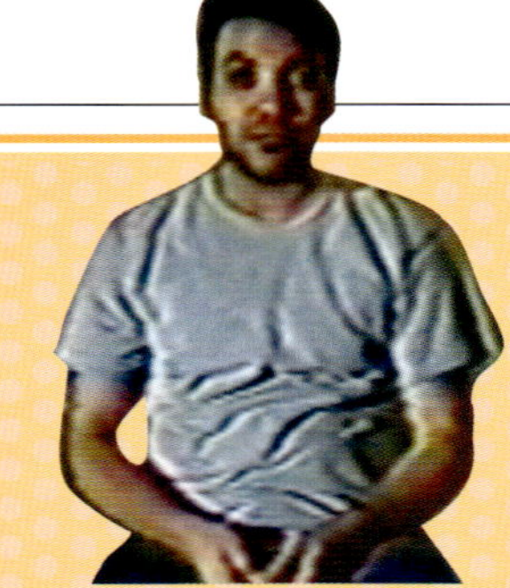

Hostage: The Bachor Tapes Tape #17 Video Still
Produced by Souheil Bachar/The Atlas Group in
collaboration with c-hundred film corp, 1999
Courtesy of The Atlas Group /Sfeir-Semler
Gallerie/Anthony Reynolds Gallery.
Copyright: The Atlas Group

Biographical Info:

The Atlas Group locates, preserves, studies, and produces audio, visual, literary, and other documents that shed light on the recent history of Lebanon, with particular emphasis on the war years of 1975 to 1990. The documents are divided between the Atlas Group's archives located in Beirut and New York. The group's "archival" material is predominantly imaginary. The conception of "imaginary research" — beguiling as it may be, along with such forms as "mockumentaries" and "fictional histories" — nevertheless provides poignant insights into the politics and visual representation of the Lebanese Wars.

Walid Raad, founder of The Atlas Group, is an artist and Assistant Professor of Art at Cooper Union in New York City. Raad's work has been included in the 2002 Whitney Biennial, New York, and Documenta XI, Kassel, 2002. His essays have been published in *Third Text*, and he is a member of The Arab Image Foundation, Beirut/New York.

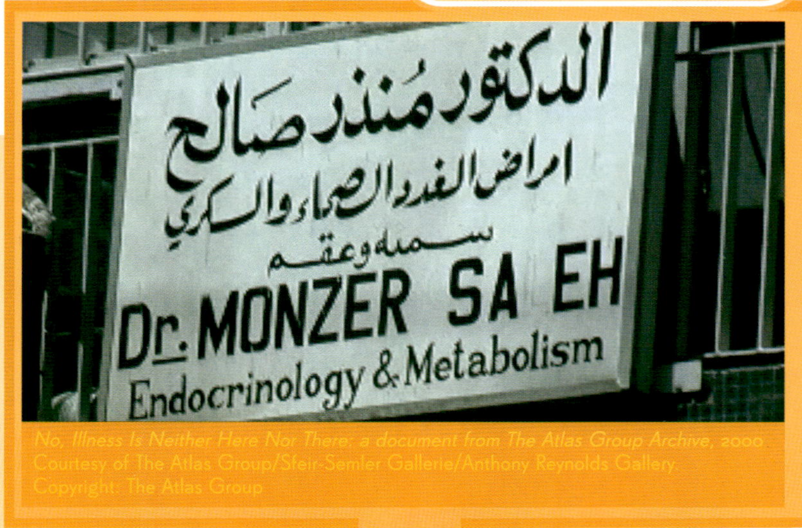

*No, Illness Is Neither Here Nor There; a document from The Atlas Group Archive, 2000.
Courtesy of The Atlas Group/Sfeir-Semler Gallerie/Anthony Reynolds Gallery.
Copyright: The Atlas Group*

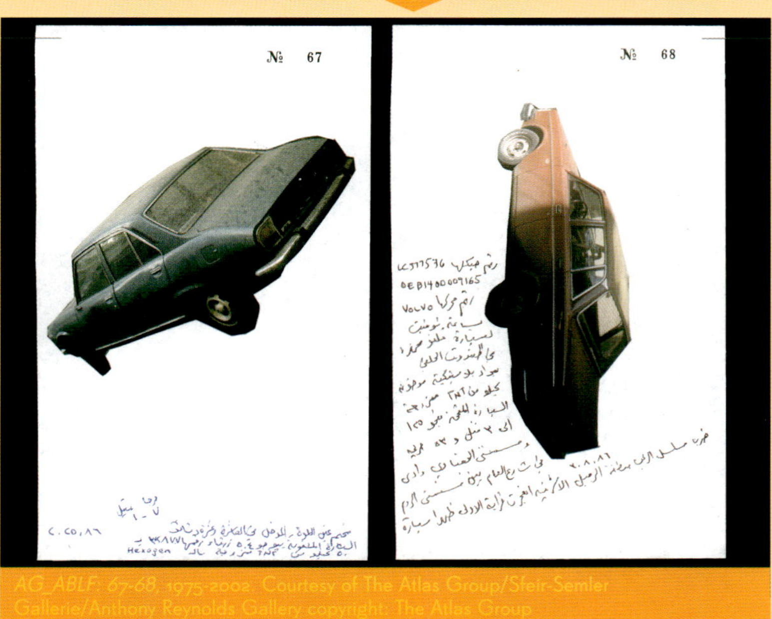

*AG_ABLF: 67-68, 1975-2002. Courtesy of The Atlas Group/Sfeir-Semler
Gallerie/Anthony Reynolds Gallery copyright: The Atlas Group*

1. The Fakhouri file includes two books, films, videotapes, and photographs. The documents in this file are attributed to an imaginary figure, Dr Fadl Fakhouri. Dr Fakhouri represents a renowned Lebanese historian who bequeathed notebooks, films and photographs to The Atlas Group upon his death in 1993.

2. The Atlas Group is a project established in 1999 to research and document the contemporary history of Lebanon. One of our aims with this project is to locate, preserve, study, and produce audio, visual, literary and other artifacts that shed light on the contemporary history of Lebanon. In this endeavor, we produced and found several documents including notebooks, films, videotapes, photographs and other objects. Moreover we organized these works in The Atlas Group Archive.

3. The only photographs of Dr Fakhouri consist of a series of self-portraits he produced during his one and only trip outside of Lebanon, to Paris and Rome in 1958 and 1959.

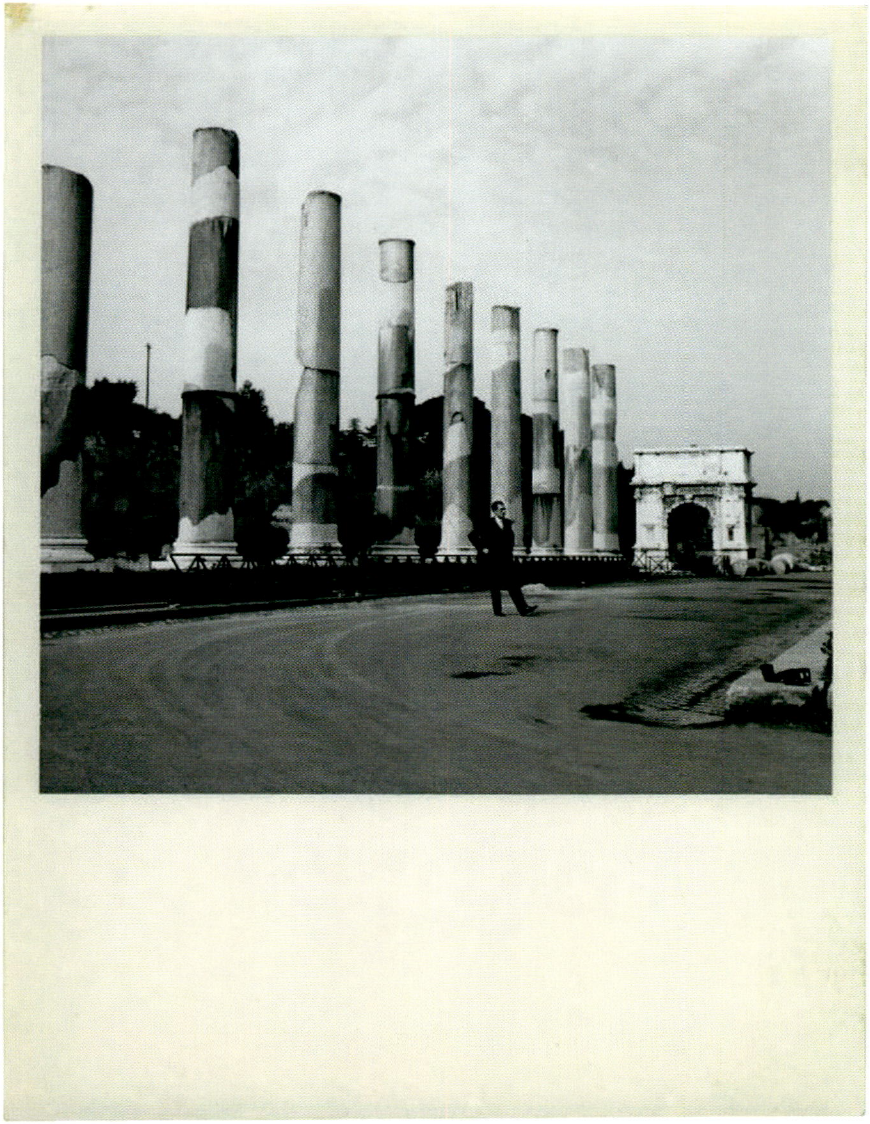

Civilizationally, We Do Not Dig Holes to Bury Ourselves?
Documents from the Fakhouri File in The Atlas Group Archive?
The Atlas Group / Walid Raad

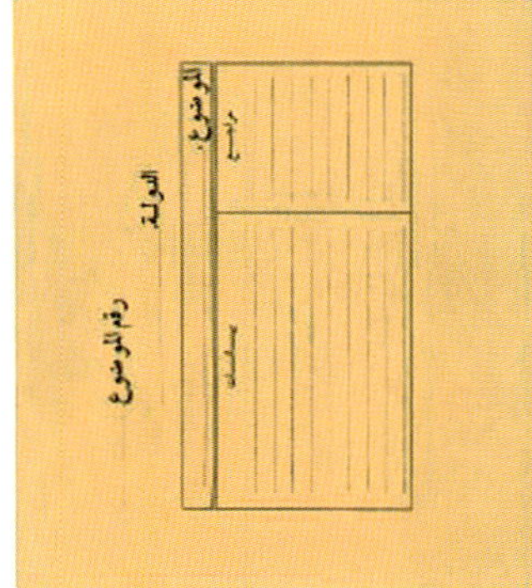

Civilizationally, We Do Not Dig Holes to Bury Ourselves _ p139, (1959)
Courtesy of The Atlas Group/Sfeir-Semler Gallerie/Anthony Reynolds Gallery. Copyright: The Atlas Group

Project Description: This presentation displays the Fakhouri documents from The Atlas Group Archive. The displayed documents consist of all the documents attributed to the (fictional) historian, namely two notebooks, two film/videotapes, and a collection of photographs.

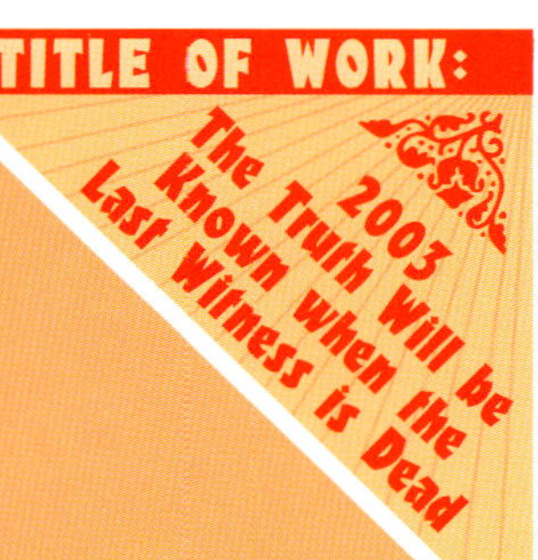

Critical Art Ensemble with Beatriz de Costa

Members from: Tallahassee, FL, Buffalo, NY, Tempe, AZ, Beatriz da Costa: Long Beach, CA

Founded 1987

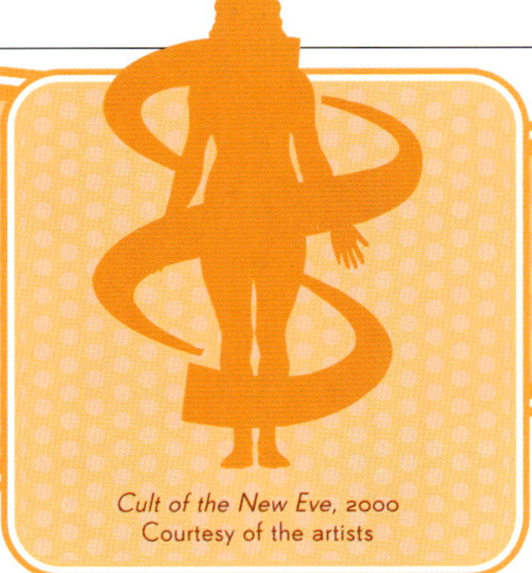

Cult of the New Eve, 2000
Courtesy of the artists

Biographical Info:

"Tactical Media is situational, ephemeral, and self-terminating. It encourages the use of any media that will engage a particular sociopolitical context in order to create molecular interventions and semiotic shocks that contribute to the negation of the rising intensity of authoritarian culture."

Critical Art Ensemble (CAE) is a collective of five "tactical media artists" — Steve Kurtz, Steve Barnes, Dorian Burr, Hope Kurtz, and Beverly Schlee — whose various specializations include computer graphics and web art, film/video, photography, text art, book art, and performance. CAE exploits the intersections of art, critical theory, technology, and political activism. Its seminal 1994 book, *The Electronic Disturbance,* has made the collective synonymous with the term "Tactical Media." The collective continues to write and produce projects and over the past eight years has focused on the social and political implications of biotechnology. Since the summer of 2000, CAE has collaborated with artist/researcher Beatriz da Costa. De Costa is a machine artist and tactical media practitioner who is currently Assistant Professor of Studio Art, Electrical Engineering, and Computer Science at University of California at Irvine.

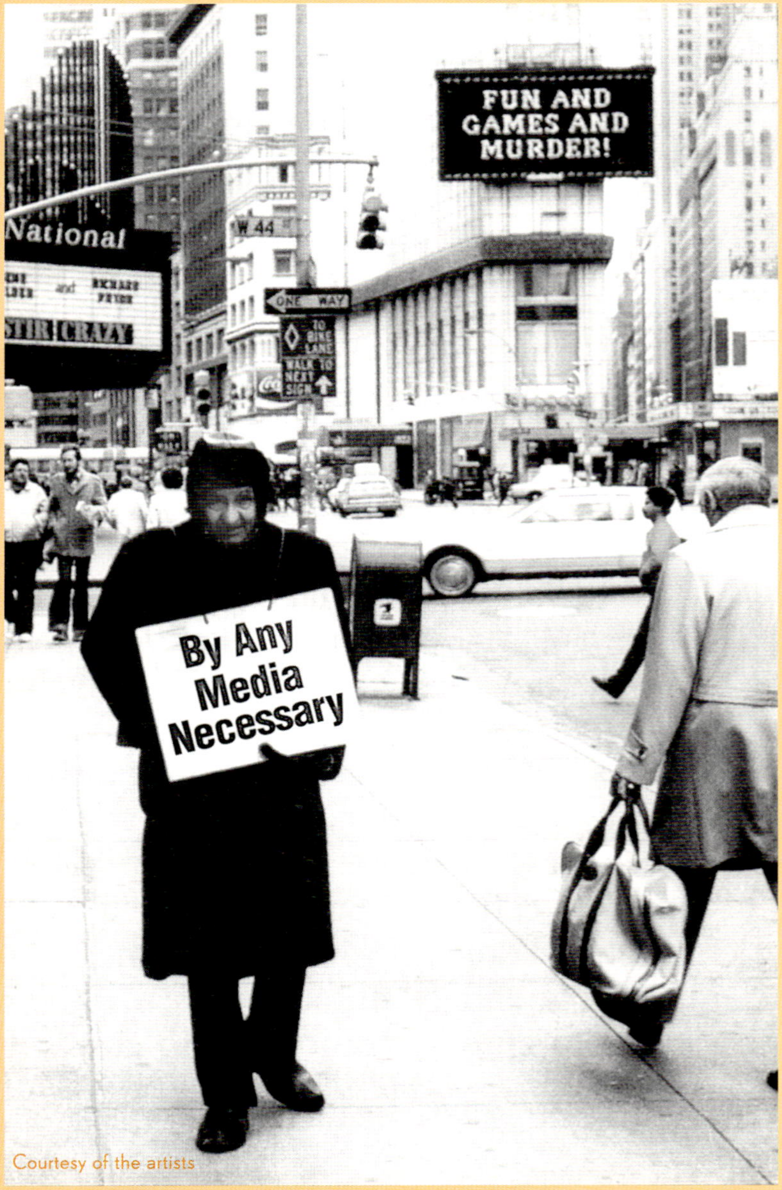

Courtesy of the artists

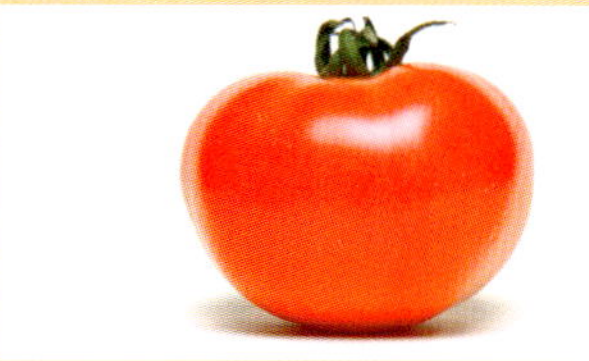 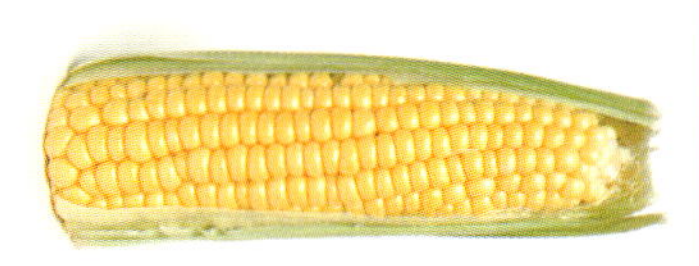 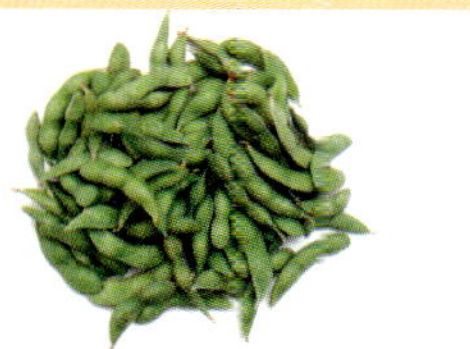

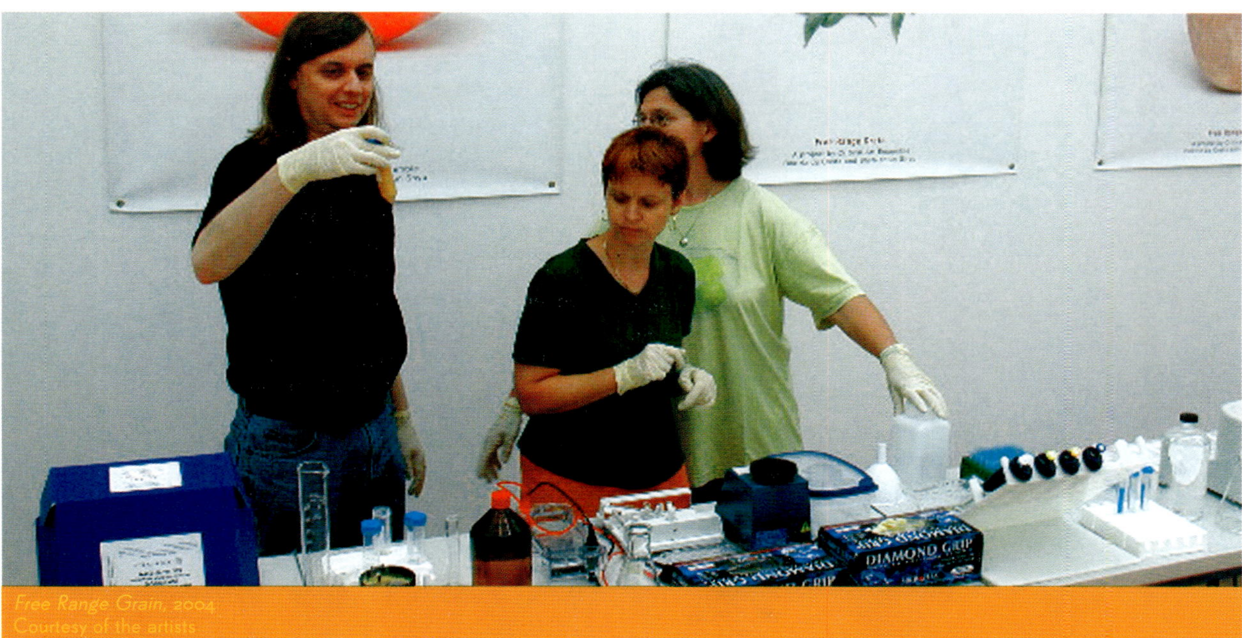

Free Range Grain, 2004
Courtesy of the artists

Project Description: "In executing projects such as this one, we hope to contribute to an idea of public science by focusing on issues (such as food production) that are of direct interest to people, and so contribute to making the meaning of scientific initiatives immediate and concrete, as opposed to the vague abstractions they tend to be." (2) *Free Range Grain* was initially installed and performed at the Schirn Kunsthalle in Frankfurt in reaction to the rising idea of the European Union as "Fortress Europe." Through the use of an on-site laboratory, CAE tested foods brought in by visitors for Genetically Modified Organisms (GMOs). The appearance of GMOs would call into question claims by EU bureaucrats that border-control policies were preventing the entry of these organisms (in the body of fruits, vegetables, and grains) onto the continent. *Free Range Grain* has been adapted for North Adams, where the subject of research has shifted to the still vague term "organic." Their project poses the question: is "naturalness" possible in the world today, and what do we mean when we say "natural" and "organic"?

TITLE OF WORK:

2004 *Free Range Grain*

2. From Critical Art Ensemble's website: www.critical-art.net

Critical Art Ensemble

Interviewed by C. Ondine Chavoya
January 26, 2004

Which practices and/or movements associated with the visual culture of the 1980s were you most engaged by, influenced by, or active in?

In the 1980s, the AIDS movement had the greatest resonance for CAE. ACT UP, Gran Fury, and Group Material all had a big influence on the type of practice we were trying to develop.

What are the different fields or networks that you operate in (not just aesthetically but specifically)? How do you view these various facets of your activity?

We use a broad range of knowledge systems and media to produce our work. We are a little more leery of networks. They are too practical and pressure producers to respond to the most immediate demands placed upon the network. So while we hover around the tactical media movement, for example, we have never become deep organizers in any way.

What spheres do you find appropriate for your work?

An anti-capitalist can act anywhere, as there is no space that does not speak the values of capital. All that is required is a project right for the space. There are no inappropriate spheres. When we do tactical media workshops, the participants pick the site of intervention, and no one has picked an inappropriate one yet.

How do you see your work operating in larger social movements?

At best, CAE is a satellite of larger movements. We see ourselves as doing independent experimental research for anti-capital resistance movements. We try to find new methods of intervention, explore new territories, and develop tools that could be of use.

How do you use preexisting visual forms or discourses in your work? To what end(s) do you use them?

They are the material for work. One primary interest of CAE's is in dialogic practices. To successfully create such situations, we must use a language that is common and well understood within the territory where we are working. We subversively use the language and forms of the space in order to communicate effectively what cannot be said about, or within, a given space.

What do you consider the advantages and/or disadvantages to collaboration, compared to individualized forms of art production?

No member of CAE has had an individualized practice, so we cannot speak from experience. We do know that none of us individually could have accomplished all that we have if we were not working together.

How do you see humor as functioning in your art?

It's useful at times, but it's not a magic bullet. It can set people at ease, and allow them some amusement. And, it is certainly fun to not be so serious all the time. That gets tiresome.

How do delight and pleasure function in your work?

For CAE, there is always delight in learning and the pleasure from the feeling of autonomy when a project works as intended. For the viewers, we try to do work that is active and engaging. Our biggest fear is boring people, because nothing of value can be exchanged under such conditions.

How does technology function in your work? In general, what is your relationship to technology?

CAE's relationship is very practical; we believe in using what you need. We have no fixed relationship to any particular piece of technology.

In the past two decades, public space has become increasingly privatized as private space and private lives have become increasingly subject to the expanded structures and technologies of surveillance. How might your work respond to or demonstrate this scenario?

Our work has been quite focused on how surveillance will act as a means of body invasion — that every strand of DNA in our bodies, every molecule will be visualized, mapped, and ordered to better serve capitalist interests.

The word intervention is central to the exhibition: what constitutes an intervention?

The appropriation of material, knowledge, and territory for the purpose of undermining or revealing the authoritative and repressive structures and vectors that produce and manage a given territory.

Can there be revolutionary art without a revolution?

No. There are resistant or contestational cultural or political movements, campaigns, and actions, but not revolutionary ones.

C. Ondine Chavoya

is Assistant Professor of Art at Williams College where he teaches courses on contemporary art and Latina/o visual culture.

His writings on art and urban space in southern California have appeared in journals such as *Wide Angle*, *Performance Research*, and *Afterimage*, and in anthologies such as *Customized* (2000), *Space, Site, and Intervention* (2000), and *The Ethnic Eye* (1996).

Chavoya's research interests revolve around the social production and use of space and the ways artists have represented and intervened in the urban landscape.

Spurse

Transnational:
Finland, Kenya, USA, Canada, Italy, Taiwan, Germany, Mexico, Great Britain, India, Ukraine

Founded 1998

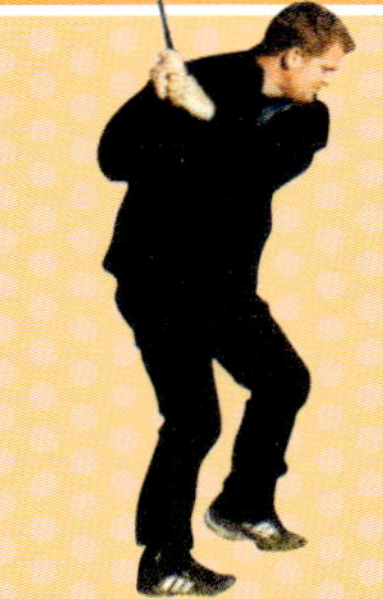

Judd Golf detail; Performance of a round of golf done in Marfa through Judd's large concrete sculptures. With the aid of a Mebane Grant 2001. Courtesy of the artist

Biographical Info:

Spurse describes itself as an international architectural collective with no fixed content or members dedicated to experimentation with a transurban milieu. Since 1998, they have produced numerous interventions ranging from buildings to performance to installation to texts. Spurse is concerned with developing new forms of collectivity and the commons (hence their collaboration with both William Pope.L and J Morgan Puett in this show). Spurse has a fluctuating membership (approximately 40). Originating in Austin, Texas, their collective now includes members in Canada, Finland, India, and Mexico City, as well as multiple locations in the United States.

With over half the world's population now living in urban environments, Spurse's binding interest is in this increasingly urban condition of existence. They question and rethink urbanism in terms of new forms of distributed agency and a refusal of the nature-culture divide. In their 2003 project at the State University of New York at Oswego, *Haeceitas/ Quaestiones Quolibetales: Settling in Question*, Spurse set out to archive and diagram "everything" not as a static thing but in terms of it being a dynamic event and, through cross-referencing, rethink the qualities and nature of urban existence, radical artifice and the natural.

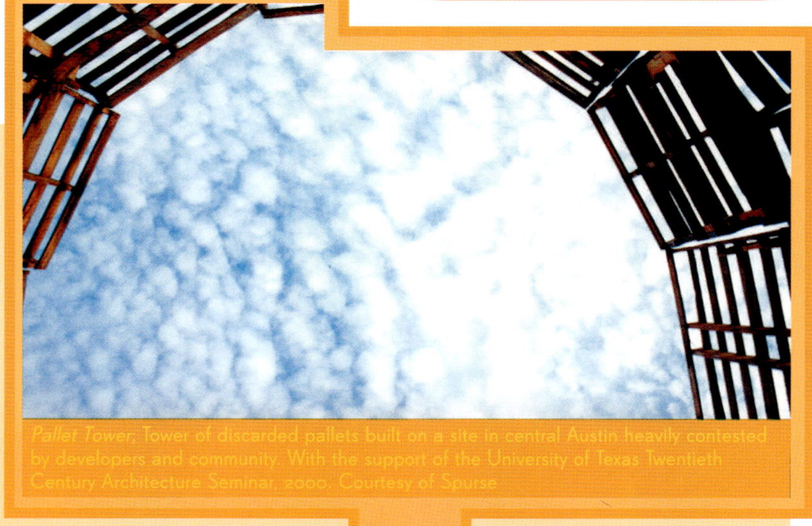

Pallet Tower; Tower of discarded pallets built on a site in central Austin heavily contested by developers and community. With the support of the University of Texas Twentieth Century Architecture Seminar, 2000. Courtesy of Spurse

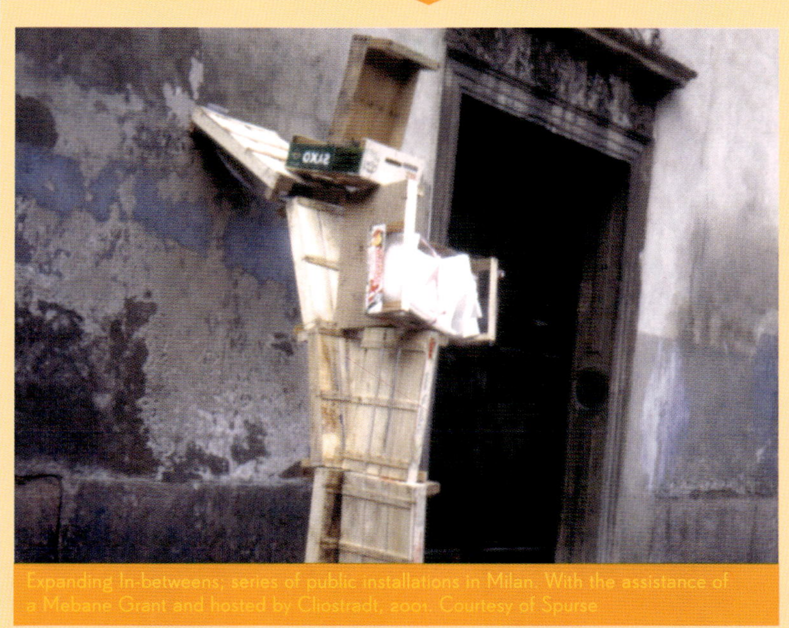

Expanding In-betweens; series of public installations in Milan. With the assistance of a Mebane Grant and hosted by Cliostradt, 2001. Courtesy of Spurse

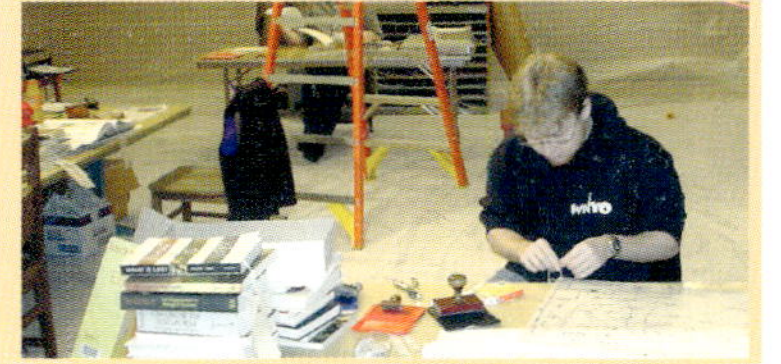
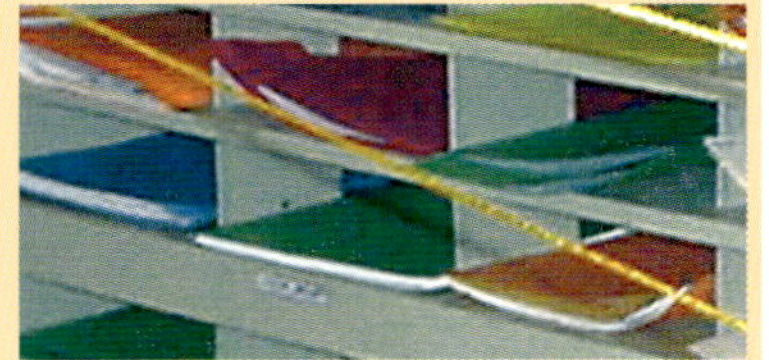
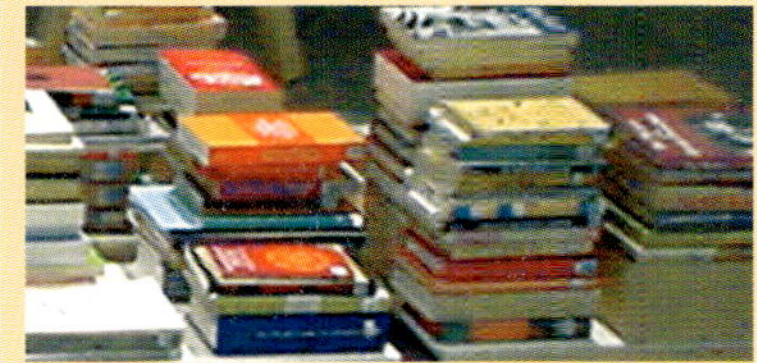

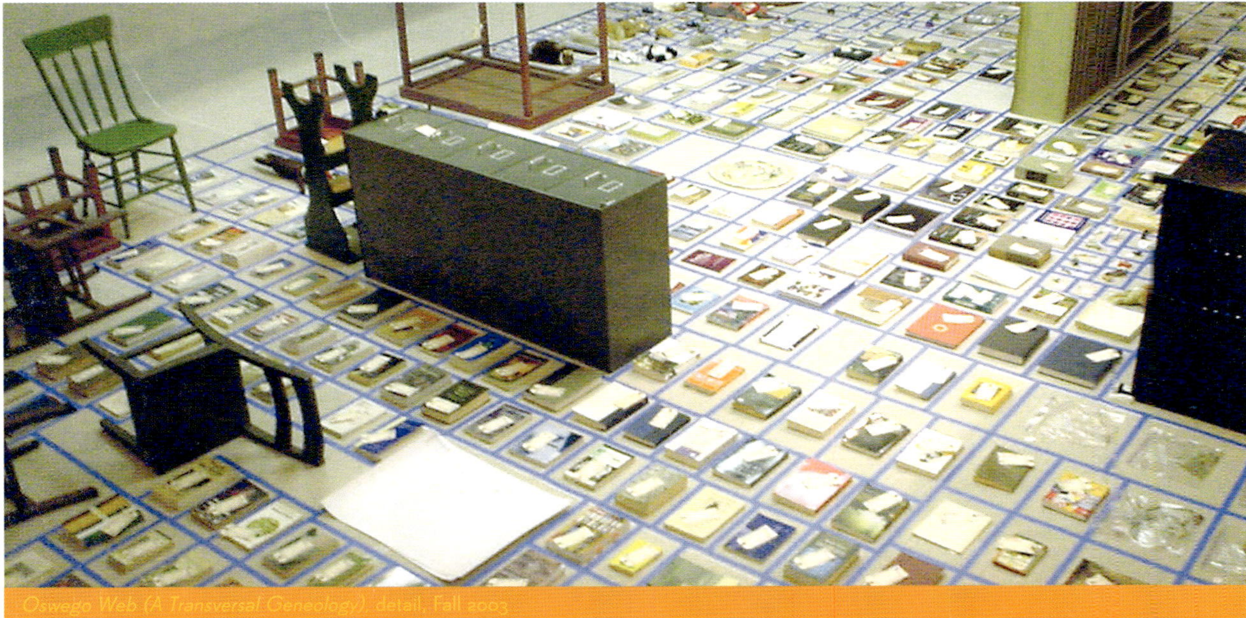

Oswego Web (A Transversal Geneology), detail, Fall 2003
SUNY Oswego Gallery. Courtesy of Spurse

Project Description: In *Sans Terre* (by Spurse and others) Spurse starts with the unconventional proposition that Mexico City is North Adams and North Adams is Mexico City. This strange statement makes evident Spurse's belief that urbanism functions – to use their phrase – "vectorally" and ignores static and dated conceptions of space such as nation states, regional boundaries, and distinct biological systems. This methodological definition of urbanism allows a rethinking of the natural as a form of the urban rather than vice versa. In order to test their vivid hypothesis, Spurse applies the same methodologies to North Adams that they have previously used to study Mexico City. In addition to this they have allowed other artists and urbanists to intervene/collaborate in this investigation.

What makes their research particularly unusual is their refusal to use any form of hierarchy in sorting data that would reinforce nature/culture distinctions and subject/object metaphysics. Spurse collects their data (interviews, found materials, and photographs) by following an algorithmically generated path which is the same path that members walked in Mexico City. They follow the route exactly: through backyards, into mountains, across streets, and into businesses. As they walk, they ask whomever they encounter questions such as, "describe your houseplants" or "What was happening the last time you looked at the ground?" If they see trash, they pick it up, and at times they take photographs. This assortment of quasi-randomly procured material is then displayed in a floating Plexiglas archive alongside the materials from Mexico City and many other locations.

subRosa

Chicago, IL
Pittsburgh, PA
Rochester, NY
Athens, GA
USA

Founded 1998

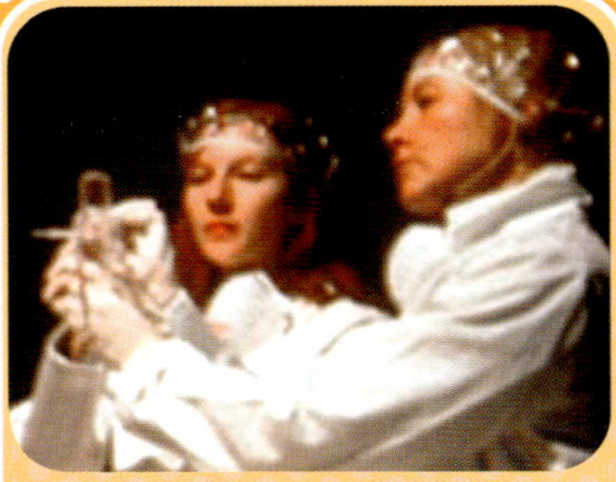

Expo EmmaGenics (Trade Fair Performance), Intermediale Festival, Mainz, Germany, 2001. Courtesy of subRosa

Biographical Info:

subRosa practices a situational embodied feminist politics nourished by conviviality, self-determination, and the desire for affirmative alliances and coalitions. The cyberfeminist art collective subRosa consists of five members: Faith Wilding, Hyla Willis, Lucia Sommer, Laleh Mehran, and Steffi Domike. The name subRosa is meant to honor other politically charged "Rosas" of history, including Rosa Luxemburg, Rosalind Franklin, Rosa Parks, and Rosie the Riveter. subRosa's work centers on the uses and implications of biotechnology as it applies to sexual difference, race, and transnational labor conditions. Their research/production takes many forms including performance, video, publishing, web projects, and teach-ins.

In 2002, subRosa produced a project at Bowling Green State University titled *US Grade AAA Premium Eggs*. Under the guise of a recruiting campaign set up in the student union, subRosa performed an educational demo about sex and gender in the "biotech century," and then asked students to estimate the dollar value of their eggs, sperm, and organs. Students employed a computer program that calculated the "flesh-worth" of their genetic material on the basis of factors of race, illness, gender, sexual orientation, national origin, and abnormalities. subRosa's first book project, *Domain Errors! Cyberfeminist Practices* (Autonomedia) was published in 2002.

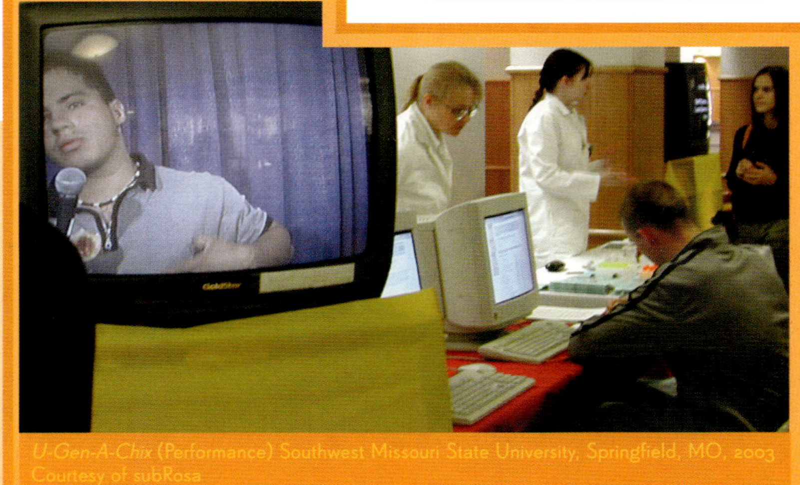

U-Gen-A-Chix (Performance) Southwest Missouri State University, Springfield, MO, 2003 Courtesy of subRosa

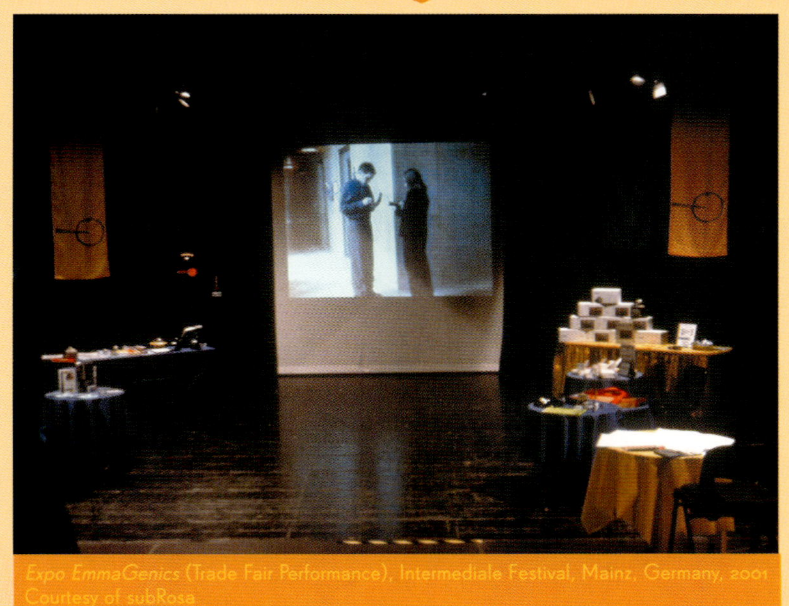

Expo EmmaGenics (Trade Fair Performance), Intermediale Festival, Mainz, Germany, 2001 Courtesy of subRosa

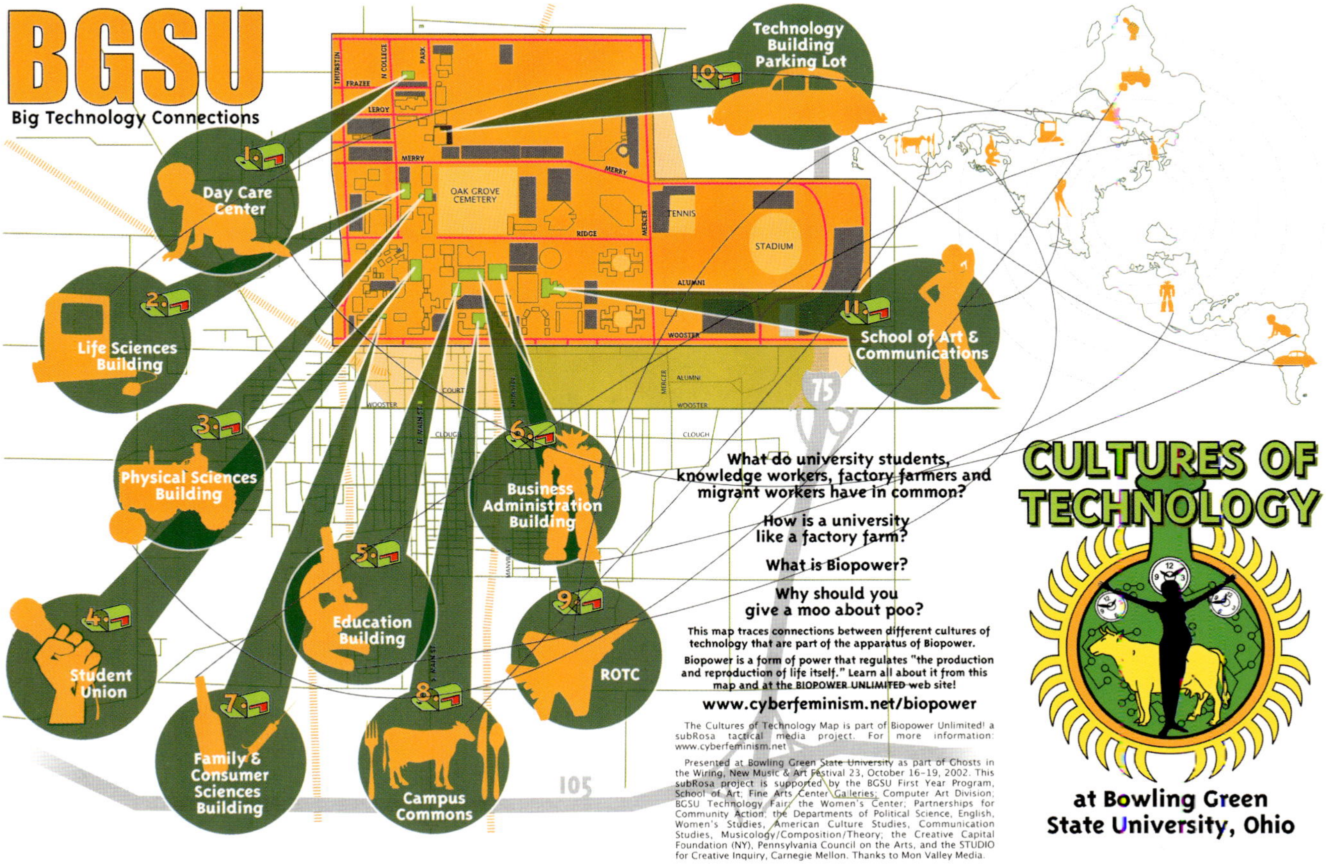

BGSU
Big Technology Connections

Day Care Center

Life Sciences Building

Physical Sciences Building

Student Union

Education Building

Family & Consumer Sciences Building

Campus Commons

Business Administration Building

ROTC

School of Art & Communications

Technology Building Parking Lot

What do university students, knowledge workers, factory farmers and migrant workers have in common?

How is a university like a factory farm?

What is Biopower?

Why should you give a moo about poo?

This map traces connections between different cultures of technology that are part of the apparatus of Biopower.

Biopower is a form of power that regulates "the production and reproduction of life itself." Learn all about it from this map and at the BIOPOWER UNLIMITED web site!

www.cyberfeminism.net/biopower

The Cultures of Technology Map is part of Biopower Unlimited! a subRosa tactical media project. For more information: www.cyberfeminism.net

Presented at Bowling Green State University as part of Ghosts in the Wiring, New Music & Art Festival 23, October 16–19, 2002. This subRosa project is supported by the BGSU First Year Program; School of Art; Fine Arts Center Galleries; Computer Art Division; BGSU Technology Fair; the Women's Center; Partnerships for Community Action; the Departments of Political Science, English, Women's Studies, American Culture Studies, Communication Studies, Musicology/Composition/Theory; the Creative Capital Foundation (NY), Pennsylvania Council on the Arts, and the STUDIO for Creative Inquiry, Carnegie Mellon. Thanks to Mon Valley Media.

CULTURES OF TECHNOLOGY
at Bowling Green State University, Ohio

Biopower Unlimited! (Technology Fair Performance), Bowling Green State University, Ohio, 2002. Courtesy of subRosa

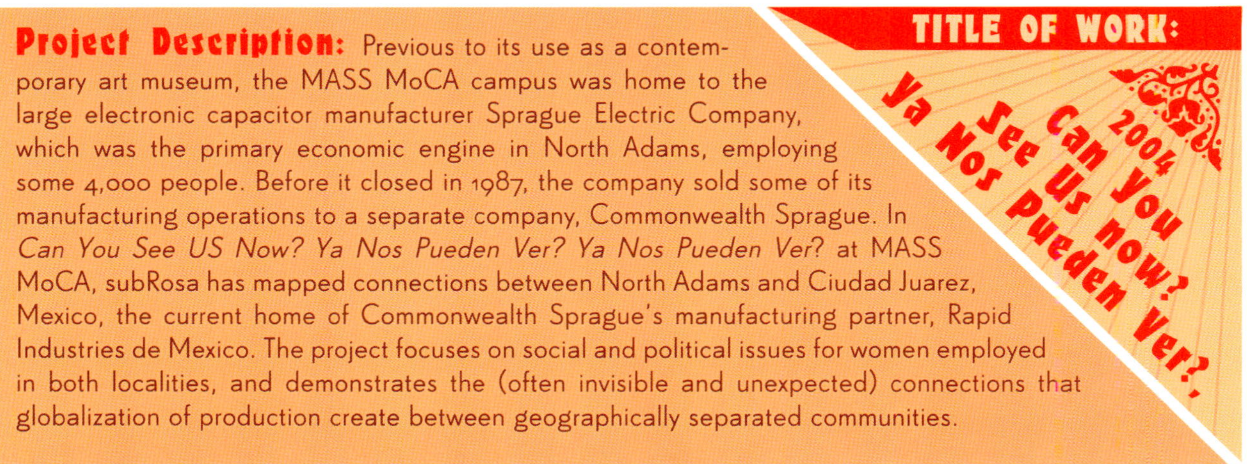

Project Description: Previous to its use as a contemporary art museum, the MASS MoCA campus was home to the large electronic capacitor manufacturer Sprague Electric Company, which was the primary economic engine in North Adams, employing some 4,000 people. Before it closed in 1987, the company sold some of its manufacturing operations to a separate company, Commonwealth Sprague. In *Can You See US Now? Ya Nos Pueden Ver? Ya Nos Pueden Ver?* at MASS MoCA, subRosa has mapped connections between North Adams and Ciudad Juarez, Mexico, the current home of Commonwealth Sprague's manufacturing partner, Rapid Industries de Mexico. The project focuses on social and political issues for women employed in both localities, and demonstrates the (often invisible and unexpected) connections that globalization of production create between geographically separated communities.

Tandem Surfing the Third Wave

Interview with subRosa, by Ryan Griffis (a longer version of this interview was published in *Next Five Minutes 4 Reader*, Amsterdam, September, 2003)

RG: Could you briefly discuss cyberfeminism and how it relates to other historical versions of feminism and critical theory?

sR: The question of how to define cyberfeminism is at the heart of the often contradictory contemporary positions of women working with new digital technologies and feminist politics. [1] Cyberfeminism (CF) appeared toward the end of the '80s as a promising new wave of (post)feminist thinking and practice that began to contest technologically complex territories. In 2004, cyberfeminism is still a controversial and puzzling term which, like feminism, has very different connotations for different generations of women.

Members of subRosa differ in our politics, practices, and everyday life situations, but we agree that one of the most urgent issues for cyberfeminist and feminist practice and theory currently is that of seeking female affiliations that respect and explore difference — especially sexual difference — and create productive projects in solidarity with others who are working on similar issues, though often from very different points of view and situations.

subRosa takes the position that cyberfeminism should be theoretically and historically grounded in feminist philosophies and embodied in political, cultural and social practices. Crucially, CF needs to be informed by postcolonial theories and critiques of technological culture and representational politics. Areas of CF intervention and practice include research on the specific impact of ICT (Information & Communications Technologies) on different populations of women globally—including highly educated professional women in academia, the sciences, medical, and computer industries, as well as clerical and factory workers in the just-in-time telecommunications and home-work industry, and rural and urban women working in electronic parts factories and assembly sweatshops. In order to strategize CF practices we must examine the impact of the new bio and digital technologies on women's sexuality and subjectivities; the conditions of production and reproduction; gender roles, social relations, and public and private space; and we need to contest the naturalized value placed on speed and efficiency when they take no heed of the limits and needs of the organic body. In the aftermath of colonialism, there are more migrants, refugees, and exiles than ever before, and many of these migrants are women. As women from developing countries increasingly become the home-service and child-care workers employed by wealthier families — as well as the world's electronic parts manufacturers, assemblers, and data maintenance workers — the lives of women are mutually reliant across divisions of race, class, and nationality. Far from being subjects irrelevant to electronic media theory, and cyberfeminism, these migrant populations are often the result of devastations caused by the interventions of empire. We must begin de-colonization in our own networks and embodied relations. CF must also research, critique and contest developments in bio-genetic technologies that profoundly affect environmental and human futures. Cyberfeminists could spearhead activism and education about Advanced Reproductive Technologies (ART), transgenic crop production, stem cell technologies and cloning and the distributed maternal body, and new eugenics practices, to expose how profoundly traditional concepts of women's bodies and gender roles are implicated in the deployment of these technologies. bell hooks' definition of feminism proposed almost two decades ago remains relevant to cyberfeminists. In her words, feminism "is not simply a struggle to end male chauvinism or a movement to ensure that women will have equal rights with men; it is a commitment to eradicating the ideology of domination that permeates western culture on various levels — sex, race, and class to name a few — and a commitment to reorganizing U.S. society so that the self-development of people can take precedence over imperialism, economic expansion, and material desires." [2]

RG: How do subRosa's theory and practice fit into this schema?

sR: At present (2003) subRosa consists of five new genre artists who produce our projects. For our book, *Domain Errors! Cyberfeminist Practices* (available from <www.autonomedia.org>), we collaborated with cultural theorists and postcolonial scholars Maria Fernandez and Michelle Wright, and invited the participation of 12 contributors from different countries and fields of cultural and technological research and practice. We are currently working on a new collaborative project, *MatriXial Technologies*, with a group of artists, scholars, and researchers in Singapore including Irina Aristarkhova, Margaret Tan, and Adeline Kueh. The project concerns itself with mapping global flows of human tissue and bioinformatics, and the varying meanings and effects these have on different populations of women. sR practices an embodied "female affiliation" of welcoming, solidarity, and inclusion. For example, when we are invited to do a project, organize a panel, or speak at a conference, we extend that invitation to women with different experiences and views whose voices have not been heard, or who do not usually travel on the circuits that we travel in. subRosa consciously tries to embody feminist content, practices, and agency within the electronic technologies, virtual systems, and RL (Real Life) spaces in which we operate and live. We politicize and problematize how both the content and form of our work and social relations are mediated by digital technologies.

RG: Since subRosa has been addressing different aspects of science and technology, which are now harder to separate than ever, what areas have become important targets for the group to critique?

sR: One big area is always the language and practices of science and of commodified biotech. Thus, for example, we have critiqued the appropriation of the feminist notion of "choice" to support commodified development of ARTs (Assisted Reproductive Technologies). We also point to the ways in which the promissory language of science and of many new medical and genetic technologies work to naturalize the new uses of biology in genetic and transgenic food and medical production. For example, in the area of cloning and stem cell technologies there is great mystification and hype that use words like "magic," "immortal," and "totipotent" to describe various kinds of stem cells. There is also the promise of "putting death to death," of "rejuvenating" and "revivifying" organs, aging bodies, and the like, not to mention "saving lives" and "extending life indefinitely." Then, we are also very concerned with capitalist science's practices of privatization and patenting of intellectual property, biological processes, knowledge production and life materials. We have talked with scientists and lab researchers in both private commercial (corporate-supported) and academic (usually also corporate-supported) institutions and have often heard them complain about the constraints that privatization and patenting put on their research and the exchange of knowledge and materials with other scientists. But for the public (as guinea pigs and eventual consumers) these are crucial issues of concern that need to be acted on. However, most people don't really understand what is involved and have long since given up trying to keep up with what science is developing. This is where we can intervene as contestational artists and activists who are willing to do the necessary research work to be able to involve the public in a different kind of understanding and experience of these biotechnologies.

For sR a central concern is also the ways in which biotech and various digital technologies affect the lives, livelihoods, bodies, roles, and subjectivities of women in different ways than they may for other sectors of the population. The bodies of women have literally become parts-supply and production laboratories for many aspects of the reprotech, stem cell and cloning biotech industry. For example, pregnant women are now routinely being advised to have their baby's umbilical cord blood collected and cryogenically stored as an eventual source of stem cells that may one day "save the whole family," or, as in ART, asking women to donate super-ovulated eggs or "excess embryos" for therapeutic stem cell research. But new biotech and genetic engineering affect women in other ways too; for example, in food production and subsistence farming, which is still done mostly by female labor in many countries. For example, during the "Green Revolution" in India, U.S.-imported farming technology deprived millions of women of a living and of their traditional agricultural work. This led, in many cases, to further devaluing of women and consequently to increased infanticide of female children, or of sex-selective abortions after amniocentesis. In sR's experience, attitudes and beliefs about sexual difference are often suppressed through a crucial element in scientific research and in the way various technologies and scientific processes are deployed. This needs much more research. Finally, we are also interested in questions of difference and of the division of labor in scientific research and digital technologies. For example, we did a project for n.paradoxa examining the "Economies of ART" in which we looked at the integrated circuit of workers and knowledge that go into "making a baby" with ART.

RG: I'm curious about subRosa's Refugia BAZ project. Could you discuss that project and what its context is?

sR: Our Refugia BAZ (Becoming Autonomous Zones) project is a series of modular projects (funded in part by a generous grant from the Creative Capital Foundation) that explore political, cultural, and biological aspects of "refuge" specific to various places or groups. Though sR has not previously developed projects around a particular activist sociopolitical campaign, we are planning to do so in certain ways in our project *Can You See US Now? Ya Nos Pueden Ver?* Ya Nos Pueden Ver? for the *Interventionists* exhibition. The North Adams mills that now house MASS MoCA were formerly occupied by Sprague Electric, an electrical capacitor manufacturing plant that employed many local women. In 1986, Sprague Electric — the company in North Adams for 50 years — sold its capacitor manufacturing to Commonwealth Sprague and shut down its main plant in North Adams. In 2000, Commonwealth Sprague relocated capacitor manufacturing to the maquiladora of its partner Rapid Industries de Mexico in Ciudad Juarez, Mexico, thus removing the economic mainstay of North Adams.

Labor industrial and "postindustrial," much of it by women and children, is the source of wealth produced in the factories that previously occupied the MASS MoCA buildings, and for the industrial revolution, and the ICT revolution and accompanying globalization. Labor created and now sustains the museum and the newly globalized 'network society'. Commodity production has largely moved across the border where women's jobs can cost them their lives. [3] sR's project investigates conditions of invisible female and feminized labor in the manufacturing, service, culture, and tourist industries that help sustain the economic basis of "post-industrial" towns.

Our mapping of the economic and cultural effects of the outsourcing of labor in North Adams, Massachusetts, and Ciudad Juarez, Mexico, will make visible the role of interactive telecommunications (ITC) and high-tech production in the process of globalization and economic change. [4] In solidarity with activist interventions on behalf of the murdered and disappeared women in Ciudad Juarez — and with women workers there and in North Adams subRosa is collaborating with the Los Angeles Center for the Study of Political Graphics, as well as with activist women's anti-violence and human rights groups, to create visibility for these issues in our museum project. By focusing primarily on women, we hope to learn more about how new cultural and service economies under mobile capital are produced and sustained through (female) labor.

Notes:

1) Much of this section contains material from Maria Fernandez and
Faith Wilding, "*Situating Cyberfeminism(s)," the introduction to
Domain Errors! Cyberfeminist Practices, a subRosa project,*
Autonomedia Books, 2003. See also: *"Where is the Feminism in
Cyberfeminism"* (Faith Wilding, n.paradoxa, No. 3, London,
1999); *"Notes on the Political Condition of Cyberfeminism"*
(Faith Wilding and Critical Art Ensemble, CAA Journal, NY,
Summer 1998).

2) bell hooks, Ain't I a Woman: *Black Women and Feminism*
(Boston: South End Press, 1981), pp. 194-195.

3) In the Mexican border factories (maquiladoras) operating under
NAFTA agreements, wages are extremely low, and working/living
conditions for the thousands of female maquiladora workers are
generally deplorable and dangerous. In the last ten years, over
280 women have been murdered and at least 350 more have disappeared in Ciudad Juarez. Many of these women were workers
in the maquiladoras; they were murdered under brutal circumstances, including sexual assault, torture, and mutilation.

4) sR gratefully acknowledges the enthusiastic research assistance
and collaboration of Smith College students in the
classes of Professors Lisa Armstrong and Donna Riley, as well
as students from Chatham College, Pittsburgh.
As well, we thank the residents of North Adams and
Ciudad Juarez who have contributed immeasurably to
this project.

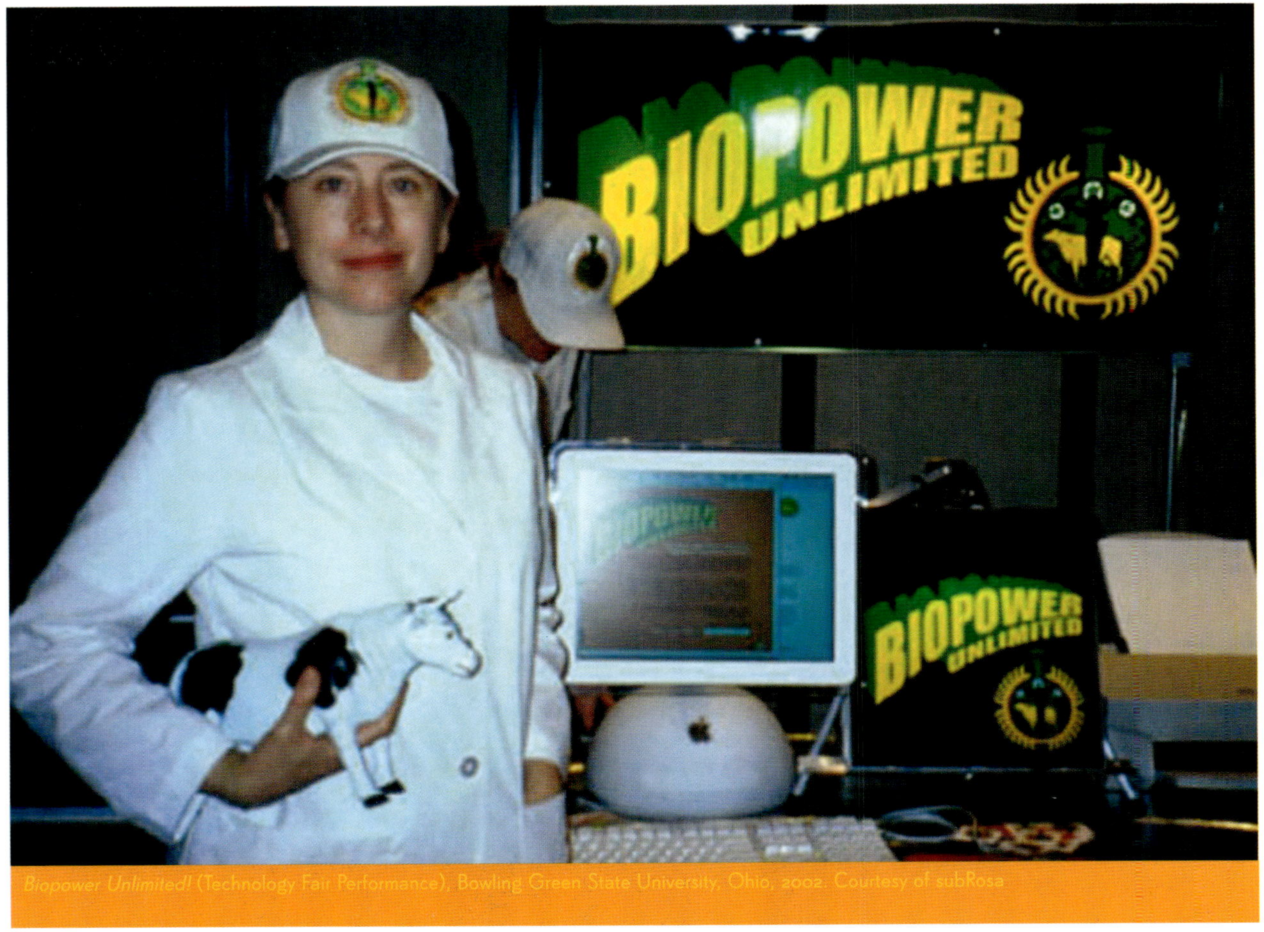

Biopower Unlimited! (Technology Fair Performance), Bowling Green State University, Ohio, 2002. Courtesy of subRosa

Tana Hargest

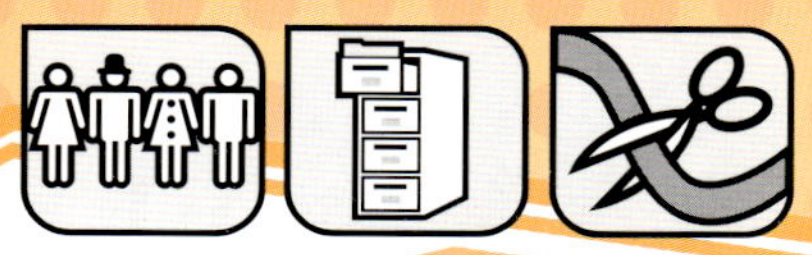

Boston, MA
New York, NY
USA

Born 1969

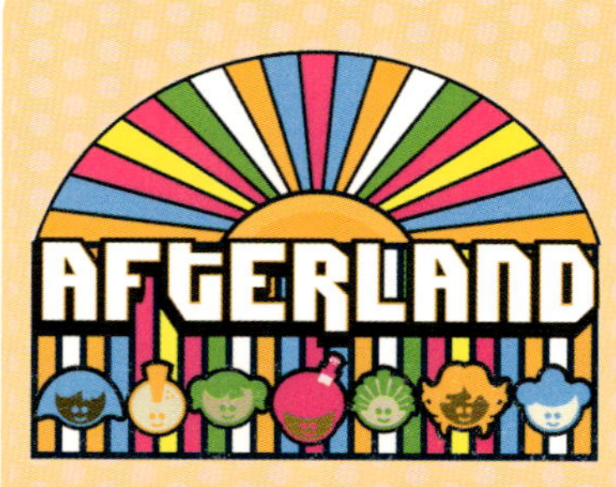

From *New Negrotopia*, 2004

Biographical Info:

Tana Hargest's work confronts questions of race in modern times, often through a fictitious corporation of her invention called *Bitter Nigger Inc.* (BNI), of which she is CEO. BNI promises to sell a race-free future. Emulating the promises that permeated the 1990s regarding a "race-blind" internet, BNI uses the internet to market lifestyle products for confronting social tensions, including Privitrol, the "privilege cessation dermal patch."

Hargest received her Masters of Fine Art in Photography from the Rhode Island School of Design in 1999 and has been honored with recent awards from Creative Capital, the Jerome Foundation, and the New York State Council on the Arts.

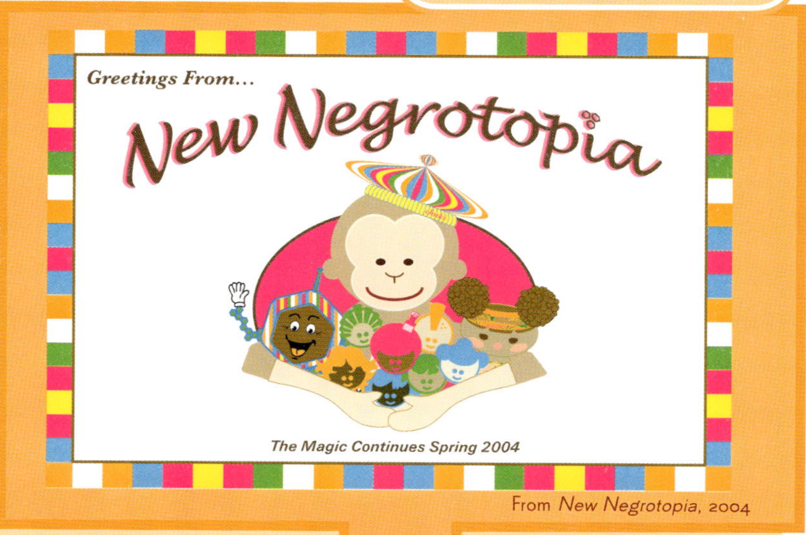

From *New Negrotopia*, 2004

From *New Negrotopia*, 2004

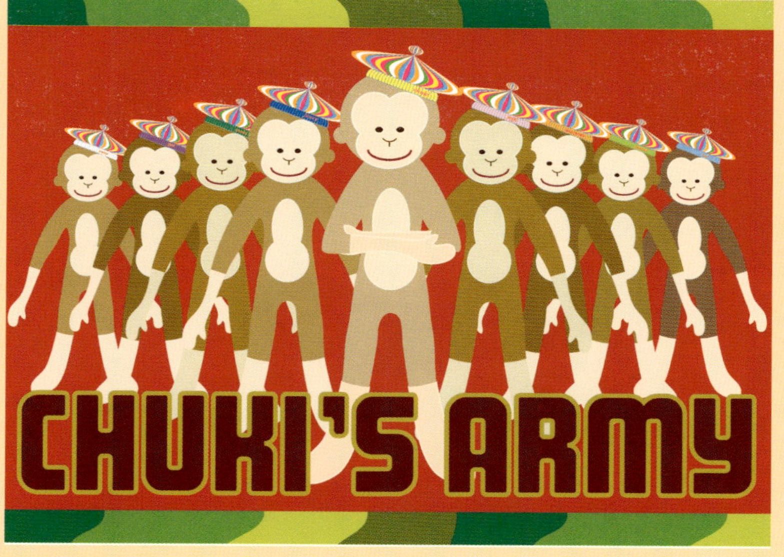

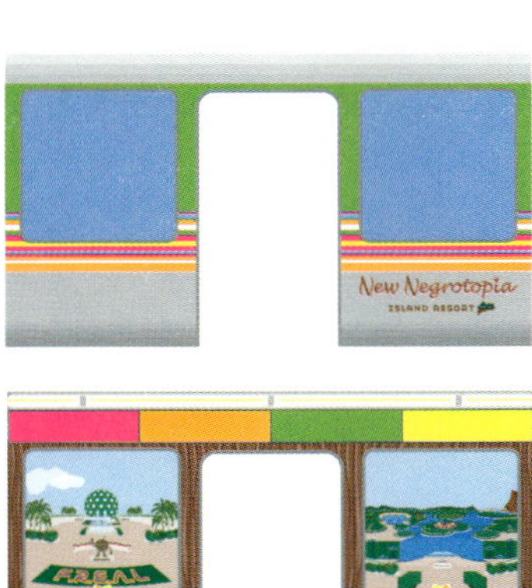

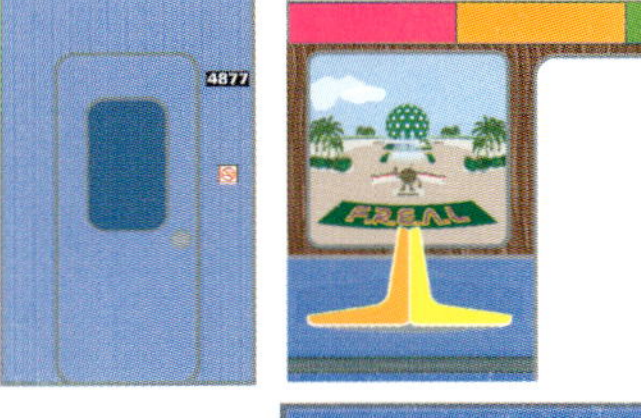

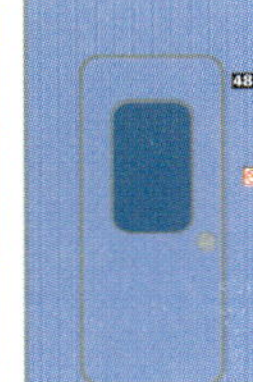

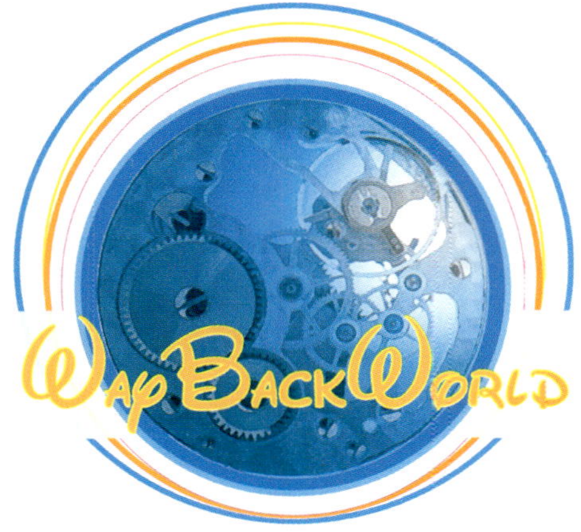

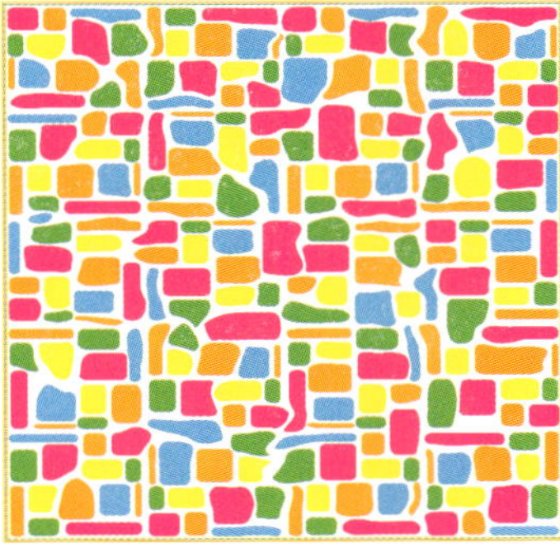

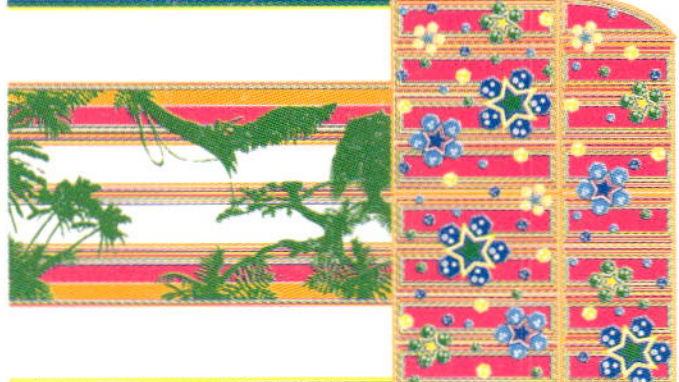

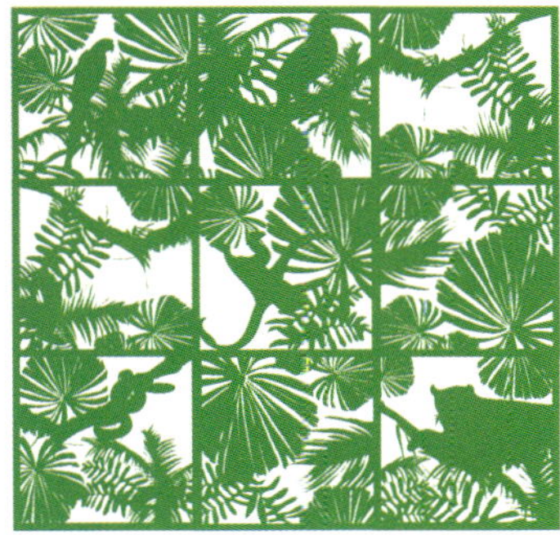

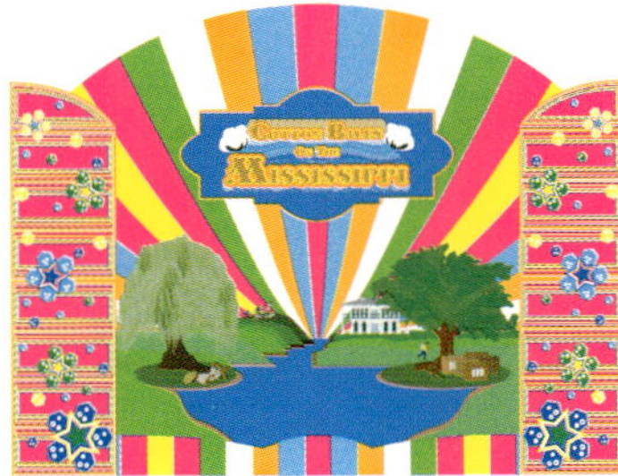

From *New Negrotopia*, 2004

Project Description: In this project, *Bitter Nigger Inc.* has proposed "a theme park beyond race" titled New Negrotopia. Bitter Nigger Inc. presents New Negrotopia at trade shows seeming to troll for investors. Comprised of a promotional video, a website, and actual trade show booths, New Negrotopia is presented as a virtual island resort and amusement park in which visitors can travel through their own racial history. New Negrotopia consists of several interactive environments, including: Atlantic Adventure, a 3-D interactive experience of the Middle Passage; the Cotton Bales on the Mississippi water ride; and The Institute of Thinking, a mock-academic think tank located in paradise.

TITLE OF WORK:

2004
New Negrotopia

J. Morgan Puett

Born 1957

Beach Lake, PA
USA

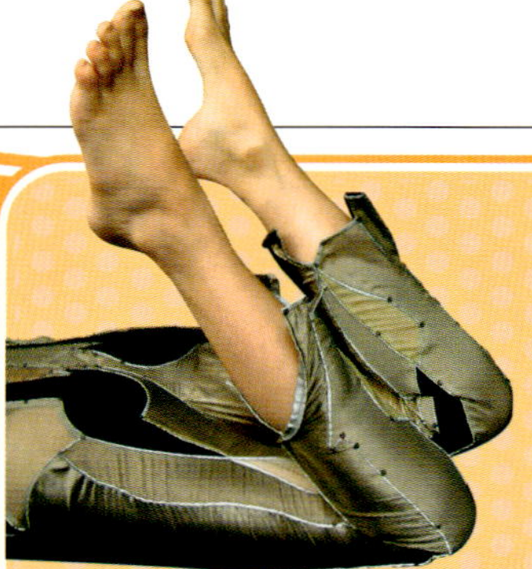

RN; The Past, Present and Future of the Nurse's Uniform, detail; J. Morgan Puett and Mark Dion, in collaboration with the Fabric Workshop and Museum 2003-04. Courtesy of the artist. Photo: Jorge Colombo

Biographical Info:

After **J. Morgan Puett** received her MFA in Sculpture and Filmmaking at the School of the Art Institute of Chicago in 1985, she moved to New York City and opened a series of unlikely, but eventually quite successful, fashion boutiques. Since leaving the business in 2001, Puett continues to investigate the intersections between labor, textiles, history, and imagination.

In 2002, as part of the Spoleto Festival in Charleston, South Carolina, Puett produced a project titled *Cottage Industry*. Working with local weavers, seamstresses, and dyers, Puett turned an abandoned building in Charleston into an operating contemporary clothing factory. Garments were developed by sewing historic textiles collected from museum sources, architecture plans, and everyday clothing. As ready-to-wear collages, the clothes provided an unexpected insight into the histories of racism, class, labor, and migration that surround the site. In her most recent project *RN: the Past, Present, and Future of the Nurse's Uniform* (2003), in

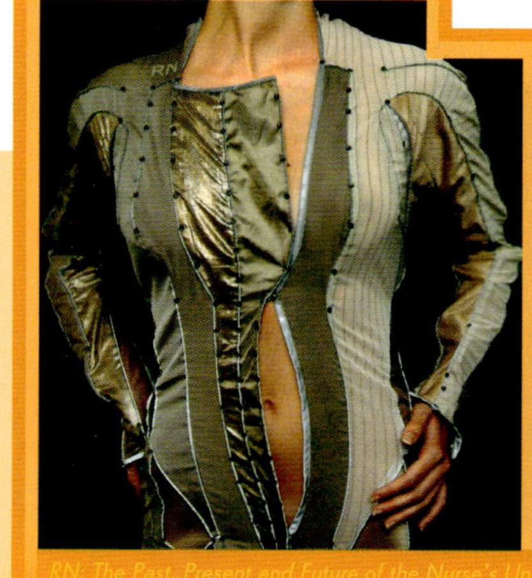
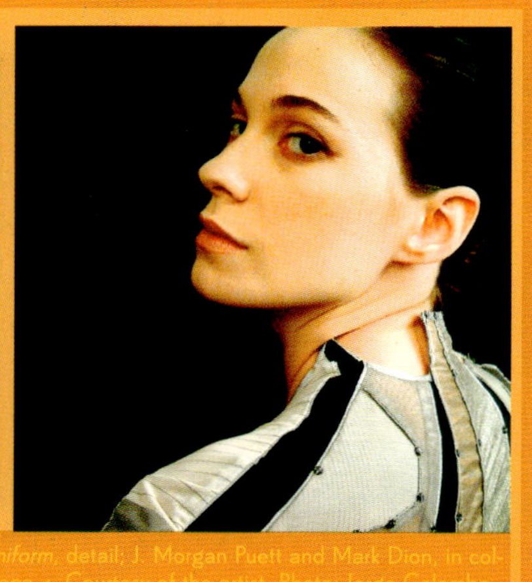

RN; The Past, Present and Future of the Nurse's Uniform, detail; J. Morgan Puett and Mark Dion, in collaboration with the Fabric Workshop and Museum 2003-4. Courtesy of the artist. Photo: Jorge Colombo

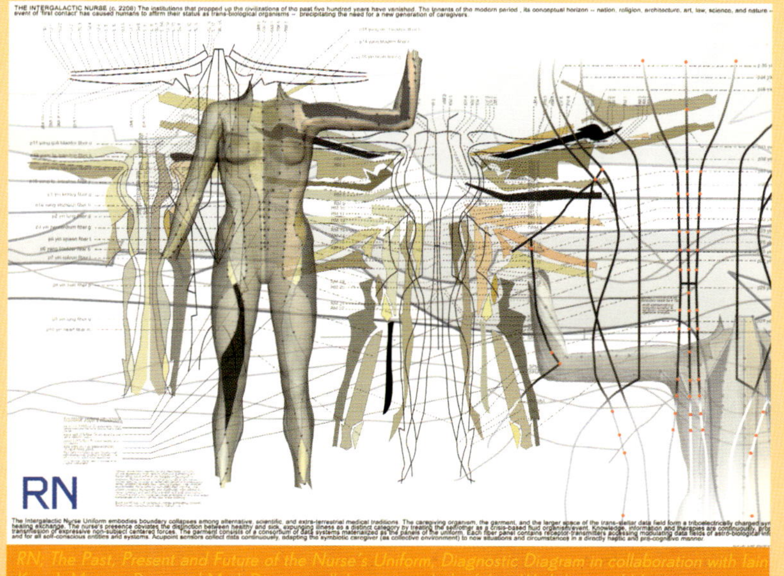

RN; The Past, Present and Future of the Nurse's Uniform, Diagnostic Diagram in collaboration with Iain Kerr, J. Morgan Puett and Mark Dion, in collaboration with the Fabric Workshop and Museum 2003-4. Courtesy of the artist. Photo: Jorge Colombo

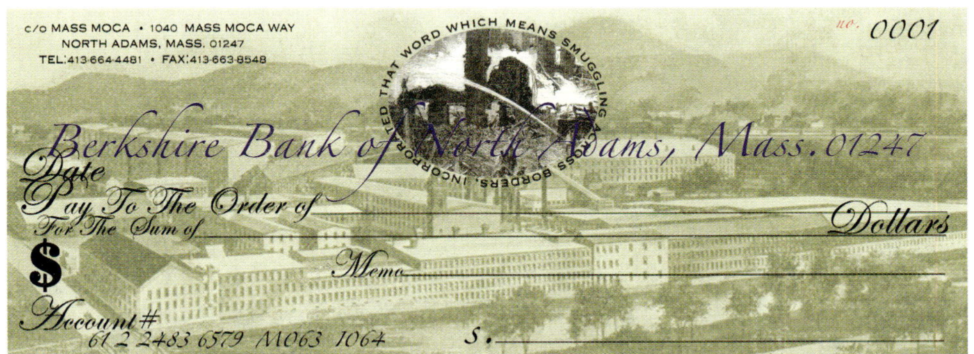

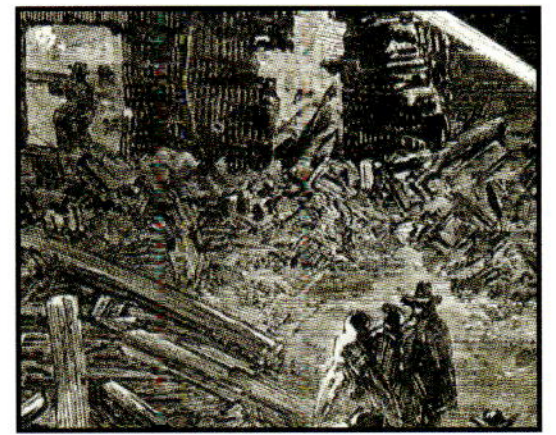

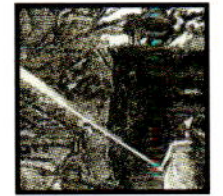

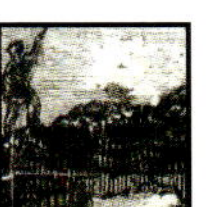

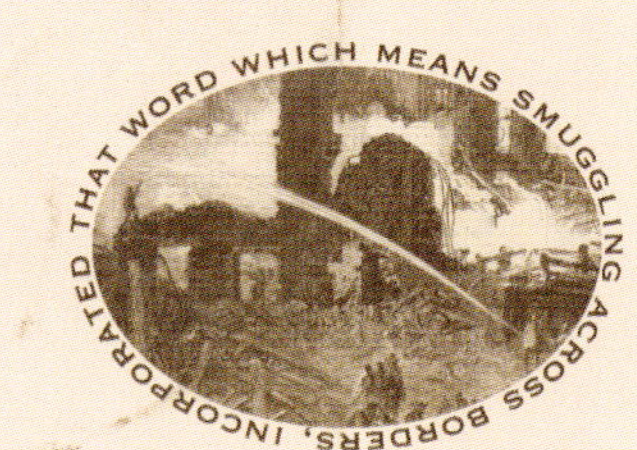

Project Description: Puett's oeuvre defies easy explanation because it combines entrepreneurial ventures with imaginative and historically informed installation. Inspired by the MASS MoCA site's origination as a textile mill, Arnold Print Works (1860-1942), Puett has embedded an unusual clothing business in the burnt-out rubble of an abandoned factory. Her project is not a facsimile or representation of a business, but, in fact, a real business called *That Word Which Means Smuggling Across Borders, Incorporated.* The company produces suits. During its hours of operation, a tailor will take orders and fit and sew suits for willing, and paying, customers. The suit itself is the operating metaphor in the project, as the artists reimagine the meaning of the suit and the history of this particularly charged attire. The suit's patterns are derived from insurance maps of the site during its use as Arnold Print Works.

TITLE OF WORK:
2004 THAT WORD WHICH MEANS SMUGGLING ACROSS BORDERS, Incorporated. (THE SUIT. PART I)

Bio Continued:

collaboration with — and installed at — the Fabric Workshop Museum in Philadelphia, Puett collaborated with Mark Dion in an investigation of the history and possibility of the nurse's uniform. Puett and Dion exhibited historical nursing uniforms alongside "the ideal nurse's uniform, which Puett and Dion attempted to produce with the assistance of nurse focus groups. And for the future, they produced science fiction inspired diagrams with the collaboration of Iain Kerr detailing future nurse garments, including the *Intergalactic* (ca. 2206) and *Post-Apocalyptic* (ca. 2030) *Uniform.*

All images from Cottage Industry, 2002. Courtesy of the artist

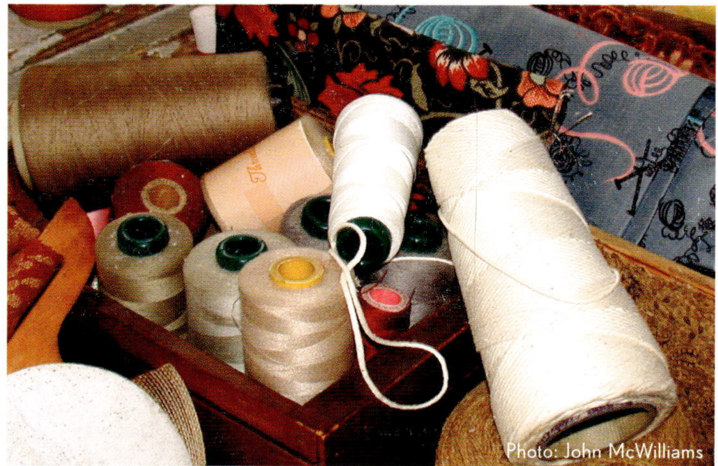

Photo: John McWilliams

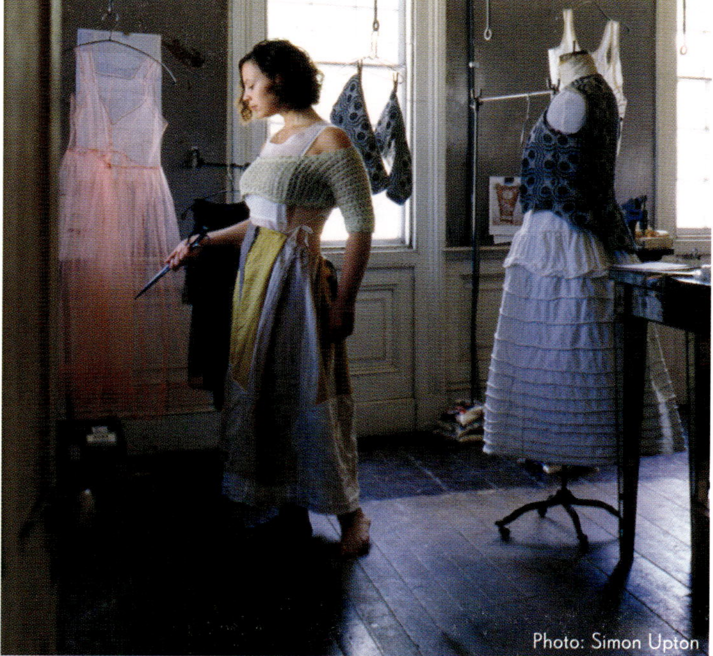

Photo: Simon Upton

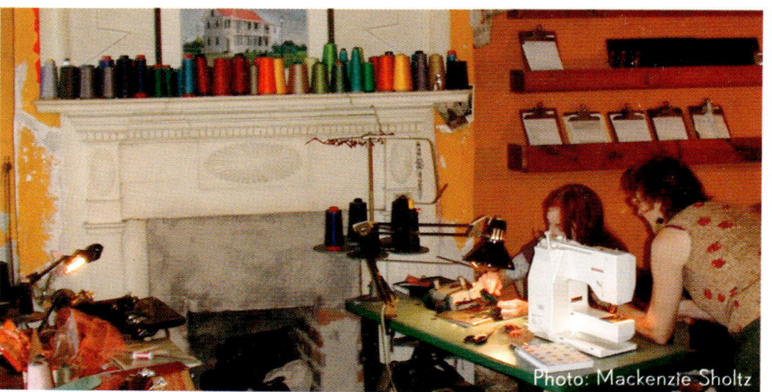

Photo: Mackenzie Sholtz

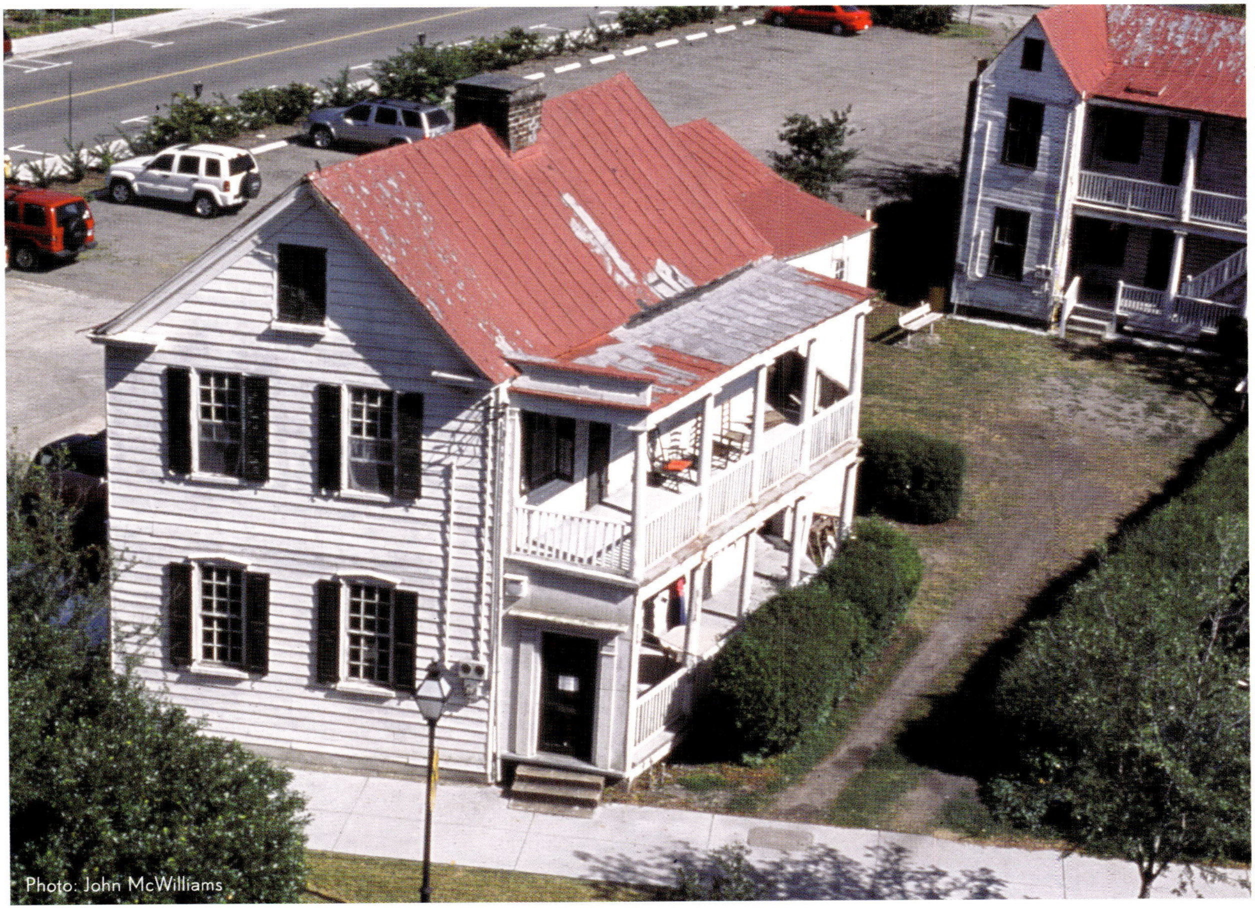

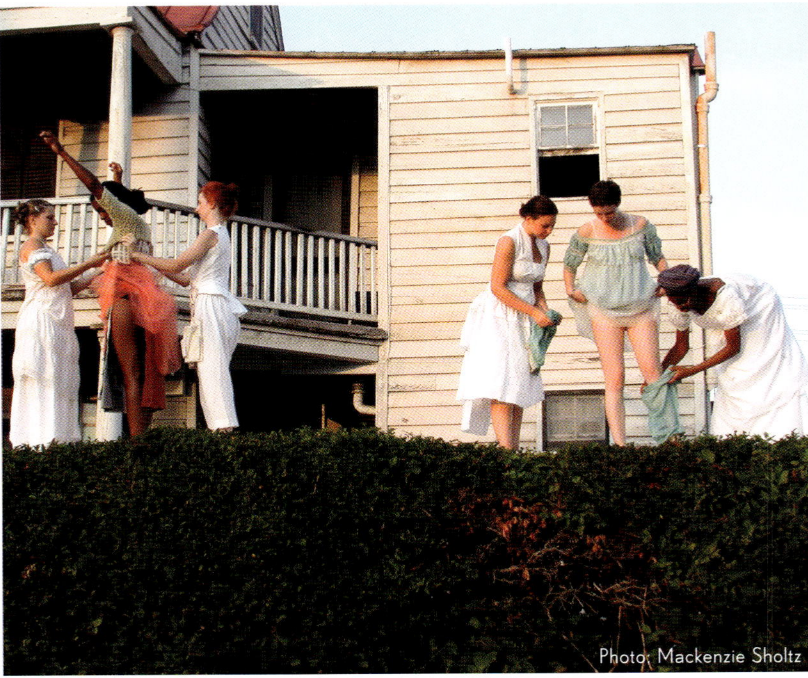

Photo: John McWilliams

Photo: Mackenzie Sholtz

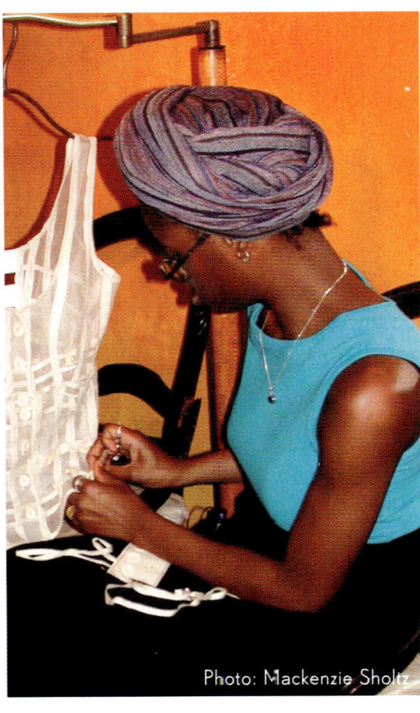

Photo: Mackenzie Sholtz

Interventionism and the historical uncanny

Or: can there be revolutionary art without the revolution?

By Gregory Sholette

April 2, 2004

"Art into Life!"…"Art into Production!"…"Liquidate Art!…," proclaimed the slogans of the Soviet avant-garde. They likened themselves to engineers standing "before the gates of the vacant future,"[1] as centuries of Russian monarchy collapsed in a matter of days. Men and women of diverse artistic temperament, including El Lissitzky, Klucis, Stepanova, Popova Tatlin, Rodchenko, Gabo, Pevsner and the Stenberg brothers, described themselves variously as Constructivists, Objectivists, Engineerists, and Productivists. Their goal was nothing less than a "universal human culture" founded on reason, collective production, and technological utility[2]. Some expressed loathing for conventional artists describing them as the "corrupters of the human race."[3] Others abandoned their studios and sought to enter factories, extolling standardized production processes modeled on Henry Ford's assembly line. They developed designs for workers clubs, portable propaganda apparatuses, and art laboratories where experimentation with new Constructivist principles ideally preceded real world implantation. The artist Tatlin, who is credited with coining the slogan *Art Into Life*, even designed a flying bicycle that would grant every Soviet citizen aeronautical mobility.

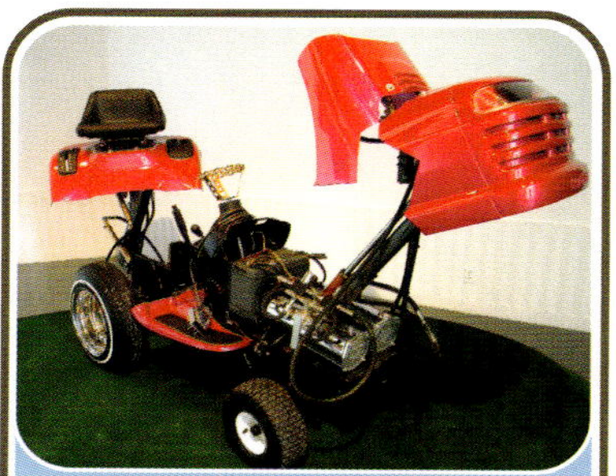

Garden of earthly delights, 2003
Rubén Ortiz-Torres

More than eighty years after Mayakovsky proclaimed "the streets shall be our brushes - the squares our palettes," a discordant collection of interests once again seeks the liquidation of artistic detachment by staging a fresh assault upon the tenuous boundary between art and life.[4] These forces include not only artists and intellectuals, but also philanthropic foundations, government agencies and — above all — global corporations, the contemporary locus of hegemonic power, a point I return to below. For the moment it is enough to note that within this constellation of interests a particular subset of individuals understands this conflict as a site for critical, artistic engagement within the public sphere. Those gathered here under the rubric of interventionists represent compelling examples of this tendency. And because the subsidiary theme of the exhibition is artist as tool provider, comparison to Constructivist and Productivist, post-revolutionary Russian art is unavoidable. Needless to say, this essay steers directly into this potentially turbulent correlation. It asserts that despite far more modest ambitions and radically different circumstances, the contemporary, so-called interventionist reveals a definite congruence with the historic avant-garde program, enough to make qualified comparisons worth pursuing.[5] At the same time there is significant variance raised by the comparison, thus complicating the thesis in ways hopefully productive for future research and debate.

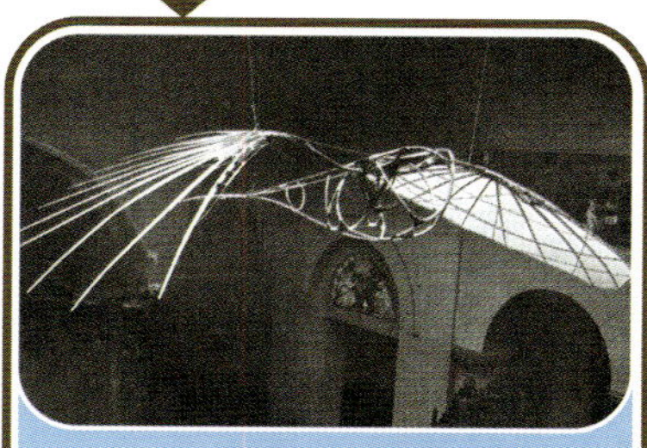

Vladimir Tatlin, *Letatlin* circa 1930. Model reconstructed from original parts, 1960s.

The Soviet avant-garde artists of the 1920s and early 1930s sought to intervene directly into life by developing an art that would be useful for the advancement of an unprecedented revolutionary society. If the magnitude of this task did not lessen artistic arguments and mutual denunciations, it nevertheless inspired a surprising degree of harmony regarding one objective: Art would never again be treated as mere décor or serve as a luxury item for the wealthy. It would instead be integrated directly into the lives and labor of the masses as a useful activity, an organizational tool, and a universal "mathematical consciousness of things."[6]

Predictably, the definition of utility varied from artist to artist, and from manifesto to manifesto. Yet, around one point this complex movement converged. A new conception of pragmatic art would cast aside conventional notions of industrial design and applied art. It would aim instead at something far more sweeping in scope. As Lyubov' Popova asserted, under the fast-changing circumstances of the 1920s, "organization was the principle of all creative activity, including artistic composition, " and the "artistic organization of the object" would inevitably become "the principle guiding the creation of even the most practical, everyday things."[7] Rodchenko carries this logic to extraordinary lengths, claiming that "contemporary art is a conscious and organized life that is able to see and build. Any person who has organized his life, his work, and himself is a genuine artist."[8] Or as El Lissitzky states, "The private property aspect of creativity must be destroyed, all are creators and there is no reason of any sort for this division into artists and nonartists."[9]

Such sentiments argue for a diffusion of creative work throughout a singularly transfigured society rather than the lock-step discipline of an avant-garde elite leading the cowed masses. They also echo the remarks of the young Karl Marx and Frederick Engles who argued that:

"The exclusive concentration of artistic talent in particular individuals, and its suppression in the broad mass which is bound up with this, is a consequence of division of labour. ... In a communist society there are no painters but only people who engage in painting among other activities."[10]

If socially useful art is ultimately determined by the society it serves, the artist as tool maker must, by necessity, look to the public sphere, and not to the realm of art, for the logic of her work. It also means that the success of any radically expanded idea of art is ultimately measured by its very disappearance into the daily life of the masses. In a revolutionary moment, such an objective introduces extraordinary possibilities. It also presents risks, not only for artists, but for citizens and even for the state as vanguard aesthetics appear to appropriate the very dynamic of the revolution itself. No doubt this same ambition made these artists, together with other, semi-autonomous movements in post-revolutionary Russia, threatening to the increasingly centralized and aesthetically traditional Communist Party.[11] As is well known, by the mid 1930s, most of the radical artistic practices I refer to had either been absorbed into orthodox forms of industrial design or sidelined by the official Stalinist aesthetic of socialist realism. Yet while Constructivist ideals of disseminating art amongst the masses gave way to the outright displacement of the avant-garde itself, the desire to

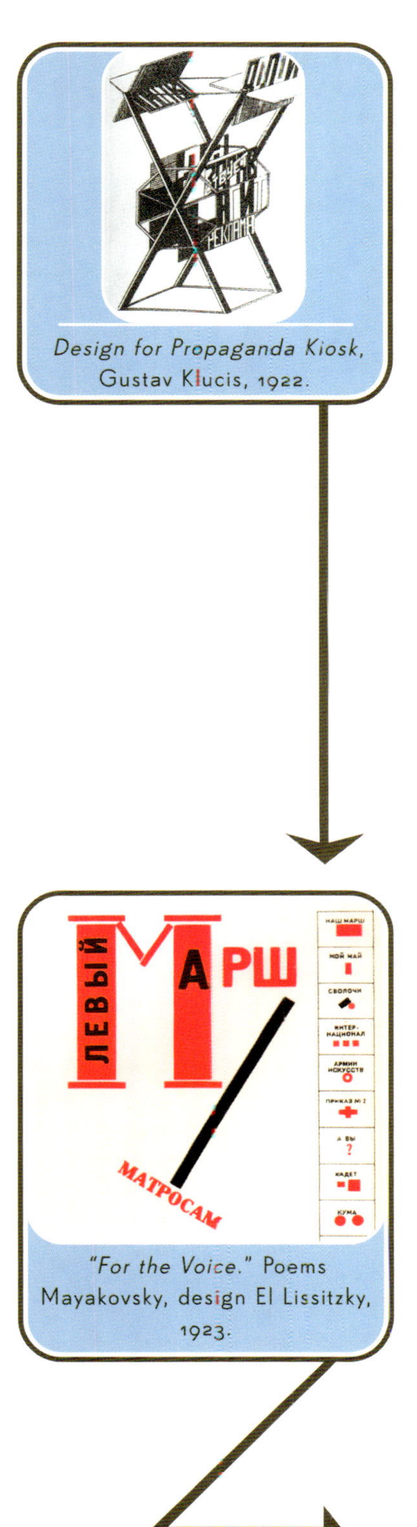

Design for Propaganda Kiosk, Gustav Klucis, 1922.

"For the Voice." Poems Mayakovsky, design El Lissitzky, 1923.

Continue

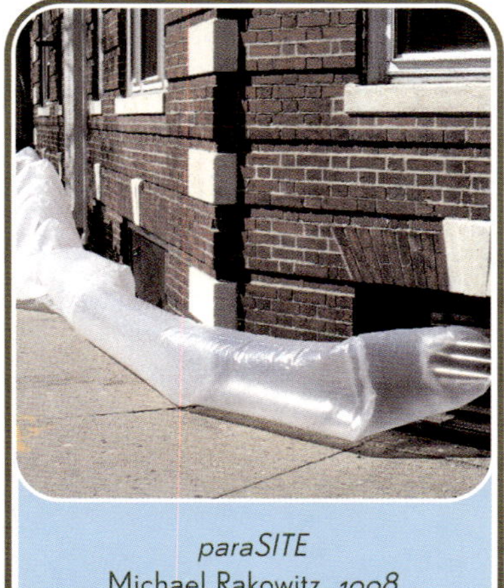

paraSITE
Michael Rakowitz, *1998*

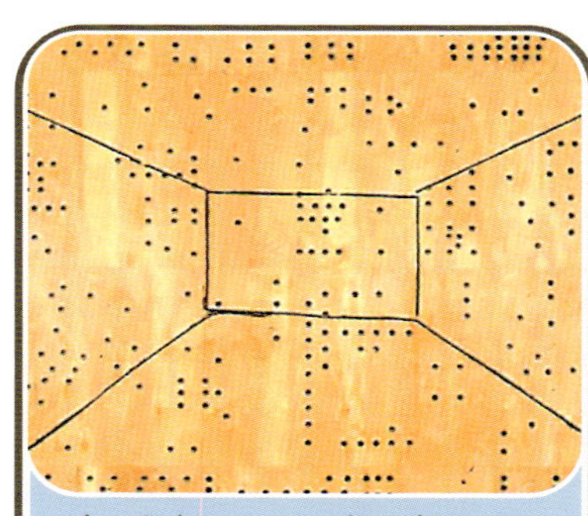

Art & Language Incident in a Museum, Madison Avenue 1986
Courtesy Lisson Gallery
and the artists.

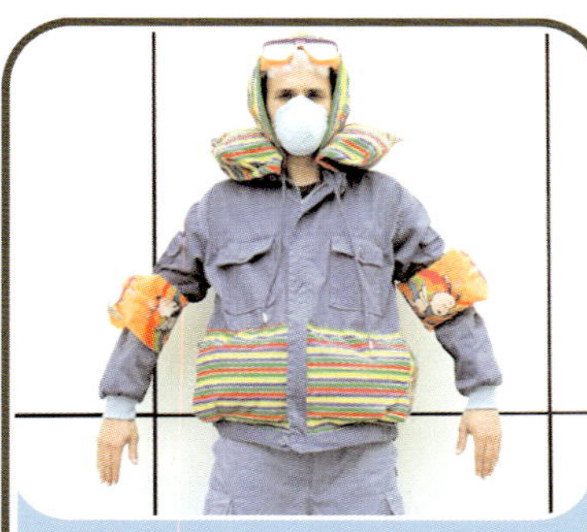

Pret A Revolter, "Ready to Revolt"
Protest Wear, Las Agencias, *2001*

drag art into life remained central to most 20th–Century avant-garde movements, including the Surrealists, the Situationists and Fluxus. Never again, however, did it foment the astonishing range of prototypes, theories and artistic programs aimed at not merely subverting existing norms, but at reinventing human existence in toto. Nor was art spared retrogression back into its familiar, rarified, commodity form as art historian Benjamin H. D. Buchloh has asserted.[12]

Nevertheless, the radical legacy of early 20th–Century art remains broadly detectable today, much in the same way background traces of radiation evince a distant, primeval universe. Take the test yourself. Visit any survey of recent art and try to locate a single participant who is not compelled to make some reference to the world beyond art, be it political, personal or through appropriation of popular media or youth culture. At the same time, however, if all one can argue is that a trace of social engagement lingers on today, as an artistic theme or curious academic problem, then certainly the grouping of past revolutionary art alongside its tepid, contemporary progeny offers a questionable family portrait. Fortunately, there is a wrinkle in this picture. Within its folds is a different interpretation of, as well as an alternative genealogy for, contemporary art itself.

Low–cost shelters for homeless people, birthing tents, graffiti–spraying robots, machines that process racial attitudes, food–testing units, mobile message boards and apparel designed for civil disobedience: on the face of it these projects might just as easily belong in a science hall rather than an art museum. (And I suspect some of the participants would actually be pleased with that alternative.) An apparent disregard for the category of art is the first conspicuous similarity between the artists in this exhibition and the Soviet Constructivists and Productivists. Approaching this more recent work as art, however, with all the historical and formal logic this implies is the premise of this text, but with this important proviso: no claim is made that contemporary interventionist artists consciously set out to emulate the work of Tatlin, Rodchenko, Stepanova and their colleagues. Nor am I promoting this tendency as an incipient neo-avant-garde, especially given assertions still to come, that the very concept of an artistic vanguard has today lost all credibility as a critical, cultural endeavor. Instead, what resemblance exists arrives by indirect routes. This includes professional training in art school and exposure to the activist art of the 1970s and 1980s, but also via a renewed interest in the Situationist theory of the detourne' as curator Nato Thompson puts forward in his introductory essay. Then again, this semblance between far-flung artistic forms might be described as sharing by way of an *historical uncanniness* in so far as there is something strangely familiar about two distant historical moments in which all existing social and productive forces are brought under the domination of a single ideology, even if this jurisdiction was specific to the Soviet Union in the 1920s and is today a global phenomenon.

The most striking similarity between the artists in this exhibition and the historic avant-garde is a mutual interest in temporal systems of organization and public circulation rather than the traditional practice of creating discrete, fixed art objects. Significantly, this indifference towards the valuable artwork is different from that of Conceptual Art in the 1960s and 1970s since it is neither calculated to be an end in itself nor intended to function as a critique of art's institutional circumstances. Instead, this recent work turns outward and away from the institutional art world. Its immaterial bias is not fixated on rejecting commodity fetishism, a near impossible objective, so much as it is focused on scattering art into the public sphere in the form of publications, software, performances, machines, temporary architecture, social services and even conversation. In this sense, the work ideally becomes the property or experience of an unknown recipient. She or he is likely to be a non-art layperson carrying out the logic of the intervention without necessarily recognizing its artistic origins. Again in theory, such dissemination within a public space forms a temporary gift economy that is quite unlike the managed parsimony of the mainstream art market. In this exhibition, Indimedia, YOMANGO, Critical Art Ensemble, Michael Rakowitz, HaHa, and Krzysztof Wodiczko most clearly represent aspects of this practice, although applies in part to most if not all interventionist artists. Needless to say, in the absence of any economic market for their work the early avant-garde manifest a comparable desire to disseminate art into the social body.

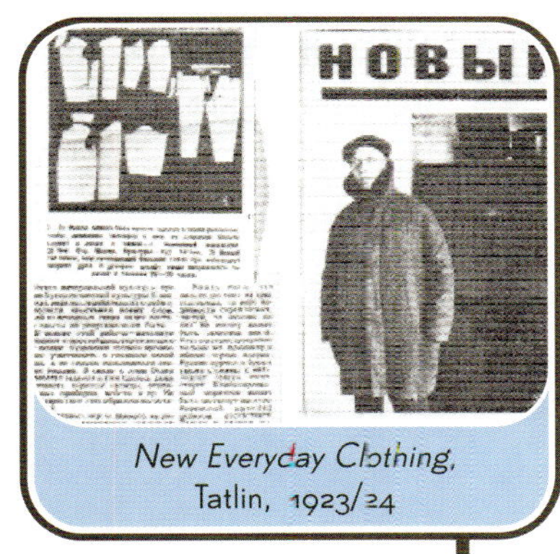

New Everyday Clothing,
Tatlin, 1923/24

There are several additional similarities between recent interventionist tendencies and the artistic program of historic Constructivism and Productivism. Insofar as tool – making is premised on a degree of research and development, we find a mutual interest in experimentalism or laboratory art, as well as the incorporation of new technology into artistic practice. Still, what distinguishes the interventionist approach under discussion here from the broader art and technology scene, as well as from such forerunners as ZERO and E.A.T., or Experiments in Art and Technology in the 1960s, is the instrumental or "tactical" approach taken to technology. In practice this amounts to the incorporation of new, as well as old, methods for advancing social analysis, communal pedagogy, or the enhancement of civic life based on particular needs, rather than technology as a spectacle or as an end in itself. Consider the tent-like pouches that, Dré Wapenaar explains, permit "people to feel secure, calm and friendly," or the Center for Tactical Magic's combination of magic and microcircuits aimed at encouraging "responsible citizenship through social action." How can one avoid being reminded of Tatlin's slogan, "not the old, not the new, but the necessary"?[13]

Because this experiment in utilitarian art goes hand-in-hand with an inattention to traditional notions of individual, artistic expression, it also reveals a distrust of overt aesthetic display in favor of an economy of form and an investment in transparency of expression. The Constructivists, of course, went so far as to describe their artistic program as engineering. And one finds a similar expediency at work in the projects of HaHa, N55, Krzysztof Wodiczko, Lucy Orta, Dré Wapenaar, Valerie Tevere (who is also a part of the group Neurotransmitter) and Michael Rakowitz, et al. But there is also a pragmatic lucidity found in the pedagogical interventions of Atlas Group, Yes Men, subRosa, and Critical Art Ensemble, and in the vernacular and amateur idioms adopted by Rubèn Ortiz-Torres, Alex Villar, Craig Baldwin, YOMANGO, and the Center for Tactical Magic.

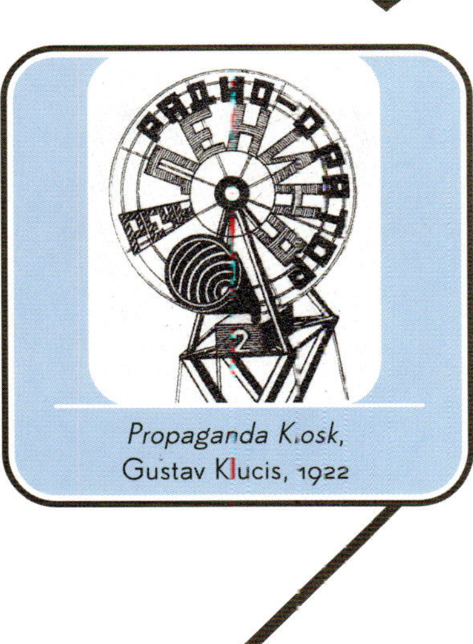

Propaganda Kiosk,
Gustav Klucis, 1922

What is most striking in this regard, as well as markedly different from the type of art favored by mainstream discourse for the past several decades, is the absence of any weighty preoccupation with making the form of the work problematic in itself. It suggests that the recently dominant paradigm of postmodernism, with its emphasis on allegorical representation, irony and pastiche, is no longer operative, raising yet another curious parallel with the Soviet avant-garde in—so—far as the latter sought to

Continue

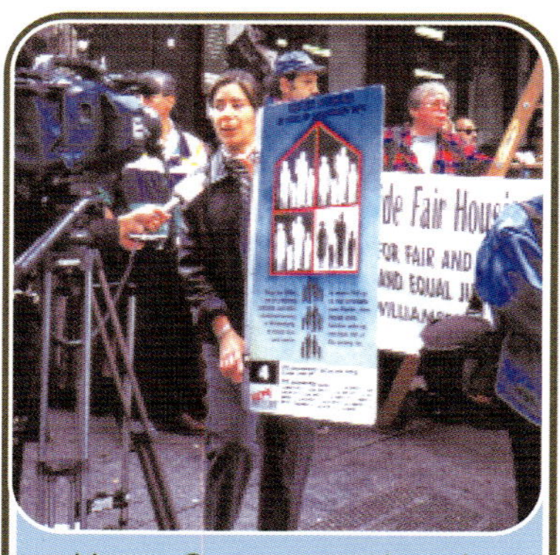

Marina Gutierrez speaks with reporters about her controversial public art work for REPOhistory. NYC, 1999

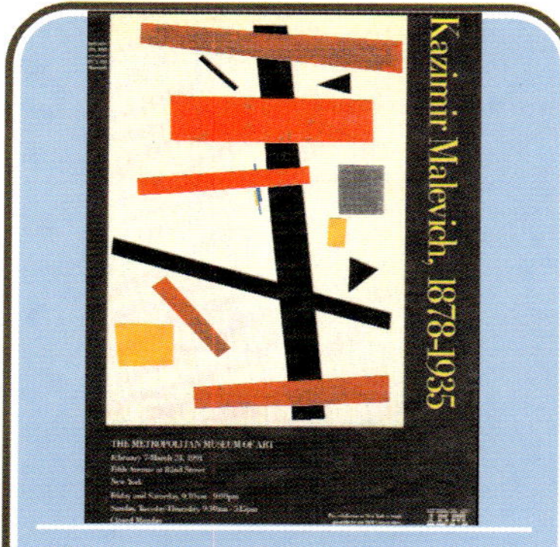

IBM Advertisement, *New York Times Magazine* January 1991

supplant all representational forms of art—making with material structures, primary forms, and de-mystified systems of objective, artistic production. However, this is also the place where dissimilarities most clearly come into play between now and then. This is so in large part because under present historical conditions the objective, material world appears radically different from that which inspired the post-revolutionary Russian artists. Yet, by examining one final area of correspondence, a shared proclivity towards collective art—making, the strangely inverted relationship between certain current art practices and the historic Soviet avant-garde will become most apparent, and my thesis productively detoured.

For much of the early avant-garde, collectivism was axiomatic. It was bound up with modernist concepts of historical progress, and unprecedented societal reform. This was frequently expressed in utopian terms and involved technological and political change but at times took the form of rejecting modernism, yet did so in a manner that nevertheless remained linked to it through negation. Regardless of which aspect of modernism or anti-modernism dominated a particular artistic inclination, the individual members of a given movement were expected to identify categorically with its convictions. According to historian Nina Gourianova, even the pre-Constructivst, anarchist-inflected art of Malevich's Supremitism, called on artists to create,

"...not an individual reflection of the soul, but a universal idea presumably free from the individual psychology and emotions of the artist, the liberation of the spirit through creativity." [14]

For the Constructivists and Productivists this greater calling meant equating art with the massive, material reorganization of society then under way within post-revolutionary Russia as everything from factories to farms was modernized, collectivized, and made pragmatic.

Fast—forwarding to the present we find a remarkable degree of collaborative and collective organization amongst the interventionist artists. Each is different, however. They range from spuriously labeled bureaus, institutes and centers to a legitimate, yet sardonic corporation in *Bitter Nigger Inc.* There is even a "factory" that simulates industrial processes and public service workers who monitor potentially hazardous forms of production such as genetically modified food." [15] Yet, contrary to early 20th century art movements, contemporary art groups, as if reflecting the plasticity of identity formations in the post-industrial world, might be said to perform or enact collectivist modes and organizational forms rather than embody them. Incongruity, pluralism and informality have come to supplant notions of unanimity and revolutionary discipline. Tactical conditions — not grand, unifying principles — compel their formation, which explains perhaps why so many engage in self-mockery and irreverent play. For example, the Critical Art Ensemble describes itself as a "cellular collective construction" exercising "solidarity through difference."

Logically, discrepancies also emerge in terms of the audience for this art. While the Constructivists, following Lenin, believed rapid industrialization held the key to radical, social transformation, and therefore understandably looked towards factory workers as the ideal audience/participant for their program, by contrast, no contemporary artist volunteers to enter the work place any more than they anticipate mass-producing utilitarian artworks.[16] Gone is the positive expectation that modernization once inspired and with it the privileged role of the laboring class. Michael Rakowitz and his cohorts Bill Stone, George Livingston and Freddie Flynn for example focus on the urban indigent rather the industrial proletariat by creating polyethylene shelters for homeless people that are inflated by heat exhaust from city buildings and subways. Similarly, the Danish group N55 offers individuated sanctuary with their Snail Shell System. It rolls as well as floats and can tap into the city's electrical grid through the base of street lamps like some municipal parasite, but the occupant it is aimed at is not the worker but an alienated nomad. YOMANGO's line of shoplifting apparel and accessories allows the plebeian consumer to perform everyday acts of sabotage against the homogenizing effects of trans-national corporations. In each case, the intended audience for this work is less working class than simply the masses or what Antonio Negri and Michael Hardt term the multitude.[17] But equally significant is the way this new wave of useful artistry functions as an ideal model for acts of civil disobedience rather than a practical strategy for defeating global capitalism.

If, for the Constructivists, experimenting with the mundane routines of labor promised something far grander than well-designed teapots, then redemption of utilitarian art was unconditionally linked with the imminent rebirth of humankind: living and working collectively, creatively and rationally thanks in large part to avant-garde art itself. By contrast, interventionist art is a symbolic and at times farcical comment about specific social problems. In other words: to the degree this work is pragmatic, it is also ironic, and to the degree it is aimed at public intervention, it cedes no transformative powers to any one group party or class. Not that this represents a deficiency so much as the logical response to current political and economic conditions. Still, it is a departure from the earnest teleology of classical avant-gardism as well as from much of the art activism of the 1970s, 1980s and early 1990s.

The Art Workers Coalition, Red Herring, Artists Meeting for Social Change, The Los Angeles Women's Building, Heresies Magazine Collective, Guerrilla Art Action Group, Paper Tiger, S.P.A.R.C. (Social and Public Art Resource Center), General Idea, PAD/D (Political Art Documentation and Distribution), Border Arts Workshop, Group Material, Gran Fury, Godzilla, the Guerrilla Girls and later REPOhistory to name only some of the artists' groups founded between 1969 and 1989 certainly had no unified program or aesthetic.[18] They did generally share however, an analyt-

ical approach to cultural criticism and a desire to use art as an instrument for revealing to a broad, non-art public concealed institutional, political, and historical power. For example, by staging sustained public demonstrations against the Museum of Modern Art in the late 1960s, The Art Workers Coalition is credited with forcing this and other New York museums to offer a free admission day. Group Material's 1983 subway car intervention, Subculture, encouraged riders to reflect on working conditions and U.S military involvement in Central America. Gran Fury and Act Up rewrote the rulebook regarding activist iconography in the mid-198s by appropriating sophisticated media strategies for enlightening the public about the politics behind the AIDS crisis. In the early 1990s REPOhistory installed temporary street signage on city streets with images and texts that offered passersby a site-specific window into historical events and people misrepresented or ignored by dominant culture including workers, women, children and minorities. And since 1985 the Guerrilla Girls, who along with Paper Tiger is the only organization listed above that remain active today, have campaigned to reveal the numerical absence of women and minorities within the mainstream cultural establishment.

Along with this strong pedagogical and analytical inclination, these groups also shared a spotty kinship with Conceptual Art, especially in terms of the latter's emphasis on language, and its de-emphasis on the sanctity of the art object. But perhaps most significantly these diverse organizations also converged around the cultural politics of the New Left: a polyglot amalgam of feminists, progressive labor, minority and community activists that, despite increasing fragmentation, appeared, until recently, to be capable of coalescing into something resembling a single movement. PAD/D went so far as to propose an entire alternative arts network linking a variety of venues, including university art galleries, community centers, union halls, even churches into a sort of shadow art world that in turn would connect with non-art oriented activists. Very much not avant-garde in approach, PAD/D sought to transform preaching to the converted into a bona-fide, counter-cultural community that anticipated some of the rhetoric surrounding the World Wide Web.[19]

While these lessons are not lost on the new wave of activist art, according to curator Nato Thompson the interventionists, "do not preach. They do not advocate. As opposed to providing a literal political message, these artists pro-

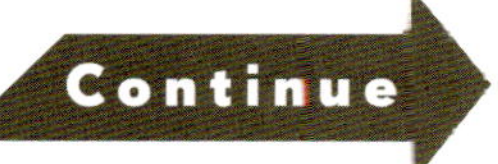

vide tools for the viewer/participant to develop their own politics. In this sense, the political content is found in a project's use. They supply possibilities as opposed to solutions." [20]

Perhaps the softer political tone of most of this work reflects a healthy disillusionment with expert culture as well as an acknowledgement that even when preaching social awareness artists remain a privileged class. And if some interventionists openly align themselves with the mass activism witnessed in Seattle, Genoa, Quebec, and so forth, their politics are, generally speaking, as informal and fragmentary as the wildly heterogeneous counter-globalization movement itself. They signal a rejection of traditional Left wing institutions. At the same time it is equally preposterous to imagine any of these artists openly embracing their own, national government in the way Constructivists and Productivists intended their art to help build communism in the USSR. This holds true despite the receipt of modest to strong federal funding amongst the artists. Instead of grander political goals, analyses, and strategies therefore we find a call for self-determined cultural, and social autonomy. However, there is a legislative model that contemporary interventionists somewhat resemble. It is the Non-Governmental Organization or NGO. Independent, unaffiliated, and ecumenical, groups such as GreenPeace, Médecins Sans Frontières, and Amnesty International stress pragmatic and tactical action over ideology. Nevertheless the question must be raised; can there be radical art without a revolution?

Ironically, or inevitably, it is not interventionist artists who lead the charge to collapse the allegedly transcendent into the merely secular, that is to say art into life. Instead this pressure comes primarily from the legitimating demands of the modern, managerial class who make up what historian Chin-tau Wu calls enterprise culture: the unfettered privatization of all public life and services. Enterprise culture is a force that has come to dominate both the US and UK and is linked with the conservative governments of Ronald Reagan and Margaret Thatcher. According to Wu, it has also produced significant effects within the cultural realm. She writes,

"Contemporary art, especially in its avant-garde manifestations, is generally assumed to be in rebellion against the system, [but] it actually acquires a seductive commercial appeal within it." [21]

The codependency between the captains of enterprise culture and contemporary art is plainly articulated by John Murphy, former Executive Vice-President of Philip Morris Corporation when he states:

"There is a key element in this 'new art' which has its counterpart in the business world. That element is innovation — without which it would be impossible for progress to be made in any segment of society." [22]

Perhaps Tatlin's revolutionary slogan should now be rephrased as "art into business," assuming that the latter has already incorporated most aspects of autonomous, daily life into itself. And clearly everything today can be market-branded from the war in Iraq to coolness itself as social critic Thomas Frank argues. [23] At the same time the language and logic of commerce has deeply permeated the art world. In art schools, students express concerns about how to market themselves. Once graduated, the emerging artist is keen to focus on product placement within prominent museums, journals and biennials. But why should this surprise us when the leading lights of the art world, from Matthew Barney to the managers of the Tate Modern, present high art as a spectacle of abundance, even of excess, in which success is measured by how many fabricators one commands and who throws the swankiest openings? And all of this shock and awe appears to be thanks to the marriage of high culture and corporate largess. In terms of artist as tool provider, therefore, the boasting of Thomas Hoving, former director of New York's Metropolitan Museum of Art sums it up decisively:

"Art is sexy! Art is money-sexy! Art is money-sexy -social-climbing-fantastic!" (Wu, 127).

The call for art to merge into life returns today under the most improbable of circumstances. Not only has the decrepit Soviet Union completely vanished, but, as if history were a glove pulled inside out, so has the once widespread aspiration that society be grounded in equanimity, fraternity and reason rather than profitability, competition, and market speculation. Socialism, the driving force of the Russian avant-garde, has become, in the words of Jacques Derrida, a specter. It haunts the totality that is, at the start of the 21st Century, global capitalism. What is so very odd, therefore, is the degree to which current historical circumstances are exactly opposite those surrounding the Soviet Avant-Garde, and yet simultaneously analogous in so far as the private interests of capital permeate the entire fabric of society now to the same degree collective ideals once saturated Soviet culture. The strongest opponents of globalization comprehend this fact. They also grasp the importance of expanding the notion of working class resistance to include the type of immaterial, symbolic production created by service and intellectual laborers. Interventionist art exists at the crossroads of these realizations.

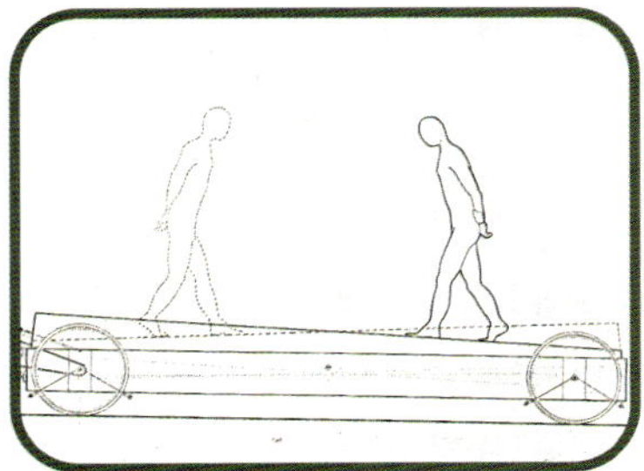

Drawing for a vehicle in which the rider must walk back and forth on a seesaw platform to power it. Krzysztof Wodiczko, 1970s

The current wave of artistic utilitarianism does indeed produce useful, tool-like art. And, these acts of resistance practiced within everyday life are witty and at times inspiring. Nevertheless, they remain disconnected from comprehensive visions of radical, social transformation. Their politics are vague or at best subdued.[24] It is worth noting by way of an admittedly oblique answer to the question raised about radical art and revolutionary politics that some of the most ambitious projects in the USSR in the 1920s, including Tatlin's Monument to the Third International and Rodchenko's *Workers Club*, never left the prototype stage. Perhaps foremost among these unrealized social interventions was the *"people's air bicycle,"* or Letatlin, a peculiar combination of the pragmatic and the fantastic that Tatlin fabricated in the seclusion of the Novodevichi Monastery outside Moscow in the early 1930s. The personal flying machine at once signaled the possibility that every Soviet citizen could be mobile, travel freely; even temporarily withdraw from the collective. But more than that, one can read into Letatlin a sly, critical stance towards the increasingly bureaucratic and centralized Soviet state.[25] In other words, is it possibly Tatlin's merging of autonomy and critique, rather than his call of art into life that most clearly prefigures today's interventionists? Perhaps the problem of representation is not obsolete after all? At the same time, how can one not afford to attempt the radical transformation of present art and society, with or without a revolution imminent?

NOTES:

1. From the *"Realistic Manifesto,"* N. Pevsner and N. Gabo, Second State Printing House, August 1920, in *Art into Life: Russian Constructivism 1914-1932* (Seattle/New York: Henry Art Gallery & Rizolli: 1990), p 61.

2. K. Medunetskii, V. Stenberg & G. Stenberg, *"The Constructivists Address the World,"* Janurary 1922, in *Art Into Life*, p 81.

3. Ibid.

4. Mayakovsky from his poem "Order to the Army of Art," in *Camilla Gray, The Russian Experiment in Art: 1863-1922* (London: Thames & Hudson, 1962), p 224.

5. Note that both my caution and enthusiasm regarding this historical comparison is indebted to the important research and writings of Benjamin Buchloh, Hal Foster and Christine Lodder on the revolutionary avant-garde.

6. V. Stenberg from *Art Into Life*, p 68.

7. Lyubov Popova,"Commentary on Drawings," December 1921, in *Art Into Life*, p 69.

8. Alexander Rodchenko, "Slogans," February 22, 1921, in *Art Into Life*, p 71.

9. El Lissitzky, "Suprematism in World Reconstruction," 1920, in *El Lissitzky: Life, Letters, Texts*, (London, Thames & Hudson, 1967), p 333.

10. Karl Marx and Frederick Engels, *The German Ideology, 1845-46*, (New York, International Publishers edition, 1970), p 109.

11. Historian Boris Groys has recently suggested that the Soviet Avant-garde was a threat to Stalin not because they rejected his aesthetic of Socialist Realism, but because their totalizing artistic project literally competed with Stalin's on the same ideological terrain. Groys revisionism however neither accounts for the ironic tendency found especially in the later work of Tatlin nor, more significantly, does it explain the call to make the division between artists and non-artists disappear in a liberated communist society. See, "Stalinism as an Aesthetic Phenomenon," in *Tekstura: Russian Essays on Visual Culture*, edited and translated by Alla Efimova and Lev Manovich, (Chicago, University of Chicago Press, 1993), p 115 - 151.

12. See especially B. Buchloh, "Figures of Authority, Ciphers of Regression," reprinted in *Art After Modernism: Rethinking Representation*, edited by Brian Wallis, (New York, The New Museum of Contemporary Art, 1984), p 107- 136.

13. *Art Into Life*, p 38.

14. Nina Gurianova, "The Supremus Laboratory-House: Reconstructing the Journal," in Drutt, Mathew, ed. *Kazimir Malevich:Suprematism*, Guggenheim Museum Publications: New York, 2003, p.44-59

15. *Observations on Collective Cultural Action*, The Critical Art Ensemble, http://www.critical-art.net/lectures/collective.html

16. At least this is true in the US today. However, some notable exceptions from an earlier generation of artists include: Mierle Laderman Ukeles who has worked with the New York City Department of Sanitation as their artist-in-residence for more than twenty years as well as such artists as Fred Lonidier, Mike Alewitz, Alan Sekula, Marty Pottenger and Toronto, Canada: Carol Conde and Karl Beveridge.

17. Antonio Negri and Michael Hardt, *Empire*: (Cambridge: Harvard 2000).

18. For more about these groups see: *But Is It Art: The Spirit of Art as Activism*, ed. Nina Felshin, (Seattle: Bay Press, Inc. 1994); *Alternative Art New York: 1965-1985*, ed. Julie Ault, (Minneapolis, University of Minnesota Press, 2002); *Grant Kester's Conversation Pieces: Community and Communication in Modern Art*, forthcoming from University of California and *Collectivism After Modernism*, eds Stimson & Sholette, forth coming from University of Minnesota Press.

19. I take up the notion of a shadow or dark matter art world in several recent essays including *"Some Call It Art From Imaginary Autonomy to Autonomous Collectivity,"* available on-line at: European Institute for Progressive Cultural Policies: http://www.eipcp.net/diskurs/d07/text/sholette_en.html

20. *Trespassing Relevance*, (*The Interventionists: Users' Manual for the Creative Disruption of Everyday Life*, MIT Press, Cambridge, MA/London) Nato Thompson, 2004

21. Chin-tao Wu, *Privatising Culture: Corporate Art Intervention since the 1980s*, (London/New York, Verso, 2002), p 161.

22. Ibid, p 125.

23. Thomas Frank, *The Conquest of Cool: Business Culture, Counterculture, and the Rise of Hip Consumerism*, (Chicago, University of Chicago Press, 1997).

24. Regarding Iraq see Noel C. Paul, *"Selling War: Marketers Weigh in on How Well Bush Is Branding the Battle with Iraq,"* *The Science Monitor*, March 26, 2003, and online at: http://abcnews.go.com/sections/business/World/iraq_selling war_csm_030326.html). And in terms of political explicitness I am focusing on a general tendency but acknowledge there are significant differences between subRosa or the Critical Art Ensemble on one hand and e-Xplo or N55 on the other.

25. Perhaps it is not coincidental that the shrewd, humorous reflexivity of contemporary interventionist art also resembles art made during the cold war in what was termed the "eastern bloc"? For example Krzysztof Wodiczko's ironic, conceptual art projects made before emigrating from Poland.

"political art" that remains as separate from the action as the art we're educated to make. While we want to move beyond the isolation and alienation of the art world, it is important to us to remain artists, to maintain contact with our roots as image makers, to recognize the social importance of making art. We'd like to encourage the fearless use of objects, and encourage and support disenfranchised people in making their own uncolonized art. We reject the way the art market has denied art's social function and defuses it by setting up false dichotomies between abstraction and figuration, "political and formalist", high and low culture. Perhaps the most insidious idea we have to combat is that you have to give up art to be involved in the world, or give up the world in order to be an artist (the alternative being that impotent neutral ground currently offered artists by the dominant culture).

PAD wants to restore the central role of art in our culture.

We want to become a channel through which artists can take responsibility for their own and other lives. We are convinced that it is possible to overcome the conflict between "my own work" and outreach, between collective work and "getting back to my studio." Individual talent, or the self, is not lost but clarified and enlarged through social practice. So far, the most visible models for understanding the personal/political fusion have been provided by feminists, but we all know a number of people invisible to the mainstream, who are doing equally important work to dispel the negative separation between the personal and the political.

PAD recognizes the complex dialectic underlying creativity in social contexts. We do not see the individual artist's gifts and needs being replaced by a dogmatic notion of "social work." Instead, we see one of PAD's central tasks as a conscious and patient investigation of the historical twists and turns of interaction between artist and society.

We have to criticize and accept criticism. We have to stop putting down everybody who's not making the same kind of political art we are — which is a classic product of artworld competition. As such, PAD can not serve as a means of advancement within the artworld structure of museums and galleries. Rather, we have to develop new forms of distribution economy as well as art, open up the old forms and, most important, support eachother in our efforts to understand the process of doing so. We have to identify our primary audience. We have to stimulate the invaluable dialogue between artists and the people we think we're working for. Art is about matter, material, reality, whether it's abstract, or representational, or conceptual. It's about real life, about how we see, touch, experience, feel. Art and politics have in common the capacity to move people. But we have to be very clear about who we are moving and why, whose reality our artwork reflects.

Artists can be useful and powerful allies.

In a nation where oppression is primarily carried out on an ideological level, through control of communication, we recognize the central importance of making powerful cross cultural images, of creative opposition to the dominant culture. One of PAD's most crucial tasks is to build an understanding of the importance of the artist in the con-

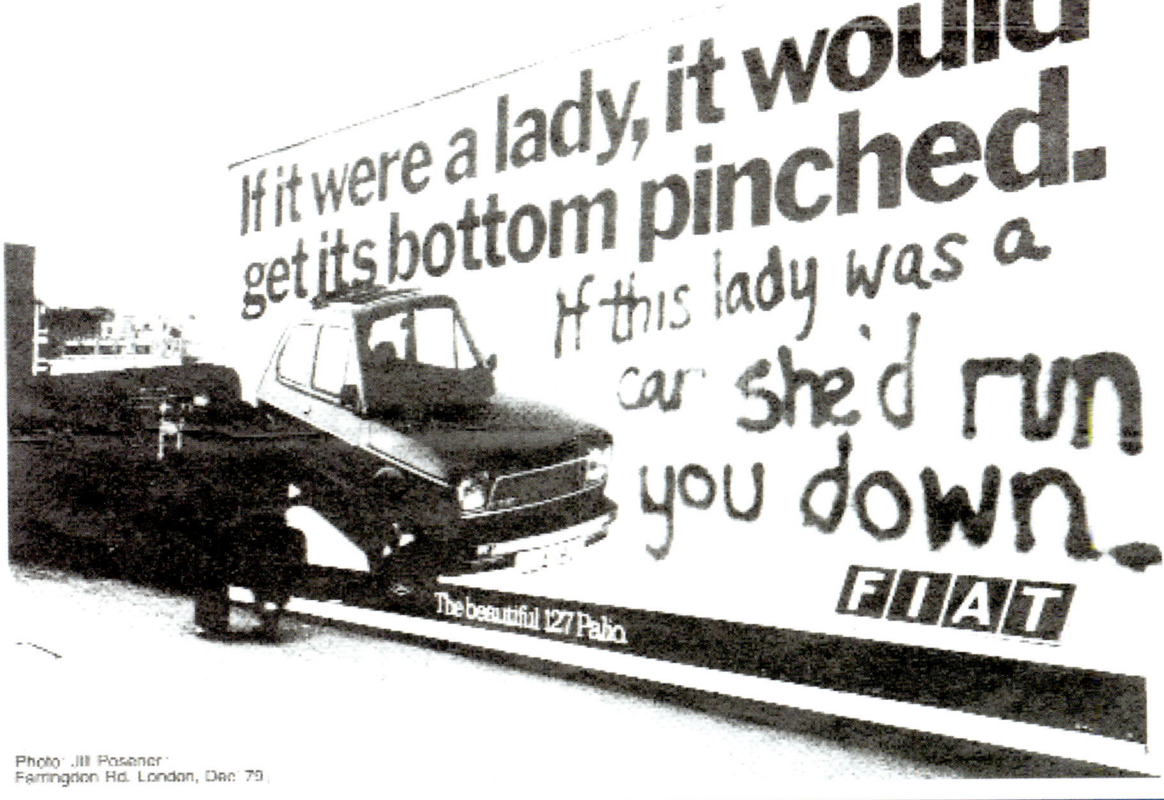

Anarchy in the ruins: dreaming the experimental university

By Nicholas Mirzoeff

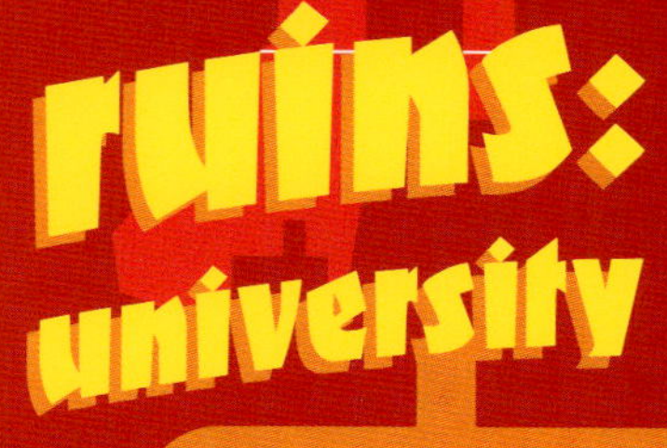

Nicholas Mirzoeff, a professor of Art History and Comparative Literature at Stony Brook University, is seen as a leading theoretical voice and protagonist for the study of visual culture.

Imagine for a moment that you do not know what a university is or, more exactly, what it might have been. Imagine that you set aside all the reams of boilerplate and platitude produced by today's universities in search of a purpose to ask yourself what a university will have been by the time this exhibition is over. The future perfect — the "will have been" — is the tense of the ghost, which will have returned. The ghost in this case is precisely the imagined university that haunts the ruins of the university as it is today.

The late Edward Said used to declare that the university was the last utopia in Western society. The slightest glance at any report by a senior university official will quickly make it apparent that no hint of utopia remains, with its language of incentivizing the faculty, naming students as customers and claiming the benefit of the institution is to function as an economic multiplier. Did that utopia simply evaporate to join the long list of unfulfilled millenarian dreams? The new "realism" among university administrators would say so, but the interventionists of this exhibition suggest otherwise. For as the ghost of the university continues to return, it demands that we consider that the university is in fact yet to come. The utopian university is not the ghost in the machine but rather, as Deleuze and Guattari might put it, it is a machine. This machine produces knowledge, not information, and there is a difference. This university-machine did not die but has become dispersed into the expanded field: beyond the museum, beyond the lecture hall, and into everyday life. Experience the intervention of the experimental university and realize that the dream was not necessarily about those places with the name "university" on the door. The existence and emergence of utopian spaces to eat, live, dream and imagine take place in between the ruins of the museum and those of the university. It is not a revolution. It is a moment of clarity.

Instead of thinking of the university as a locus of national policy by which the elite recruits new members, perhaps it might be a place in which people encounter each other. This sideways encounter is inspired by the German writer and critic Walter Benjamin's vision of the Arcades, the 19th-century covered iron-and-glass arena for shopping, strolling and — perhaps above all — observation.

Benjamin took this social and architectural innovation and transformed it into what he called a dream-image. The dream-image expressed his sense that the Arcades were an especially important site in which people were trying to dream the future into being. Taking seriously Said's sense of the university as a utopia would make it the 20th-century equivalent of this dream, trying to create tools, images and ideas for the 21st century. Of course, this kind of rhetoric is close to that used by universities themselves with their insistent claims to prepare people for the future and improve the world we live in. Said's view was far more expansive than the narrow socioeconomic amelioration now offered to students and their parents in exchange for their ever-rising tuition fees. This university might be a place of emancipation rather than instruction, formed by critique rather than the transfer of information. The emancipated university was not accomplished in the past but dreamed by it. Like the Arcades, it was a vision of the refiguring of social space or, more exactly, the rendering of space such that its social nature becomes apparent. That is to say, there is no such thing as empty space because all space, or the sensation of space, is socially produced. Unlike the Arcades, the university is a space of production rather than consumption, in short a machine. Here is the connection with contemporary art, which Sarat Maharaj has called a form of knowledge production. In this view, the distinction between the university (each with its own museum) and the museum (each with its own education department) is getting productively blurred. In this interface of artwork, museum and university, knowledge is produced as a dream of an emancipation that is yet to come. The emancipated university in the expanded field is, then, a dream machine.

There is much work to be done in developing this idea. Let's begin with the question of emancipation. Emancipation is the legal or biological process by which a minor attains status as a subject. To be emancipated, one might come of age; or be set free from bondage in slavery or indentured servitude; or have the legal burdens of civil disability set aside, such as those prescribed against Jews and other minorities in European nations prior to the French Revolution. In short, emancipation is an act of what French philosopher Michel Foucault called "biopower," the intersection of life with power. Biopower sets the age at which one attains subject status at 30, 21 or 18; figures the "age of consent" to sexual relations; renders certain forms of sexual practice not just illegal or immoral but as a separate species, such as the "homosexual"; permits children to be tried "as adults"; determines what forms of embodiment are "disabled" and which are not, and so on. In the European Enlightenment, the philosopher Immanuel Kant answered the question posed by a German newspaper "What is enlightening?" as emancipation, or "Man's quitting the nonage occasioned by himself." Nonage was the legal state of minority which required emancipation. In Kant's instance, "Man" — by which he normally means the white, male, European, free, able-bodied Gentile — is able to emancipate himself by the public use of Reason. The difficulty inherent in this concept of emancipation is that Reason has also been used to create the barriers to its enactment for those people who did not fall into the category of "Man."

To make an assertion that will perhaps seem too quick, the experimental university would be a space for a collective and interactive deployment of criticism and other modes of inquiry that are not circumscribed by this limited definition of the human. In discussing Kant's essay on enlightenment, Foucault argued that criticism was now to be framed as "a historical investigation of the events that have led us to constitute ourselves as subjects of what we are doing, thinking, saying....But if we are not to settle for the affirmation or the empty dream of freedom, it seems to me that this historico-critical attitude must also be an experimental one." By this, Foucault meant that such projects must be local and specific rather than seek to create the "new man that the worst political systems have repeated throughout the twentieth century." The empty affirmation of freedom is all around us at present even as its local and specific forms seem to be under consistent and widespread erasure.

In the context of art and visual culture, there is a notable omission from Foucault's definition of the activities of the subject: namely, seeing. His work was built on the theory of the "interpellation" of the subject, developed by his colleague Louis Althusser in 1960s Paris. Althusser described interpellation, or hailing, as something "which can be imagined along the lines of the most commonplace everyday police (or other) hailing 'Hey, you there!'" When we respond to that call by looking around or asking "do you mean me?" we recognize our interpellation. This recognition is the means by which an individual locates herself in time and space. Inherent in that little moment is also a visual surveillance that leads to a moment of detection or recognition. The actions of the subject are suspicious, but their actions clearly exist.

Rather than an exchange between individuals on foot, as presumed in Althusser's theory of interpellation, his former colleague Jacques Rancière has recently argued that the modern anti-spectacle now dictates that there is nothing to see and that instead one must keep moving, keep circulating and keep consuming: "The police are above all a certitude about what is there, or rather, about what is not there: 'Move along, there's nothing to see.'" One of the new camps for migrants or refugees concealed in a remote area of the countryside is a good example of this object of visuality which is there and not there at once. The police are not just the uniformed officers of the police force but what Foucault called "an administration heading the state, together with the judiciary, the army and the exchequer." Contrasting this generalized sense of the police with the practice of politics, Rancière continues: "the police say there is nothing to see, nothing happening, nothing to be done, but to keep moving, circulating; they say that the space of circulation is nothing but the space of circulation. Politics consists in transforming the space of circulation into the space of manifestation of the subject, be it the people, workers, or citizens. Politics consists of reconfiguring that space, what there is to do there, what there is to see or name there. It is a dispute about the division of what is perceptible to the senses." Insofar as that dispute concerns the visual, necessarily interfaced with the other senses, this politics of bringing the subject into presence in space is visual culture. For when the police say there is nothing to see, they are not telling the truth, nor are we supposed to infer that they are. Rather they mean, "while there is something to see, you have no authority or need to look at it." By being simply a citizen, one does not necessarily attain the full authority of the visual subject, the person who is allowed and required to look in all circumstances.

In the experimental university, new forms of looking are being enacted that would allow for the formation of visual subjects in the new spaces of globalization, with or without the permission of the police. With the Atlas Group, we look into the archive of the Lebanese wars of 1975-1991 that seems to be a precursor to much of the current dramas of terrorism. The Atlas Group is described by Walid Raad as "an aesthetic and cultural laboratory." The archive offered presents film, photography, documents and commentary but Raad adds: "It is important to note that some of the documents, stories, and individuals I present with this project are real in the sense that they exist in the historical world, and others are imaginary in the sense that I imagined and produced them." All pertain to making the situation in Lebanon visible and imaginable. But the interweaving of creative and documentary material places the viewer in a far more active position than that of a simple witness or consumer. In making this "division of what is perceptible to the senses", the viewer becomes a visual subject. But whereas the ordinary university accomplishes these tasks based on a comfortable guarantee that the information offered is true in commonsense terms, the Atlas Group Archive makes us question how and why archives come into being. Knowledge becomes a problem as well as an answer.

Clearly this work is political, but it is not politics as we have become accustomed to it in American art of recent years. Interestingly, critics as diverse as TJ Clark and Sarat Maharaj have recently called for a reconsideration of anarchism, the space between the artist and Duchamp's "anartist." Clark has gone so far as to say that socialism's epistemic crisis began with the break with anarchism in the 1890s, for which he has been soundly critiqued by scandalized Marxists in wealthy private universities. To look at 1890s anarchist concerns with race and racism, ecology and the politics of food, prison reform, and a decentered political system is to get a shock of Walter Benjamin's Jetzeit (the time of the now). Anarchy also recalls the fashion, music and politics of 1970s punk that are again visible in suburban streets.

Continue →

So to think of anarchism is not to disavow mass political action because that is the exception to everyday life, as in the recent anti-war demonstrations that were mobilized from people's houses via the internet. That action was anarchist, in the sense of a political action committed out of sight of the police. It is closer to the anarchist trend within modern criticism that runs from Oscar Wilde and Camille Pissarro in the 1890s to the "theocratic anarchism" of the young Walter Benjamin in Weimar, Germany, the Situationists of the 1950s and '60s, and many contemporary strands of theoretical practice, perhaps especially those connected with the philosophy of Gilles Deleuze. This is not to suggest that the artists here should simply be thought of as anarchists, because many of them would disagree. At the same time, it is not to adhere to the violence committed as "anarchism." The point is to bring that strand of concern with the politics and practice of everyday life that was addressed by anarchism, and often overlooked by other forms of the political, back into the practice of the experimental university.

The possibility of an experimental university has emerged in considerable part thanks to the emergence of digital culture. Computer technology blurs the distinction between amateurs and professionals and threatens to make information available as simply as photography did for the image. It is intriguing in this context to recall that Eric Raymond's famous essay, "The Cathedral and the Bazaar," one of the classic texts of digital culture, concludes with a passage from Peter Kropotkin's *Memoirs of a Revolutionist*. Raymond's essay highlights the creative possibilities of "open-source" programming using the Linux operating system with the top-down, all-controlling in-house system (implicitly that of Microsoft). After hailing the "bazaar" of open source as superior to the "cathedral" of in-house (and without addressing his own Orientalism), he turns to Kropotkin. Kropotkin had turned away from a career as a government reformer to that of a radical and revolutionary in Czarist Russia of the 1860s. He had witnessed what he considered the failure of government-led reform in Siberia, while gaining a devotion to the peasants and ordinary people that was to shape his subsequent career. The passage cited by Raymond turns on Kropotkin's reflecting on his life within a serf-owning family — a serf being a person "owned" by a landowner as the labor for that land only to then experience emancipation in 1863. Having lived through this emancipation, Kropotkin came to "appreciate the difference between acting on the principle of command and discipline and acting on the principle of common understanding. The former works admirably in a military parade but is worth nothing where real life is concerned, and the aim can be achieved only through the severe effort of many converging wills." That effort of many converging wills was what sustained the anarchy of the internet before it was reined in by Microsoft and AOL. Seen more broadly, Kropotkin's belief in the convergence of wills is perhaps the first theory of everyday life as a form of resistance and as an alternative to centralized power, for all its 19th-century baggage of "civilization" theory. More widely still, this is the ethos of the experimental university. Indeed, Kropotkin used museums and libraries as examples of the principle of "to every person according to their needs."

Yet needs can be met in a variety of ways. Discussing the growth of public kitchens in the 1890s, Kropotkin shuddered that "to make a duty of taking home our food ready-cooked, that would be as repugnant to our modern minds as the ideas of the convent or the barrack." By connecting mass-produced food to the disciplinary institutions of church and state, Kropotkin linked everyday life to power through the basic means of subsistence. It has recently been estimated that ten corporations supply over half of all the food and drink consumed in the United States. The number of people now working as farmers is less than one per cent of the working-age population, for all the endless evocation of the needs of farmers by the governing class. When you hear "farmers," think "agro-business." Now that nearly all but the most dedicated of us take home our bread ready-cooked, Critical Art Ensemble with Beatriz de Costa plan to make us reexamine that connection by testing loaves for the presence of genetically modified grains. We are told that these are safe. Exactly what knowledge will be produced by this experiment is unclear. This is the difference between an artistic experiment and a scientific one that is created to demonstrate a theorem. It challenges the coziness of the "museum visit" with its promise of quiet viewing, rewarded by a visit to the gift shop and café. In the experimental university that has taken its place, it remains to be seen what happens next. The point at which this will start to get interesting will be when the artist-educator loses the edge of surprise over the experimental student. Learning curves are very short these days.

The cybernetic hope of anarchic freedom implied in Raymond's citation of Kropotkin had already been imagined as a cityscape by the Situationist architect Constant in the 1960s. He called it "New Babylon." A Dutch painter who had come to abandon art in favor of the new practice of urbanism, Constant may well have invented the Situationist strategy. Inspired by his vision of a mass culture freed from the routine of subsistence labor by cybernetics, Constant imagined that automation would generate huge amounts of "so-called free time." Rather than think of this time as "leisure," Constant and the other Situationists were inspired by the Dutch historian Johann Huizinga to think of free time as play and in turn to consider play as freedom. In elaborating his theory of New Babylon, Constant quoted the cybernetic theorist Norbert Weiner who "compares the electronic machine to the imported slaves of antiquity." This new emancipation from the necessity to work would be for all, rather than the minority supported by slavery. It will generate "unprecedented freedom, an undreamt-of opportunity for the free disposal of time, for the free realization of life....The freedom won as a result of the disappearance of routine work is a freedom to act," which he called the "lived work of art." In this society, traditional forms of art would be revealed as a "surrogate" for this kind of freedom. New Babylon was to be the site of "the real practice of freedom — of a 'freedom' that for us is not the choice between many alternatives but the optimum development of the creative faculties of every human being." Freedom was not to be seen either as an absence of constraint or as the self-enabling choice among variables, which is presented by American apologists today, but as the possibility to play. Constant envisaged New Babylon as a world without frontiers, which he called "a camp for nomads on a planetary scale." Rather than an exclusionary camp that seeks to detain and deport the nomad, like the new detention camps for migrants and refugees created in the European Union, Australia and the US borderlands, New Babylon opened a space for them to play as they chose without having to become settled to do so. This new cityspace was inspired by the old Babylon of the ghetto and marginal space: "these areas of the historical cities, where the outcasts of the utilitarian society stick together, these poor quarters where racial minorities, artists, students, prostitutes, and intellectuals are living together." The subRosa group creates maps of cities from alternative points of view in the hope of forming a refugia, a New Babylon that actually exists. In this case, they will have traced the places in North Adams that connect gender and production, looking at the ways in which MASS MoCA itself is housed in a former factory. Their project is going to be controversial because gender is always troubling and is exemplary of the experimental university that is yet to come. It has clear links to art and politics of the past but tries to create a new future. However, that new future is not a calm utopia but a place where ideas, identities and knowledge are troubled rather than reinforced. The risk is that knowledge production simply becomes knowledge commodification. It is in that space between the museum and the everyday that the experimental university tries to establish itself. Both museums and universities have sought to evade the charge of elitism by organizing themselves to appeal to ever-larger numbers of people. The blockbuster show is, in this sense, on par with on-line courses, part-time degrees and the promotion of lifelong learning. If there is to be a cultural and political significance to this expansion beyond the simple pursuit of numbers, then these institutions must face the challenge of anarchism, experimentation and utopia presented by this show.

Nicholas Mirzoeff
Professor, Art History and Comparative Literature
Stony Brook University

Encyclopedic Entries

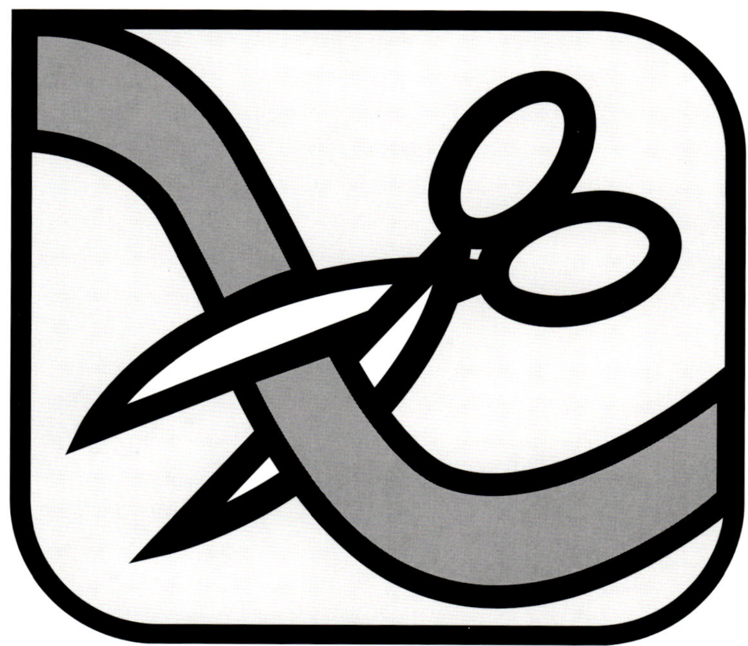

The Amateur

Critical Art Ensemble

The word "amateur" is very rarely used in a positive sense. It is a disciplinary term used to discourage hybridity and maintain profitable professional and social separations. For the most part amateurs are second-class citizens in the area of knowledge production. However, in the context of political and cultural intervention, amateurs have a significant and vital role to play. They can have the ability to spot contradictions and rhetorical cover-ups within the dominant paradigms, are freer to recombine elements of paradigms thought dead or unrelated, and can apply everyday life experience to their deliberations with greater ease than can specialists. In this manner amateurs can reconfigure the terms of action within the terrain of a given discipline.

Most importantly, however, amateurs are not invested in institutionalized systems of knowledge production and policy construction, and hence do not have irresistible forces guiding the outcome of their efforts, such as maintaining a place in the funding hierarchy or maintaining prestige-capital. This is not to say that amateurism should be promoted for amateurism's sake. The amateur's relationship to the expert is a necessary one in many ways. For the sake of efficiency, to limit mistakes, to teach fundamental processes and protocols, and to reinforce good ideas, dialogues with experts remain a key part of the amateur's process.

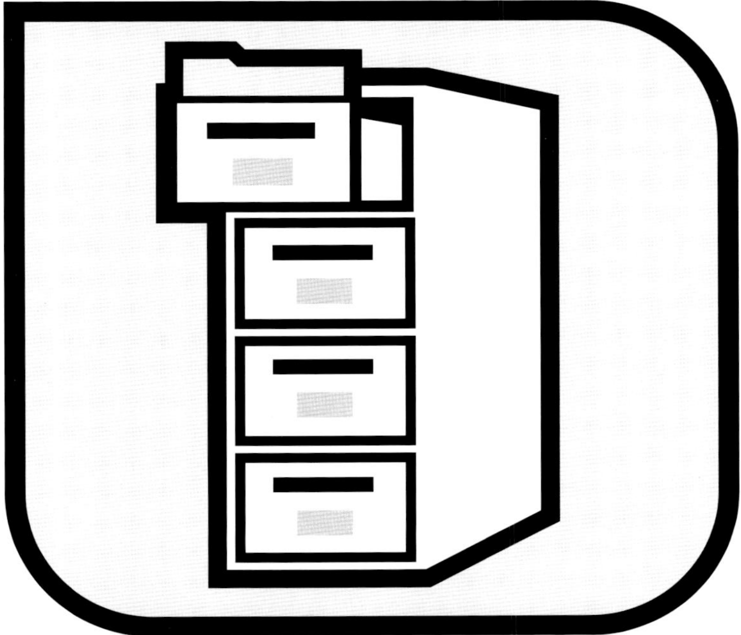

The Archive:

Spurse

The archive is often seen to be tied to the documentation of a past event — an event that has receded far into the past so as to be only accessible through documentation housed in the archive. The archive becomes thus situated as a space for the complex and contested production of histories. In Foucault's alternative sense the archive is the site of the spacing-out of a history so as to turn history upon itself and uncover the discursive and non-discursive regimes of what is sayable or visible at a given moment. The Foucaultian archive becomes a site of ontological — or perhaps heterological — investigation/production and experimentation. Critical to this form of the archive is that there is a nascent cartographic function to the archive — where it begins to trace out weaknesses, aporias, new paradoxes, and new modes of becoming latent in the mass of housed materials (always in relation to questions of the present). This is what Foucault himself saw as the shift into genealogical modes of inquiry (and what Deleuze termed the "cartographic"). Perhaps, then, it is not all that much of a morphogenetic shift to see the archive as an open experiment in the production of what is in common — where this conceptualization of the "commons" is being posed as a zone of problematization.

Here in the development of a temporary parallel space or event of inquiry one finds interesting resonances following the archaic root of the word archive — "Archeia" — the town hall — a public gathering, the space of civic engagement. "Archive" then as a space for the production of a public. The archive becomes a strategic zone of stopping midstream to allow the unformedness of ideas, things, events, places, identities, individuations of any scale and forces to fold in upon each other as an experimental problematization of the given — a pause — a slowing-down of acting to allow the givenness of a new situation to reshape one's mode of acting and doing.

Given the global context of action and vastly distributed nature of agency, there is a need for this form of situated condensation and slowing-down of agents, forces, spaces, and events. A strategic temporary parallel institution — the archive is at once a collection, a system of collecting, a series of relations (to peoples, groups, regions, terrains, events, things and other beings, etc.) and an unfolding collective space in which to experiment with these (now collective). The archive becomes a way of investigating and experimenting with the present through the collective development of a system of problematization.

A system is needed to move from the space of problematization towards the production of an archive. Here one needs to develop a methodology of tracing out immanent forces at the point of emergence. A score that directly engages outside of the structural subjectivities of scientific, aesthetic and others produces an archive that can move outside of itself, making it possible for the archive to become an active force in its own reshaping. The generation of archival objects through the scores creates an open set, in which any object, image, sound, smell, or agent can become an element of the set if collected from the environment using the specified methodology, thus permitting the discovery of unanticipated elements and associations. The archive demands an engaged participation that over time must respond to the changing problematic that the archive itself calls forward. The spatio-temporal contingency of the archive and archival process is fundamental and thereby as a process sustains a dynamic continuity, remaining open to intervention, aberration, and inflection. So, the etymology of the word "archive" as an interaction of forces maps onto the praxis of the archive as a collection. It is a repository of motion and speeds; a collection of open agencies, sensible and prone — the production of a people(s) and a space/spaces still to come.

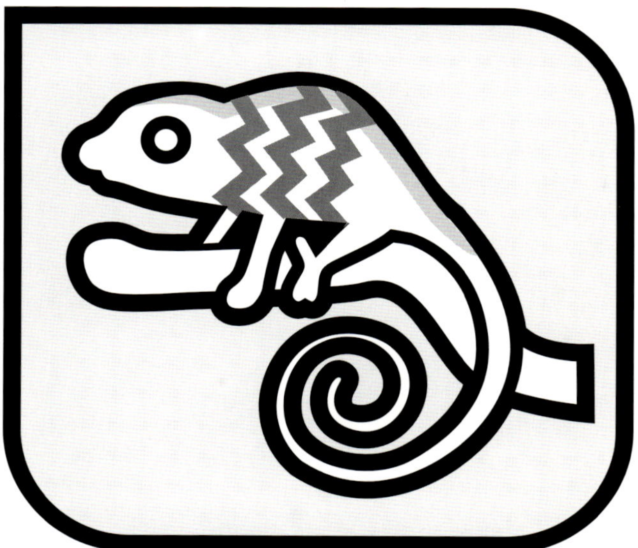

The Chameleon
The Center for Tactical Magic

Clandestiny for the Multitude
There is no set formula for cloaking oneself successfully in today's society. Merely changing appearances like the skin of a chameleon will not enable you to elude scrutiny. Each context must be carefully considered on an individual basis. Only then can you effectively shift perception.

The Ninja
To act clandestinely does not merely mean wearing a black mask in the cover of night's shadows. The "nin" in ninja is most commonly translated as "concealment" yet it also can be defined as "forbearance," "patience," or "self-control". So, we come to see that hiding, camouflaging, and masking are only the most obvious ways to not draw attention. At the core of concealment strategies we find an applied understanding of time and space — not as separate from us, but as a part of us. Thus, effective concealment must consider the individuals' (all who are involved) relationship to time and space. This often involves the control, manipulation, or adaptation of space, as well as special attention to timing.

The Private Investigator
The basis for private investigation is the acquisition of information that others wish to conceal. Regardless of whether the hidden information pertains to an identity, a location, or particular activities, the private eye must see without being seen. From the private investigator's careful observations of human behavior and psychology, several strategies for covert action take form:

Humans are creatures of habit. Fit in with their habits or fit well outside of their habits, and you will disappear from their view. Even some of the flashiest, gaudiest, most ostentatious acts go unnoticed when you follow habitual flows. Act nervously and suspiciously, and people take notice. Act bored and self-obsessed like everyone imagines strangers to be, and you completely blend in. Fit in to their most meager expectations. Conform to their lowest standards. Act like you don't give a damn, and chances are they won't.

The Magician
Magic can mean many things to many people, but most will think first of the conjuror's illusions or of the occult's arcane practices. In both cases, we are asked to contemplate that which is hidden, obscured, and shrouded in mystery. Throughout history we find that there are three common strategies employed to hide something of value:

1) You can build a fortress around it. But by doing so, you alert everyone to the fact that a treasure lies within. As such, a conflict is inevitable; those who seek to obtain it will contest those who seek to protect it. Over time, the guardians will ultimately fall to a more powerful adversary.

2) You can hide it away and try to keep it a secret. But secrets are rarely kept once shared. When people know that a treasure is hidden, they come looking, and the treasure becomes vulnerable to those who are resourceful and determined.

3) You can veil it in illusion, in an air of dismissal. When people are convinced that there is no treasure, that it's fantasy, myth, or child's play, then they no longer seek it out. Therefore, there is no longer a need to guard it. The treasure can be left in sight, in arm's reach, without risk of losing it.... Such is the case with magic. (Of course, this is also the case within politics, advertising, and many authoritarian structures, both religious and secular).

Consider your own dismissive tendencies. What have you been taught to disregard? What is treated as insignificant, trivial, or absurd? What is commonly accepted as "true" without question or investigation? Illusions surround us, working their wonders so well, because we are so willing not to see them.

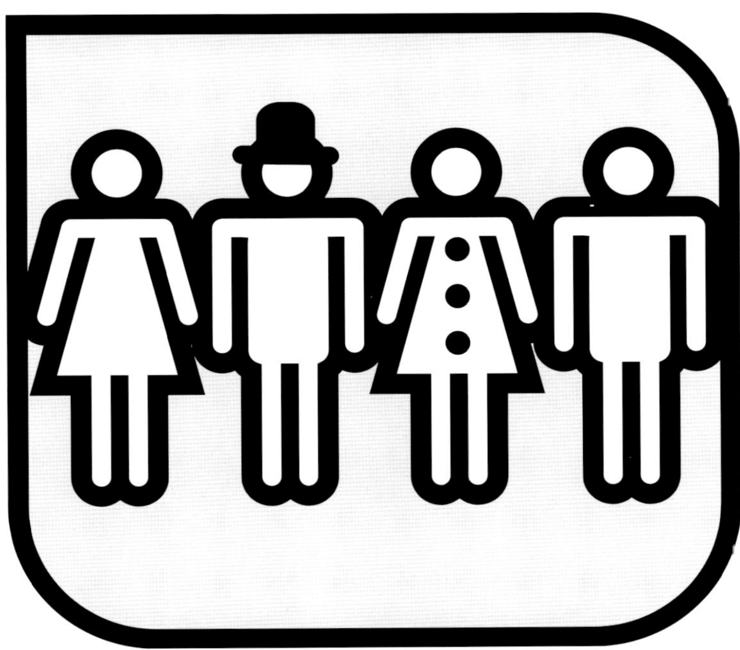

Collectives

Gregory Sholette and Blake Stimson

The desire to speak in a collective voice has long fueled the social imagination of artists. Futurism, Constructivism and Surrealism shared this aim early in the 20th century, as did collectives such as CoBrA, the Situationist International, Gutai and the Lettristes after World War II; Fluxus, the Art Workers Coalition, Art & Language, and others in the 1960s; Group Material, S.P.A.R.C., PAD/D, and Gran Fury, among many in the 1970s and '80s; and organizations such as The Guerrilla Girls, RTMark, Critical Art Ensemble, Temporary Services and Las Agencias, more recently.

At any given moment, the particular form of collectivism has varied depending on specific historical conditions. For example, if the earlier ambition was, as Mondrian once put it, to struggle "against everything individual in man" or to become, as Malevich termed it, "world-man," then the aspiration of collectivism after the Second World War has been imagined differently. The governing artistic posture of collectivism after modernism, as it might be called, has rarely claimed to find its unity as the singularly correct avant-garde representative of social progress. Instead new collectivism gathers itself around decentered and fluctuating identities that leverage heterogeneous character of any group formation.

In keeping with Theodor Adorno's critical judgment that modern collectivism and modern individualism "complete one another in falsity," artistic collectivism in the last 50 years has found its purpose in skirting both untruths. This aim to rework social imagination has become all the more pressing and all the more prescient in light of the various social, economic and political pressures that have been lumped together under the label "globalization."

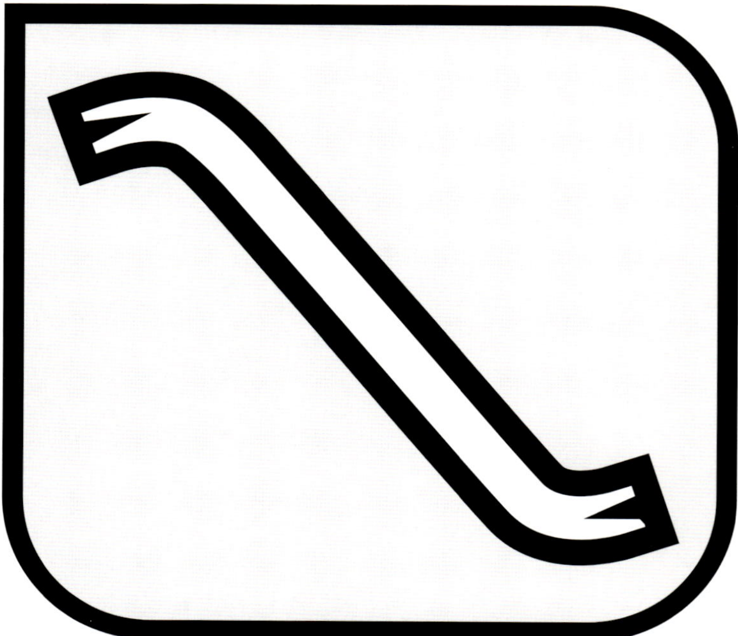

Détournement
Nato Thompson

"Since opposition to the bourgeois notion of art and artistic genius has become pretty much old hat, Duchamp's drawing of a mustache on the Mona Lisa is no more interesting than the original version of that painting." -Guy Debord and Gil J. Wolman, "A User's Guide to Détournement"

Originally conceived by the Situationists in the 1950s, détournement can be re-conceived as a form of existence: That is to say, making meaning within the landscape of a dominant system is a form of life. Détournement can take the form of a billboard manipulation in which one modifies an advertisement to propose a radical alternative to its original intent. Détournement can also derive meaning by trespassing, or by modifying the rules of engagement. The radical implication of détournement is that meaning is connected to a relationship with power. We find contemporary examples in "culture jamming" where popular media (commercials, television shows, popular music) are modified guerilla-style to produce critical re-interpretations. The popular Canadian magazine *AdBusters* has found a radial marketing niche for this very type of subversion.

However, as Debord and Wolman point out, dancing on top of the visuality of a dominant system may only be the beginning of a successful détournement. The trick is to reveal the underlying power relationships behind an image and then channel them into a productive, potentially ambiguous, sphere.

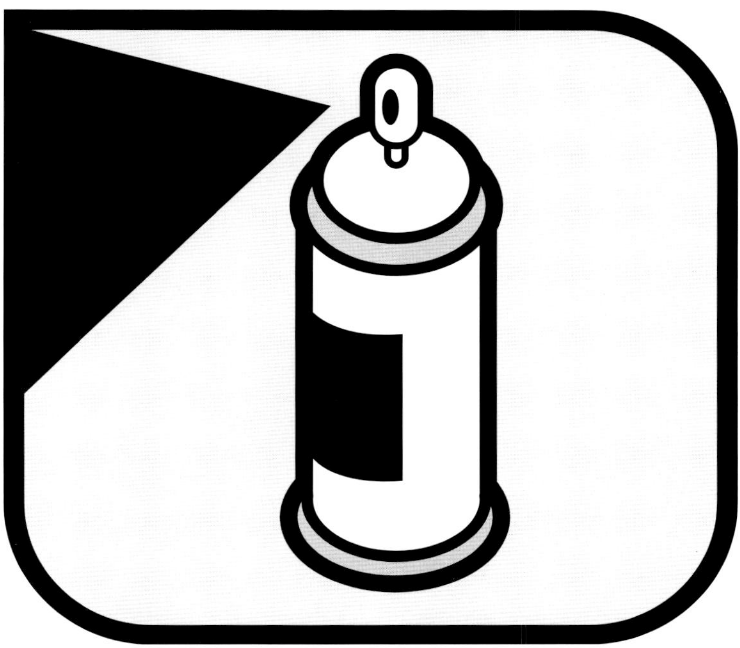

Illegality
YOMANGO (Spanish for "I Steal")

You must realize that YOMANGO is not a collective formed by individuals who dedicate their time to shoplifting. First, it is not a collective. Second, there are no "YOMANGO individuals". YOMANGO is everywhere, but it is hard to grasp. So how can "the followers of YOMANGO" get arrested? You don't "follow" YOMANGO. YOMANGO happens.

Nonetheless it is true that when YOMANGO occurs certain physical entities, such as security personnel or store workers, do what they possibly can to avoid it, thus making visible the person who is enjoying a YOMANGO moment. This person, at that very moment, could be percieved as a thief. But nothing is farther than the truth.

YOMANGO is a gesture which provides you with everything advertising promises but the reality of capitalism prevents you from having: the prospect of adventure, self-fulfillment, creativity, sharing, community...YOMANGO is a transformative act of magic. It does not recognize the laws of physics nor does it acknowledge definitions such as legal or illegal. It does not recognize borders or security arcs. YOMANGO liberates objects and liberates your desire. It liberates your desire which is trapped within objects which are trapped inside large shopping malls, the same place where you yourself are trapped. YOMANGO is a pact between co-prisoners.

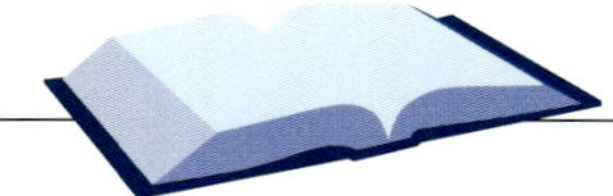

Laughannilingus

William Pope.L

Despite (and probably because of) its enormous and enduring popularity, comedy has never enjoyed the critical prestige of, say, the so-called serious forms such as drama or the documentary or the novel...

Comedy can be both anti-authoritarian and socially transformative. However, just because a person is against authority does not mean he or she is pro-society. And even if so, which society? Maybe the only society worth being for is that which one is willing to stand against.

When comedy shifts from its proper focus — that is, against convention, the law, the uppity and the socially powerful — and turns its attack on the weaker and the oppressed, it keeps things the same and assists in maintaining the status quo. Comedy then becomes a strategy to keep people in line, their desires in their panty and their pleasure routine.

Some feminist historians consider comedy a feminine form: "ancient, tribal, [and] used to celebrate" the wank of a thing; always moving dramatically toward conclusions in which people are united through divorce and lots of parties; made whole through dissipation and so on and so on...

Benedict Anderson's notion of nations as "imagined communities" comes in handy when thinking about comedy. Why? Because when a nation has its mouth open, anything can happen...

Adapted from: *Comedy, Melodrama and Gender: Theorizing the Genres of Laughter*, Kathleen Rowe in Classical Hollywood Comedy, ed. K. B. Karnick and H. Jenkins, 1995.

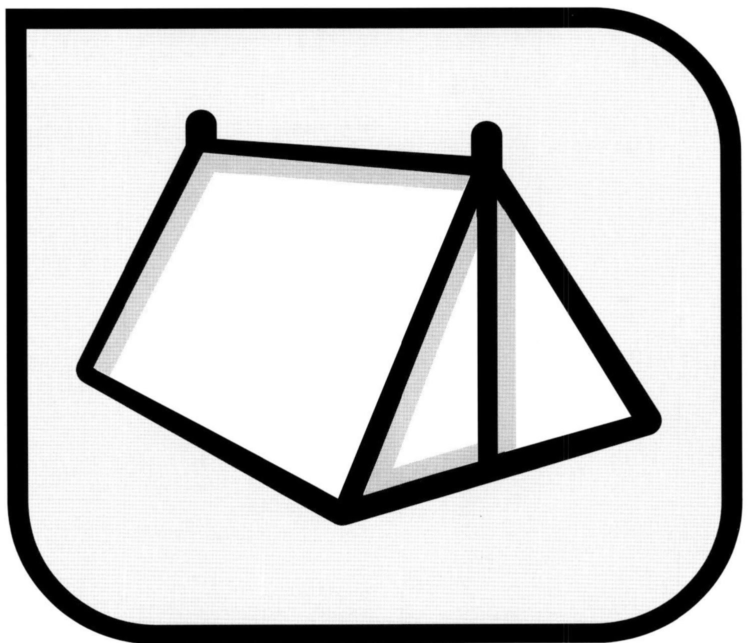

The Tour
By e-Xplo

It is a difficult assignment, to trace how one arrives at a particular strategy or medium, and the task is made more difficult because of the collaborative nature of our work.

Touring is more than just a metaphor for the "society of the spectacle" or for the increasing industrialization and mobilization of culture for economic purposes.

The tour conjures more than tourism; it implicates and puts into play numerous forms of movement, across and between borders, not just of people but of images, of sounds, of resources, of capital, of labor, of cultures.

The tour can be a pointed critique or a reflexive method of involving/implicating ourselves within the physical and discursive terrain of frames such as public art, site specificity, sound art, mobility, land art, sculpture, architecture, film, music or performance.

It can also be seen as a tactical response to the increased policing of "public" space, in which walking or wandering gets redressed as trespassing or loitering.

It can also be said that the tour is linked to previous politically motivated artists who have taken to the streets, such as André Breton (Surrealists) with his strategy of objective chance or Guy Debord (Situationists), who proposed *dérive* ("a technique of transient passage through varied ambiences") as a method for studying terrain, emotionally disorienting oneself, as well as an intermediate step toward the realization of a larger field of study of psycho-geography, fostering among other things the creation of maps in which specific regions of the city would be noted for arousing particular affective or aesthetic responses (not to forget the ultimate goal of social revolution).

The tour could also be a useful technique for confronting critical and timely questions raised by Paul Virilio, Elizabeth Grosz and other thinkers addressing issues (e.g., movement, architecture, cities, technology, virtuality, space, time, duration, transformation, and memory) related to our work.

Touring can be seen as a proposal for a way of exploring cities, tourist sites, and off-sites or, for that matter, the site of tourism.

The tour is also more than all of the latter points; it is a context, a situation, a form, a techné, a tool, an architectural proposal, a quasi-memorial to duration, passage, the present, transformation.

Touring may not even be touring. At times it can be more akin to Barthesian cruising: not swaddled in the stereotypes of monuments, the cruiser is more aware of the world around her/him or at the very least more aware of the very process or act of moving.

Postscript:
To quote Guy Debord quoting Karl Marx, "Men can see nothing around them that is not their own image; everything speaks to them of themselves. Their very landscape is alive."